POLITICS, FEMINISM AND THE REFORMATION OF GENDER

Why do men always dominate political elites? If women want to change the world, are they going about it in the right way?

Caught between their female gender and their aspirations in a public sphere founded on the gender role of men, women face a problem that is more intractable than either conventional or feminist political analysis has fully recognised. In this book, Jenny Chapman addresses both the substance of the problem and feminist strategies for change.

Part 1 focuses on a key aspect of the male political world. Male dominance of political elites is virtually universal and yet there is no general theory of recruitment to account for this; there is even a serious lack of real recruitment studies in the academic literature. Drawing on feminist and mainstream theory, Jenny Chapman uses a rigorous comparative study of political recruitment to show why different models of recruitment among men produce virtually identical gender results, irrespective of context. The emphasis is on men's recruitment patterns and the data come from countries as varied as the USA, the USSR and Scotland (where extensive new survey and interview data has been collected for the purpose); self-selection is analysed as well as the role of political parties and other institutions.

Part 2 looks beyond this universal pattern to its gender basis and strategies for change. The rise of feminism as a social movement poses problems of organisational and gender strategy which different strands of feminism have tried to resolve in very different ways. Jenny Chapman's review of feminist strategies ranges from early communitarian socialism to Nordic feminism today, with historical case-studies of Finland and revolutionary Russia and studies of contemporary Norway, Iceland and the German Greens. A critical review of women's gender theories and their policy implications provides the touchstone for identifying a convincing feminist strategy.

Jenny Chapman is a lecturer in Politics at the University of Strathclyde.

POLITICS, FEMINISM AND THE REFORMATION OF GENDER

Jenny Chapman

ROUTLEDGE

London & New York

First published 1993
by Routledge
11 New Fetter Lane, London EC4P 4EE

Simultaneously published in the USA and Canada
by Routledge
a division of Routledge, Chapman and Hall, Inc.
29 West 35th Street, New York, NY 10001

Typeset in Baskerville by Witwell Ltd, Southport
Printed and bound in Great Britain by
Biddles Ltd, Guildford and King's Lynn

British Library Cataloguing in Publication Data
A catalogue record for this title is available from the British
Library.

ISBN 0-415-01698-3

Library of Congress Cataloging in Publication Data
Chapman, Jenny, 1941–
    Politics, feminism, and the reformation of gender/
Jenny Chapman.
        p.   cm.
    Includes bibliographical references and index.
    ISBN 0-415-01698-3
    1. Women in politics.   2. Women political activists.
    3. Feminism.
I. Title.
HQ1236.C47   1992   92-9372
305.42—dc20   CIP

CONTENTS

CONTENTS

vi

FIGURES AND TABLES

FIGURES

TABLES

PREFACE AND ACKNOWLEDGMENTS

Three inter-related strands in my experience produced the impetus to write this book. Chronologically speaking, the first of these was practical involvement in conventional politics as an activist and parliamentary candidate in the 1970s; this revealed surprising *lacunae* in the political science literature some of which this book attempts to fill. The second was a deepening concern with feminist ideas, which seemed to me to provide profound insights into the nature of politics and the world in which we live but without answering some of the most difficult questions modern women have to face, in employment, in politics and in their family lives. It became increasingly clear to me that these were very basic questions the women's movement had met and foundered on before; if history was not simply to repeat itself, they should be confronted and, if possible, resolved. However, it is a third factor, my role as a mother, which has held me to the task. This is partly because my particular experience of motherhood (in the very different contexts of shared and single parenthood but always as a breadwinner) has forced me to apply my mind to uncomfortable facts which feminism often seems inclined to fudge. Still more compellingly, however, it has given me a sense of obligation to the future which has made this book a personal responsibility impossible to evade.

The task could not have been accomplished without help. In particular, I am greatly indebted to the Trustees of the Nuffield Foundation for funding my research and providing the Fellowship which got the writing underway; without their support and confidence the work would have been impossible. The same can be said for the candidates and councillors who responded to my questions and thus provided the raw material for part of the analysis; I thank them all for their time and trouble and their good humour and goodwill. I am also indebted to my friends and colleagues for their encouragement and advice. Without the moral support of Mark Franklin in the early stages of the work and Professor Jeremy Richardson towards the end it might not have been completed; I am especially indebted to the latter for making our department at the University of Strathclyde an environment in which such long-term projects are still feasible for individual members of the teaching staff, even in the present climate of pressure on the universities. I am also grateful to Tom Mackie for his companionable interest in my work, to Jack Brand for technical advice and to Stephen Tagg, Ann Mair and Sarinder Hunjan of the Social Statistics Laboratory for their unfailing helpfulness. Further afield, I should like to acknowledge a debt to Anne Phillips, whose timely advice gingered me to further, vital efforts. I am also grateful to Ronald J. Hill for permission to make new use of his Soviet data and to the Routledge editors and readers for their advice. Above all, however, I must thank my family, Howard, Keith and Sarah Robinson for their long-suffering support; it is to them that I should like to dedicate this book.

INTRODUCTION

The great interest with which issues of gender and politics are received today undoubtedly has its roots in the changes which have taken place in women's situation in the modern world, and particularly in their widespread access to the kind of education which creates a public for ideas and the thinkers and communicators to provide them. At the same time, this interest is engendered by frustration, for women are a 'public' which is largely outside public life. With a very few and arguable exceptions among industrialised nations, women remain outside the centres of decision-making throughout the world and the forms of status, influence and power which are available to men continue to elude them. Cultural values continue to marginalise their identity and interests (even though commercial interests are only too eager and able to exploit them) and public policies continue to reflect the priorities of men.

This has led to much impatience with the rate of change achieved by women within existing systems and inconclusive argument about the nature of the obstacles they face and how they may be overcome. Some feminists have concluded that the only way forward is to reject these systems altogether and opt instead for either revolution or deliberate non-participation. For other feminists, who are probably the vast majority, the idea of a women's revolution is too fantastic to be entertained, while non-participation seems tantamount to a negation of the struggle; it seems the only hope is to progress by means of incremental change. In the end, women's participation may afford them sufficient leverage to make radical changes in existing systems *from within*, with or without the help of men.

The irony, however, is that women who take part in order to modify or even revolutionise the system face the same basic problem as those who simply want to share the spoils on equal terms with men: how to reach decision-making roles at all? To the extent that they succeed, they face an even more profound and taxing question; how best to use their new-found influence in pursuit of further change? Even if proportionality with men is all that women seek from public life, it seems clear that great changes in society and politics will be required before this can be achieved. Unfortunately, it is by no means easy to agree on what these changes ought to be. The strategy that feminists employ will obviously depend on what they think stands in their way, but whether they succeed, in any sense of the word, will depend on how correctly the obstacles have been identified, and also on how willing other women are to adopt their feminist goals. The kind of changes that will promote women's advance in politics can hardly leave their broader social role and interests untouched; feminism is controversial among women precisely because of its profound implications for all women's lives. Whether the women's movement is trying to work within existing systems or against them, it must eventually confront the same unanswered question that was posed by Freud, 'What *do* women want?'

It is to both these crucial feminist issues – the 'why' and 'how' of women's difficult advance – that this book is addressed. Its central argument is that women, caught between their female gender and their aspirations in the world of men, face a scissors problem which is as old as gender itself and more intractable than either conventional or feminist political analysis has fully recognised. The foundation of the public sphere and its dominant values on the gender role of men is one dimension of the scissors; the other is the female role and its exterior location in the partly 'private' sphere. Thus women's situation cuts two ways; as participants in the essentially hierarchical systems devised by men they are but one of many out-groups and subject to the same competitive rules as men, and yet by virtue of their gender women are uniquely set apart, not just an out-group but *outsiders* too. On the one hand, it is impossible to explain the limited progress of women in the public sphere without an understanding of the principles on which it is constructed and their effects on men as well as women. At the same time, no strategy for changing women's situation can possibly succeed which does not fully take account of women's gender role as well as men's. Without a grasp on both dimensions of the gender scissors, the situation of women can be neither understood nor remedied.

Although the whole history of feminism could be described as an unsuccessful effort to escape the gender scissors, it is a problem which seems to take feminists in every generation by surprise, leaving them divided not only among themselves but from the mass of ordinary women. Each repetition of the movement's cycle finds it trapped in the identical pattern which is the hallmark of the scissors problem, of half-acknowledged inconsistencies among its goals and a profound, but unacknowledged conflict between the stated aims of feminism and the underlying, long-term gender implications of the policies that feminists pursue. Along with this goes a recurring tendency to lose sight of the realities on which male politics are based, leading to over-optimism about what can readily be achieved and the disillusionment which this inevitably brings in its train.

The need to mark out both dimensions of the scissors problem clearly and measure feminist strategies according to how well designed they are to deal with it, has therefore been the principal motivation for this book. The task has gained a special urgency from the recent appearance, for the second time this century, of what look like new departures in feminist conceptions of their strategy and goals, coinciding as they did before with cases of unusual access on the part of feminists to positions of political power. The hopes aroused by the advance of Nordic feminism, in particular, demand our urgent scrutiny and at the same time make it all the more important to analyse the failures of the past, lest we repeat them now.

The scope and structure of the book reflect the nature of the scissors problem and its two-dimensional effect on women's lives. It is in two parts, integrally related by their common theoretical framework and ultimate object, but each more closely concerned with one dimension of the scissors: Part 1 with the existing, male-dominated order and the obstacles it presents to women's political advance, and Part 2 with women's situation and the way the scissors problem bears on feminist strategies for change. Like the male and female worlds of which they treat, the themes and perspectives of these parts are intertwined and often overlap but are also very unalike in some respects.

For one thing, although the questions asked are inextricably linked – until we really understand things as they are, how can we hope to change them according to our will? – the research demands they make are very different. Being equally at home myself in quantitative and more traditional approaches to political science, I have felt free to go about each part of the problem in what seemed the most appropriate way, but this has led to considerable differences in the methods and materials used. Whereas the longer, second part (ironically, in view of its more radical content and perspective) is largely traditional in its analytical approach and the 'literary' kind of sources used, an intensive empirical investigation is conducted in Part 1, where most of the data, whether quantitative or qualitative, are of survey origin. The theoretical, historical and cross-cultural range of the book is also more than usually wide. Driven by the universal nature and profound significance of the issues in question (and also being anxious to do justice to those feminists whose ideas I have felt bound to challenge in Part 2), I have tried to create as strong a comparative framework and empirical basis for both parts of the book as is within my powers. Like others before me, I have also found it quite impossible to confine the issue of women's situation within the frontiers of a single academic discipline. The result is a fairly long and complex work, which enters in some detail into the experience of men

xiii

and women in different countries and at different times, and draws on the insights of several disciplines in the analysis of feminist ideas. Some of its elements might even stand alone as case-studies of their kind: for example, the three empirical chapters of Part 1 as self-contained studies of different aspects of recruitment (and all three together as a single work); Chapter 8 as a critical review of women's gender theories; and other sections of Part 2 as separate studies of feminism and political change in specific countries at specific times. This is incidental to the plan, however; each element is conceived as being essential to the whole.

The first objective of the book is to examine the virtually universal pattern of male dominance in the recruitment of political elites. Why *are* men always dominant, irrespective of the immense differences in culture and political system which exist even within the developed world, let alone between the industrialised nations and the rest? How is it possible, too, for such identical effects to be produced in almost every case: firstly that more men than women seek entry to elites and proportionately even more succeed and, secondly, that the higher up a political hierarchy we look, the smaller is the proportion of women to be found? What are the conditions, if any, in which the pattern may be changed?

It may seem surprising that a phenomenon so universal and also, nowadays, so problematic as the gender pattern of recruitment should still require an explanation. One reason is that the subject of recruitment in itself has been less systematically studied than one might suppose. Although a lot of work has gone into identifying different stages in the recruitment process and the range of possible selectors, and a link between political recruitment and individual socio-economic resources has been observed (or else assumed) in some studies of a single setting, no attempt has been made to develop this into a general theory or extend into comparative research; the contrast with the field of mass political participation, with its highly developed comparative theory and empirical findings, is remarkable. Indeed, there is no general theory of recruitment at all and much of the 'recruitment' literature scarcely deserves the name; so-called recruitment studies are often mere descriptions of elites.

It thus devolves on women, as the interested parties, to provide the theory and demonstrate the laws by which they are excluded. However, although contemporary feminist political analysis has provided immensely valuable insights into the nature of politics in general, it has been less successful in relating them to specific issues like recruitment and testing general theories in the field. Athough the feminist perspective has made it impossible any longer to ignore the political character of male–female relations and women's experience is now accepted as a legitimate field of study, neither theory nor findings have been fully integrated into the mainstream of political research. As a result, the strength of women's studies has ironically had something of the same marginalising effect as the sexism of an earlier generation of male political scientists who dismissed the virtual absence of women from the public sphere as a 'natural' function of their apolitical outlook and private role; it focuses attention on women themselves as the key to their problem rather than the nature of the systems in which they are obliged to act. Reinforced by contemporary academic interest in secondary, personal/psychological explanations for political behaviour, it is one source of the widely held but questionable idea that women's situation can be changed by changing women, without also changing (or even fully understanding) how men have organised the world.

Part 1 sets out to redress the balance by combining a feminist perspective with the insights of traditional political analysis and the methods of behavioural research. The dual object is to develop a theory which explains the universal nature of the gender pattern of recruitment in terms of the systems where it is produced and then to demonstrate the theory in the field. Starting from the universal dichotomy of male and female gender, Chapter 1 draws on the common properties of all male systems to present a general theory of the relationship between political values, socio-economic resources and elite recruitment which explains recruitment patterns among men. As for the gender pattern, the key lies in the scissors problem. In terms of recruitment, the first blade of the scissors is that whatever resources are associated with success among men, women as an out-group will have less of them, their situation in this respect being the same as that of other out-groups; women are like 'losing' men. The second blade of the scissors is that whatever distinctive attributes women possess by virtue of their gender will be of little use to them when they compete on 'equal terms' with men; the only 'right' resources are those possessed by 'winning' men. The theory not only accounts for the gender pattern in general but explains specifically why it remains unmodified by quite substantial variation in the basis of recruitment among men, such as occurs when 'modifying' institutions intervene in the recruitment process on behalf of disadvantaged groups; very different kinds of men succeed in different cases but the gender outcome virtually always is the same. A set of hypotheses is proposed which actually predict the gender outcome very precisely in all cases from the patterns of recruitment among men, irrespective of the selectors involved, the political context or the models or recruitment which are at work.

These hypotheses are tested in a comparative, empirical study of recruitment which employs a more rigorous methodology than sadly is usual in this field. The investigation has three parts, dealing respectively with major party, non-partisan and minor party recruitment and drawing on a large body of new survey and interview data collected by the author for the purpose, as well as secondary data and other published sources. It is located in a broad range of institutional frameworks and political cultures, including the three very different partisan settings provided by the USA, Scotland and the former USSR in Chapter 2; Scottish and American contexts of 'non-partisan' recruitment in Chapter 3; and a range of Scottish and other European examples of minor party recruitment in Chapter 4. Although this research is not cross-national in the strict sense of an identical study performed in different countries at a single point in time, the comparative framework is an intrinsic part of the research design; given the universal rules that the scissors hypotheses are intended to explain, it is essential to demonstrate them at work in the greatest possible diversity of political cultures and system-types. At the same time, particular use has been made of the unusually rich and detailed seam of local Scottish data, which not only meet all the standards of design, depth and precision laid down in Chapter 2 but also permit an extended analysis of individual experience in Chapter 3, where in-depth interviews are the focus of analysis and the links between socio-economic attributes and personal/psychological orientations and experience can be made explicit.

The results of all three studies are remarkably consistent. What they reveal is a world so structured by male values and the hierarchical relationships which they sustain in economy, society and polity, that the parameters of change are very narrow even for men. Where women are concerned, the finding is the same in every context and irrespective of whether it is the role of individuals, political parties or other institutions in the recruitment process which is being analysed: that without an absolute revolution in *either* the distribution of resources *or* the political criteria employed by men, no significant and lasting change in women's access to elites is feasible. The only open door (and it is but very slightly ajar) is that of education, with its two-way, but inherently limited effects, on the attributes of women and the attitudes of men.

If the only purpose of this book were to describe things as they are, the matter could rest here. It is our capacity to change these things, however, which is its ultimate concern and the function of Part 1 is to lay the groundwork for Part 2. In order to explain the gender pattern of recruitment, it has opened a window on the nature of male-dominated systems and the place of women in them, in the process identifying the prerequisites for change. Unfortunately, however, the gender scissors are not just the key to patterns of recruitment, but a summary statement of women's whole situation in a gendered and male-dominated world. In such a world as this, is it really in women's power to achieve the kind of internal revolution in the public sphere which a significant change in their political status would require? Can anything as universal as the exclusion of women from political power conceivably be changed unless we look beyond existing systems to their origins and make the changes there? Or are such changes already taking place? If so, what role can feminism play in change and how will it affect our lives? The theory and empirical findings of Part 1 thus provide the framework and, at several levels, the questions to be answered in Part 2. The framework is the gender scissors and the problem it creates for women in a political world which has been organised by men; the questions are identified by the way the scissors works against them and the nature of the underlying obstacles to change.

At one level, this new emphasis on change involves the continuing theme of recruitment and empirical enquiry, albeit of a rather different kind. Are those very few but striking instances, past and present, in which the gender pattern has apparently been breached merely minor variations in the pattern, or are they possible harbingers of a more widespread change? Have they occured because of changes in the distribution of resources between the sexes, or in male values, or in both? In any case, how could such change occur? These questions lead directly to the next level of enquiry. Changes in the distribution of education and its valuation by men have been signalled by Part 1 as the most likely reason for exceptional advance on women's part. However, is not education also a crucial factor in the rise and development of feminism as a social movement? Certainly, feminism of one kind or another has been a highly visible feature in the context of every deviant recruitment case. What contribution has been made by the political consciousness and strategy of *women* in the exceptional cases? Why did the feminism of earlier generations fail to live up to its promise, even in the relatively favourable context of these special cases? And has it more potential now? In short, if women want to change the world, are they going about it the right way?

The approach required to tackle questions of this kind is necessarily of a very different order from that adopted in Part 1, even where recruitment is concerned. While the object of earlier chapters is to prove the general rule, the focus is on the exceptions now and qualitative rather than quantitative methods are more appropriate to an understanding of the historical, socio-economic and cultural contexts from which they spring and the role in them of feminism. However, the differences from Part 1 are necessarily much more profound than this.

Political scientists are notoriously better at describing things as they are than at predicting change and a tendency to conceive the world in static terms is implicit in an empirical investigation of the kind presented in Part 1; the explanation for the gender pattern also sets the bounds on change. The importance of socio-economic factors in explaining politics (and they are crucial in the present case), also reinforces this deterministic bias and the pessimism it breeds. Yet human affairs are never static and the role of ideas in achieving change, albeit unquantifiable, can never be ruled out. Part 1 has made the obstacles extremely clear, but an emphasis on change and the potential role of feminism in promoting it implies that human will and understanding are significant elements in the scheme of things.

Up to a point, the concept of feminism as a social movement offers a conventional framework for this more dynamic and voluntarist approach but although the aims, origins and strategic dilemmas of the women's movement can be compared with those of other social movements (just as women are compared with other out-groups in Part 1), a new perspective is also required. It is impossible to analyse the situation and interests of women and evaluate the competing strands of modern feminism without being confronted by the gender basis of the public sphere and the fact that women are not only participants inside male-dominated systems but, as females, stand outside them too. This is the second dimension of the gender scissors, and the only perspective which can bring it fully into view is that of women themselves. No movement which seriously intends to change the situation of women can afford to overlook the values and functions of the female role, any more than it can ignore the male-centred basis of the public sphere. The only appropriate feminist strategy is one which recognises *both* dimensions of the scissors and is at heart a strategy to deal with them. If no escape route from the scissors can be found, whichever way they turn, then gender itself is the issue women must address.

The foundation for this new approach is laid in Chapter 5, where the character and significance of feminism as a social movement are discussed in terms of social movement theory and the gender problem. These themes are further developed in Chapter 6, where the role of education in the development of a favourable climate for feminist ideas and the strategic options open to the women's movement are discussed. Two great and enduring strands in modern feminism are those of equal rights and socialist feminism, both of them closely associated with competing male ideologies and structures, as well as with historical cases of exceptional, but unsustained advance on women's part. Since both these kinds of feminism continue to inform and divide the women's movement throughout the world (and between them probably have more adherents among women politicians than all the rest), it is vitally important for feminists to assess their strategies and identify the long-term implications of their aims. The analysis reveals much common ground between the two and in spite of their considerable achievements it points to gender and its origin in reproductive roles as a trap which neither has escaped or even fully understood.

Chapter 7 tests this analysis of equal rights and socialist feminism in the setting of two remarkable late nineteenth- and early twentieth-century exceptions to the general recruitment rule. The first case is that of Finland during and after its constitutional struggle for independence, when the proportion of women elected to the first Riksdag in 1908 and the mobilisation of women to the feminist cause was far greater than in any other Scandinavian country until the 1970s (or than Westminster or the US Congress have experienced yet). The second is that of Russia before and after 1917, when the recruitment of women to revolutionary elites and the apparent integration of feminism into the political programmes of men had reached levels which have yet to be surpassed. In the event, neither capitalist, democratic Finland nor state socialist Russia fulfilled their feminist promise and the object here is to discover why these unusual opportunities for women arose in the first place and show why feminists could not use them as a basis for more long-term, incremental change.

Both levels of analysis, theoretical and empirical, point to gender strategy as the key to women's active role in change. Yet whereas the related issue of organisational strategy has been addressed by feminists (and even by a few political scientists) the very need for the women's movement to have a gender strategy at all is rarely recognised. Nor have the gender implications of contemporary feminist policies and current social trends been thoroughly explored. This is certainly not for want of theoretical material; nearly all the most creative feminist political thinkers have written extensively, and in some cases exclusively about gender, while its relationship with reproductive roles has exercised the minds of many women anthropologists and students of psychology. The trouble is that this body of work is rarely reviewed and analysed in terms of strategy; not surprisingly, the result is that a vast gulf exists between theories of gender on the one hand and, on the other, the development of feminist programmes of action and the choices made by individual women in their personal lives. The object of Chapter 8 is to bridge this gap by returning to the work of women gender theorists in order to compare their ideas and establish what constructive gender strategies can be derived from them.

The diversity of these ideas and the wide range of disciplines on which they draw makes this an intellectually challenging, but most rewarding exercise. Even if feminists remain sharply divided and often inconsistent in the remedies they prescribe, there is nonetheless a considerable degree of consensus about the sources of the gender problem and how far it is susceptible to conscious strategies for change. If these ideas are pursued to their logical conclusion, the outline of a coherent gender strategy does emerge and, along with it, a basis for evaluating public policies and social trends in feminist terms.

Whether the path this study indicates is one that many women would wish to take is quite another matter. Social trends suggest that women in general are, to say the least, ambivalent about the kind of change in gender roles it would involve; indeed, with the insights given by this study, we can even say that the main new path they are pursuing for their liberation is more likely to reinforce the gender *status quo* than change it. The question then must be how the contemporary women's movement is matching up to this dilemma; are feminists aware of the true nature of the problem and are they developing coherent and potentially effective policies to deal with it? Or are they really, like so many of their predecessors, tending to defeat their object by trying to face two ways at once?

Once again, the best arena for observing feminist strategies in action is where women have gained unusual access to decision-making roles and hence, perhaps, the chance to start a process of sequential change. The final chapter therefore returns to the exceptional recruitment cases and in the process draws together both dimensions of this enquiry: the political world of men with its inbuilt parameters of change and the women's movement's struggle with the fundamental gender problem. Three contemporary case-studies are presented, chosen to represent the widest possible range of favourable political contexts and recruitment opportunities and the most developed feminist strategies available to women at the present time. The first is that of the West German Greens, which up until the reunification of Germany was not only the most conventionally successful of the 'new' social movements in Europe but uniquely open to the mass mobilisation and recruitment of women to elites. The second is Norway, where the numerical advance of women has not only cut across the party system and brought parity in government itself, but is also being carried over from elected office to the corporate structures which play a crucial role in Nordic policy-making; Norwegian feminists have played a prominent part in these developments and in the process have developed a distinctive, unusually gender-oriented strategy. The third is Iceland, where the wholly female and feminist Kwennalistinn suddenly acquired a pivotal role in the Icelandic parliament, mainly on the basis of a 'women's vote'. Once more, the case-studies are largely self-contained but invite comparison, not only with each other but also with Finnish and Soviet experience. Between them, these cases represent the most advanced frontiers of feminist political thought and action in the present day and offer an unparalleled opportunity to compare immensely varied feminist strategies and visions of a better world. If the problem nature has dealt women is not in fact insoluble, then this is where the answer is most likely to be taking shape.

Part 1

1

GENDER AND RECRUITMENT: THE NATURE OF THE PROBLEM

THE GENDER PATTERN IN ELITE RECRUITMENT

In the last hundred years women in advanced societies have generally achieved the right to own property, enter paid employment, vote and hold political office. They have also gained universal access to formal education on more or less equal terms with men, thus acquiring an attribute which a long line of researchers from Lipset onwards have found to be associated with the development in men of a disposition to engage in political activity.[1]

The effect of these changes on the political behaviour of women, both in absolute terms and relative to men, has been in some respects dramatic and immediate. For example, as soon as they were given the opportunity women began to vote in large proportions and the first women to win election to the national legislatures of Britain and many other western societies did so within a matter of months after becoming eligible.[2] In some respects, however, change was more gradual. Indeed, when political scientists began seriously to study patterns of participation after the Second World War it was not the speed of women's assimilation which they found striking, but the fact that in almost all respects they had still not caught up with the male participatory norm. It was not until the late 1960s and 1970s that the gender gap in forms of what is usually described as 'mass' participation was found to be diminishing rapidly.[3] These changes have still, in the 1990s, not seriously impinged on men's dominance of political elites, even though in countries such as Britain and the USA the disparity in low level participation has nearly disappeared. Two 'almost iron' laws of women's elite penetration are found to be in general operation even now:

1 That wherever political rewards exist which are desirable to men, relatively few women will be found seeking, and even fewer securing them.

2 That wherever there is a hierarchy of such rewards, then the higher up the hierarchy we look, the smaller the proportion of women will be.

The operation of the first of these contemporary laws is both straightforward and obvious. At every level of contested election for public office, anywhere in the world that we choose to look, we find that female candidacies are grossly outnumbered by those of men, even after anything up to eighty years of becoming eligible to stand. Even in Scandinavia the proportion of women among parliamentary candidates has on only two occasions been reported as over a third.[4] It was not until 1983 that women as a percentage proportion of candidacies for the House of Commons even got into double figures for the first time and that position has not yet been reached in the United States.[5] At the local level women are usually more likely to appear as candidates in most advanced societies, but still not at all in proportion to their presence in the electorate.

It is also an almost invariable feature of competition for office, local as well as national, that the success rate of women candidates is lower than that of men. In Britain indeed, the gap between women's aspirations to office and their success in achieving it has become more, not less pronounced with time; until 1987, the increase in women as a proportion of parliamentary candidates in post-war elections was actually correlated negatively not only, as one would expect, with the *proportion* who succeed but also with the *absolute number* of women MPs.

The resulting pattern is well known. Governments throughout the world are dominated by men, notwithstanding the occasional appearance of a personally dominant female head of government, such as Mrs Thatcher; such women rulers have to be looked at in the context of the whole population of rulers and have never been more numerous across the world than can be counted on the fingers of one hand. Norway at the time of writing, is the only, and first ever, exception to this general rule; of the eighteen Cabinet members, nearly half (including Prime Minister Gro Harlem-Bruntland) are women. In national legislatures, or their functional equivalents in one-party states, the highest female represent-ation is also to be found in Scandinavia, but even there it lags considerably behind that of men.[6] More characteristic is Britain, where over half the population but only 6.3 per cent of the MPs elected in 1987, were women (a female success rate of only 8.3 per cent, compared to 27.2 per cent for men).[7] This derisory figure was not only the highest proportion of women there had ever been in the House of Commons, but represented a *recovery* as much as an advance. The previous highpoint of 4.6 per cent was in 1964, after which the proportion declined to around 3.6 per cent, almost exactly the proportion that was found in the Central Committee of the Communist Party of the Soviet Union[8] and still obtains in the United States Congress. In the case of the Labour party (which paradoxically claims to be the only party a genuine feminist should support in Britain), the last time this party reached its 1987 total of twenty-five women MPs was in 1945. Of fifty-six states cited in a recent overview, nearly half had a female presence in their national legislatures of 5 per cent or less and only eighteen had 10 per cent or more.[9] Even after the general election of April 1992, Britain could not be numbered among the latter: at only 9.2 per cent, the proportion of women still has not made it into double figures.

The second 'almost iron' law – that the proportion of women will vary inversely with the hierarchy of rewards – is slightly less obvious in its operation, though no less reliable. Although in most cases it operates as straightforwardly as in Britain, where the proportion of women rises to 22 per cent of district councils in England and Wales (19.5 per cent in Scotland), in the United States only 10 per cent of mayors and local council members were female in the 1980s[10] and this proportion is 3 per cent *less* than is found at the higher level of state legislatures. In Scandinavia, the proportion of women in local councils varies between 21 and 29 per cent, but this is not very different from the proportion to be found in national legislatures.

If we look more closely, however, and bear in mind that we are concerned with the *rewards* of office and not its constitutional status, it becomes clear that most if not all cases which appear to break the rule are really illustrations of a consistent relationship between rewards and gender. In political systems like the British where the formal hierarchy of office, ranging from national to local office, coincides with the hierarchy of rewards – such as money, status and power – the hierarchy of female under-representation coincides exactly with the pyramid of office. Similarly in the Soviet Union (where the proportion of women could be as high as 50 per cent in the local soviets but real power resided in the Communist Party committees), there was a sharp decline in female representation when one moved up the local hierarchy. In fact, when the relative status of local soviet and Party office are taken into account, the British and Soviet cases are both perfect illustrations of a direct relationship between the hierarchy of office and the gender pattern. There is in both cases a strong element of service involved in local government office and for most people little or no prospect of career advancement or financial gain. Rewards must be measured in terms of power, which is severely limited by that of central government in a unitary system, (and by that of the Party in the Soviet case) and status, which reduces sharply as one moves down the formal hierarchy from national office. The hierarchical pattern is therefore perfectly straightforward. In the United States, the real distribution of rewards is rather different and local office may be prized and hotly contested by men for the power and pecuniary advantage it brings.[11] It is *within* the levels of state and local elites that the pyramid effect is to be found, with the proportion of women varying inversely with the size of the state legislature and the members' pay[12] and with the salary and scope of the local office.[13]

We thus have a universal gender pattern in political elite recruitment which rests upon the three components of our 'almost iron' laws; the under-representation of women among the candidates for office; their lower success rate than that of men; and the inverse relationship of their participation and success to the rewards of the office sought. The problem is that no satisfactory explanation for the universal character of this pattern has yet been advanced.

THE LIMITATIONS OF EXISTING EXPLANATIONS

Although most socialists and some feminists have claimed to have the key to women's political equality, the universality and durability of the gender pattern has confounded their expectations as well as those of political scientists; women have been failed not only by traditional power structures but also by socialist states and active women's movements. The Soviet Union was committed to sex equality since its inception, with the education of women and their induction into the paid labour force being articles of public policy as well as dogma throughout its history. Yet the results of seventy-three years of Soviet power brought women no nearer the centres of political power than, for example, seventy-three years of traditional male chauvinism in Mediterranean Greece. Nor do the claims of socialist parties (or trade unions) in Western Europe to be the natural vehicle for women's progress stand up to examination. On the other hand, where women in the USA have pioneered the modern women's movement and made vigorous use of their own structures as pressure groups within the arena of interests, the same derisory results are found as in Britain, where no coherent and structured women's movement exists at all, and in the Soviet Union, where feminists 'from below' until recently risked jail or deportation.[14]

There is one other aspect of political systems which has attracted such considerable attention as an explanation for variation *within* the gender pattern as to be treated by some people almost as an adequate explanation for the pattern itself; this is the kind of electoral system in use. However, while it is true that a cross-national comparison of national legislatures in recent times shows a definite relationship between the incidence of proportional representation and the proportion of women elected,[15] this explanation does not stand up when examined over time; before the sudden improvement of recent times, proportional representation systems had already existed for decades in Norway and Denmark with the same infinitesimal proportion of women legislators as everywhere else.[16] Electoral systems clearly do not offer a primary explanation in themselves but provide conditions which are more or less responsive to changes in the real, underlying causes of the gender pattern.

The theory and findings of political participation research are equally unable to explain the gender results. The most fruitful emphasis of this research has been on the centrality of socio-economic status in defining population categories which are more or less likely to participate in politics, with education identified by Almond and Verba as the crucial determinant of 'civic' or participatory political orientations[17] and commonly regarded as the best independent 'predictor' of actual participation. Yet even at the level of grass-roots participation there are gender gaps which appear to resist this explanation, so that after controlling for education and any other participation-related variables they may have at their command, such analysts as Duverger, the authors of *The American Voter* and Verba, Nie and Kim resort in their turn to sex roles as the residual explanation for sex differences.[18]

The problem at the elite level is of course much greater, for the spread of education has had scarcely any impact there, with some of the worst levels of female representation in national legislatures occurring in the most advanced societies. Among the latter, indeed, it is in America, where further education is more generally available to women than anywhere else in the world apart from the former Soviet Union (there being even more college-educated women in the USA than men) that some of the worst female elite participation outcomes are recorded, even at the local level.

Empirical participation research also poses another conundrum. Cross-national study has shown that the relationship between socio-economic status (ses) and grass-roots political participation is modified in favour of low-ses individuals when the institutional context includes redistributive institutions, i.e. institutions like trade unions, socialist parties and other organisations which seek to redistribute social goods in favour of less advantaged groups. As Verba, Nie and Kim have shown, one of the things which gets redistributed by these agencies is the pattern of grass-roots political participation.[19] Where they are active, mobilising members of their low-ses constituency and providing an organisational framework for their political activity, the participation gap between the high and the low ses-groups begins perceptibly to close. That is to say, it begins to close *among men*; low-ses men participate at a rate closer to that of high-ses men. Low-ses women, however, do not. In fact, the existence of redistributive institutions is actually found to increase the *gender* gap; not only are women less likely to join the institutions concerned than are the men, but the unequalising effects of this are compounded by the fact that when they do join 'such affiliation has less payoff in terms of increased political activity' for women than it does for men.[20] Indeed, the only country where the political activity of women is found to gain as much as men's from their affiliation to politically involved institutions is the USA, where no redistributive institutions are held to exist.[21]

Thus the empirical study of participation leads to exactly the same paradox as confronts the feminist who puts her trust in socialism: redistributive parties *ought* to advance the interests of women relative to men (and they frequently *profess* to do so) but somehow, mysteriously, they do not.

The questions the gender pattern demands, then, are why, and how, are these invariable effects produced? If the spread of education has not closed the gender gap in political elites; if a commitment to feminism, either from 'above' in state or party policies, or from 'below' in the form of the women's movement makes no real difference; if the electoral 'rules of the game' can vary without an invariable effect on the pattern; and if the main conclusions of participation study (which explains so much in the case of men) do not explain the gender outcomes, there is certainly a mystery here to be solved. Small wonder that so many men have side-stepped the problem by concluding that there is something intrinsically wrong with women which accounts for it (such as their supposedly 'apolitical' nature) and that some women have retaliated with the counter-proposition that there is indeed something wrong, but with the nature of men, not women.

It is more constructive, however, when we fail to come up with answers, to ask ourselves if it is not the approach which has been at fault. In the following pages, a new theoretical approach to the problem is conceived, which draws on anthropological and historical as well as political science perspectives to explain the universal gender pattern. Precise hypotheses are constructed, which predict the gender outcome in vastly different settings and in subsequent chapters are put to the proof.

TOWARDS AN EXPLANATION OF THE GENDER PATTERN

Such a universal phenomenon as the gender pattern of recruitment obviously requires an equally universal explanation. It should be equally obvious that this explanation will not be located entirely in the situation and behaviour of women themselves. Nor will a single setting suffice for its detection and demonstration. The problem demands a comparative approach, and must encompass men as well as women. There are two main reasons for this.

8

In the first place (as anthropologists first pointed out more than fifty years ago), although in all societies women are distinguished from men because they bear the children, and the differences in reproductive role are always the kernel around which gender roles are culturally constructed, the way these roles are constituted and the connections which are drawn between reproduction and other aspects of adult life are extremely variable. As a result, the actual content of gender roles and the degree of their differentiation vary enormously from one society and culture to another.[22] What is women's work in one place and time, is men's in another and vice versa. Thus, for example, the medical profession is a male preserve in the industrialised west, but was predominantly female in the Soviet Union. Farm work is regarded as too physically demanding for women in most of Europe and North America, yet most of the (unmechanised) agricultural labour in many Third World countries is done by women, and the rural work-force is predominantly female in the former Soviet Union, too. Until the early years of this century, clerical jobs in all societies were almost exclusively performed by men, yet have been regarded ever since as 'women's work' in the industrialised world. The variations which existed from one primitive society to another were apparently no less startling; deep sea fishing, we are told by Lewenhak, was normally the preserve of men among Polynesians, but off Cape Horn, of all places, it was the role of women and only girls were taught how to swim.[23]

The degree to which societies recognise a difference between the worlds of men and women and demand their separation varies even more strikingly. Women's questioning of the 'female role' has surfaced mainly in advanced societies, yet from the perspective of institutions of sex-segregation like purdah, gender differentiation in the west appears so slight as to be almost non-existent. In fact the only cultural response to biological sex that does not vary from from one society from another, as the anthropologists have also pointed out, is that the attributes assigned to men, whatever they may be, are everywhere more highly valued and rewarded than those of women.[24]

In practice, then, there are only three fixed characteristics of gender roles. The first is the fact of their universal existence. The second is that women everywhere have primary responsibility for childcare. The third, and least adequately explored in its implications, is that one set of values – those of men – is always dominant.

What this means is that the dominance of male values has crucial implications for men as well as women, for these values determine not only the relationship between men and women but relations among men themselves. Whether the source of these values and their supremacy lies in the innate characteristics of men or in a universal cultural response to the existence of two sexes with very different reproductive roles – or in a

9

combination of the two – is not the point at this juncture, though it will be crucial to any assessment of the prospects for a society without any gender (as opposed to reproductive) roles at all. For the moment, it is enough to note that when women seek to do the same things as men: when, for example, they begin to compete for entry to political elites, they do so within systems which have been set up by men for their own purposes and which reflect their values.

This brings us to the the second, interrelated reason why we must look beyond the experience of women in order to explain it – the fact that a general condition of subordination is *not* specific to women, but one which they share, because of the nature of male values, with many men. In terms of the political system, what this means is that women are never the only political out-group. Indeed their uniqueness lies in being the only out-group which does not include men. Political systems as we know them – that is, male-dominated political systems – abound with out-groups, such as ethnic, racial and linguistic groups; slaves or serfs; groups or classes identified by their relationship to the productive process, such as peasants and industrial workers; religious sects; and, of course, 'those who are always with us' – the poor. An explanation of the gender pattern which is rooted in the female gender role cannot account for the existence of these other out-groups any more than colour, creed or class can be used to explain the problems of women in general.

When women encounter a problem within the systems of men (like that of access to political elites) *and this is a problem for men too*, it should be obvious that the explanation for the problem cannot lie solely in the unique and culture-specific features of their own, female situation, precisely because it is unique to women. Even if we are careful to take a comparative approach and succeed in distinguishing a common core of female gender everywhere, a theoretical approach which is confined to the general consequences which flow from women's gender role and ignores their interdependence with those which flow from the dominance of men can never provide more than a partial explanation for a phenomenon which is rooted in both. To understand the universal political implications of gender and how they are related to the equally universal implications of out-group status for groups that are all-male or mixed, we must look to *both* the general character of gender relations *and* the common properties of the systems in which women are seeking to advance, recognising that the common denominator of both is the dominance of men, over women in the one case and over men as well in the other.

It is a fact, none the less, that the tendency of theoretical approaches to the gender problem has been either (a) to marginalise it as secondary to such primary male concerns as socialism or (b) to concentrate more or less exclusively on the social-cultural situation and characteristics of women in particular contexts, emphasising such overlapping concepts as gender socialisation,[25] social role constraint[26] and even 'lifestyle',[27] which are to a large extent inevitably culture-specific and also add as much to our knowledge of the consequences as the causes of male dominance. Valuable as some of these latter contributions are in themselves, their findings are limited by the lack of scope for generalisation and the need for a more thorough exploration of their relationship to the situation of men.

Empirically these approaches encounter problems, too. History has shown that it is only too easy to realise socialist objectives without altering the condition of women relative to men at all. On the other tack, the findings of socialisation studies on both sides of the Atlantic are inconsistent and at best inconclusive[28] and though it seems obvious that women's social roles must severely inhibit their participation at the national level of politics, none of the variants on the social role theme can account for women's gross underrepresentation in local politics, their lower success rate at all levels, and the fact that the most striking source of variation in the proportion of women in national legislatures is not, as this perspective would suggest, the local variation in women's social roles but is instead the kind of electoral system in use. Thus the proportion of women in the Italian legislature is frequently higher than in Britain and the United States[29] and the recent numerical advance of Scandinavian women in the traditional political structures has not, contrary to the popular impression in other countries, been the result of any major shift in childcare responsibilities or the female gender role.[30] Furthermore, the European Parliament, with its extraordinary inconveniences of distance and alternating locations in two different cities, has turned out to be comparatively attractive to women political aspirants in some of the more peripheral parts of Europe; 18 per cent of the UK's candidates in 1984 were women, which is only 4 per cent short of the proportion which stood in the Scottish District elections of the previous month and compares with 11 per cent of the candidates in the General Election of 1983. In addition, although the lowest proportion of women elected to any of the national contingents in the European Parliament was 8 per cent from peripheral, male-chauvinist Greece, this is nearly twice as great as the highest proportion of women 'liberated' America has ever sent to Congress.[31]

There are clearly other forces at work here than socialisation and social role constraints and since the pattern occurs independently of variation not only in gender roles but also in levels of industrialisation and democratisation, we cannot look to the latter for a primary explanation either. The evidence points strongly to the objectives of men and the nature of their political relations as the place to start looking for the explanation. It is the second of our 'almost iron' laws which is at work

11

and we must seek its foundations not so much in women themselves as in the values and behaviour of men.

THE NATURE OF MALE-DOMINATED POLITICAL SYSTEMS

There are two common properties of all the systems created by men: their competitive inegalitarianism and the interdependence of social, economic and political resources. The whole history of men is one of competition for the objects they value, which are consequently always in short supply. Relations among them, like those of men with women, are based on the unequal distribution of these values and are therefore always those of hierarchy and dominance – hence the very existence of elites and of in- and out-groups in the first place. Indeed, the very function of politics, according to such disparate sources as Locke, Rousseau and Marx, is to defend and regulate this inequality and, as Dahl reminds us, the relationship between resources in the different spheres is always a dynamic one.[32] Socio-economic resources are converted into political status and the polity is a principal arena of competition among men precisely because political power serves in its turn to defend, maintain or challenge the distribution of resources in the other fields.

This dynamic interdependence between social, economic and political status is at one and the same time the explanation of the ability of in-groups to become self-perpetuating elites (i.e. to resist change) and the reason why the reverberations of change in one field, such as economic relations, are invariably felt in the others and may lead to the actual replacement of incumbent elites. While it is in the interest of everyone, some of the time, to have sufficient social, political and economic stability to enjoy what he has in peace, the complete absence of competition is rarely in anyone's interest, because it is difficult to be satisfied with what he has got when there is a possibility of getting more. Hence the perpetual pursuit of peace *and* war, co-operation *and* conflict. Hence, too, the constantly shifting perceptions of what constitutes the best kind of political system and the most desirable set of international relations, as political values and goals respond to changes in the distribution of competitive forces and expectations.

It follows that when women compete with men for access to political elites, they do so on the terms already established by men for competition among themselves and in political systems which already contain out-groups of men. The success of women in politics, like that of any male out-group, cannot be achieved within such systems without displacing, or replacing an existing elite and without some change in values, and it cannot occur independently of fundamental changes in socio-economic as well as political relations. Of course, without a clear understanding of the way men regulate their own access to political elites, the conditions which govern that of women will remain obscure.

Observation suggests that there are two basic mechanisms which have been used to regulate access to political power among men, providing both a framework for competition and a means of setting bounds upon it. In many traditional societies and those modern dictatorships which are similarly characterised by the close unity of political, social and economic status, the principal means used by elites to maintain their relative position has been simply to exclude other men from competing altogether. This exclusion of out-groups *per se*, or discrimination as it is nowadays perceived, is a device which may come to be enshrined in convention and law but from which the threat of physical coercion is rarely very far removed. Historically it has taken such 'constitutionalised' forms as slavery; qualifications such as birth, religion and property for political office; a limited franchise and so on. Discrimination may also take more subtle, cultural forms, such as the development of in-group and out-group stereotypes which work informally on people's expectations to qualify the one and disqualify the other for access to convertible resources. Discrimination may be open, or in the case of elites under severe pressure, disguised by a semblance of equal opportunity; it may be conscious or take the unwitting form of prejudice.

It is incontrovertible that outright exclusion has been the first line of male defence against women, through sex qualifications for entry to property ownership, education, occupations which are valued by men and political rights. Under some systems of exclusion, such as the English, women after marriage have even been denied any social existence by the law. In some cases the restrictions on women's access to resources can be traced to remote historical times, while in others they have been a response to the new conditions created by capitalism or have not been introduced until women actively sought the entrée to new rights enjoyed by men. While this kind of overt discrimination is still practised in many parts of the world, it has had to be abandoned in recent times in advanced societies, just as it has in respect of ethnic minorities and the poor, because of its incompatibility with the ostensibly egalitarian values of modern men. It would, however, be quite uncharacteristic of the behaviour of male elites if more covert and informal, to say nothing of unconscious forms of discrimination did not continue to be practised none the less, against women as they are against men.

However, there is a second mechanism which is more characteristic of advanced societies in modern times; it consists of institutionalised conflict, through structures which convert socio-economic and other contingent resources into political rewards in an open and regulated competition for political power. Its development was necessitated by the advent of capitalism, which wrought significant changes in the underlying conditions of competition among men.

One of the major effects of capitalism was to create new resources which led to the expansion and proliferation of elites and the relative dispersal of social, economic and consequently political status. It became increasingly difficult, and self-defeating, for traditional elites to practise outright exclusion in the face of the rising expectations and socio-economic resources of newly emergent groups. Political systems were opened up, by peaceable or violent means, to accommodate this wider social base of competition but, in order to regulate the distribution of resources and above all to prevent its becoming too general and egalitarian for their liking, the incumbent elites and their competitors had recourse to such protective mechanisms as differential systems of education; informal patronage networks; exclusive professional, business and other occupational associations; and the development of new political institutions to regulate access to political power. It was particularly in order to take advantage of the extension of the franchise that political parties arose; institutions designed to harness the popular vote to the pursuit of political office by competing elites.

Thus the basic features of contemporary political systems emerged, including of course those elements of the recruitment process which are to be found today not only in competitive party systems but to some degree wherever their influence is felt:

1 self-selection;
2 what Prewitt described as institutional-selection, but might more accurately be called external-selection (since individuals and informal groups as well as institutions may act as agents of recruitment); and
3 voter-selection.[33]

On the face of it, all three pose distinct risks to both the continuity and stability of political systems and the inter-related interests of existing elites. If anyone can come forward, then why not the 'have nots'? And since the relatively disadvantaged are always in the majority, the popular franchise could be used to put them in power. The more open the competitive system, the more opportunity too for challengers to the *status quo* to organise themselves and impinge on the recruitment process through their own institutions. The result could in theory be a rapid and revolutionary redistribution of resources, with the formation of new in-group and out-group identities or even, as some have hoped, the end of competition altogether. In practice, however, political change in competitive systems has been evolutionary rather than revolutionary and the complete dispossession of elites is the exception rather than the rule.

The reason, of course, is that very same interdependence of socio-economic and political resources which underpins the whole history of human political values, roles and practices and led to the opening up of competition in the first place. Whatever the available forms of political action may be, and whatever mix and balance of elements may be found in the recruitment process, there is a basic tendency for those who act and come forward to be 'haves' rather than 'have nots'. At the lowest levels of political activity, this tendency is so pronounced that Verba and Nie have described it as the 'standard model' of participation.[34] As far as political elites are concerned, their tendency to be dominated by socio-economic elites has been so inexorable as to call to mind the 'iron law of oligarchy' which was proposed by Michels, and it is not difficult to see why this should be so. The very same attributes which identify people as members of socio-economic elites – property, income, occupation and education – are those which render people more likely to take part in politics. They also give them what used to be described as 'a stake in society' and, consequently, a sense that politics is relevant to their lives. On the other hand, people who do *not* enjoy high status in their own or others' eyes are by the same token exposed to exactly those forces which will make it difficult to participate at all, let alone seek entrée to elites: such factors as their lack of the 'civic orientations' which flow from education and a sense of one's worth, the expectation that elite roles and the modes of political thought and action which go with them will require people with superior attributes to perform them correctly, and the fear that by putting themselves forward they will be construed as challenging the *status quo* and will be punished accordingly. In any case, the material conditions of life which are necessary to take advantage of what Seligman has called the 'political opportunity' structure[35] – economic independence, control over one's time and appropriate funds – are a function of status too. This does not mean that political recruits are necessarily always pursuing the narrow interests of their dominant class (indeed, history shows that the sufferings of the most deprived are sometimes introduced to the political agenda not by their own kind, who are non-participant, but by people from the most privileged sectors of society), but it does mean that where elite-based institutions apply selection criteria which advance high status individuals through the recruitment process, they are swimming with the tide.

Of course, where these institutions are concerned, it must be expected that strong motives of self-preservation and political interest will reinforce the self-selection bias. It is only logical for their selectors to prefer high status candidates, for these are the people who exemplify the attributes they value themselves and share their motivations. Neither their interests nor the perspectives on which they draw will normally be served by choosing people of a different kind to advance and represent them. Because the kind of people they prefer will also be of the kind who

15

mostly *want* to be involved, this will seem both natural and inevitable, too. The only tension within the recruitment process is likely to come from the fact that parties have to attract a popular following among low-ses groups in order to win elections or maintain their legitimacy in a 'popular' dictatorship. In practice the advent of mass-based democracies has given the parties a crucial role in mediating between the tendency of self-selection and the interests of the mass electorate. The standard outcome is the curious balance that exists in most advanced societies, between the socio-economic elite attributes of political leaders and the mildly redistributive content of their policies.

Change does take place none the less, within competitive political systems as well as by the revolutionary overthrow of traditional elites. This century has seen major adjustments to the distribution of political power, and consequently to the distribution of socio-economic resources through political action; the rise of socialist parties in Western Europe and the creation of the British welfare state are cases in point. These changes may have been accepted by incumbent elites, but their source has lain outside them, in the political advance of organised out-groups, and their implementation has been associated with the advance into political elites of individuals whose participation does not conform to the 'standard model'. That this has been possible at all is due, yet again, to the intrinsic nature of capitalism. Instead of the socio-economic polarisation which many on both sides of the nineteenth-century class conflict came to expect, capitalism in most advanced societies led instead to a more complex stratification based on two different kinds of socio-economic resource.

The development of capitalism gave rise not only to new elites composed of highly resourced individuals but to a new, collective kind of resource. One of its effects was to concentrate workers in circumstances favourable to the development of their political consciousness whilst providing them with a weapon in its own dependency on the continuity of their labour. Large social groups emerged, made up of individually powerless, low-status men, who could none the less wield considerable collective power by virtue of their strategic location in the capitalist economy and their essential skills. Workers in large concerns, with sufficient money wages to support unions and strikes and the self-confidence which went with the possession of highly valued skills, were particularly well placed to take industrial and political action; in trade unions and socialist or labour parties they found the means to do so. Another collective resource, political this time, lay to hand in the popular vote and though they had to compete with elite-based parties for the support of low-ses voters, the fact that socialist parties were derived from the working-class and identified with it in their programmes helped them to reap the advantage that working-class votes were both numerous and

16

geographically concentrated and could thus be effectively mobilised to win elections.

What then of the selection criteria of parties which originate in the collective resources of low-ses groups? It is logical to expect that similar motives to those of elite-based selectors will lead to a different socio-economic tendency on the part of low-ses selectors within parties committed to redistributive policies. The people they too can be expected to value are those who exemplify the attributes from which their party identity and strength derive. These will be people like themselves, to whom the ethos and goals of the party are most familiar, comprehensible and dear. In any case, to the extent that the overthrow of existing elites is one of these goals, logic and the need for credibility suggest that there will be electoral and psychological costs in choosing elite individuals as candidates. The fact that the party is also modifying the standard model of *grass-roots* participation by recruiting members from low-ses groups, means that they will have an adequate pool of non-standard self-selectors on which to draw.

It would be naïve, all the same, to imagine that the effect of such parties' intervention will be to *invert* the standard model of participation where their recruits are concerned. It is true that in the short term this might appear to be the case. For example, the composition of the British House of Commons changed quite markedly with the election of the first wave of Labour MPs after the First World War; 70 per cent of them were workers, and mostly manual.[36] However, the working class is not a homogeneous mass of equally skilled, equally valued and equally unionised individuals. The collective resources on which its political movements are based are not equally distributed and it is from the most-resourced sectors of this class that the most powerful unions and the greatest levels of political consciousness are derived. If labour movements tend to favour recruits who exemplify their own most valued attributes, then from a middle- or upper-class perspective these people may be indistinguishable from any other workers, but they are actually most unlikely to come mainly from the least collectively resourced sectors of the working class even if these least-skilled and lowest-paid comprise the majority of that class.

Unfortunately, experience also suggests that once redistributive parties have established their access to elite positions (which in the case of free elections among mass electorates involves the entrenchment of partisan rather than personality-oriented patterns of electoral behaviour) the effect of such institutions tends to become blunted by the infiltration of the standard model of recruitment within the parties themselves. Thus the tendency of the Parliamentary Labour party in Britain has been to 'converge' in its socio-economic characteristics with its elite-based rival, the Conservatives.[37] A similar process can be observed within the party

organisation and the unions too, where time and organisational elaboration have produced their own internal stratification and career
structures. In the Soviet Union, the elitist tendency of the CPSU since the
1930s, notwithstanding its claim to be the party of the working class, was
also well attested, of course.[38] In both cases the revisionist effect of the
standard model has been most pronounced in higher-level elites. The
long-term tendency of such institutions is thus to modify, rather than
invert, the standard model and we can expect to find that even this effect
is strongest in the early period of their existence and thereafter at the
lower levels of the political hierarchy.

It is thus within a complex context of competition, resources and
recruitment among men, in which resources may be individual or
collective, the motivations of the parties conservative or redistributive
and the tendencies of recruitment either 'standard' or 'modified' that the
question of the gender pattern must be posed. It was only at the end of
the basic processes of change which gave rise to modern party systems
that the question of women's access to political elites first seriously
arose. The last social group to achieve the vote and qualify for public
office at all, they entered the competitive arena only after the modern
processes of elite recruitment had taken shape and without the benefit of
either socio-economic resources or a physically concentrated female
vote. Neither the expectation that women's entry to the public sphere
would be followed rapidly by their integration to political elites, nor
the hope that they would be among the principal beneficiaries of redistributive parties, has been borne out. It is the relationship between
these two variables – the out-group status of women in the world of
men, and their failure to penetrate political elites – which must now be
addressed.

WOMEN AND RECRUITMENT: THE 'SCISSORS' HYPOTHESES

The theoretical approach

That the key to the problem of the gender pattern lies in large part in the
socio-economic basis of male recruitment will become obvious, if we start
from the premise that (a) wherever women are seeking access to political
elites they are doing so through the medium of institutions created by
men and (b) whatever the attributes may be which are valued by men,
women in a male-dominated society are less likely to possess them. From
this foundation it is possible to develop precise hypotheses (which can be
tested empirically) about the way in which the effect of socio-economic
resources on the recruitment of *men* determines the outcome for *women*,
and why this outcome – the gender pattern – is always the same,

18

irrespective of both the political system which is involved and the selection criteria which are being used.

It has not, of course, entirely escaped political scientists that there is a relationship between socio-economic resources and the gender pattern in elites. In Britain, Vallance has suggested that there is a connection between women's absence from political elites and the higher levels of other hierarchies.[39] She and others have pointed out that even high-ses women lack the resource of occupations which particularly 'converge' with national office among men. Similar observations have been made in the United States, where Welch has attributed 'a substantial part' of women's political under-representation to their absence from the 'eligible pool' of business and professional occupations[40]; Deber's observation[41] that the candidacies of women are 'targeted to lose' and Merritt's hypothesis that women candidates will resemble male losers[42] are also significant theoretical advances.

However, all this progress has been made on a culture-specific basis and within the conceptual framework of the standard model. When the evidence does not fit, as in the case of the British Labour party, there is no attempt to accommodate this theoretically. Instead, commentators who have begun by ascribing women's slow start in participation in general and their problem of elite recruitment in elite-based parties in particular to their lack of high, individual socio-economic resources either ignore the issue of socialist or labour parties altogether or shift their ground, ascribing the problem there to a lack of political resources instead. With the possible exception of Hernes and Hanninen-Salmelin, who go to the heart of the matter by observing the *'systematic character'*[43] of socio-economic elite representation (and women's under-representation) in the corporate structures of the Nordic countries and in passing suggest a parallel with the composition of elected structures, the opportunity to integrate the gender pattern findings in order to construct a general and comparative theory of recruitment and resources is being lost.

The basis of such a theory must be that women as an out-group by definition lack the attributes of status in all fields of social relations and in particular the profiles of characteristics which the institutions of men are designed to convert into political status, influence and power. Of course, not all elite positions are equally attractive to all men, even among those who seek political office. The resources which are relevant to any particular contest will depend on the distribution of values in the male catchment area for the office in question.

To the extent that maleness itself is a prerequisite for success, women's problem may be described as sex discrimination, and straightforward discrimination by male gate-keepers against women seeking nomination to winnable seats has been proposed by Rasmussen as a reason for the low success rate of women candidates for elective office.[44] Although he has nothing but circumstantial evidence to present for this assertion and the only systematic search for discriminatory attitudes (among Labour party selectors) found none,[45] the proposition that men (and women) discriminate against women as such is difficult to disbelieve in a society which values maleness more. Even so, sex discrimination can be only a partial solution, for it cannot explain either the patterns of success and failure among men or the fact that some women succeed in competition with men. It is more to the point that the nature of male dominance ensures that among the correlates of sex will also be the correlates of success and failure among men.

Where there are winners, there must also be losers, and, in the perpetual competition among themselves, the majority of men are losers. What distinguishes these losing men is exactly what distinguishes women too – their lack of the attributes of success among men. Where men and women have the same attributes but men are more successful in the process of selection, we may put this gender gap down to discrimination; where there is a lack of women with the attributes of success among men, we do not need this variable to explain the lower rates of either participation or success among women.

Men, women and the standard model

Where men are competing for entry to a political elite, and it is the standard model of recruitment which is operating among them, the attributes in question are those of high socio-economic status. Losing men will be distinguished by their relative lack of resources, low-ses men being less likely either to come forward or to succeed when they do. Of course, male elites compete among themselves and have their own internal hierarchies, so that the competitors (and the attributes of success) will vary according to the office in question; in politics as at the races, there are 'horses for courses'. Only the careful and detailed comparison of winners and losers in each case will show which resources are most relevant, and which configuration most commonly associated with success.

As an out-group, women are by definition lacking in all aspects of status compared with men. Since low-ses individuals are less likely than other people to self-select, the first effect of this will be a smaller pool of potential female candidates than male, even if women self-select at exactly the same rate as comparable men. Indeed there is no need to look any further for an explanation of the frequently observed fact that women 'do not want to come forward'. Given their socio-economic location, and applying the same causal model to women's participation as we do to men's this is exactly what we should predict. Most men do not want to

20

come forward either, but the minority who do come from clearly defined socio-economic groups.

Women's lack of resources will bite again at the point where external selectors intervene. Even those women who do aspire will tend to have less resources than high-ses men, so that even fewer will appeal to institutional and other selectors, especially for winnable seats. In their lack of both resources and success, women will resemble losing men. If only those women were to stand whose resources were the equal of the most eligible men, then the proportion of women candidates would be very small (if indeed there were any at all). In practice, the proportion of women can be expected to outstrip their possession of resources, producing the invariable effect that women, in their lack of the relevant resources for success, resemble losing men.

It might be asked, on the one hand, why will women compete when they do not have the requisite resources to succeed, and, on the other, if it still true anyway, given the spread of education, that women are seriously disadvantaged compared to men. Of course the generic questions are, 'Why does *anyone* compete without the right resources?' (for the majority of losers are usually men) and 'What *is* the relationship of education (in distinction to the other constituents of socio-economic status), with winning, as opposed to seeking, office? The first question cannot be fully answered without answering the second question in the process.

To the question 'Why do losers compete?', one set of answers is systemic. To win, one has to risk losing, and no one knows for certain who will win until the final choice is made. Also, a competitive system needs competitors, and this can generate pressure on relatively ill-endowed individuals to take part. People who feel that it is 'undemocratic' for someone to be elected unopposed may feel obliged to stand themselves in order to maintain the system's norms, even if they think they have no chance of winning. Political parties, too, will put pressure on people to stand in unwinnable seats rather than 'lose their credibility' by failing to put up a candidate. In both cases, it is effectively a loser who is being recruited (which is usually why conditions of candidate shortage arise in the first place) and this will both make self-selection easier and relax the criteria applied by external selectors. The tendency of education to produce a sense of civic duty will make educated people particularly vulnerable to this kind of pressure, even – or indeed especially – when they lack the other, more crucial attributes of success and have 'nothing to lose' by being defeated. However, the gender role of women (with its service orientation) and that of men (with its fear of failure) may reinforce this effect for the former, and inhibit it for the latter.[46]

Another reason is socio-economic change. The habits of mind which go with status may outlive the decline of its material base and, conversely, the rise of newly resourced groups may be impeded (and indeed disguised) by the entrenched position of existing elites. In both cases, the key is a lack of fit between the expectations of a group and the real opportunities its members have for entry to political elites. In traditional societies, both socio-economic change itself and the expectations of outgroups are severely inhibited, but in a modern competitive system it is normal to find groups with expectations which are not being met – and indeed may never be. One of the main reasons for this is the spread of education – a potent source of systematic mobilisation and disappointment which affects both sexes but produces special effects in the case of women.

Education, as we know, is peculiarly associated with the development of a disposition to take part in politics. However, it is only one of the components of socio-economic status and historically not the most important, as the analysis of capitalism (and the role of physical force and landownership in the formation of earlier systems) makes very clear. Even now, when access to an increasing number of occupations depends on educational qualifications, education in itself does not determine status in the way that property and occupation do. Access to the most valued forms of education is mediated by the non-educational resources of parents and even, in some cases, remote ancestors, and what is valued about it is often the contacts it brings as much as the qualifications. Also, many of the occupations which are most dependent on educational qualifications (like teacher, researcher and scientist) are relatively low-paid and secondary to the socio-economic structures which they serve, structures which are often – even typically – controlled and fought over by the relatively uneducated. Education may enhance people's wish to influence events, but often leads instead to a frustrating mixture of job security and dependence, in a context where it is property and other, more strategic occupations which determine the basic structure of society and the major lines of social conflict. The result is that modern societies contain fairly large groups of people whose educational resources are sufficient to create high political expectations, but too marginal to the most important dimensions of socio-economic status (individual or collective) to be able to satisfy them at anything like the rate they are created. In Britain, one consequence is the great post-war increase in the number of people who stand for Parliament, most of them representing minor parties. Since Parliament has stayed the same size, this means there are far more losers than there used to be.[47] Other effects, in Britain as elsewhere, are the proliferation of pressure groups and a growing input to the political agenda of issues (like environmental concerns) which originate with intellectuals.[48]

For women, education is the most accessible component of socio-economic status, but is also more independent of the others than is the case for men. The correlation of education with the other components of personal socio-economic status (occupation, income and property) depends on its practical exploitation. Although the combination of a high level of education and a low-status job is one which few men encounter except in times of high graduate unemployment, it is a commonplace for women, whose working lives are fundamentally affected by motherhood. The very expectation of motherhood discourages many women from ever practising an occupation commensurate with their qualifications. Some give up paid employment altogether after their children are born, becoming housewives, while those who return to work outside the home are frequently obliged to accept jobs of lower status and rewards than their level of education would lead one to expect in the case of men.[49] Thus the effect on personal status of changes in the distribution of education is much more marginal where women are concerned than is the case with men.

As far as politics is concerned, education may create the same initial expectations among females as it does among males,[50] but where the occupations of men enhance their salience and promote their fulfilment (albeit to varying degrees), women's do not. A smaller proportion of educated women than men will seek office, even though their numbers grow in comparison with the uneducated generations that came before. What is more, if virtually all the people who stand are educated, and occupation, income or property is then the variable on which male winners and losers divide, this will also be a point of difference between men and women. Thus their access to education simultaneously gives women some encouragement to aim for political status and fails to provide them with the other resources needed for success.

Men, women and the modifying model

If a modifying model of recruitment is at work, (with its very different criteria for selection) we must nevertheless expect the gender outcome to be the same. Since it is the possession of collective resources, not the absence of any resources at all, on which the identity and achievements of modifying forces are based, it is inevitable that they will be male-oriented in a male-dominated society. In the case of the working class, men have made it their business to ensure this through the power of trade unions and collaboration with employers. Though women were active in the early days of the workers' movement in most industrialising societies, by the end of the nineteenth century unions everywhere were still dominated by men and their values, as they remain to this day, even in the case of predominantly female occupations. Far from attempting to combat the separation of home and workplace developed by capitalism, the institu-

23

tions of working-class men have used their influence on the whole to reinforce the marginalisation of female labour and the socio-economic out-group status of women, through such mechanisms as the 'family wage' of men, sex-segregated employment, with low pay for women and male monopoly of skilled and economically strategic occupations, protective legislation coupled with higher rates of pay for the 'overtime' available only to men and so on.[51]

Of course, the political advance of the working class was accompanied by internal competition and stratification not only between the sexes but among men, with working-class women at the very bottom of the social heap and highly skilled men in strategic locations at the top. The power structure and achievements and, as we shall see, the elite recruitment tendencies of labour-based parties reflect quite clearly the differential resources of different sectors of their constituency.[52] It is a modification, not an inversion of the standard model of recruitment which they produce and as in the case of elite-based parties women will be less likely to have what it takes.

Lacking *either* the conventional, individual resources which are usually associated with self-selection *or* the collective ones, based on occupation and economic location, which have overcome this problem in the case of many working-class men, low-ses women will be unable to generate potential candidacies at anything like the rate of men. The most likely outcome is that very few women will stand for redistributive parties and, paradoxically, most of those who do will not be working-class. They will be the female counterparts of the upper-class socialists and ex-working-class professionals to be found in larger numbers (but as a smaller proportion) among the men. Where the modifying tendency is at its strongest (e.g. in local politics), the success rate of these women will be low, compared to low-ses candidates of either sex. Where the standard model has crept in, their numbers, resources and success rate, as ever, will be small compared to those of men.

The consequences of women's out-group status are thus the same whether the resources in question are individual or collective and whether the tendency of selectors is to reinforce or modify the standard model of the resources–recruitment relationship. They can be expressed in the form of the following two hypotheses:

1 The socio-economic characteristics of women seeking political office in a male-dominated society will be different from those of men

and

2 The attributes of women candidates will resemble those of losing men.

In the context of a study of recruitment (where winners can be compared with losers, and women with men) the demonstration of these propositions should be perfectly straightforward – so long, that is, as the different components of socio-economic status (and their varying relationships with the recruitment process) can be clearly distinguished.

Where the standard model is at work, the proof will be that women candidates, as a group, are less endowed with high individual socio-economic status than their male counterparts. Since it is this kind of resource which is associated with success among men, relatively low ses, at least in respect of its success-related aspects, will be the common factor between women and losing men, compared to winning men.

Where modifying institutions are at work, recruiting and favouring the candidacies of men who are low in individual ses but high in collective resources, the differences between women and men will appear to turn the 'standard model' on its head. Because there is no modifying intervention on behalf of low-ses women (who do not have access to collective resources), the latter will be a missing element in the overall profile of women candidates, compared to that of men; women will be almost entirely dependent on high-ses – the standard model – to stimulate their candidacies. The seemingly bizarre result will be that women (like the losing men) will have higher, not lower 'status' than successful men. The point is that this will not be status which is valued by selectors in the particular context where they are competing.

The implications of these hypotheses for women's recruitment are obvious. If they hold good for both models of recruitment (standard and modifying) and different political contexts, then the socio-economic out-group status of women is in itself a sufficient explanation for the universality of the 'iron laws' which constitute the gender pattern of recruitment, even where socialist parties are powerful and apparently committed to women's advance. As long as women's access to political elites depends upon the same process of recruitment as obtains for men, but their attributes are those of losers, how can they succeed? Realistically, their lack of resources must be expected to inhibit their advance on both dimensions of the recruitment process – mobilisation and selection – and through the elements of both self and institutional selection. The dominance of men can be sustained without recourse to sex-discrimination, as opposed to socio-economic discrimination. All other things being equal, until there are more women in society with the attributes of successful men (i.e. until women cease to be a socio-economic out-group), this situation cannot be expected to change.

PATTERNS OF SUCCESS AMONG WOMEN: HYPOTHESES 3 AND 4

Ideally, the ultimate demonstration of the socio-economic explanation for the gender pattern should be found in the patterns of success and failure among women. The success rate of 'winner-type' women should correspond to that of similar men, and women with the 'wrong' attributes should be less successful than those with the 'right' ones. Sheer lack of numbers, however, may make this proposition rather difficult to demonstrate unless, or until women's socio-economic profile becomes less unlike that of men, and the number of their well-resourced candidates begins to grow. In the extreme case, if there are no women candidates at all who have the attributes of winning men, the predicted results obviously will not be found; if they are very few, then we run into the problems which arise in very small samples, where an insignificant deviation can have a major effect on the results. It is also quite possible that the success rate of 'loser' type women in a small candidate population will be higher than it would within a larger group. Even among men there will always be factors at work to ensure that not all winning men conform to the dominant recruitment model – such contingencies as the idiosyncratic effects of personality, the rise of protest parties, and by-products of electoral systems such as marginal seats and tactical voting. Into these nooks and crannies of the recruitment process will penetrate men who look like losers and yet succeed, and with them some women who, in the small population of female winners, may well loom larger than their male counterparts among the successful men.[53]

With these technical caveats in mind, it is therefore somewhat more tentatively that the following two hypotheses are advanced:

3 Women with the attributes of winning men will be winners too

and

4 The socio-economic correlates of success and failure will be the same among women as they are among men.

Thus far we have looked at the resources which women may bring to the recruitment process from the standpoint of the male values on which it is founded. From the very different perspective of the female gender role, with its universal core of mothering responsibilities, it might still be argued that women possess distinctive attributes, over and above their lack of socio-economic resources, which derive from the peculiarities of their role and might constitute potential political assets. Such characteristics as their well-attested tendency to enter public life at a more mature and experienced point in the life-cycle than men,[54] their willingness to accept responsibility and co-operation,[55] and their expertise in somewhat specialised areas of grass-roots political participation[56] spring to mind.

The trouble is that the female gender role is not the standpoint from which male-dominated political systems are constructed and operated. Even if women candidates do possess distinct, gender-based characteristics (which are not simply either the corollary of the male monopoly of

26

valued attributes or else an arithmetical illusion caused by the *absence* among women of important categories which are found among men), the problem is that these special characteristics are not valued in politics, for it is the male gender role which is valued, not the female. Since there is no reason to believe that women will be judged differently from men by selectors – unless indeed the possession of characteristics which are distinctively associated with an out-group actually militates against their chances by accentuating their unvalued, out-group identity and the practical and moral problems it presents to elite participation – we can only incorporate this perspective on recruitment in the form of the following rather depressing observation:

5 That any distinctive attributes of women candidates which are derived from their gender role (over and above those which are simply the corollary of their lack of the winning attributes among men) will be neutral to their prospects of success, or even negatively associated with it.

The sum of all these tendencies will be to create a 'scissors' problem for women which accounts for the universal pattern of gender differences in elite aspiration and success in male-dominated societies:

Whatever is associated with success among men, women will have less of it – the first blade of the scissors. Whatever women have that men do not will be of no use to them in competition with men – the second blade.

Of course, this is not to say that male dominance is a perpetual and impermeable condition of human existence, any more than the relationships among men have remained fixed throughout their history. Women would not be the first out-group to overcome, or at least modifiy the entrenched position of an existing elite and there are some observers who believe the dominance of men already is being eroded. However, we should not attempt to make predictions about the outcome for women until we are sure we understand the systems they are trying to penetrate. How can women hope to avoid the pitfalls of unrealistic hopes and disappointment which have characterised the last twenty years of the women's movement (or distinguish those strategies which may help to shorten the odds against success) until they know precisely what the obstacles are?

The first object of the present work is to improve this understanding. In the preceding pages, a general theory has been presented which seeks to explain the socio-economic basis of political elite recruitment among men and the way this impinges upon women. In particular, this theory is designed to account for the fact that the gender pattern is always the same, not only where it is the standard model of recruitment which is at work among men, but also where modifying forces (such as collective resources and the redistributive institutions to which they often give rise) have intervened to improve the chances of those who are low in individual socio-economic status. If the propositions of this theory can be demonstrated empirically, we will have come a long way towards an understanding of what women are always up against. We will also have laid a proper foundation for the analysis of their future prospects.

The focus of the following chapters is therefore on the hypotheses which make up the first blade of the 'scissors'. In Chapter 3, new data and old are used to demonstrate the models of recruitment at work among men, and their implications for women, in the comparative framework of partisan recruitment in three very different political systems; the USA, Scotland and the former USSR. In Chapter 4, it is the basis of non-partisan recruitment, with its greater emphasis in self-selection and the unmodified impact of non-party, social institutions, which is examined, in the settings of the USA and Scotland. Whereas the data used in Chapters 3 and 4 are drawn almost entirely from local politics, Chapter 5 includes recruitment to the European Parliament and the British House of Commons as well as local politics in Scotland, and the point at issue is the possible role of minor or 'third' parties in causing deviations from the gender pattern and promoting change.

2

MAJOR PARTIES AND RECRUITMENT: THE USA, SCOTLAND AND THE USSR

The subject of this chapter is the role of major parties in the formation of the gender pattern. The object is to use the study of recruitment to test the three hypotheses which make up the first blade of the 'scissors' problem, in a comparative framework which offers a variety of institutional settings and examples of both standard and modifying models of selection. The focus, as far as possible, is on local politics, the level at which there are large candidate populations for study, including enough women for empirical analysis to be feasible, and where the modifying tendency of a redistributive institution is likely to be strongest. This is also the lowest level of political office and is thus the recruitment Rubicon for most people who seek entrée to elites.

DEFINING A RECRUITMENT STUDY

Although 'recruitment' is a commonplace political science term, it is frequently misused, not least by political scientists themselves. Especially in the United States, many studies which purport to deal with it are not really focused on recruitment at all, but deal instead with its end-product and are simply elite studies. Properly understood, recruitment is the *process* in which a political elite is formed from a general population. The basic, inter-related constituents of this process are *mobilisation* of individuals to seek these roles; and *selection*, whereby the few who will compose the elite are winnowed from the many who do not enter the lists at all and the losers among those who do. To qualify as a study of recruitment, a study must cater to these two components; it must present a population from whom to choose and a choice that has been made. To be of any value, it must identify the selectors, too, and tell us enough about the differences between the winners and the losers (or the mobilised and unmobilised) to show what selection criteria have been used. Without these basic standards of research design, we run the risk of inferring the characteristics of one group from those of another and attributing bias (or neutrality) to selectors where none may exist. Because there are so many possible steps in the recruitment process, and no single set of selectors, care must also be taken to distinguish its elements and avoid attributing the bias of one stage, and one set of selectors, to others which may have a different tendency.

In the present instance, the objective is to focus on the role of parties in recruitment, in order to distinguish the selection criteria they use in choosing among men (and the implications of these criteria for women) in different national settings. To do this, a stage in the process must be isolated in each case where the selectors are the parties. The population among whom they make recruitment choices must be identified and so must those who win or lose by the criteria they use. The research design thus requires an understanding of the varying elements and stages in recruitment; the way they interact in different contexts; and the relationship of parties, in particular, to the recruitment process.

POLITICAL PARTIES AND THE RECRUITMENT PROCESS

As well as the three distinct elements of self-selection, institutional (and other external) selection, and voter-selection, there are also three potentially distinct stages in the recruitment process to which they are in varying degrees related, each with its 'winners' and its 'losers'. In the first place, the individual must become disposed to seek (or at the very least to accept) *entrée* to the political elite. The second, although frequently overlapping stage of the process brings the criteria of external selectors and the local 'rules of the game' to bear on individual aspirations, to determine whether the individual is indeed eligible to seek office according to those rules and whether he or she meets the approval of any selectors (such as party selectors or voters in primary elections) who have the power to decide which names go forward to the final selection and/or in what guise (e.g. as official or endorsed party candidates or on a short-list). The third, and final stage, is that of election or appointment itself, which divides the approved candidates into 'winners' and 'losers'. In practice, there is enormous variation in advanced societies in both the precise mix of recruitment elements and the distinctiveness of the stages at which they are brought to bear. The intervention of institutions, however, and especially of political parties, tends to be a factor at all stages.

An obvious source of variation in the recruitment process and the role of parties is systemic. In some political systems there are no elections, so that voter selection is not a direct factor in recruitment at all. Likewise, dominant groups or institutions may be able to exclude specific categories of the population from political participation or candidacy altogether, which obviously limits the scope of self-selection. Of course, this does not mean that parties or other institutions can ever be so dominant in the recruitment process that they control it altogether. An element of self-selection can never be excluded, for it is difficult to see how any system could function if people were systematically selected for leadership roles against their will. Nor can party selectors choose people who are not visible to them. At the other end of the process, even if the mass electorate are denied the direct leverage of choosing who to vote for there will be a need to secure popular acquiescence, if nothing more, which may constrain selectors to take some account of what they think the popular criteria would be.

Within these parameters, political parties usually have a considerable hold on contemporary recruitment processes, with the degree of their dominance varying according to such factors as the type of party system; the kind of electoral system in use and the rules governing the identification of candidates; levels of party cohesiveness and organisation; and the strength of partisanship in the mass electorate. The institutional framework of recruitment may be tight, in which case one or more institutions (usually political parties) have a monopoly of the nominating process. Or it may be loose, in which case non-partisan, group-based or individual candidacies will co-exist with partisan nominations or even substitute the latter altogether. The tighter the framework, the more likely it is that some institutions will control the final stage of election as well as nomination, either by eliminating voter choice altogether or (where the system calls for party lists) by ranking the candidacies in such a way that voters have little freedom of action. Where elections are open but strongly partisan, few realistic opportunities will exist for those of the self-selected who do not meet with party approval. Equally, when party labels rather than the personal characteristics of candidates is the basis of voter choice, and safe and winnable seats can be identified by selectors in advance, it is party selectors who are effectively distinguishing the winners from the losers at elections simply by deciding who stands where and when, or in what position on the party list. In the most extreme forms of institutional dominance, such as the one-party state, both eligibility and success in every case are in the gift of a single institution.

The shape of the recruitment process varies, too, according to the local cultural context and from one partisan framework to another. In some contexts, like the USA, anyone who does not display enough self-confidence to put him or herself forward as an unusually meritorious individual is unlikely to be taken seriously. Contrast this with a Labour party branch in Scotland when the question of nominations to the candidates' panel comes up. In the words of one of the chosen, 'In the Labour party, you don't get up and say you want to be a councillor!'[1] Any appearance of personal ambition should be avoided, however dis-

31

ingenuously, and the would-be candidate who knows the ropes will be careful to employ more subtle means of bringing himself to the attention of selectors, such as exemplary attendance at meetings, seeking the acquaintance of existing councillors and taking an obvious interest in local government matters.

Even within the same party system and at the same level of the public office hierarchy, the contextual variation can be extreme. In the British Labour party, it is unusual for local government nominations where there is no incumbent to be uncontested unless they are for extremely unwinnable seats (and even these are valued as an apprenticeship), yet Conservatives frequently report a shortage of candidates for unpromising seats and even, occasionally, the recruitment of people who were not even party members, let alone activists, for winnable seats.[2] (This does not necessarily mean, of course, that they have no one who might be prepared to do the job or that they will accept anyone who chooses to come forward; what it certainly signifies is a shortage of 'suitable' aspirants). Additionally, there are some parts of Britain where both Conservative and Labour candidates may be faced not only with opponents from other parties but with people who stand as individuals (or 'Independents') and may have genuinely selected themselves.

Thus, although self-selection is always a factor, it may manifest itself in different ways, according to the political context, and different degrees according to the extent to which the idea of candidacy originates with the individual concerned or other people, or both. An individual may openly seek nomination as a candidate or, if appropriate, apply for an appointment. More tacitly, people with an eye to selection may deliberately place themselves in the eye of selectors by performing actions which suggest willingness or eligibility to be recruited, or simply by seeking their acquaintance. On the other hand, there are people whose active sense of civic obligation or other personal characteristics both bring them unintentionally to the attention of others as being suitable for office and render them susceptible to being recruited. Of course self-selection is no guarantee of selection by others and conversely, many people who see themselves as candidate material may need a nudge from other people, or events, before they act on the idea. Where political parties are active, their attitudes to particular socio-economic groups and what they convey about their own selection criteria will also help to shape the image people have of public office and of themselves, thus indirectly influencing the patterns of self-selection.

It is by virtue of all these complications that no study of the complete recruitment process has ever been carried out, or probably ever will be. Enormous problems of research design as well as finance prevent systematic identification of self-selectors in populations at large in order to measure the proportions of those who would come forward if given any encouragement; those who are discouraged, by means crude or subtle, deliberate or unwitting, before they get to the point of applying for a place on the candidate's list or for a nomination; and those whose aspirations are considered by others but rejected. Sometimes the conditions of a particular selection process make it possible to identify distinct elements among the latter category, as Holland is able to do in his study of Labour party candidate selection for the European Parliament elections of 1979, where persistent enquiry identified four categories of aspirant: people who tried actively but without success to enter the formal selection process; people who were considered but not selected as candidates; candidates who lost; and election winners.[3] However, no satisfactory solution has been found for the others, in this or any other investigation, and although Holland's is that *rara avis*, a genuine recruitment study, it would be a delusion to suppose that it is dealing with more than a part of the whole process. What it does achieve exceptionally well is to focus on the role of a particular set of selectors at particular stages of recruitment, where the winners and losers can be identified and the criteria used by selectors can be inferred from the different characteristics of these groups. It is this which makes it a study of recruitment rather than elite composition and not, as Holland seems to suggest, the fact that it encompasses more than one stage of the selection process.[4]

The isolation of the role of party selectors in recruitment and the identification of the criteria they use to divide a particular population of male elite aspirants into 'winners' and 'losers', is exactly what is required here. Only when the criteria of recruitment among men have been identified (and the characteristics of male winners and losers have been established) do we really understand what women are up against. In addition, however, this must be achieved at a comparable level of recruitment, with comparable data on comparable populations, in a cross-national framework. This is the purpose of the present study.

THE DATA

Three countries were selected for this study: the USA, where modifying institutions are generally held to be relatively absent and recruitment is said to take place in a fairly loose institutional framework; Scotland, where a dominant redistributive institution (which may be expected to advance the candidacies of low-ses men) is confronted by an equally entrenched party of the status quo in a much tighter institutional framework; and the former Soviet Union, where one party had a monopoly of power and offered the fascinating spectacle of a single institution simultaneously operating two models of recruitment. The populations selected for study in each case were candidates for local government office.

The choice of candidates, rather than populations which included unselected aspirants for nomination, was made with two main factors in mind. The most important was comparability. Even if the primary research in Scotland could have been designed in such a way as to identify such aspirants (and the parties had been willing to co-operate), the chances of finding comparable data for the USA were very slim indeed, and for the USSR were non-existent. On the other hand, the existence of Ronald Hill's study of Soviet recruitment[5] provided both the data and the conceptualisation of a Soviet winner/loser dichotomy analogous to that which is produced among the candidates of a single party by the combination of partisan selection criteria and free elections in Britain and the USA. In all three cases, the total slate of candidates for a party consists of people who are both desirous of standing for that party and acceptable to its nominating selectors. Differences between the candidate profiles for different parties tell us what kind of people are advanced by the intervention of one party rather than another and identify the socio-economic models at work. When parties pick candidates for particular seats, however, we enter another dimension of recruitment, for in a tight partisan framework they do so in full knowledge of the electoral prospects in each seat. Unless electoral conditions are especially volatile, they know which seats they can expect to win and lose, and where the imponderables lie. When a seat is safe or winnable, this is because the voters can be trusted to vote on party lines, and in choosing a candidate the party is choosing a councillor, or probable councillor, too. In dubious or unwinnable seats, it is losers they are choosing. Where election results are highly predictable, the winners and losers in elections provide a ready-made hierarchy of selector preferences. Where they are more volatile, seats can be evaluated on a more flexible basis.

In each case the prerequisite is data which enables us to identify precisely the model(s) of recruitment at work. This means we need to have detailed information about the socio-economic background of the subjects, who must, of course, include the losing, as well as the winning candidates (or their analogues in the Soviet case). It is absolutely inadmissable to infer the characteristics of the candidates as a whole and/or the losers from the attributes of office-holders alone. After all, the office-holders might be a representative socio-economic sample of the totality of candidates, or they might not. If not, who is to say whether their status was higher or lower than that of the losers? Or whether they represent distinct occupational sectors or types of education within the broad categories commonly used by social scientists? To establish the model at work, we must be able to compare the male recruits with the male electorates from which they are drawn and then compare the characteristics of winners and losers very exactly, both overall and by party where appropriate.

Only when we understand the conditions in which the women must compete can we proceed to the next stage, the comparison of women and men. If the previous step has revealed significant differences between male winners and losers, the test of our second hypothesis is that women should differ significantly from winning men, but not from losers. Where different parties are found to be operating different models, the comparison should be by party.

METHODOLOGY

The methods used in an analysis must be appropriate to its ends, which in this case means eschewing some of the more sophisticated statistical techniques available to contemporary social science research, in favour of relatively simple methods. In fact, the methods used here are very straightforward and should be perfectly intelligible to the non-numerate. This is not just for simplicity's sake, however. It follows from the exigencies of the theoretical approach adopted here, which goes beyond the broad categories of economic activity and social status (such as social class, or manual/ non manual or professional/non-professional employment) to consider the different types of resources derived from different locations in the economy and to detect the hierarchy which exists within a social class.

The occupation variable is crucial to some of these distinctions and must not be used in any form which obscures their identity. For example, we have to be able to distinguish between different categories of worker and between those professional occupations that are linked to business and management and those like teacher or social worker that are not. Above all, we have to use the occupation variable in such a way that its association with two kinds of resources, individual and collective, is not obscured. This means that two very common treatments – scaling and dichotomisation – are largely inappropriate. When we *scale* a variable, we are assuming that its properties are linear; the higher an individual is placed on the scale, the greater the possession of the single characteristic being measured. To make a linear variable out of occupation in the present enquiry would be to distort its character to the point where vital information is lost. When we *dichotomise* a variable – and dichotomisation is a form of scaling – we are assuming that its properties can best be exploiting by dividing it into two categories, signifying the presence or absence of whatever is being measured. In the present instance, although dichotomisation is the only way of isolating the effect of any one particular category of occupation, the way it is dichotomised will vary according to the category under examination; there is no single, all-purpose division to which occupation can be reduced.

These constraints mean that two common practices in participation research are unavailable here. In the first place, the creation of an *index* of socio-economic status is out, because this depends on treating all its components as linear. This is what Verba and Nie did in their celebrated study, 'Participation in America', effectively creating an index of *individual* socio-economic status.[6] When they came to analyse their cross-national data, occupation was dropped from the index.[7] No explanation for this was given, but since the distinction between individual and collective resources had by then become a central part of their argument, we may surmise that it no longer made sense to them to treat occupation as linear. Being unwilling to abandon their index, they opted to do without the variable instead, at the cost, I fear, of much essential information. Nor can it be maintained that the problem was solved by their retention of income in the index; the distinction between high *individual* status (which roughly corresponds with high individual income) and high access to *collective* resources (associated with relatively low income) is exactly what is lost when using income as the yardstick. Like education, the other component in the Verba and Nie index, it is not an indicator of access to collective resources.

An index involves the integration of two or more linear variables into a single measure. Sophisticated techniques like multi-variate regression analysis, which preserve the separate identity of the variables but still require that they be linear, are also largely inappropriate here. This is no loss either. The object of regression analysis, as with so many techniques which have been developed mainly for the study of voting behaviour, is to provide as 'elegant' or 'parsimonious' an explanation as possible for the effect under scrutiny. They are intended to reduce life to its most intelligible form, but not to reveal its complex patterns. Paradoxically, the present study is one where the more sophisticated the statistical technique, the less sophisticated the analysis will be.

There is of course a basic problem which confronts anyone who is trying to analyse complex relationships between variables, that of sample size. The greater the detail required, the larger is the number of subgroups in use and the smaller the number of cases which appear in the cells. For the findings to be authoritative, either the sample must approximate so closely to the total population under study that tests for statistical significance are irrelevant, or else the representative sample must be so big that these tests are passed. The problem of subgroup size has been a major impediment to social science research, even in the case of 'mass' surveys like those of opinions and voting behaviour. Indeed, one may reasonably wonder what is the point of collecting a lot of this information when the sample size so often is not large enough for anyone to use it. In the case of recruitment research, the problems of finance and research design are compounded by the fact that the elites themselves are small. Unless researchers start to think in terms of surveying whole candidate populations instead of representative samples, they are likely to find their efforts undermined by sheer lack of numbers. As the reader will see, this is a problem with some existing recruitment research; as the Scottish research will show, however, it can be overcome.

THE USA

The American political system offers the most complex of the three recruitment settings tackled here and is the one in which institutional selectors are usually held to be least dominant in local politics. Though Presidential and Congressional elections are of course party-based, as are most contests for state-level electoral office, local elections are often (and in some cases compulsorily) non-partisan, at least in the sense that candidates do not (or may not) stand under a party label. Such complexity would seem to offer a unique opportunity to identify and compare the criteria of party-, self- and voter selection in a context where all three are expected to operate according to the standard model of the resources–recruitment relationship. Ideally, we should wish to identify those local candidates who are recruited or endorsed by the political parties and compare their backgrounds and the patterns of success among them with those of:

1 party candidates at higher levels,
2 their non-partisan local counterparts, and
3 party recruits in other countries.

Unfortunately, it has to be with a sense of disappointment that we turn to our empirical task. In spite of the obvious challenge of the American setting to the recruitment analyst and the trail-blazing calibre of so much of early empirical work by American political scientists, the USA has most surprisingly proved the least satisfactory of the three country studies tackled here. This is because of two closely related problems; the unexpectedly undeveloped state of American recruitment research and the lack of good data, especially at the local level. In spite of the challengingly narrow base of Dahl's meticulous historical analysis of elite recruitment in New Haven;[8] in spite of Suzanne Keller's warning in 1963 that though political office-bearers were generally drawn from socio-economic elites, it remained 'an open question' how this came about;[9] and in spite of the great progress made by research into mass-level participation, the study of elite recruitment in the USA has stagnated since the early 1960s.

Lack of adequate data is both cause and consequence of this stagnation. The major recruitment studies from Lasswell through Keller,

37

Matthews and Prewitt to the national surveys by the Center for the American Woman and Politics (CAWP) in the 1980s all suffer from an absolutely fatal flaw; they are almost exclusively based on office-holders.[10] Thus, while a general consensus has emerged that the standard model holds as good for elite recruitment as it has been shown to do for mass-level participation, this consensus is based mainly on supposition and analogy, not demonstrated fact. Only at the Presidential and Congressional level is there evidence (from a plethora of sources), to show that a very high level of socio-economic resources, especially financial, is mandatory for both candidacy and election. Even the dominant voice of Prewitt, whose 1970 study of local councillors in the San Francisco area is the principal contribution of the last twenty years, is reduced as a result to speculation. He feels sure that the ultimate source of recruitment bias is the unequal distribution of socio-economic status, but the statement that the three processes of recruitment (i.e. of self-, institutional- and voter-selection) 'may operate concurrently; in fact they probably do, and thereby reinforce each other' is as far as his inadequate data will allow him to go.[11]

Unfortunately, the temptation to make inferences about what is happening from the characteristics of office-holders is too much, even for Prewitt. When he tells us that 'the social composition of municipal leaderships is a systematic distortion of the communities they govern' he is stating nothing less than the facts of his data. When he goes on to say that 'The aspirant for public office will find the going difficult if he is not among the upper two-fifths of the population in education and income' he is telling us what he does not know.[12] For all he knows, such people never join the ranks of aspirants in the first place and might win hands down if they did. Equally when he attempts to explain the fact that the very highest socio-economic strata are NOT represented on the councils, his set of elegant theories to explain why they do not stand for office[13] may be ludicrously wide of the mark: for all we know they do stand, and systematically get defeated. Close examination of Prewitt's analysis also indicates a conceptual confusion which seems to be characteristic of American recruitment analysis. When he talks about recruitment and success he fails to distinguish clearly between these concepts in the sense of candidacy, i.e. aspiration, and in the sense of being elected. As a result, the model of recruitment he has in mind is never clearly defined and the reader is always obliged to make a careful study of the context in order to decide whether he is assuming that socio-economic inequality produces (a) a homogeneous pool of high-ses candidates or (b) a heterogeneous pool of whom only middle-class individuals are likely to succeed. He is not alone in this kind of conceptual confusion. The extreme case is that of Tobin and Keynes, who repeatedly describe their research as a state legislature 'candidate' study in spite of the fact their subjects are without exception elected office-holders.[14]

The need for better data on recruitment seems to have gone unnoticed until the advent of women political scientists wishful of making gender comparisons, but even they have for the most part failed to collect it. Extensive searching in the published literature and the ICPR data archive, along with personal enquiry among American political scientists, has revealed only six complete candidate studies in the USA, of which two cover attitude variables only.[15] Two of the others, including the only dataset available for secondary analysis, are unfortunately focused on Congress. These are the Miller and Stokes dataset on Democratic and Republican Congressional candidates in 1958, (collected for a study of representation which has never been published) and Raisa Deber's study of Congressional candidates and aspirants in Pennsylvania from 1920 to 1978.[16]

Very few women stood for Congress in 1958 and the Miller/Stokes sample has in any case too small a real n (only 251 cases, 9 of them women) for detailed analysis of subgroups to be feasible.[17] The main interest of this dataset therefore lies in the light it sheds on the male recruitment process, albeit at the national rather than the local level. The data confirm what is generally supposed: congressional candidates as a whole are of such uniformly high socio-economic status that there is little room for significant differences to exist between winners and losers. The occupational profile of the two parties' candidates is almost identical moreover, with around 40 per cent lawyers in each case, nearly a quarter from what is described as a medium- or small-business or managerial background, about an eighth in government service and only about 6 per cent drawn from the 'caring' professions which in this instance include the male-dominated clergy. The candidates are also extremely highly educated, 40 per cent having a postgraduate degree.

The majority of losers in 1958 had never at any time occupied a seat in Congress. When this group (the Neverwons) are compared with the winners of 1958 plus those who had at some time in the past been incumbents (the Everwons), such differences as are found (like the over-representation of lawyers among Democratic winners and their under-representation among Republican winners) tend to cancel one another out and derive from partisan rather than personal fortunes in this election. The data do show some changes over time which reflect the growing professionalisation of socio-economic elites. When all candidates who were not actual or ex-incumbents in 1958 were analysed separately, the new Democratic winners were found to be much more likely than losers to have a college degree (96.6 per cent compared to 63.5 per cent) and lawyers were an exceptionally successful occupational group. There were too few new Republican winners for analysis. There are no data on income in this dataset, so that we cannot measure the relationship of income with winning. We do know, however, that Congressional winners are generally extremely wealthy. Indeed, according to a recent estimate, as many as a third of Senators are millionaires, while in the House there are at least thirty.[18]

Clearly nothing short of a socio-economic revolution would produce a sizeable pool of women candidates who resembled these men. The effect of the standard model of recruitment on women in the USA is illustrated by Deber's Pennsylvania study, which includes primary contests and third party candidacies and perhaps because of this finds more distinct differences between male winners and losers.[19] Only 3.6 per cent of the total bids for Congress generated over fifty years by the Pennsylvania mixture of self-, party- and voter-selection were from women. Their success rate was extremely low (3.4 per cent) compared to that of the men (10.4 per cent), providing them with only 1.4 per cent of the seats won over this period. The distinctive characteristics of male winners, apart from ethnic origin, were a professional occupation in general, the specific occupation of lawyer, and major party backing. In all these respects and almost without exception, the women candidates resembled male losers. Less than 5 per cent of the women were lawyers and we are told of the rest that 'If employed at all, they held jobs at the lower end of the occupational hierarchy'. Nearly a third of them stood for third parties, which produced only one winner, a man, over the entire period; those who had major party backing were concentrated in unwinnable seats. The effect of the relationship between occupation and political career emerges clearly from Deber's findings. Women were an infinitesimal proportion of the lawyers who stood, but no less than 56 per cent of the lawyers, as opposed to only 26 per cent of the women, were major party nominees; 38 per cent of the men who won were lawyers. The only three women to win seats from Pennsylvania were in fact the widows of recently deceased Congressmen, who may be regarded as having temporarily inherited the attributes of their former spouses, at least in the eyes of the bereaved party selectors!

Another published study, of recruitment to the Oregon state legislature in 1966, paints a similar picture at this level.[20] Although Seligman *et al.*, like Prewitt, tend to draw conclusions about candidates as a whole from the observed characteristics of office-holders; and though like Miller and Stokes they have too small a sample, with far too few women, for subgroup comparisons to be feasible, these authors' research really is a candidate study and their desire to carry out winner–loser comparisons is encouraging, even if it is frustrated at times by lack of numbers. Their claim that 'high-status occupational groups are *favoured* for legislative candidacy' as a *'general rule'*[21] in the United States may lack conclusive proof, but it certainly holds good for Oregon. Relative to the electorate, the candidates were exceptionally highly educated (even more so than office-holders in other states) and substantially more prosperous, while almost all of them had high-status occupations.

This study is valuable, too, for its equal emphasis on occupation as a source of socio-economic status, compared to the more usual concentration, which these authors note, on educational attainments in the American literature. Interestingly, although Seligman *et al.* conclude from their data that 'levels of income, education and occupation have no significant bearing on the outcome of the election', their winner–loser comparisons actually show a definite advantage to the highest occupational category, that of 'business executives, proprietors, and major professionals'. Republican and Democratic winners are respectively 13 and 23 per cent more likely than losers to belong to this group, so the lack of significance to which the authors refer is presumably statistical, and due to the lack of numbers in the subgroups of their rather small sample. At the other end of the job hierarchy, not a single person out of the small groups of clerical and technical workers and skilled workers, all of whom were Democrats, won a seat.

It is surprising that the standard model should appear to be operating so strongly to the disadvantage of lower-ses Democrats, since the overall tendency of the Oregon Democrats was to recruit from lower-status occupational groups than the Republicans, a tendency which is consistent with Sorauf's earlier observations of legislators – i.e. winners – in Illinois and other states.[22] The Democratic party appeared to be acting to a small extent as a modifier of the standard model at the state level, but whether this tendency is generally recruiting more losers than winners, as it appears to be in Oregon, and precisely which occupational groups are most likely to benefit from it, must remain obscure until we have comparative data for the other states and larger samples. Without more data, the implications for women cannot be explored either, beyond the obvious conclusion that any criteria based on occupation are likely to put women at a disadvantage.

The final and most recent US source, and the only one to focus on local candidates, is also unfortunately the least reliable. This is Merritt's study of male and female candidates in the municipal elections of 1974 in the suburban areas of Cook County, Illinois.[23] Noting the absence of existing candidate, as opposed to office-holder, studies, Merritt set out with the excellent intention of comparing the background characteristics of winners and losers among all the women candidates and a representative sample of the men. The problem arose in the execution, which left her with the exceptionally low response rate of under 50 per cent and no data on the election outcome for more than half her cases. It is a great pity that this study has to be treated with caution, because the original conception and some of the results are exceptionally interesting.

Merritt's data show the standard model at work in the recruitment of local candidates, male and female. No less than 78 per cent of the men had a professional occupation and 30 per cent a postgraduate degree. Three-quarters had incomes of over $15,000 and more than a third over $20,000. Relative to women in the electorate, the women candidates were even more of an elite than the men, but this still left them trailing the latter in socio-economic status. While the women had similar family incomes, their educational level was much lower and only 23 per cent had a professional occupation. It can, of course, be argued too that a 'family income' is generally much more freely at the disposal of a man than a woman.

Thus far, Merritt's study confirms the usual assumption that the standard model is as relevant to local as national US politics, though it does not go so far as to support a rather surprising hypothesis advanced by Prewitt that the socio-economic gap between leaders and led will actually be greater at the lower level, because of 'the lower salience of local politics for all but the more attentive.'[24] Her winner–loser comparisons, however, suggest a more complex interaction of recruitment tendencies. Income apart, it is if anything lower status which is associated with winning among men and significantly so among women and the main distinguishing characteristic of male winners is that over two-thirds of them are party recruits, compared to only 11 per cent of losers. If valid, these findings suggest the fascinating possibility that though the standard tendency of self-selection is responsible for generating most of the candidacies, a modifying tendency is also at work to produce the winners. The Chicago setting of the Merritt study and the importance of party recruitment point clearly to the Democratic party as the modifier in question. It is most unfortunate that the occcupational categories employed (professional/non-professional) and the way the data are presented do not allow us to investigate the relationship between institutional intervention and the socio-economic structure.

If Merritt's data can be trusted and our interpretation is correct, this would not actually be the first time dissident voices have been raised in America about the supposedly invariate relationship of resources to local recruitment. Two studies of local office-bearers in the 1960s, in St. Louis and Philadelphia respectively, came separately to the conclusion that their local political elites were not socio-economic elites at all, but reflected the characteristics of their communities fairly accurately.[25] These studies were cited by Prewitt only to be dismissed[26], but not, however, disproved. Given the great diversity of local socio-economic conditions in the USA and the equally well-known fragmentation of party identity and structure, one cannot but wonder how logical it is to assume that the same tendencies of recruitment will operate as universally as Prewitt and others assert. We can only regret the lack of data either to explore a research question of such significance or to provide a reliable test of our hypotheses.

SCOTLAND

None of the methodological problems encountered in the American setting arise in the case of Scotland, where extensive new data has been collected from virtually all of a large population of local candidates, men and women, winners and losers alike, for the specific purposes of this enquiry. The research was designed to test the 'scissors' hypotheses in a European setting where competitive elections permit comparison between winning and losing candidates in the context of different models of recruitment. The setting chosen for this research was the local elections of 1984 in the Strathclyde region of Scotland, an area which in its nineteen Districts embraces approximately half the country's population and the institutional selectors include the two major parties, Conservative and Labour, which exemplify respectively the 'standard' and 'modified' models of participation and recruitment in British politics.

The Labour party, a redistributive party derived from the working class, is electorally dominant in the region; so dominant that in the District elections of May 1984 it won 54 per cent of the popular vote and 68 per cent of the seats. The modifying tendency of Labour recruitment was at one time so strong that, as mentioned in Chapter 1, the majority of the first wave of Labour MPs (between 1918 and 1935, many of them sitting for Scottish constituencies) were ordinary workers, most of them manual. Though this tendency has not stood the test of time at the national level, a significant deviation from the standard model of recruitment can be expected in respect of District Council office, which is the lower of the two tiers of Scottish local government. A convenient contrast is supplied by the Conservative party which, as its name suggests, is relatively uncritical of the existing distribution of socio-economic resources and may be expected to operate the standard model.

Both Labour and Conservative parties are so long-established in the region and the habit of partisan voting is so entrenched among the electorate that the identity of core areas of support and of winnable and unwinnable seats is very clear to party selectors. The fact that as many as four major parties may be competing (due to a period of electoral volatility in the 1970s which led to the expansion of the Scottish National Party and the emergence of the now-defunct Alliance) keeps both traditional parties on their mettle but this has not posed a serious threat to the predictability of Labour wins in most seats or to Conservative control of their residual areas of core support; the 1984 results could have been almost exactly predicted from those of 1980 as could those of the most recent election (in 1988) from those of 1984.[27]

Table 2.1 Proportion of women nominated by parties, District elections of 1984 in Strathclyde region, and their success rates compared to those of men

	Proportion women %	Success Rates Men %	Women %
Conservative	31.0	29.0	16.0
Labour	15.0	73.0	74.0
Alliance	25.0	10.0	11.0
SNP	24.0	6.0	5.0

Since the function of the voter is in practice to choose between parties not personalities, it is thus the choices of party selectors which determine what kind of people will tend to win and lose within each party. Nor are these selectors necessarily limited to the pool of self-selectors within their immediate communities. In Glasgow District, with its 66 seats the largest in the region, all would-be Labour candidates have to join a single, all-District panel, to be approached at will by branches throughout the city. In a series of in-depth interviews with a stratified, random sample of the candidates carried out after the elections of 1984 (part of a larger study of participation not reported here), both examples and tolerance of candidate mobility were found to be fairly widespread in both parties except in rural areas. For example, although the majority of candidates stood in or near their place of residence, one Labour candidate in Glasgow reported being offered no less than nine other nominations.

Neither the different recruitment models associated with the two major parties, nor the religious differences between them (for Labour is generally associated with Catholic and Conservative with Protestant in West Central Scotland, as are working- and middle-class status respectively) made any difference to the gender outcome. The 1984 elections were a perfect example of the universal gender pattern of recruitment; of the 1189 candidates who stood, only 260 (21.8 per cent) were women and the proportion elected (17.1 per cent) was even smaller, a female success rate of only 28 per cent compared with 37.2 per cent for men. As Table 2.1 shows, each party made a uniquely different contribution to the working of this pattern which clearly reflects the difference in their electoral situation.

Far fewer women than men were nominated by all the parties but the party which stood to win most of the seats (Labour) was also the party which put up by far the smallest proportion of women candidates. The rest of the explanation lies in the differential success rates of the men and women candidates. The party which put up the greatest proportion of women (the Conservative party) was also that in which the female success rate was significantly lower than the men's.

The data

All 1,189 candidates were surveyed in the Strathclyde District Election Survey (SDES) of 1984, a postal survey which collected standard demographic data and extremely detailed information about the education, employment status, occupation and personal political history of the respondents.[28] The extremely high response rate of 84 per cent yielded a sample of 776 men and 227 women, of whom 321 were Labour candidates and 218 Conservatives (response rates of 82.9 per cent and 84.4 per cent respectively). Allthough the word 'sample' is used to describe the 1,003 cases in this survey population, the fact that these respondents constitute such a high proportion of the candidates who stood in these elections should be noted. In what is ordinarily meant by a sample survey, the results of analysis are not complete descriptions of what has occurred in the whole population, but estimates thereof, and tests of statistical significance are used to distinguish results which are likely to be replicated in another sample from the parent population from those which may merely reflect the idiosyncratic characteristics of the particular sample used. In the present instance, significance tests are inappropriate as the 'sample' very nearly *is* the population. Where the word 'significance' occurs in the following discussion, it is therefore being used in the substantive rather than the statistical sense.

With the SDES data, all three of the hypotheses which make up the first blade of the gender 'scissors' can be tested. The first step is to establish the socio-economic profile of male recruits in comparison with men in the general population and compare the profile of Conservatives (which is expected to illustrate the standard model of recruitment) with that of Labour candidates (who are expected to show evidence of a modifying pattern of selection). The next step is to compare male winners with male losers, in general and within each party, to identify the correlates of success and failure. Having thus identified the models of recruitment at work among men, the first two hypotheses can then be tested by comparing the resource profile of women candidates firstly with that of male candidates, and then with the profiles of the winning and the losing men. Then the third and fourth 'scissors' hypotheses can be tested, that the pattern of winning and losing among women should be the same as among men.

Patterns of male recruitment

Candidacy

When the male candidates of 1984 are compared with men in the population as a whole,[29] to determine what model (or models) of recruitment are operating at the level of candidacy in Strathclyde, the data show unmistakably that the standard model is at work. The male candidates are definitely an educational elite, for while only the very small proportion of 8.4 per cent of adult males in the population as a whole have any degree, professional or vocational qualification whatsoever, no less than 49 per cent of the men candidates have a qualification of some kind and in the case of 20.4 per cent this is a university degree. It is noticeable, all the same, that this tendency is considerably more pronounced among Conservatives: 36.8 per cent of Conservative men, compared to only 26.9 per cent of Labour men, have full-time further education.

Occupationally, the candidates are also an elite. The broad category of professional and managerial occupations is greatly over-represented among candidates whereas all kinds of manual workers are under-represented; only men in non-professional white-collar occupations are to be found in equal proportions at both levels.

In order to make maximum use of the detailed occupational information provided by respondents, the scheme of classification adopted here was CODOT, a system devised by the Department of Employment to order occupations according to the type as well as status of the work performed and used with some modification in the classification of census data. This system enables us to distinguish precisely among the occupational sectors and measure the impact of recruitment upon each. Using this system, we find that among the candidates there are 4.7 times as many men in general management and the business-linked professions (law, accountancy, etc.) as there are in the population; 4.5 times as many in the caring professions (health, education etc); 2.5 times as many from line management and small business; and 2.3 times as many from the scientific, engineering and technical professions. Only men involved in clerical work or sales at the non-managerial level are equitably represented. Of the blue-collar and manual occupations, security services are under-represented by a factor of 1.5 and men in catering, cleaning and other personal services by 1.7 times. The most under-represented sector, by a factor of 2.5, is that of industrial, transport, construction and general workers. It is noticeable, however, that there is a hierarchy of representation *within* this sector, ranging from the almost exactly equitable representation of workers in processing, manufacturing and repairing occupations down to the gross under-representation of general (mainly unskilled) workers by a factor of no less than eleven. Thus while we have every reason to regard the candidates as a socio-economic elite overall, it is equally the case that a strong modifying influence is also operating, to the distinct advantage of some, but not all, sectors of the working class. The source of this tendency becomes clear when we compare the occupational profiles of men in the Conservative and Labour parties, as shown in Table 2.2.

As Table 2.2 shows, it is almost exactly the same occupational sectors

Table 2.2 Occupational sectors, male District Council candidates, by party, compared with men in the electorate: factor of over- and under-representation

Sector	% Conservative	Labour
All professional grades:		
Business management/professions	+10.0	+ 1.9
Caring professions	+2.8	+ 5.9
Science, Engineering/Technical	at par	+ 2.2
Line Management/small business	+ 2.2	at par
Clerical	at par	at par
Sales	at par	at par
Catering/cleaning/and personal services	- 1.2	- 1.4
Industrial manufacturing/transport construction and general workers	- 6.5	- 1.7

Source: SDES,1984

Table 2.3 Non-service workers among male District Council candidates, by party, compared with men in the electorate: factor of over- and under-representation

	% Conservative	Labour
(Non-metal) Manufacturing, Processing etc	- 2.8	at par
Metal/ electrical manufacture	- 7.3	- 1.3
General workers	- 6.3	-11.0

Source: SDES, 1984

which are over, under and equitably represented in both cases. However the degrees of distortion are so dissimilar that within the general tendency to elitism these parties are actually operating very different recruitment tendencies. The Conservatives are operating the standard model to a fault, with men in general management and the business professions over-represented by a factor of ten, while at the other end of the occupational hierarchy workers are under-represented by a factor of 6.5. In the Labour party, it looks at first sight as if the tension between two recruitment tendencies has produced a fairly representative occupational profile. Look more closely and we find (as shown in Table 2.3) that this is so only up to a point, which is the appearance of the same, distinct representation hierarchy within the working-class element which we have already observed among the candidates as a whole.

Manufacturing workers in particular are pulled up nearly to par with their incidence in the male electorate. By contrast general workers, the group of least status within this hierarchy, are under-represented by a factor of eleven. At the other end of the occupational hierarchy, it is the caring professions which are most disproportionately recruited, by a factor of 5.9. These findings confirm that the Labour party is a modifying institution in the recruitment process, as opposed to the standard tendencies of the Conservative party. However this is modification of a very specific and discriminant kind, coexisting with both the over-representation of high status groups and the virtual exclusion of low-status groups within the working-class.

Winners and Losers among men

When winners are compared with losers, the modifying tendency is found to be even stronger at this stage and the contrast between the parties even more developed. The role of education is examined first and then that of occupation.

The educational profile of winners shows a strong electoral advantage for less-educated men. Only 40 per cent of winners, compared with 54.7 per cent of losers, have qualifications of any kind, so that although the winning men are still vastly more qualified than the electorate, it is clear that the parties' allocation of seats is working to modify the gap. The same effect is found in respect of university degrees, possessed by 13.8 per cent of winners, compared to 24.3 per cent of losers. The difference with respect to full-time further education is even more marked; men with full-time further education, as opposed to part-time or none, are almost 20 per cent less likely to have won a council seat. When the educational profiles of winners and losers are compared within each party, the relationship of success to further education is remarkably consistent. As shown in Table 2.4, in both Conservative and Labour parties men without any further education at all are the most likely to succeed, followed by those with part-time further education only and trailed a poor third by those for whom it was full-time. However there are marked differences in other respects between Labour and Conservative winners. Only 33.5 per cent of Labour winners report any kind of qualification beyond school-level examinations, compared to 57.1 per cent of losers, and only 14.3 per cent have a degree. In the case of the Conservatives, there was no significant difference on either variable between winners and losers.

However there are marked differences in other respects between Labour and Conservative winners. Only 33.5 per cent of Labour winners report any kind of qualification beyond school-level examinations, compared to 57.1 per cent of losers, and only 14.3 per cent have a degree. In the case of the Conservatives, there was no significant difference on either variable between winners and losers.

Table 2.4 Success rate (% winners) of male Conservative and Labour candidates, by further education

| | Further Education | | |
	None	Part-time	Full-time
Conservative	36.1	32.7	24.5
Labour	81.6	74.0	52.1

Source: SDES

When we compare the occupational profiles of all these groups, the significance of these nuances becomes clear. It is occupation, rather than education, which is the key to the electoral fortunes of Conservatives, while both variables are integrally linked to the Labour pattern of success. Looking at the candidates overall, the differences are not great in the occupational profiles of winners and losers, the main difference being the greater representation of industrial, transport, construction and general workers among winners, which is at the slight expense of all other occupational sectors, including manual service workers. However, when these results are broken down by party we find a marked reinforcement of the differential tendencies of Labour and Conservative recruitment. Table 2.5 shows the success rates of occupational sectors by party. Figure 2.1 illustrates the occupational profiles of winners and losers in both parties and compares them with the profile of the whole male electorate.

No less than 81.9 per cent of Conservative winners belong to the broad category of managerial and professional occupations; of these it is the highest status category, general management and the business-linked professions, which is by far the most advantaged, followed by the smaller group who are in line management or small business. The men who are picked to stand for safe Conservative seats are thus of a very uniform character indeed and enjoy high socio-economic resources in spite of their relatively less intensive educational background than that of losers. The likely explanation for the latter is an orientation of winners towards the general and administrative, rather than professional occupations. At the other end of the election hierarchy, the success rate of non-service workers is so low, at 8.3 per cent, that these are a negligible category among Conservative winners.

Non-service (i.e industrial manufacturing, construction, transport and general) workers are, however, one of the two categories which are advanced by an exceptionally high success rate among Labour candidates. As a result they constitute 37.6 per cent among winners, but 19 per cent among losers. An even higher success rate is enjoyed by a group of men who also enjoy high individual social status, line managers. These gains in the pool of winners are at the expense of all other groups

49

Table 2.5 Success rates (% winners) of occupational sectors, by party

	Conservative	Labour
All professional grades:	35.2	60.9
general management/professions	40.8	38.9
caring professions	n.a	63.4
science/engineering/technical	n.a.	73.4
line management/ small business	37.0	85.0
Clerical	33.4	64.7
Sales	20.0	70.0
Catering/cleaning and personal services	33.3	42.9
Manual Workers (non-service)	8.3	83.0
non-metal manufacturing	n.a.	88.2
Metal and electrical manufacturing	n.a.	79.1
(Mean success rate, all men candidates)	(30.6)	(71.1)

Source: SDES
Note: sectors with very few candidates have been omitted

and are due to two distinct factors: the separate effect of occupation itself and the way it combines with education to enhance the effect of both attributes. The independent and interactive effects of education and occupation in producing the pattern of Labour success are illustrated in Figure 2.2, which shows the comparative success rates of five groups of Labour men:

1 those who have both the wrong education and the wrong kind of job (i.e. not industrial worker or line manager);
2 men with the right education but the wrong kind of job;
3 men with the right education and the right job (workers);
4 men with the right education and the right job (line-managers); and
5 men with either of the right jobs, but the wrong education.

Two things stand out from this figure: firstly, the very much poorer success rate of the first category compared to any of the others and secondly, the fact that the very positive effect on success of both education and occupation, independently of each other, is increased by around 10 per cent when the two interact. Closely related as these variables are, they cannot be used as substitutes for each other without considerable loss of explanatory power.[30]

Looking more closely at the less advantaged occupational groups, it is perhaps unsurprising to find that the lowest Labour success rate is experienced by people in general management and the business-linked professions. Metal and electrical workers, by contrast, have a success rate of 79.0 per cent and constitute nearly a fifth of the winners; they are

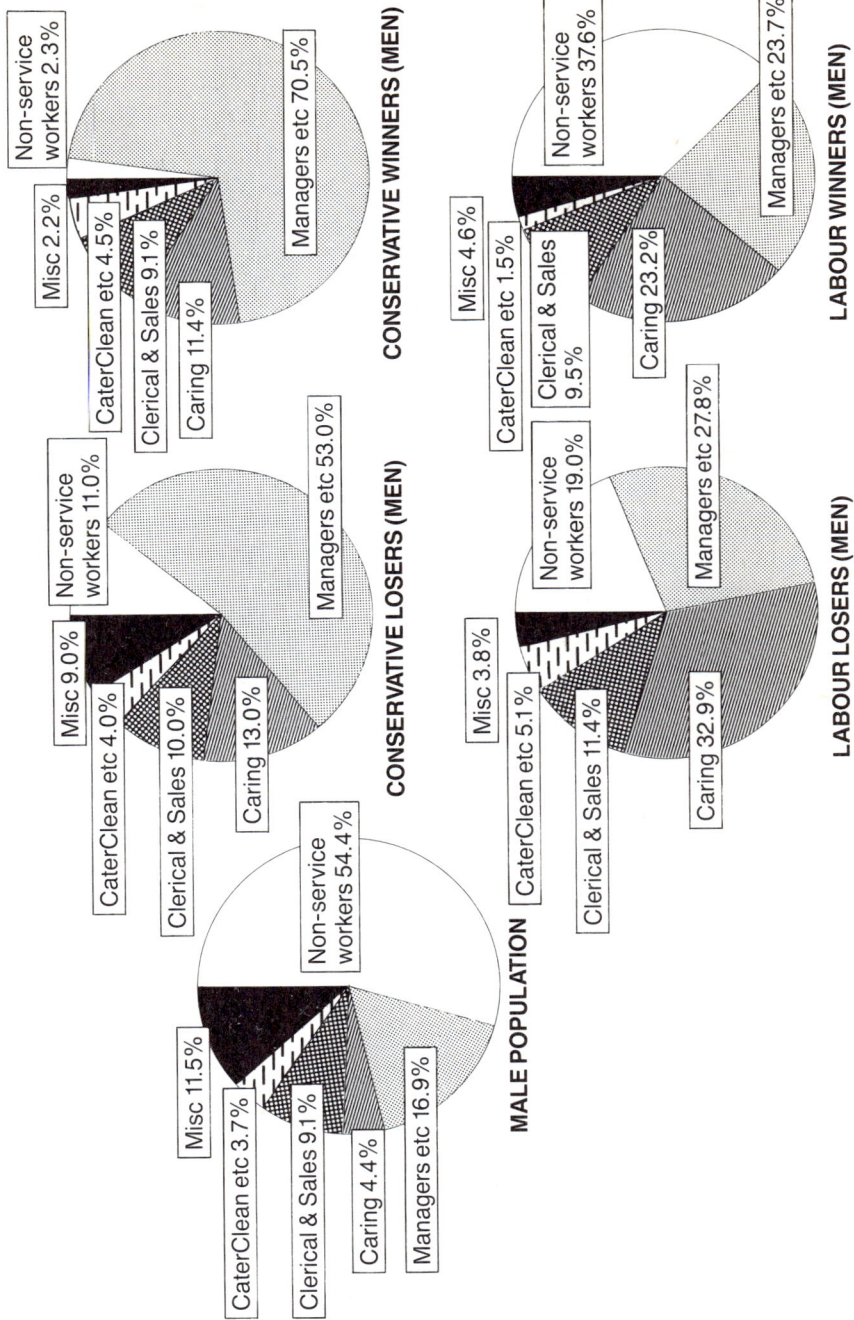

Non-service workers 2.3%

Misc 2.2%

CaterClean etc 4.5%

Clerical & Sales 9.1%

Caring 11.4%

Managers etc 70.5%

CONSERVATIVE WINNERS (MEN)

Non-service workers 11.0%

Misc 9.0%

CaterClean etc 4.0%

Clerical & Sales 10.0%

Caring 13.0%

Managers etc 53.0%

CONSERVATIVE LOSERS (MEN)

Non-service workers 37.6%

Misc 4.6%

CaterClean etc 1.5%

Clerical & Sales 9.5%

Caring 23.2%

Managers etc 23.7%

LABOUR WINNERS (MEN)

Non-service workers 19.0%

Misc 3.8%

CaterClean etc 5.1%

Clerical & Sales 11.4%

Caring 32.9%

Managers etc 27.8%

LABOUR LOSERS (MEN)

Non-service workers 54.4%

Misc 11.5%

CaterClean etc 3.7%

Clerical & Sales 9.1%

Caring 4.4%

Managers etc 16.9%

MALE POPULATION

Figure 2.1 Occupational characteristics of the male population and of winning and losing men, by party, Strathclyde, 1984.

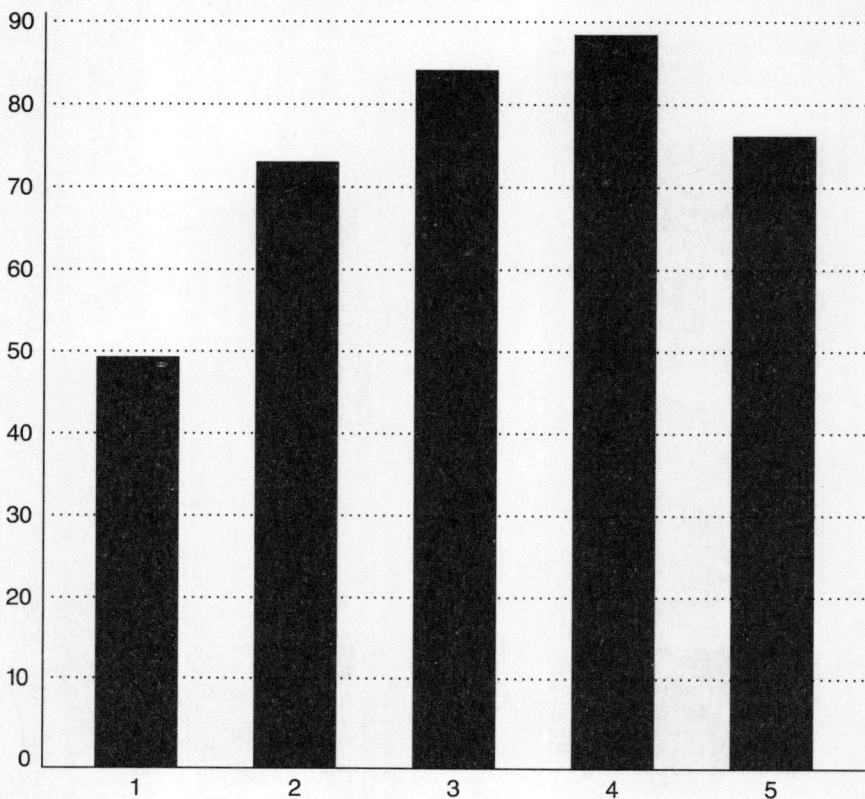

1. Wrong (i.e. full time further) education/wrong job (49.2%)
2. Right education/wrong job (72.4%)
3. Right education/right job (industrial worker) (83.3%)
4. Right education/right job (line management) (87.5%)
5. Wrong education/right job (75.5%)

Figure 2.2 Percentage of winners by education/occupation type (Labour men).

Labour's second largest occupational contingent on Strathclyde's District Councils. The largest group of councillors, as of candidates, is of men drawn from the caring professions, but their dominant position has nevertheless been eroded by a lower than average success rate (similar to that of male clerical workers). Nearly a third of the losers, compared to just over a fifth of the winners, belong to this group. The effect of the standard model has been to produce too many highly educated individuals chasing too small a proportion of the winnable seats.

It is worth noting, too, that the effect of collective, as opposed to individual resources makes itself felt even within the educated group. Analysts have stressed the importance of upward social mobility in recruitment to the increasingly middle-class and professional Parliamentary Labour party and internal elite.[31] Although the spread of educational opportunities in post-war Britain has mainly benefited the middle class, it has meant that some individuals of working class origin 'who, forty or fifty years ago, would have risen to the ranks of the PLP through the trade union movement, have . . . found different routes to the House of Commons. Others, who have retained their links with the union movement have, none the less, secured middle-class jobs.'[32] Although selectors for a parliamentary seat 'find it difficult to resist selecting well-educated and often highly articulate middle-class individuals in preference to less well-educated and sometimes less articulate individuals from lower down the social scale'[33] they can and do discriminate according to family background. Thus a crucial factor which distinguishes middle-class Labour MPs and activists from professional candidates in other parties is their 'class origin'. If not industrial workers themselves, they are the children or grandchildren of workers, which, as Rush points out, is probably why they are standing as Labour candidates anyway, rather than as, for example, Conservatives.

Exactly the same process was found to be at work in local Labour recruitment in Strathclyde. No less than 43.8 per cent of the educated men who stood as Labour candidates were the sons of industrial, non-service workers; only 23.9 per cent had fathers in the top five categories of the Codot hierarchy. What is more, the sons of non-service workers were 13.1 per cent more successful than the rest. In fact less than half of the educated men who lacked this background won their seats, against an overall Labour male success rate of 70.8 per cent in the whole SDES population. Education was always a handicap, but less so when offset by the right parental background, a neat illustration of the paradox that the Labour party is highly attractive to middle-class activists with a social conscience, but values the industrial worker more.

Thus the tendency of the Labour party in allocating seats is to reinforce the modification of the standard model we have observed at the level of candidate recruitment, though not as dramatically as in the case of the opposite Conservative tendency. It is a selective modification, moreover, which works to the advantage of lower level managers – the only group to gain in both parties – and the industrial worker, leaving the disadvantage of the general, unskilled worker unmodified. The industrial derivation and values of the Labour party, and the occupational basis of its local recruitment hierarchy, could not be more clearly illustrated.

Women different, but not equal: the 'scissors' hypotheses

The implications for women of the findings with respect to men are obviously not auspicious for their chances of success, but the validity of the 'scissors' hypotheses remains to be demonstrated. As with men, the essential first step is to identify the resource profiles of women candidates, in general and by party. Comparing them with that of the female electorate, it is possible to identify the criteria of recruitment at work among women and compare them with what was found among men. As expected, neither the standard nor modified model of recruitment work to the advantage of women, and the first of the 'scissors' hypotheses – that the resource profiles of women candidates will differ from those of men – is easily demonstrated. So is the second, crucial hypothesis, that the attributes of women will resemble those of losing, rather than winning men. Finally the patterns of success and failure among women have to be identified and compared with those of men, in order to test the third and fourth of the 'scissors' hypotheses. The result is an almost unqualified confirmation of the expectation that winning and losing women will repeat the socio-economic pattern of winning and losing men.

Hypothesis 1: women candidates compared with men

A comparison of women candidates with the female electorate and with their male candidate counterparts reveals a highly significant pattern of socio-economic profiles. The female electorate is less educated than the male and has a lower occupational status profile. Only 5.7 per cent of adult females have qualifications of any kind and (although statistics on the distribution of degrees etc. in the whole population do not exist) we know that even now, when the gap is closing rapidly, fewer female than male school-leavers proceed to university. Occupationally, over a third of women of non-pensionable age are not even 'economically active' (i.e. in or seeking paid employment) and therefore have no active occupational status at all. Of those who are economically active, the occupational distribution is different from that of men. Though the proportion of women in the professional strata is much the same (the absolute number of course being a good bit smaller) they are much more concentrated in the caring professions. The largest sector of female employment is white-collar, with 26.9 per cent in clerical and 9.9 in sales occupations, compared to a white-collar total of only 9.1 per cent for men. Of the 35.9 per cent employed in manual work, nearly two-thirds are in catering, cleaning and other personal services, a reversal of the manual sector distribution of men.

The operation of the standard model can thus be expected to produce fewer women candidates than men, simply because the pool of highly educated and high occupational status females in the population is smaller. Furthermore, since women in general are less educated than men, it would not be surprising to find an even larger gap between the generality of women and the few who stand for office than is the case for men, at least where educational attributes are concerned (the occupational gap being perhaps somewhat offset by the higher proportion of white-collar female workers). These expectations are in fact met by our data, but what we also find is a result which incontrovertibly confirms Hypothesis 1 – that women candidates will be different from men – but is entirely untypical of the operation of the standard model in a male-dominated society: that the women candidates have higher socio-economic status than the men!

Among the whole sample of candidates it is educationally that the superiority of women is most marked. Though fewer women in the population than men have a qualification of any kind, the proportions are reversed among the candidates. Fully 33.5 per cent of women candidates have a university or college degree or diploma, compared to only 25.4 per cent of the men. No less than 49 per cent of the women have had full-time further education, but only 34.3 per cent of the men. The occupational profile of women candidates, like that of men, is strongly skewed towards the higher status occupations but in ways that reflect the differences between men and women in the general population; even allowing for this, the female profile is even more top-heavy than that of men. About the same proportion as men (53.8 per cent of women, 60.7 per cent of men) are professional in status, though the women are so much more concentrated in the caring professions that these account for no less than 36.1 per cent of all the women candidates. Clerical workers are represented roughly at par, as was the case with men, and are consequently a much larger element among the female candidates. However from this point down the scale the similarity with men comes to an end, for women in sales occupations are under-represented by a factor of three and the degree of under-representation of all sectors of manual labour is much greater than for men. The proportion of women in personal service occupations is three and a half times smaller among women candidates than in the female electorate and for other (mainly manufacturing) manual women workers the position is even worse. On the other dimension of employment status, the distorting effect of female recruitment is equally strong; only 15.9 per cent of female candidates are housewives.

The inescapable conclusion from these data is that the modifying factor we have found at work in the recruitment of men is not affecting women, who are thus being recruited almost entirely on the basis of individual socio-economic status. In comparison with the men, there is a missing element in the pool of women candidates; the female equivalents of the low-ses men. Since the latter were almost entirely recruited by the Labour party, herein lies the main explanation for the anomalously small proportion of women among Labour party candidates. We can demonstrate this more precisely with a comparison of the attributes of Conservative and Labour candidates by sex.

In contrast to the overall pattern of male–female differences, Conservative gender profiles conform closely with what we would expect where the standard model is operating (i.e. that women will have lower individual socio-economic status than men) especially where occupation is concerned. Women candidates are approximately 9 per cent less likely than the highly qualified Conservative men to have qualifications of any kind and 8 per cent less likely to have a degree. However, they are just as likely as men to have had full-time further education, the aspect of socio-economic status which was not associated with the winner/loser dichotomy among Conservative men. Occupationally, the differences are very striking: women are 37 per cent less likely to be in paid employment for a start and their occupational profile is not only different from the men's but comparatively less skewed to the very top of the occupational hierarchy. Some 73 per cent of male conservative candidates, but only 52.8 per cent of the women, are drawn from professional and managerial occupations and women trail no less than 19 per cent behind men in the highest grade of all, general management and the business-linked professions. The shortfall is made up by the far greater proportion of female white-collar workers, the absence of manual workers being as marked among female as male Conservatives. Given the occupational distribution differences among men and women in the population, these are just the kind of candidate differences we would expect to find where the standard model is exclusively at work.

In the Labour party, the direction of gender differences is just the opposite and is as marked in educational as occupational terms. Though only slightly more likely to have a qualification of any kind, Labour women are 10.5 per cent more likely to have a degree, diploma or professional qualification. Most startling of all, 45.7 per cent had had full-time further education compared to only 26.9 per cent of Labour men. The occupational profiles vary in the same direction and are clearly linked with the educational variables. The proportion of women from the professional strata is slightly greater than that of men but the concentration of these in the caring professions (where high-level educational qualifications are indispensable) is much greater. Next in line, white-collar (mainly clerical) workers amount to 20.9 per cent of Labour women compared to 9.9 per cent of the men. The result is that only 18.8 per cent of Labour women are drawn from manual occupations, compared to 37 per cent of the men. The reason is the gross under-representation of women in catering, cleaning and other personal services. Because there are so few women Labour candidates to begin with, this means that the absolute number of manual workers among them is tiny. In fact the ratio of Labour women manual worker-candidates to women manual workers in the population is only 1 : 17,907, compared to a ratio for men of 1 : 4,020. Even this understates the under-

Table 2.6 Proportion (%) of Conservative candidates from general management and the business-linked professions: a comparison of male winners, male losers, and women

Candidate	Proportion (%)
Conservative men winners	45.5
Conservative men losers	29.0
Conservative women	14.9

Sources: SDES.

representation of women manual workers compared to men, since the large proportion of women in the general population who are housewives must contain a sizeable element of former manual workers who do not appear in the census occupational count at all.

In spite of this disproportionate preponderance of the educated among Labour women, their absolute numbers are of course very few none the less. The failure of the British higher education system to recruit working-class girls compared to boys is if anything even more striking than its middle-class bias, with the effect that the pool of educated Labour women who are more acceptable to selectors because of family background is necessarily very small. Inevitably, although 57.1 per cent of the educated Labour women candidates were the offspring of non-service workers there were less than a third as many of them as there were among the men. Even in this indirect fashion, lack of collective resources is at work to depress the number of Labour women candidates.[34]

Hypothesis 2: women resemble losing men

We have already seen that the allocation of winnable seats serves to reinforce and accentuate the differential recruitment tendencies of the Labour and Conservative parties. From what we now know of gender variation within each party's total set of candidates, it is obvious that the content of male winner–loser differences will have an adverse bearing on the chances of both candidacy and success among women. When we compare women candidates within each party with the winners and losers among the men, we find a conclusive demonstration of our central hypothesis: that the attributes of women will resemble those of losing men.

In the Conservative party, it is the occupational dimension which we have found to differentiate male winners and losers. As Table 2.6 shows, whereas nearly half of the male winners are drawn from general management and the business-linked professions, the proportion of male losers with this occupational attribute is only 29 per cent and it is even smaller (only 14.9 per cent) among women.

Table 2.7 Proportion (%) of Labour candidates with full-time further education: a comparison of winning men, losing men, and women

Candidate	Proportion (%)
Labour men winners	19.8
Labour men losers	44.3
Labour women	45.7

Sources: SDES.

Table 2.8 Proportion (%) of Labour candidates from a caring profession: a comparison of male winners, male losers, and women

Candidate	Proportion (%)
Labour men winners	23.2
Labour men losers	32.9
Labour women	41.7

Source: SDES.

Table 2.9 Proportion (%) of Labour candidates with a non-service manual occupation: a comparison of winning men, losing men, and women

Candidate	Proportion (%)
Labour men winners	37.6
Labour men losers	19.0
Labour women	6.3

Source: SDES.

In the case of the Labour party, both educational and occupational dimensions of socio-economic status were implicated in the differentiation of winners from losers. Labour women candidates resemble losers, not winners, in both cases. The level of full-time further education for male winners, male losers and women among Labour candidates is shown in Table 2.7. Whereas 45.7 per cent of the women and 44.3 per cent of the losing men had full-time further education, the proportion of educated men among the winners was only 19.8 per cent.

In terms of occupation, the main differences between winning and losing Labour men were the greater proportion from the caring professions among the latter and the greater proportion of non-service workers among the former. The proportion of women candidates from a caring professional occupation are compared with those among winning and losing men in Table 2.8.

Yet again, the contrast between the women and the male winners is extreme and in this case the women are considerably more disadvantaged than the male losers, too. In the case of a non-service manual occupation, the same result is found and is shown in Table 2.9. Male winners are nearly 20 per cent more likely than losers to come from a non-service manual occupation, and no less than 31.3 per cent more likely than women.

The ordering of these scores (on both the occupational attributes) is exactly the same as for education (and for occupation among Conservatives). Not only do women resemble male losers rather than winners; they actually have even less of the desired attribute (or more of the undesired) than male losers do.

Hypotheses 3 and 4: patterns of success among women

Turning to the success rate of women with 'winning' attributes (for Hypothesis 3) and the differences on these variables between winning and losing women (for Hypothesis 4), the tendency of the data to confirm both hypotheses is so strong that it transcends the numbers difficulty. Of the tiny band of nine Labour women manual workers (six service and three non-service), *every single one was successful*. The even smaller group of women in the 'line management' category had a success rate of 83 per cent, virtually the same as that of their male counterparts. The success rate of women without either of these occupational advantages was only 66.6 per cent. In Table 2.10(a), where the sex of Labour candidates is cross-tabulated with the occupations most advantaged among men, the cell entry in each case is the percentage success rate of the people with that particular combination of sex and occupation. If sex, not occupation, is the determinant of success, then the figure in the bottom left cell (where the 'wrong' sex is combined with the 'right' occupation) should be substantively lower than that in the upper left corner (combining the 'right' occupation with the 'right' sex). Success rates across the bottom row (both occupational categories of women) should be the same.

On the contrary, as Tables 2.10 (a) and (b) show, people with the 'right' occupations win, and those with the 'wrong' ones are more likely to lose, *irrespective of sex*. In the case of further education, as shown in Table 2.10(c), the success rate of the less-educated follows the same pattern; 'winner-type' women are winners. This pattern is further embellished by the finding (not shown) that the effect of collective resources at one remove is the same for Labour women as it is for men. Educated Labour women who had a non-service worker for a father are 8.3 per cent more successful than their fellows.[35]

Table 2.10 Success rates (%) of Labour candidates by sex and socio-economic characteristics

---

(a) Sex by industrial manual occupation

	Industrial manual	Other[A]
Male	83.0	63.6
Female	100.0	71.8

(b) Sex by line management[B]

	Line management	Other[C]
Male	85.0	63.6
Female	83.3	71.8

(c) Success rates by sex and education

	Full-time further education	
	Yes	No
Male	78.3	52.1
Female	76.0	71.4

Source: SDES.

Notes: [A] Excludes people in the other 'right' job category (Line management).
[B] Category includes small business people, but there are none in the Labour sample.
[C] Excludes people in the other 'right' job category, industrial manual worker.

In all three cases, the occupational pattern of success among Labour women also reflects the pattern among men; 'loser-type' women are less likely to succeed. However, as anticipated in Chapter 1, 'loser-type' women have a slightly higher success rate among the small population of female candidates than they do among the far more numerous men. (In fact, as a subsequent series of in-depth interviews with these candidates was to show, many of these were women whose seats had been regarded as unwinnable when they were first selected; they had come to success by dint of exceptional standards of personal campaigning or unusual persistence.)

The only inconsistency with Hypotheses 3 and 4 arises in the case of the Conservatives, where the outcome for the small group of eleven women of managerial-level occupations was disastrous; only one took her seat. However closer examination reveals that even this setback is more apparent than real. Only three Conservative losers came within 2 per cent of success in 1984. All three of them were women (with a margin of defeat which was actually less than 1 per cent in each case), and two of these fall into the 'managerial' occupational group. Both women were ex-councillors, who had first been selected for these seats when they were already in Conservative hands and had thus been selected to win; only the relentless pressure of the Labour tide in 1980 and 1984 combined with minor party intervention has turned them into losers. In such a small 'n' of 'winner-type' women, a tiny variation in the popular vote would have given them a success rate of 27.0 per cent, not as good as the men's rate of 40.8 per cent, but superior to the 19.0 per cent of other women. What this suggests is that Hypotheses 3 and 4 are valid for Conservatives too, with the caveat that the residual gender gap leaves room for the suspicion that sex discrimination is an active factor too.

Looking ahead to the prospects for women if the number of their candidacies were to grow, it is striking, of course, that the candidacies of women in Strathclyde are concentrated in those socio-economic groups which have the lowest male success rates, i.e. where too many men are already chasing too few favourable openings. In the case of the Conservatives, where there is the highest proportion of women candidates, the result is a low female success rate. While the success rate of Labour women is very high (even in the 'wrong' categories), there are so few of them that this seems less significant for the future than the acute shortage of women with the occupational and educational attributes of winning men. Certainly it does not indicate that Labour women are finding different resources than men to secure election. Though 44.0 per cent of winning women have full-time further education and 41.7 per cent were drawn from the caring professions, the absolute number involved in either case is still far smaller than the number of men with the same 'losing' attributes who nevertheless succeed against the odds. The unfortunate implication is that an increase in female candidacies, unless they were candidacies of a markedly different character from what has emerged so far, would simply lead to a depressed female success rate. The root of the problem, of course, is the out-group status of women in the male occupational hierarchy which is the basis of both Conservative and Labour elite recruitment. To achieve a female candidate profile resembling that of men would require a major redistribution of socio-economic resources in the population at large.

The possibility could not be excluded, nevertheless, that changes were already taking place to the advantage of women: changes which would be disguised by the electoral advantage of incumbency. In particular, the decline of manufacturing industry in the West of Scotland might have rendered the traditional occupational values of the Labour party obsolete (although it is not easy to imagine what might replace them). To test for this possibility, the whole analysis was repeated for the subsets of incumbent and non-incumbent candidates and the results compared. This exercise was also a way of testing for changes in the socio-economic profile of women candidates. Extraordinarily little change was found over time. The only trend was a very slight upward tendency in educational levels across the board. The patterns of success and failure (when non-incumbent winners were compared with incumbents, of whom virtually all retained their seats) and the comparative occupational and educational distributions of men and women were almost identical. A further comparison, of men and women candidates up to 30 years old, found the patterns to be if anything more sharply defined in this age-group.

It is quite clear from these findings that both the standard and modifying tendencies of institutional selection in Strathclyde are firmly grounded in the socio-economic relations of men, not women. The result is a local political elite who very precisely reflect those elements of the male occupational hierarchy from which the two main parties are derived, both overall and within the industrial working class. Because the occupations of women are of low or marginal status within this hierarchy, their chances of recruitment within the existing socio-economic framework and through the medium of male-dominated mixed political structures are very slim.

It is a curiously illogical outcome, when we consider the functions of Scotland's District Councils. Their main function and point of expenditure is publicly-owned housing: a 'council house' is the theatre in which no less than 61 per cent of Strathclyde's women perform their traditional role. So wholly are housing matters considered to be 'women's business' in the local culture that, as one (male) councillor put it to me, '90 per cent of the people who come to see me are women, on housing matters. Anything to do with housing is considered the women's sphere around here.' Thus a powerless female clientele face an industrial-based male political elite across territory which is almost entirely occupied by a 'women's issue'.

THE USSR

The study of Soviet recruitment has moved from the arena of current affairs to that of history since the dismantling of the Union in December 1991, but Gorbachev's efforts to reform the system had already thrown Soviet electoral politics into a state of flux.[36] There are consequently two versions of Soviet local recruitment on which we can draw: the familiar system dating from the Stalin period, which remained essentially unchanged right up till 1989, and the short-lived Gorbachev alternative, which changed the basis of Soviet recruitment quite dramatically, but in the end proved to be too little, too late. Of the two, it is paradoxically the former which is infinitely more interesting from a gender and recruitment point of view. For this reason, the following account of local Soviet recruitment is located in the system before Gorbachev, in the early years of that period of remarkable political stagnation known as the 'Brezhnev era'. In spite of the limitations of this system, the negative implications of the Gorbachev reforms for female recruitment will become only too clear.

The two main organs of local political leadership in the USSR were the local soviet and the local committee of the Communist Party of the

Soviet Union (CPSU), each with its internal elite of soviet executive committee (ispolkom) and party bureau respectively.[37] These organs overlapped in function and personnel, but the party committee was by far the more powerful of the two. Although members of both were self-selected in the sense that they were not recruited against their will, the principal determinant of membership was selection by the party. For party bodies, membership of the party was of course a prerequisite for recruitment; in the case of soviets it was not essential but it had always been the rule (pre-Gorbachev) that candidates be party-approved and nominated (which in practice means appointed) through a procedure controlled by the party.

There was not, however, a single set of selectors involved in either case. Recruitment could be direct and *apropos* of the soviet or committee itself, or indirect through the nomenklatura system of party-controlled appointment to all 'responsible' posts in Soviet political, economic, social and cultural life. Whenever possible (which meant almost invariably), nomenklatura posts were filled by party members so that responsible officials were directly subject to party discipline and values. In order to integrate public affairs in every sphere under party leadership, a core of party members was used to penetrate all public bodies, departments, etc. and control them from within, usually from their leading positions. Conversely, anyone with elite potential was recruited to the party membership and leading individuals in non-party agencies were frequently members of the appropriate level of party committee. Lateral movement, from party to non-party post and vice versa was also common, especially in the careers of general administrators. The result was an exceptional degree of unity between political, social and economic status, all of it dispensed by the process of party selection in one form or another. Lower level nomenklatura posts included key positions in local affairs, party and non-party, which carried ex officio membership of either local soviet, or party committee, or both. They also included a wider pool of eligibles on whom selectors may have felt advised to draw: the more important the nomenklatura post, the higher the level of party selectors who would have been involved in making the appointment. However, in the case of ordinary deputies to local soviets, other agencies such as Komsomol and trade unions had some part to play in selection too, but under party guidance and control.

The party's monopoly of the recruitment process meant that the composition of local elites was always an accurate reflection of their selection criteria; there are no risks attached to inference from office-bearer characteristics here. Nevertheless, there are two reasons why the pattern of local elite composition was a complex one: the hierarchy which existed within a local elite and the fact that traditional Soviet political recruitment was the product of the tension between two quite distinct (and equally deliberate) recruitment models. The first of these models was based on the representative principle and its tendency was modifying. As with party membership, it was an object with Soviet selectors to see that local soviet and party organs (particularly the former) reflected significant features of the general Soviet population. From the ideological perspective of the party, it was the class composition of the population which was its most important dimension and the workers the most highly valued class. As a result the primary goal of this tendency was to recruit low-ses individuals. The other model was derived from the notion of the party as vanguard, incorporating 'leading communists' from all spheres of life, and exercising a leading role in everything. It was on this principle that the nomenklatura system was based and its tendency was of course elitist in a highly centralised, state-interventionist and hierarchical social economy. As in the case of the modifying tendency, it was occupation which was the crucial determinant of political status, but now it was higher-, not lower- ses individuals who had to be recruited, in a heavily reinforced version of the standard model.

The data used here to illustrate the working of these models and evaluate their effect on the gender composition of local Soviet elites were collected by Ronald J. Hill in the Moldavian city of Tiraspol and published in 1977 in what must be one of the most interesting contemporary studies of political recruitment anywhere.[38] Hill's findings cover both city soviet and city party committee (gorkom) in the industrial city of Tiraspol, a former republican capital, over the years 1950 to 1967. They are based on detailed information about the background characteristics of people who served as soviet deputies or gorkom members in this period. The stability (or stagnation) of Soviet politics throughout the Brezhnev period left these findings as relevant in 1988 as twenty years before and makes them an extremely useful touchstone for the changes currently being considered in the former Soviet Union.

It is clear from Hill's results that the tension between the two recruitment models was resolved by the systematic, if tacit recruitment of two different types of people, to perform two different functions at different levels within the local political elite. The keys to this dichotomy are institutional status and turnover. There are three respects in which Soviet local elites were dichotomised by institutional status. The party committee was superior to the soviet, the soviet executive committee was superior to the ordinary deputies, and the party bureau was superior to the ordinary members of the party committee. In respect of turnover, the dichotomy was between the vast majority of short-stay recruits (serving two to four years on the soviet and one to five years on the gorkom respectively) and the small minority of long-stay individuals who more or less coincided in each case with the internal structural elite of ispolkom and bureau (especially the former).

The Tiraspol soviet and party elite could thus be divided on four overlapping dimensions into what Hill calls 'strong' and 'weak' clusters. The 'strong' belonged to gorkom rather than soviet, to the ispolkom rather than the ranks of ordinary deputies, and the party bureau rather than just the gorkom; they are long-stay rather than short-stay deputies or party committeee members. The different functions of the 'strong' and 'weak' recruits were identified by their location and experience. The function of the 'strong' was to take decisions, head the local administration and be accountable to superiors at higher levels of party and state. At the highest level the party bureau seemed in Hill's words, to have been 'deliberately composed to create an effective decision-making unit, with all the most responsible officials in the town present'.[39] Within their respective structures, the 'strong' were equipped by experience, seniority and status to dominate the proceedings and did so.

The function of the weak was to embellish the soviet and party committee with a representative character, in which the occupational dimension of class was the crucial attribute; to listen and give assent to the responsible decision-makers; to pass the messages they received on to a wider public; and to perform the day-to-day routines of dealing with constituency problems. The one was active and power-oriented, the other was relatively passive and service-oriented. Though by no means an exact equivalent, the categories of 'strong' and 'weak' will bear comparison with the categories of 'winner' and 'loser' in the free elections of the West, especially in the case of the Soviet 'strong' and the winners of highly partisan, party-selector- controlled elections such as those of Strathclyde. In both cases, the attributes associated with 'winning' identify the values and priorities of the selectors.

On all four dimensions, the attributes associated with Soviet 'strong' or 'winning' locations compared to 'weak' or 'losing' were found to be the same. 'Winners' were more likely to be party members, older, industrial managers, party or (except in the case of the party bureau) state administrators, and male. 'Losers' were more likely to be non-party, younger, production workers, engaged in trade, press or communications, and female. The inter-relationship of all the 'winning' attributes is self-evident and so is the crucial role of occupation in shaping the cluster. The most complete set of Hill's data to illustrate these findings relates to turnover and length of service of deputies and party committee members. These data have been recalculated to provide the percentages from each occupational sector and these are illustrated in Figure 2.3, the first two lines of which compare the composition of the deputies and committee members as a whole and subdivided into 'long-stay' (strong) and 'short-stay' (weak).

Industrial production workers, so essential to the 'correct' socio-economic profile of the soviets, amounted to fully half the total tally of deputies but accounted for only 24.7 per cent of those who were renominated more than once. Of all the members of the gorkom, only 13.1 per cent were workers and of long-stay members the proportion was only a tiny 2.8 per cent. Clearly the worker element on these bodies was decorative rather than powerful, and few workers ever had the chance to become senior and experienced politicians through public office. The advantage is all with management, whether in the form of industrial managers (the group which actually enjoyed the longest mean length of service on party bodies) or party and state administrators. (The small group of lawyers, markedly successful at party bureau level, have been included in this group for the sake of comparability with the Scottish occupational data). Only 13.6 per cent of deputies and 24.1 per cent of party committee members belong to the industrial management category, but they provide no less than 23.5 and 37.1 per cent of the respective long-stay groups. General administrators (their equivalents in the state and party bureaucracies) were equally dominant. Only 10.1 per cent of deputies fall into this category, but they were nearly a quarter of the long-stay group. In the party committee it is party, not state officials who are dominant, constituting nearly half of the long-stayers. The only stable group of size across these boundaries was that of the caring professions (education and medicine); other occupations, including the particularly disadvantaged trade sector (i.e. sales and distribution workers) were associated with weakness.

Of course the Soviet Union had a one-party system and a nationalised, centrally planned and directly administered economy, so the distinctions between party, state and economy were very fine ones indeed. The people who managed all three were powerful adminstrators, separated by structural rather than socio-economic or ideological boundaries. As Figure 2.3 shows very clearly, the Soviet local elite was characterised by the extreme dominance of its effective levels by the managerial element; in the case of the party committee (line 2 of Figure 2.3), this dominance was almost total.

It is instructive to compare these Soviet findings with the results of the recruitment process in Strathclyde. The overall outcome in Strathclyde is illustrated in the third row of Figure 2.3, the Labour and Conservative results in Figure 2.1. Though the managerial element among long-stay Soviet deputies was somewhat greater, the distribution of occupations among this group was in fact very similar to that of Strathclyde's councillors. Both attest to the modifying effect of selection in their respective contexts. The other similarity, and a most striking one indeed, is between the composition of the local Soviet party elite, especially at its higher levels, and the pattern of success among Strathclyde Conservatives.

Women: losers again

As noted above, sex is one of the attributes associated with the 'strong/ weak' dichotomy. This is not surprising when we consider the attributes which distinguish male from female recruits. As Table 2.11 shows, the attributes of women deputies were the demographic, political and socio-economic correlates of 'weakness', while those of men were the correlates of 'strength'.

Three-quarters of the men were party members, only a third of women. Almost all the men were over 30, and two-thirds over 40, whereas nearly two-thirds of the women were under 40 and therefore ineligible in terms of seniority for really responsible jobs. Only 7 per cent of the women, but a quarter of the men, were in party or state administration; nearly half the men, but only 10 per cent of the women, were in industrial management. The largest group of women deputies were in fact of that lowly species, the industrial worker. By their occupations, these women were simply ineligible for the power-elite. Their destiny was to make up the quotas on class, sex, age, etc. and perform the basic surgery service which was expected of the soviet deputy.

Given the socio-economic status of women in the Soviet Union, it is hard to see how it could have been otherwise. Even in 1981, after a drive in the 1970s to recruit more women, they still amounted to no more than 26.5 per cent of the Party's membership, though women outnumbered men in the eligible age groups by 18 million.[40] According to the census of 1959, which fell exactly in the middle of Hill's period, only the infinitesimal proportion of 0.19 per cent of all the employed women in Moldavia were in industrial or administrative posts at that time. On this showing it is surprising that any women at all reached the local power elite. In the lower ranks, it is clear that people were being recruited for a short stay who were young, female and workers, in order to meet the requirements of three quotas simultaneously.

Bizarre though the attributes of selected women are in the Soviet Union, compared to what we have found in either Britain or the USA, our hypothesis is yet again conclusively demonstrated. Whatever the attributes may be which are associated with success among men, women have less of them. It is losing, not winning men whom they resemble. The traditional Soviet outcome is a perfect illustration of the inverse relationship of women's elite penetration to the rewards of office (the second 'iron law' of the universal gender pattern). From 37. 4 per cent of all the deputies, the proportion of women drops to a quarter in the ispolkom, to an eighth of the party committee and finally to a derisory 5.3 per cent of the real seat of local power, the party bureau.

Did Gorbachev's reforms affect female recruitment? The essence of the changes had been to undermine party control of the recruitment process.

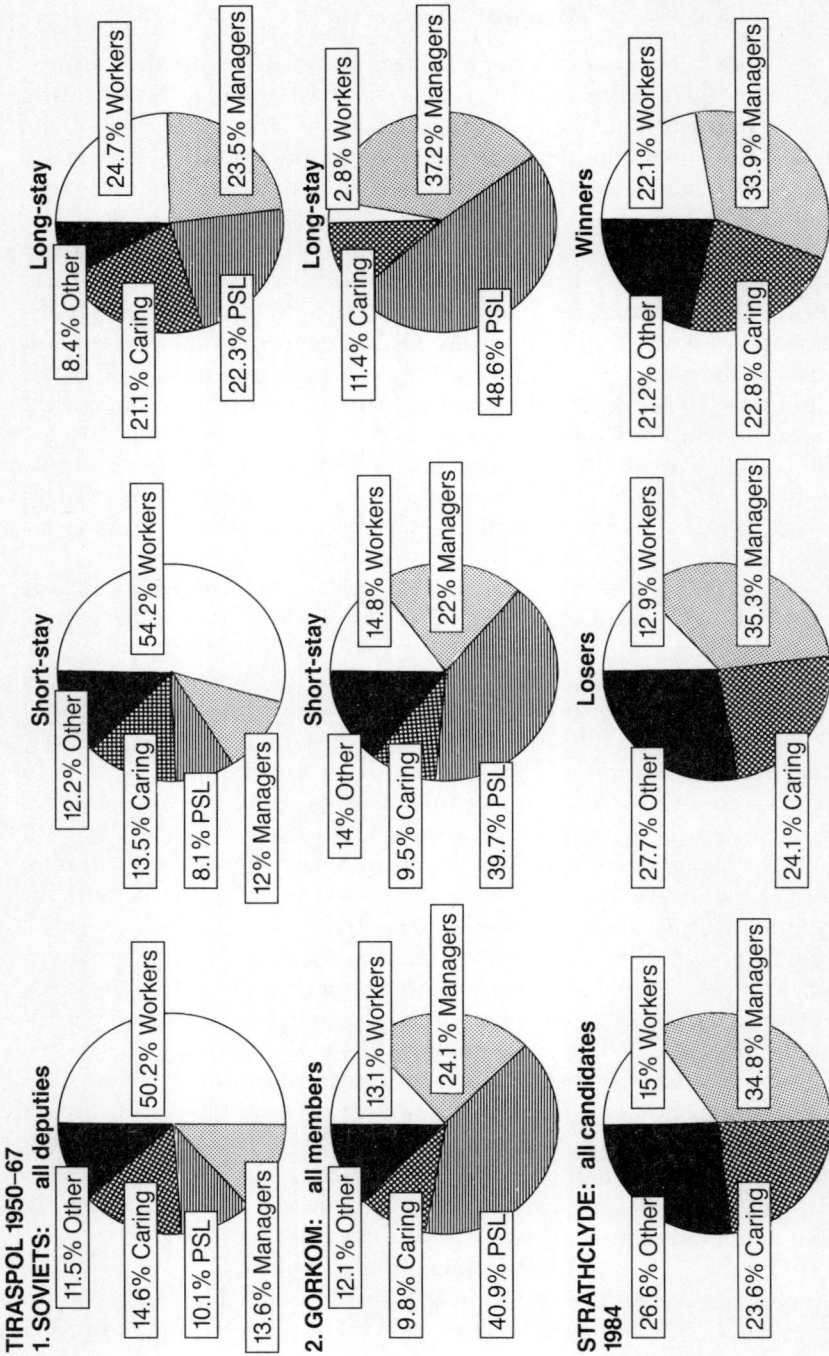

TIRASPOL 1950–67
1. SOVIETS: all deputies

Long-stay
24.7% Workers
23.5% Managers
22.3% PSL
21.1% Caring
8.4% Other

Short-stay
54.2% Workers
12.2% Other
13.5% Caring
8.1% PSL
12% Managers

all deputies
50.2% Workers
11.5% Other
14.6% Caring
10.1% PSL
13.6% Managers

2. GORKOM: all members

Long-stay
2.8% Workers
37.2% Managers
48.6% PSL
11.4% Caring

Short-stay
14.8% Workers
22% Managers
39.7% PSL
9.5% Caring
14% Other

all members
13.1% Workers
24.1% Managers
40.9% PSL
9.8% Caring
12.1% Other

STRATHCLYDE: 1984

Winners
22.1% Workers
33.9% Managers
22.8% Caring
21.2% Other

Losers
12.9% Workers
35.3% Managers
24.1% Caring
27.7% Other

all candidates
15% Workers
34.8% Managers
23.6% Caring
26.6% Other

Figure 2.3 'Winning' and 'losing' in Tiraspol and Strathclyde (PSL= Party, State & Law).

Table 2.11 Characteristics of Tiraspol Deputies, 1950–67, by sex

	(%)	
Characteristics	*Men*	*Women*
Party membership	76.1	33.7
Aged over 30	93.2	60.6
Aged over 40	65.3	35.2
Industrial occupation (all)	52.5	62.8
Industrial management	44.5	10.6
Production worker	29.1	56.,1
Administration	25.3	7.0
Service/caring professions	14.5	29.2

Source: Ronald J. Hill, *Soviet Political Elites* (London, Martin Robertson, 1977).

The original idea was certainly not to abandon this control altogether but to share it with major, established non-party institutions which traditionally chafed at the extent of party interference in their affairs but were to a large extent the creatures of the party. The main point of popular intervention was to be the elections themselves, where voters would select the winners from a set of acceptable nominees. However, popular nominations and unofficial sponsorships were made possible as well and the effects greatly exceeded Gorbachev's probable intentions. In the first elections to the new Congress of People's Deputies, diverse groups and organisations emerged to sponsor opposition candidates and unpopular party figures, especially in the major cities such as Moscow, were defeated by popular candidates associated with reform. Only the inbuilt insurance provided by the system of indirect elections to the actual Soviet itself (so that the party was effectively able to decide which Congress deputies actually served the first time round) enabled the leadership to salvage a 'parliament' which it could more or less control. The republican elections of 1990 advanced this process beyond the point of party control.

However, this upsurge in democracy did not encourage the recruitment of low-ses individuals, including women; on the contrary, there was a truly massive drop in the proportion of women candidates and winners in the new-style elections, as compared with the old. Women deputies were down from 32.8 per cent in the former Supreme Soviet to only 17.1 per cent (including 75 reserved places) in the new Congress of People's Deputies[41] and the proportion of women among candidates for the Soviet of the RSFSR in 1990 was reportedly as low as 7.6 per cent.[42] This outcome was entirely predictable, given the nature of traditional Soviet recruitment, for one of the obvious effects of weakening party control was to eliminate the source of the traditional modifying principle. It was the party which wanted Soviets to reflect the demographic structure of society, and in the traditional system it could afford to see that they did.

By packing the Soviets with low-ses, short-stay individuals they were actually killing two birds with one stone, simultaneously ensuring the ideologically 'correct' deputy profile and providing a backcloth of docile dogsbodies for the high-powered men in crucial occupations who were the lynchpin of the system. After Gorbachev's reforms, the party's priorities had to be very different. In the first place, competitive elections meant that the position of these key individuals was no longer assured but had to be fought for, and this – the standard model in recruitment terms – had to be the party's primary concern. Secondly, there was nothing to be gained, and much to be lost, by putting forward 'nobodies' as supplementary candidates, for unless the voters strongly endorsed the party's modifying values, people like this would be easy targets for well-resourced opposition nominees. In fact, post-Soviet sources now describe the demographic principle of selection as inappropriate and obsolete. Without the particular source of institutional intervention which was entirely responsible for the modifying principle in Soviet recruitment, it might be expected that the standard model will become increasingly dominant in Russia and other republics, expressing the values of the new selectors and their new priorities. For women, this means the kind of sharp reduction in their prospects of recruitment which has already taken place.

CONCLUSION

This analysis has used a comparative framework to identify the socio-economic basis of male political recruitment in three very different institutional contexts and cultures. It has pinpointed the role of institutional selection in the process of converting socio-economic resources into political status and shown how the criteria of selectors never work to the advantage of women, irrespective of whether their tendency is to reinforce or to modify the standard model of recruitment among men. We have seen how women, by virtue of their out-group status, lack exactly those attributes – of occupation, education and income – which the institutions of men exist to convert into political power. They lack the high individual status which would render them eligible in the eyes of Soviet party chiefs, Conservative constituency selection committees and American party selectors and voters. They lack also that share in collective socio-economic resources which would give them access to the avenue of Labour party recruitment in Strathclyde. Their greatest share has been in the lowest level of the Soviet local elite, where their role begs comparison not so much with local office-bearers in Scotland and the USA as with the army of women social and political activists who run the unpaid, voluntary services of local communities and the routine work of some political parties, like the Scottish Conservatives.

What then, are the prospects for an improvement in women's access to elites? Systemic changes do not seem to hold out much hope. Mr Gorbachev committed the former Soviet Union to competitive elections, but it is men, with their superior resources, who stood to gain from open competition. On the other hand, the possibility of a change in the electoral system in Scotland has been mooted several times in recent years, in connection with the project for a Scottish parliament (in abeyance under a Conservative government) and the Liberal commitment to proportional representation in the UK as a whole. PR is no guarantee, in itself, of proportionality for women but in some circumstances party selectors might feel constrained to look for women candidates in order to attract a 'women's vote'. Indeed, the unofficial Scottish Constitutional Convention in 1990 came close to recommending sex quotas for elections to the putative Scottish Parliament and the Scottish Conference of the Labour Party has gone so far as to adopt this as official policy, a startling development which of course does not affect existing local and parliamentary seats and could not be implemented without undermining the existing party's character. The conditions which give rise to quota commitments of this kind, the potential they offer women and the continental models which have influenced the Scots will be discussed in Part 2.

One final possibility, the direct intervention of women's institutions in the recruitment process, is nearest to being realised in the United States. Bipartisan women's caucuses, PACS and coalitions have begun to make their appearance, with some small effect on women's access to campaign funds, party support and executive appointments.[44] The effect is restricted, however, by the extremely limited resources American women control; in such a money-oriented system, the sex disparity in income (which is definitely not closing)[45] can be decisive on its own.

Thus, in the USA as everywhere else, it will require nothing less than a socio-economic revolution before women can present a candidate profile resembling that of winning men in comparable proportions. The only alternative is a change in the selection criteria, either through the advent of new and powerful selectors with radically different values or through a change in the priorities of existing selectors. Eventually, anyone who studies women's role in politics must come to grips with these alternatives and the questions that they raise. Is such a socio-economic revolution possible, and if so, in what conditions? Or, alternatively, what kind of political system would it be, where political priorities were so different? In Part 2, these questions will occupy the stage. In the meantime, however, the possibilities of existing systems have not been exhausted. It can be argued that the dominant party systems are the villains of the piece and that other criteria (in the context of 'non-partisan' elections), and/or radically different selectors (in the form of

71

minor, new and protest parties), are already with us. If these suggestions are well-founded, then what women need is not a revolution in socio-economic or political values, but a better grasp of the existing options. The following chapters take up these points in turn, starting with 'non-partisan' political recruitment.

3

CHANGING THE SELECTORS: NON-PARTISAN RECRUITMENT

The comparative study of partisan recruitment in Chapter 2 has shown how the dominant political parties in three very different political settings are a vital part of the process which converts male status in one sphere into resources in the other and how women, without status in either, cannot be the beneficiaries. Socio-economic factors are crucial, and the importance of occupational sector in explaining the patterns of male recruitment, whether it is the modified or the standard model of the resources–recruitment relationship which is at work, has been a particularly significant finding, since the measurement of socio-economic resources by education alone, or with income, has been characteristic of much previous participation research. We now have a more exact and theoretically better grounded understanding of what is going on, which has depended upon an unusually refined use of both the occupation and education variables. However, this investigation has by no means exhausted the range of recruitment contexts, even within the set of countries we have observed. As far as the Soviet Union was concerned, it is true that the total dominance of the CPSU had been the whole story of elite recruitment until very recently indeed, but in western democracies the looser institutional framework leaves room for the intervention of minor and protest parties which might be harbingers of change and for cases where non-partisan elections are the rule.

Both the non-partisan and minor party alternatives have been proposed by some as more propitious frameworks for women's access to elites than those provided by the major parties and the detailed examination of these options is the object of this chapter and the next. Two basic questions must be answered: do these alternatives even now constitute breaches in the systematic dominance of politics by men and, if so, do they offer a basis for continuous advance on women's part to parity with men? In this chapter, data on non-partisan recruitment from the USA and Scotland (including in the latter case in-depth interviews with non-party candidates) allows the broad cultural context to be held constant while we consider the implications for women of a change in the

73

configuration which gives more weight to self-selection and the unmediated intervention of social and economic institutions. The arguments for and against the non-partisan alternative are reviewed first, before proceeding to an empirical investigation which follows the same basic structure as in Chapter 2.

NON-PARTISAN ELECTIONS

In Britain, we are so used to the domination of our political life by political parties that it easy to forget that there are other ways of organising political relationships – even competitive ones – and other bases for choosing between people who want power. Non-partisan elections are those in which individuals do not stand for office under a party label. Either they do not want to be identified with a party, which is the case in those parts of Scotland where people stand as 'Independents', or party identification is prohibited by electoral law, which is often the case in the United States of America. Thus 'non-partisan' simply means 'not party'. Whether the absence of party label is merely a legal formality (where everyone really knows what party a candidate supports and which party endorses which candidate) or whether it means that political parties are really not involved at all will depend on circumstances. 'Non-partisan' in its formal sense is therefore a perfectly straightforward term but its substantive meaning can never be taken for granted.

Interest in non-partisan elections arises from the feminist search for political alternatives which would be more congenial to women than the dominant party systems. It is sometimes argued that the role of institutions is so inimical to women's recruitment, especially for winnable seats, that a system which minimises their intervention or excludes it altogether will offer women a better chance of advance, through self- and voter-selection. The fact that British voters do not effectively discriminate against women as such[1]; that discrimination against them is declining in the United States[2]; and that in some circumstances the votes of women have been mobilised behind female candidacies in Finland and Iceland[3] can be cited in support. There is also a school of feminist thought which holds that non-partisan elections should be more attractive to women – or at least less repulsive – because they are not invested with the institutionalised conflict of the party system. This argument rests on the belief that the female gender role (and possibly their innate propensities too) predisposes women to co-operative rather than conflictual behaviour, in contrast to the competitiveness of men.

To the present writer, both kinds of reasoning seem to understate the inherent problems women face in this avenue of recruitment. The first argument rests on two very dubious assumptions, that a) 'non-partisan' means 'non-institutionalised' or even entirely 'self-starting' and b) a change of *selectors* is equivalent to a change in the *criteria* of selection. Against the first, we must be careful not to underestimate the informal role of institutions, political parties included, in the initiation and nurturing of ostensibly non-partisan candidacies. As for the second, the criteria of self-selection and the identity and criteria of any non-institutional external selectors who may be involved are clearly crucial here.

Even if the voters do not discriminate among the candidates on the grounds of either sex or socio-economic status (which would have the same net effect), but assess them on some other basis which is less unfavourable to women, they cannot vote for people who do not stand, i.e. who do not self-select. The trouble is that self-selection leads us straight back to socio-economic resources as the independent variable which sorts people into those who are more, and those who are less likely to see themselves as candidate material. To the extent that it is governed, as we must expect it to be, by the standard model of the resources–recruitment relationship, it is a process in which women are handicapped by their relative lack of individually high socio-economic status.

Furthermore, what the Scottish and Soviet findings have shown, and the American data suggested, is that as far as institutional selectors are concerned, occupation is as vital a resource as education, whether it is the standard or modified model of recruitment which is at work; it is both the *interaction* of occupation with education in the underlying distribution of socio-economic values and the independent effects of both variables which explain the patterns of recruitment. The educational gender gap in the population at large is relatively easy to close, but unless occupation is found to be less relevant to non-partisan recruitment than we have found it to be where major parties are concerned, the much more resistant occupational disparity between the sexes will be a major obstacle to women here too.

Of course the ownership of property is an even more fundamental and ancient source of dominance among men, and by men over women, than occupation. We must still be prepared to encounter settings where property is as important as either occupation or education in assigning socio-economic status (and determining income), as it was in former, less diversified societies. In Scottish rural areas, for example, where the ownership or tenancy of land is a prerequisite for the high-status occupation of farmer, this form of property carries more social weight than anything else and is also relevant to local office in a way that the ownership of industrial capital or liquid assets is usually not.[4] Control of the land is intrinsic to economic development, the provision of housing and the availability and disposal of employment, so that landowners and occupiers are simultaneously influential in local affairs and vulnerable enough to wish to take part in them.

Precisely because occupation and property, as well as education, are so integral to the male status hierarchies on which the *parties* draw, predictions about self-selection must take them into account too. What is more, when self-selection is not only the basis on which men come forward but is also the main platform on which they seek election, it is only logical to expect that the most-valued aspects of their socio-economic status will assume even greater importance, in their own eyes and perhaps in those of voters, than is the case where individuals are bolstered by the endorsement of party selectors.

Where gender is concerned, it seems likely that in such circumstances a woman who is highly educated but lacks the attributes of occupation or property on which male self-selection is based will still feel unequipped to compete. Like the American wives who were found by Jennings and Niemi to require a great deal *more* education and income than their husbands before they could *equal* them in low-level political participation[5], a woman will have to be exceptionally well-educated if this alone is to compensate for her lack of the other sources of status among men! Indeed, this is probably the clue to one of the best-publicised 'gender gaps' in the history of empirical research: the alleged failure of Verba, Nie and Kim's female subjects to 'convert' their socio-economic resources into active participation at the same rate as men.[6] The reliance of these investigators on education alone as a measure of socio-economic status[7] means that a great deal of potential explanatory power is unavailable to them and that when they compare similarly educated groups of men and women they are assuming a socio-economic equality which is very unlikely to exist. The most plausible explanation for the 'gap' is that it measures the effects of the occupational inequality of equally educated members of the two sexes. A by-product of this inequality is the lower *personal* incomes of women, who may be earning some of the family income but almost always much less than their husbands and in many cases none at all. This may be of little relevance when it comes to grassroots participation but, as we shall see, may present particular difficulties in the case of non-partisan candidacy.

In fact, even the most superficial consideration of modern political trends suggests that education alone will be of limited use in explaining patterns of non-partisan recruitment. If this were not the case, we could expect the spread of education to have a pronounced, positive effect on both the absolute number of people seeking office without party support and the proportion of women among them; more men would stand in non-partisan elections as they became more educated, and more women would come forward relative to men as well. However, the evidence does not support this proposition. The tendency throughout the western world has been for politics to become more, not less partisan over the period when education has become more widely available and it is partisan, not non-partisan candidacies which are increasing in number with the rise of new parties in European countries and the decline of the one-party state in the USA.[8]

The problems with the second, feminist argument for non-partisan elections are twofold. One is that in removing the party character of an election we do not remove the conflict. We may reduce the element of dogma and sterile party-bashing but at the cost of intensifying the bitterness of personal attacks and removing the safety valves for the individuals involved (who can no longer contain the conflict to their party persona and enjoy a comradely half-pint together in their private capacities after the debate). The other difficulty with the feminist case is the very same gender role on which it is based. One of the best-attested handicaps of women, and one which they share with other out-groups, is low self-esteem. Few attributes could be considered less appropriate for non-partisan political candidacy. Standing under the umbrella of a political party provides the legitimacy and shelter which may embolden a fragile ego to expose itself. In addition, the person who has been taught to serve instead of lead has the comfort of seeming to serve a greater cause than simply herself. Logic suggests that standing as an individual is a psychologically much more difficult political act for anyone, but especially for a woman; there is no shelter nor justification other than a sense of her own merit, and votes are being solicited directly for herself. Nor is there strength to be gained from the fact that most non-partisan elections are fought at a very local level, where individuals are likely to be canvassing support from people they already know. For a woman who is typically circumstanced and typically insecure, this lack of anonymity is likely to make things worse; there is no escaping from her 'real' identity, as woman, wife and mother.

All these reservations suggest the hypothesis that genuinely non-institutional settings will be extremely unpropitious for women unless or until they acquire the same socio-economic characteristics as men. In the meantime, the most likely outcome is that only the exceptionally well-endowed will come forward. Their success rate may be high, but this does not mean that it is realistic to expect other kinds of women to come forward without the intervention of institutions which are prepared, for whatever reason, to recruit them. It will tend instead to support our emphasis in this research on the process of institutional-selection and on socio-economic factors rather than sex as explanations of the gender pattern.

The remainder of this chapter is focused on the empirical evidence for this hypothesis, looking first at the American context to illustrate some of the general points of this discussion and then at the Scottish case, where more extensive data makes it possible to delve deeper into the personal, political histories of candidates to identify the patterns of male non-partisan recruitment, and their consequences for women, very precisely. For the United States, in addition to the sources used in the previous chapter, the analysis draws on the recent surveys of male and female holders of elective office conducted from the Centre for the American Woman and Politics and on the extensive American literature on state and local politics.

NON-PARTISAN RECRUITMENT IN THE USA

On the face of it, the United States offers considerable scope for the investigation of non-institutionalised recruitment but no comfort at all for feminist advocates of non-partisan politics. In a political system where non-partisan local elections are frequently the norm (and sometimes compulsory) and women's electoral performance (in terms of percentage vote) is slightly better in non-partisan elections, women have one of the worst local recruitment records in the developed world. Closer inspection obliges us to regard the superficial impression of an extremely weak institutional framework for local politics as an over-simplification, but *not* to conclude that non-partisanship is in itself of any help to women.

It is certainly true that of the three settings we have examined so far, the USA is the one in which institutional selectors are least dominant and the onus is greatest on self-selection, with its dependence on the standard model, to bring individuals to the point of candidacy. As we would expect, and have seen in Chapter 2, candidates in general are well endowed with the individual resources of education and occupational status which are generally associated with a strong sense of personal efficacy and 'civic' orientation and are less available to women than men; the resource gap in Merritt's sample was predictably even greater between the women candidates and the general female population than was the case for men, but women candidates were still at a disadvantage compared to the men. High income is also found to be a candidate characteristic, again predictably, because the American system makes peculiarly high financial demands on aspirants. There are no limits to local campaign expenditures and personal resources will be almost indispensible even if the candidate expects to raise money from individual and group supporters; fund-raising itself requires an initial investment and time spent raising money is time lost from campaigning. Money will count even more when it comes to winning, especially for genuinely non-partisan candidates who cannot rely upon partisan loyalties to identify and mobilise the vote.

At the level of candidacy, then, the American data support the hypothesis that the standard model, operating via self-selection, is the basis of local elite recruitment and represents a built-in barrier to women.

However, this picture of the recruitment process is an over-simplification all the same, for it obscures the important part which institutions really play in it, especially when it comes to winning elections. A national survey of local council members (i.e. winners) in 1980 found that nearly all of them (84 per cent) had either been recruited as candidates by a political party or gained party support after deciding to stand.[9] This is entirely congruent with Merritt's findings that

1 two-thirds of her sample of candidates 'were brought into the political arena through institutional political structures; individual political leaders or groups such as local parties, homeowners' associations, or caucuses'[10] and
2 the main distinction between her male winners and losers was the fact that over two-thirds of the institutionally recruited men, but only 11 per cent of the others, were successful.[11]

In this light, the claims that only a third of the 1980 council members had fought in a 'partisan' contest and that the elections in Cook County, Illinois, the location of the Merritt study, were 'non-partisan'[12] have to be treated with caution. The non-partisanship of local American contests is frequently more formal than substantive, for a strong institutional framework of recruitment is clearly being brought to bear in many cases on both the initiation of candidacies and the mobilisation of group or party loyalty to separate the winners from the losers. In areas of the United States where party loyalties are strong and their organisations active, the struggle to gain party endorsement, declared or implied, must be considered the functional equivalent of a nomination process. In other areas the dominance of one party is so great that what some observers may describe as 'non-partisan' politics looks more like a one-party state from another perspective; the absence of visible party organisation, which is often periodic, simply reflects the lack of effective opposition against which to organise. The confusion arises because in Mayhew's words, 'getting a sure handle on organisation in many of the country's nominating environments is close to a hopeless task even when good accounts are available: the softer forms of party or partylike organisation, perceivable as nods, nudges and rumours, are hard to distinguish from nothing at all and act as a minimal constraint on individual candidates' in contrast to traditional party organisations which 'are fairly easy to follow.' The most minimal of constraints is, of course, that the candidate should be acceptable to the dominant interests in the *status quo*, and as Mayhew goes on to explain,

> as a practical matter, nonpartisan elections offer the same sort of opportunity that standard partisan primaries do to organisations who wish to promote sets of candidates. In both cases a lack of

widely available information that might be used to identify either potential candidates or candidates appearing on an undifferentiated list in a ballot . . . invites unofficial slating or endorsements. In fact some kinds of organisations confine their activities to one type of process or the other, but traditional party organisations have operated indiscriminately in both, promoting candidates wherever the opportunity arises.

This author also points out that in some contexts it is 'hard to tell whether political organisation operates independently of economic organization or as just another expression of it.'[13] Another comparative study of American state politics concludes that institutions of some kind are almost always involved in recruitment and that even the common hypotheses that party recruitment varies with levels of urbanisation and partisan competitiveness are not really supported by the evidence.[14]

I have already regretted the lack of adequate data to identify the socio-economic criteria of this kind of institutional selection of winners among American local candidates and noted the possible presence of modifying selectors in the case of Illinois. The Scottish and Soviet findings suggest strongly that investigation would find occupational criteria to be a crucial factor, both in male patterns of success and in the very low rate of female participation. However, before turning to other, and possibly more genuinely non-partisan elections elsewhere, we must consider an alternative hypothesis, advanced by Merritt, about the criteria of recruitment in the American case.

Merritt's expectation was that female 'non-partisan' candidates would differ from the men not only in their background characteristics, which was certainly to be expected, but in the relationship of their attributes, socio-economic and political, with success. In other words, Merritt was suggesting that the criteria of recruitment would be different for women than for men. On the face of it, her findings appeared to confirm this hypothesis, particularly in respect of political experience. Women who had held appointive office were much more likely than other women to win, which was not significantly the case for men. A history of extensive community involvement was also associated with female success but not male. The limited nature of the data and the very small subsample involved in the case of male community involvement render these findings extremely tentative, but what is even more arguable is the interpretation Merritt puts on them. The conclusion she draws is that experience of voluntary work in the community is the 'functional analogue' for women of male occupational experience, so that women are approaching office by different routes to men and using different resources to do so. This is an interpretation which requires careful scrutiny. Although it has superficial attractions as an explanation of why the resource profiles and the winner/loser differences of women candidates differ from those of men, it seems to me essentially spurious.

So long as some major routes to candidacy and election, such as the most advantageous socio-economic attributes, are closed to women, then the resource profiles of men and women candidates are bound to be different. (In addition, women will exhibit more, and men less, of those kinds of behaviour and experience which are derived mainly from the female gender role.) Inevitably those routes and attributes which *are* open to women will bulk larger in their profile than they do for men. This is a matter of ordinary arithmetic and will be the case even if there are actually far fewer women approaching by their most open routes than there are men, simply because there are so few women candidates anyway. In Scotland, for example, the proportion of Labour women with higher education was much higher than that of men, among both winners and losers. However, this was not because there were a great many educated women; they were actually outnumbered greatly by their male counterparts, among both winners and losers, and the significant factor was the *lack* of less well-educated women.

The only difference found between Scottish male and female candidates which was not socio-economic in character is another good illustration of this point. A much larger proportion of women (19.8 per cent) than men (8.4 per cent) in the SDES population came from a family in which at least one member had held public office before the respondent herself first stood, (though in neither sex was this attribute associated positively or negatively with success). What these figures tell us is not, as the incautious might conclude, that a highly political family background is a politicising factor for women but not for men. The number of men involved was actually much greater than that of women (sixty-five men and forty-five women) and what the figures really indicate is that a) not even such a propitious background as this generates as many female candidacies as it does male and b) a smaller proportion of women are coming to candidacy from other kinds of background. It is only when the greater proportion of women using a particular route is also a greater absolute number that we can seriously claim that women are following a 'different' route from men.

It might still be argued on substantive rather than statistical grounds that a higher success rate for women with a specific kind of experience than for men with the same background is significant even if the relative number of women is smaller. Could it not mean, as Merritt is proposing, that selectors are evaluating this kind of experience more highly when it is possessed by a woman than they are in the case of men? Of course, this would imply that there are not one but two processes of recruitment going on, one for men and the other for women, employing different values but the same selectors in each case.

81

While the hypothesis might have a certain superficial plausibility in respect of contests where the competitors are all women, both arithmetical and political logic are really against it. If civic activism is the only kind of relevant attribute politically active women have, then the selectorate in all-women contests are being asked to choose between people who have some resources and people who have none. In choosing the candidates who have some, they are behaving exactly as they would do with men. Where the contests are mixed and analysis reveals that women civic activists and political appointees are significantly more successful than other women, whereas male civic activists and appointees are not more successful than other men (the Merritt example), we should be cautious about accepting this finding at its face value. In the case of the women, the candidates who do not have civic or appointive experience are likely to have no valued attributes at all. It is quite the contrary in the case of the men, for we know that in their occupations they do indeed have another, crucial kind of attribute, the very kind that women lack. Like is not being compared with like.

SCOTLAND

For the study of gender and non-partisan recruitment in Scotland, there is a wealth of primary data, much of it gathered for the specific purposes of the present enquiry. The data have three principal components:

1 election returns showing the incidence and success rates of partisan and non-partisan candidates of each sex over four elections(1974–84);[1]
2 the basic survey of 1984 (SDES) to which the reader was introduced in Chapter 2; and
3 a series of personal interviews with virtually the entire subset of Independents in Strathclyde, which was designed to identify, among other things, the relative contributions of self- and institutional-selection in each respondent's route to candidacy and the substantive significance of non-partisanship in local Scottish politics.[2]

In Scotland, non-partisan contexts have certainly not proved favourable to women's recruitment so far. Although there had been an increase of over two-thirds in the absolute number of Scottish women standing in District elections over the decade since reorganisation, bringing them from only 14.4 per cent of the candidates in 1974 to 21.5 per cent in 1984, this had been accounted for entirely by a rise in partisan candidacies; the number of women standing as non-partisan candidates (or Independents as they are usually known)[3] had fallen, as it had for men. Furthermore, of all the major candidate types (Conservative, Labour, Alliance, SNP and Independent) it is among the Independents that the proportion of women is lowest, slightly trailing even that of the Labour party in every election since reorganisation. The parallels with Labour do not end here. Though the success rate of women Independents is extremely high (71 per cent in Scotland as a whole and 55.5 per cent in Strathclyde) this is a reflection of the high proportion of incumbents among them.[4] The trouble once more is that there are so few of them, amounting to only 15.7 per cent of the total number of Independent councillors – exactly the same as the proportion of women among Labour winners.

For an explanation of these puzzling similarities in the gender outcomes of partisan and non-partisan elections, and an indication of the conditions in which non-partisanship might offer greater opportunities to Scottish women, it is necessary to start with the distribution and context of non-partisanship in Scotland. Although the number of Independents in Scotland is declining, they are still one of the major categories of candidate in rural areas. Where they occur, it is often as the dominant form of candidacy and a manifestation of strong local resistance to the idea that local politics is 'about politics' at all. They have the highest success rate of any kind of candidate, Labour included, over the decade since reorganisation, with anything from a fifth to over a third standing unopposed and an average success rate of 62 per cent. In Strathclyde region, they are concentrated in two Districts (Argyll and Bute in the West Highlands and Clydesdale in the Lowlands) with a success rate which (at 50 per cent in 1984) was lower than that of Labour but 25 per cent better than that of the third-ranking Conservatives. Inside these Districts, only two Independents were defeated by a party candidate rather than another Independent; outside them, only six Independents were successful throughout the whole of the rest of the region, and one of these (a woman) was elected by an island offshoot of a mainland District.

One reason for this geographical distribution is the weaker resistance to party intervention in urban areas, where local loyalties may be relatively less strong, individuals more likely to be anonymous and their identities when known less clearly marked. In rural areas, conversely, lack of anonymity may also deter people from declaring their party colours, for fear of alienating employers, customers or neighbours.[5] Another reason is the greater population size of urban wards, especially since the reorganisation of 1974 which did away with a system of many small authorities, closely linked with their communities, in favour of the broader capabilities associated with a much smaller number of larger units. This structural change led to a swift and sudden partisan domination of local politics in almost all non-rural areas, as the parties moved in to take advantage of the discontinuity. In fact reorganisation created expectations of the need for partisanship even among existing councillors who were non-party themselves, and this was for personal reasons as well as because of the greater resources of the new authorities. Along with the new system came an amalgamation of wards, so that in most cases one councillor had to serve where there were several before. The result was a campaigning problem of a quite different order from the 'good old days', with ward electorates as high as 11,000 in some city wards. Faced with the alternatives of raising the money and organisation to reach a large electorate on their own, or have a party foot the bill *and* capitalise on its voter loyalty, most of those who might have preferred to stand as Independents have felt that there was no real choice. The unlikely event of a re-reorganisation which broke up the local govern-ment authorities into smaller and (in today's policy terms) less viable units, seems to be the only way that non-partisan elections could be considered feasible again in urban areas.

Even in rural areas, the Independent candidacy was not expected at the time to outlive reorganisation. The words of a man whose experience as a councillor in Argyll spanned nearly a decade on either side of reorganisa-tion illustrates both this unfounded expectation and a common rural attitude to parties in local government even among those who know where their sympathies lie.

> When re-organisation came in, it was thought that the new council would be very politically weighted. I don't care much for the party machines at local government level but I stood as a Conservative. When I got in, I found that there was absolutely no requirement for party politics at our level and I went back to being an Independent thereafter . . . the best way to operate was as an Independent and take total advantage for your own area of any party that came along; quite mercenary.[6]

However, Regional elections in rural areas present candidates with similar problems to those of urban Districts, with the result that some people who have contested District elections as Independents feel obliged to appear as party candidates at the regional level, even if their enthusiasm for the party of their choice is distinctly lukewarm. Although it might be said that some of these people are thus appearing in their true colours (with their Independent status in District elections being more fictional than real), personal interviews reveal that expedience is just as likely to work the other way, even to the extent of overcoming a marked distaste for the party concerned, in search of an identity with which to reach voters in areas where the candidate is personally unknown or lacks the personal resources to campaign effectively.

Here is confirmation already of the fact that resources are a crucial element in the recruitment of Independents and that circumstances exist in which political parties offer an easier option to potential candidates. With this in mind, it is easier to understand why even in rural areas the number of Independent candidacies is declining; non-partisan candidacy is simply a more difficult political act, for men as well as women.

Expense is part of the problem. In partisan campaigns the disposable personal income of a candidate is of little relevance because the party pays the bill. By contrast, although some Independents are supported by private donations in money or kind, many, if not most have to pay their own way from personal savings (it being absolutely taboo in the Scottish context to mount an open fund-raising drive for a personal candidacy). The amount of non-monetary help some candidates feel they ought to accept from other people is also limited, morally or for electoral reasons. The result is a tacit, but absolutely crucial financial barrier to recruitment, which is often exacerbated by the costs of transport in sparsely populated but far-flung rural areas. Ironically, this is a problem of which many Independent candidates appear to be entirely unaware, their own circumstances being sufficiently comfortable for the outlay of a couple of hundred pounds on an election (expenditures being strictly limited by law) to seem quite trivial. It transpired in interviews that it was mainly those few candidates who were themselves low-paid who had previously considered what a deterrent this might be to ordinary rural workers, who will with difficulty accumulate even so small a sum and will have to be ruthless indeed to divert the money, when they do, from family needs to an electoral gamble on their own behalf.

The hazards of such a gamble bite deeper, however, than the direct commitment of time and money. We can expect that the most basic and powerful deterrent to political action on the part of low-ses individuals will arise from their situation of dependence on those whose positions as property-owners and employers give them control or influence over the lives of the less-resourced. Without the collective resources from which redistributive institutions arise, among which are the solidarity and safety in numbers of the industrial work-force, low-ses individuals in rural society are likely to be too constrained by their very real economic dependence on high-ses individuals, and the habits of mind to which this gives rise, to mount what might be construed on both sides as a challenge to the *status quo*. It is only those people whose sources of livelihood lie beyond the influence of the immediate community who are likely to feel free of material inhibitions on this score and we can expect that the psychological constraints of dependency will require equally unusual circumstances to be overcome. Men may in general be less self-doubting than women, but they too are likely to find it particularly difficult to put themselves forward as individuals even if they have the 'right' combination of socio-economic attributes, but especially if they do not. After all, it is by overcoming such inhibitions that modifying institutions are able to extend the socio-economic range of recruitment and in their absence it seems reasonable to expect very few low-ses men to come forward.

There is yet another material aspect of the non-partisan context – and one of which most councillors were very much aware – which may have a seriously inhibiting effect on candidacy, especially among the lower ses orders. Rural Districts tend to be large in area, and though this is not such a problem in Clydesdale, it reaches ludicrous proportions in Argyll and Bute. This is the largest District in Scotland – possibly the largest basic level unit in the UK – and has quite extraordinary problems of internal communication. With 2,500 miles of coastline, indented by hundreds of miles of sea-lochs and fringed with no fewer than twenty-six inhabited islands, the logistics of travelling from a local community to the District Headquarters in the village of Lochgilphead can be daunting. There are no internal air routes, ferry services are infrequent and time-consuming, and bus services on some routes to Lochgilphead (which has no sea-borne connections at all) are non-existent. Mainland councillors must have cars and sufficient control of their time to be able to spend inordinate amounts of it on the road; islanders must either have cars *and* spend a great deal of their nights in mainland hotels or else resort to such fantastic route-plans as the Tiree councillor who flies out to Glasgow in the morning (overflying Lochgilphead on the way), drives by hired car the 75 miles back to his committee meeting in Argyll and reverses the journey at the end of the day to be back at work on his croft by nightfall. It is the scale of this problem which leads to the frequent (though by no means accurate) assertion on the part of Independent councillors that the only people who can do the job are 'the self-employed, the retired and the unemployed'.[7]

In the light of so many adverse factors, it is not surprising that Independent incumbents have the highest proportion of uncontested elections. This does not mean that the office itself is less attractive in rural areas – the interviews revealed that this is far from being the case[8] – but is a measure of the difficulty of this kind of participatory act. It might seem, indeed, that we already have in this difficulty a sufficient explanation for the low levels of female non-partisan recruitment.

However, there is an alternative theory of non-partisan recruitment, which has been foreshadowed in the discussion of non-partisan elections in America and implied in the quotation above from the reluctant regional party candidate. Professions of non-party Independence on the part of local politicians are often distrusted (not least by their own fellow candidates and councillors) and it is held by some that the whole concept of the Independent councillor should be discounted as a smokescreen for the the active intervention of political parties in both the processes of recruitment and the operation of ostensibly non-partisan councils. Given that some individuals even appear in both guises simultaneously, turning up as a party candidate for the Regional Council while actually serving as an Independent councillor in one of its Districts, this is an argument that must be taken seriously. More subtle, indirect forms of partisan intervention are also possible, if local community or occupatio-

86

nal associations act as fronts for the less acceptable face of party politics – a form of intervention which from another perspective could of course be described as more crude, being the direct action of material interests on the process of political recruitment. To understand fully the processes of male recruitment and their significance for women, we must first be clear as to what kind of men really come forward as candidates, and who the winners are. Thereafter, it is essential to identify the role of institutions and other external agents of recruitment in the selection process and to discover how the models of the ses-recruitment relationship which these selectors employ interact with the recruitment tendencies of self-and voter-selection. In the following sections we look first at the characteristics of male Independents and the winners and losers among them, then at the relationships these people have with political parties, and finally at individuals' routes to candidacy and the institutional component in their recruitment.

Male Independents

A total of sixty-six people (fifty-seven men and nine women) stood as non-partisan candidates in the 19 Districts of Strathclyde region in 1984; nearly all of them responded to the original basic survey (SDES) and between this and the later series of personal interviews, background data were collected on 92.4 per cent of these (fifty-four men and seven women). Close examination of these data shows that the kind of men who stand as Independents, and especially those who win, are a perfect illustration of non-partisan recruitment as a process of socio-economic elimination.

At first sight, this might not appear to be the case, for male Independents are by no means very highly educated. In fact they are the least likely of all the candidate groups to have had full-time further education, bearing in this, as in their high success rate and gender pattern, a strong resemblance to Labour party candidates. Closer examination, however, reveals that this is just an example of how badly adrift we can be taken by over-reliance on the education variable. Although only 18.9 per cent have had full-time further education and nearly half have had none at all since leaving school, the majority of these people are unquestionably drawn from socio-economic elites. The point is that their status is measurable mainly in property and occupation, not education. Some 68 per cent of the total population of male Independents (and no less than 81 per cent of the winners) are people of high individual occupational status, with the direct ownership of property in land or business assets also a feature of approximately half these cases.

It is true, however, that over a third of all the men who stood as Independents in Strathclyde were mavericks, standing as isolated non-partisans in areas which are dominated by party candidacies. In these

Table 3.1 Socio-economic characteristics of Independent men

Characteristics	Proportion (%)
Full-time Further Education	26.5
Owners/Operators of Land or Business Assets	50.0
High Individual SES	64.7

circumstances, Independent candidacies are as likely to arise from internal feuding within the parties, as from the non-partisan tradition. As the marginal products of exceptional local circumstances, their candidacies may thus have a substantive significance quite different from those of Independents in areas where non-partisanship is the dominant mode and their personal characteristics might distort our vision of the 'real thing'. For this reason, the enquiry is confined hereafter to those Independents who stood in one or other of the two Districts – Argyll and Bute, and Clydesdale – where the tradition of non-partisanship has survived local reorganisation as a dominant mode. Between the original basic survey and the subsequent series of in-depth interviews, background data were collected on all but two of the forty-one non-partisan candidates in these Districts and 90 per cent (thirty-one men and six women) were interviewed.

Repeating the basic socio-economic analysis of men for this core population, similar results were found all the same, as shown in Table 3.1.

Only a quarter have full-time further education, but over two-thirds fall into the top five categories of the Codot occupational classification and half, including a small group of major landowners, either own or control significant concentrations of land or business assets. The only difference is that on neither characteristic was there any appreciable variation between winners and losers in 1984.

These findings obviously attest to the dominance and occupational/ property base of the standard model, at least as far as candidacy is concerned, and are as damning in their implications for women as they are for the generality of men. However, we already know that both the socio-economic patterns of rural life and the patterns of competition among non-partisan candidates are different from those of urban, suburban and rural/urban areas where the parties dominate. If we further refine the occupation variable and adopt a somewhat different perspective on the distinction between winners and losers, three aspects of the non-partisan pattern come into view which demand further investigation. The first is that nine-tenths of the candidates fall into one of four very distinct occupation/employment sectors. The second, inter-related phenomenon is an unmistakable manifestation of the bimodal tendency

Table 3.2 The occupation/employment groups of Independent men

Group	%
1: Farmers/landowners[A]	20.6
2: Business[B]	29.4
3: Nationalised industry employees	23.5
4: Employees of other external agencies	17.6
5: Other (miscellaneous)	8.8

Notes: [A] Not including crofters.
[B] Mainly small business proprietors, but includes local company director and partner in business-linked professional firms.

of recruitment – standard *and* modified – which was found earlier among Conservative and Labour candidates. The third is a longitudinal pattern of winning and losing which seems to reflect this bimodal tendency, though more tenuously, at the point of election as well.

Two of the four main occupational sectors represented among Independents and shown in Table 3.2 are entirely predictable manifestations of the standard model at work.

Group 1 is an agricultural 'upper crust' of farmers and landowners, whose control of the land makes them the most prestigious human element on it and the main, resident source of strictly rural employment; they also, of course, inherit a class tradition of civic involvement. The agricultural counterparts of the urban managers and business-linked professionals who were found in the previous chapter to be so numerous and successful among Conservatives, they amount to a fifth of all non-partisan candidates. A still larger group is drawn from the village and small town elite. These are the businessmen (Group 2), nearly all of them working in the local community and consisting mainly of small business proprietors, such as shopkeepers, traders, restaurateurs and so on along with a very few business-linked professionals; they include some self-made men but are often heirs of long-established family businesses. They, too, enjoy the status of local employers and between them control a great deal of the economic life of the community; like their agricultural counterparts, they also inherit a tradition of local civic activism and are people of high individual socio-economic status and resources, measured in property and/or occupation. Between them, these two groups of local *prominente* comprise exactly half the candidates.

How we view the rest of the candidates depends on our perspective. The most obvious distinction between them and Groups 1 and 2 is that whereas the latter are self-employed, all the rest are (or were, if retired) employees. Strictly in terms of occupation, however, they are a motley collection of the skilled and the unskilled; the highly educated (a small minority), part-educated and minimally educated; the white-collar and the manual worker. They range from a former government research scientist to the only three crofters (as opposed to farmers) in the candidate population, all of whom, as the exigencies of crofting demand, are in paid employment (mainly low-ses) as well. They also include the only two representatives of the 'caring' professions, both of them teachers. It is only when we consider the character of their *employers* that a second common factor falls into place which gives these candidates their distinct socio-economic identity and signficance: virtually all of them (fourteen out of seventeen) are the employees (or retired employees) of agencies which are based *outside* the District. In two instances this means that the individual's whole working life was spent elsewhere (abroad in one case) but for the rest, it means employment *inside* the District, but for external employers. Look more closely at these employers, and another part of the puzzle falls into place. The candidates who are (or were) employed by central or regional government agencies or private firms are mainly individuals of fairly high individual status, whereas almost all of the men who do not have high individual resources of education and professional status are local employees of the nationalised industries: telephone engineers, electricity board officers, postmen, an airport authority fire-man and so on. We thus have two further occupation/employment categories: men of low-ses externally employed by the nationalised industries (Group 3, containing nearly a quarter of the total candidates) and a smaller group who are employees (mainly high-ses) of other external agencies (Group 4). Most of the latter possess, in their educa-tional and employment status, two mutually reinforcing characteristics which can foster a personal inclination to participate quite apart from their independence of local employers. In the case of the former, lack of individual resources appears to be offset by peripheral access to the collective resources of a large-scale, strategically placed and highly unionised work-force which is not only economically independent of the local community but, as we shall see, exceptionally well-placed to convert these socio-economic and psychological resources into individual political status. The hypothesis that independence of local employers would be an important factor in low-ses recruitment in rural areas is amply confirmed, but the evidence also suggests that employment in a nationalised industry has been a positive, modifying force in non-partisan recruitment which makes these men the non-partisan equivalents of the industrial employees selected and favoured elsewhere by the modifying tendency of Labour party recruitment.

Following the same structure as in the earlier study of partisan recruitment, the next step should be a comparison of the attributes of winners and losers. There are special circumstances, however, which make this exercise less than straightforward among non-partisans. For one thing, non-partisans (unlike the candidates of a single party) may stand against each other. In socio-economic terms, this may mean that voters are faced with options as distinct as those which characterise, for example, Labour and Conservative candidates, but it will be difficult to judge whether non-partisanship is being used as a front for party intervention in such cases or whether it is due to chance. Likewise, if similar kinds of people are found opposing each other, this could result equally from lack of partisan alignment or from the absence of an authoritative selection procedure to decide which one ought to go forward. If, for example, there is no formal process to give an elderly councillor the nudge into retirement, he may simply soldier on until faced with a younger counterpart on the ballot paper. Success and failure may thus measure different things in different cases.

Another problem is the small proportion of losers and their uneven distribution, due to the high incidence of uncontested elections among Scottish non-partisans. In the two districts under investigation, over a third were wholly unopposed in 1984 and a further two individuals were opposed only by a party candidate (Labour in one case, Conservative in the other). Once again, success and failure mean different things. Where a candidate is unopposed, his success tells us something about the nomination stage of recruitment and nothing about the attitude of voters. It is only contested elections which involve voter-selection, and it would clearly be imprudent to come to any very firm conclusions about the preferences of voters who are given so little opportunity to express them.

A further difficulty arises from the fact that nearly all the candidates are either incumbents or ex-councillors. There is thus a high proportion of ex-councillors (seven out of eleven) among the defeated, most of them former members of the District Council itself, the others of its predecessors under the old system. Indeed, there is hardly an Independent candidate to be found who has not been endorsed by the electorate, or else stood unopposed, at some stage in his political career. As the interviews revealed, these men are overwhelmingly dedicated, one might even say addicted to local politics. Slightly over half were already in office in the geographically smaller Burgh, District and County Councils which existed before reorganisation and some of the older ones have a history of public office which goes back to the 1950s. Most of them are councillors still (some of them very old indeed) but there are also a few who did not survive the transition and have been trying to get back into office ever since. The post-reorganisation contingent are even more likely to be councillors. As a scrutiny of past elections shows, few of the post-1974 entrants who were defeated have stood a second time.[9] A full analysis of voter choice would really require information about these past losers too, but this is unavailable.

The question of winning and losing must therefore be approached

Table 3.3 Proportion (%) of each occupation/employment group who had ever lost an election (the Everlosts)

Group	Ever lost
1: Farmers/landowners	14.2
2: Business	27.2
3: Nationalised industry employees	37.5
4: Employees of other external agencies	66.6
5: Other (misc.)	66.6

with considerable reservations. Also, as already noted, no clear socio-economic patterns emerge from a comparison of winners and losers either by education or the straightforward occupational sector categories. Indeed the only obvious characteristic of voter-selection among non-partisans is a decided preference for incumbents over challengers. However, when we analyse the candidates' electoral histories longitudinally and crosstabulate various aspects of these histories with the fourfold occupational/employment typology, a pattern does emerge.

From a combination of the interviews, with their complete candidate histories, and the available election returns, it is possible to distinguish both those candidates who have never won an election (the Neverwons) and those who have ever lost one (the Everlosts). Since nearly all the candidates have been successful at some time, interest focuses on the Everlosts, who comprise just over one-third of the cases.[10] A tendency for these men to be more educated than the rest is too slight to be regarded as significant, but the variation according to occupation/employment criteria is more substantial, as Table 3.3 shows.

Only one of the farmer/landowners (Group 1) has ever been defeated, and this was an elderly and infirm landowner being retired by a youngish farmer in 1984. Less than a third of the businessmen (Group 2) and scarcely any more of the employees of the nationalised industries (Group 3) have ever lost an election. It is the remaining categories – the unpropertied, fairly educated employees of other external agencies (Group 4) and the small residue of unclassifiable cases (Group 5) whose vulnerability stands out; in each case, they are almost twice as likely as any of the other groups to have suffered defeat at some time. It is also interesting to observe that if the 1 to 5 numbering of occupational/employment Groups which I have used above is treated as a ranking order, then in all eight instances of defeat at the hands of another Independent candidate in 1984, only one candidate lost to an individual who was lower in this hierarchy; either the election was lost to someone of the same type, or more usually, to someone higher up the scale.

These findings certainly suggest that the same bimodal pattern of candidate recruitment is being sustained at the point of election by the preferences of voters, whose deference to high-ses individuals coexists with considerable concentrations of support for a very specific category of collectively resourced, low-ses individuals. Nevertheless, we should not read too much into this; uncontested elections not only exclude voters from recruitment altogether but have an indirect bearing on the kind of choices that are open to them in the elections which *are* contested. Taking the four sets of District elections from 1974 as the database, over half of the candidates of 1984 have enjoyed at least one uncontested election (and in some cases several) since the District councils were set up, but there is no evidence that any of the socio-economic categories is more or less advantaged in this respect. It is in the characteristics of contested elections that a pattern is visible which throws additional light on the choices made by voters. One of the main reasons why farmers/landowners and nationalised industry employees are seldom defeated is that they almost never stand against fellow-members of their socio-economic group; this kind of internecine competition is only slightly more common among the businessmen. The other is that these categories rarely compete with each other either, though when they do this invokes the reinforcing hierarchy of voter preferences. The competitive pattern gives the distinct impression that there are rather more small proprietors with a hankering for office than there are council seats for them to fill, but that they and the other two entrenched socio-economic groups form an almost impenetrable political establishment with the others – Groups 4 and 5 – cast mainly in the role of challengers and the generality of the male population excluded from the contest altogether.

The question is how, in the absence of overt political party intervention, are these results being achieved? Is non-partisanship just a front either for the parties (as the absence of competition *within* the top three groups would seem to suggest) or for occupational groups which are so strong that they can afford to dispense with parties altogether? Alternatively (where recruitment patterns are grounded mainly in the self-selection process) are socio-economic resources important mainly because of their effect on the psychological orientations of individuals, or because of the material circumstances they entail (or both)?

For the answers to these questions, we can now turn to the interview data. In so doing, we are also moving from the level of socio-economic variables, where broad patterns enable us to distinguish the greater or lesser likelihood of recruitment from different groups, to the level of the individual, where each person's history is unique and brings the particular and the personal to bear on the issue of which individual stands for which office. By using both levels of analysis, it should be possible both to explore the substantive political content of non-partisanship and identify the links which bind the experience of the individual to the characteristics of larger groups to which he belongs.

A warning is in order here, however. Individual case-histories are a level where we must expect to find a great variety of idiosyncratic reasons for political involvement and personal factors which may cut across the boundaries of socio-economic status which have proved to be so important in distinguishing the pools from which participant individuals are drawn. The reader must not be deceived by this into thinking that these case-histories somehow invalidate the findings of socio-economic analysis. The psychological bases of aspiration (interest in politics, the development of a sense of personal efficacy, and so on) are the same for everybody, irrespective of socio-economic circumstances. So is the basic range of possible agents of recruitment (themselves or other people). It is quite impossible that aspiration and recruitment should not cut across the boundaries of subgroups within the candidate population, for they are the constants which defined the total population in the first place. What the preceding analsyis has shown is that some socio-economic groups throw up more cases of candidacy than others and nothing we find at the level of individual case-histories can invalidate this finding. What we are looking for is further insight into how this happens (and in particular how far parties and other institutions are involved) in the case of Independents.

Political parties and non-partisan politics

The interviews were designed to offer two distinct approaches to the problem of defining the relationship of Independent candidates to political parties. The first was grounded in 'hard' data relating to party membership and activism; party involvement in the initiation of candidacies or election campaigns; and stated party identification. The second centred on the candidates' own perceptions of their relationships, as self-styled Independents, with party politics. Neither approach on its own does justice to what has proved to be a complex pattern, with very real differences in the substantive significance of 'non-partisanship' from one candidacy to another and even variation over time within the experience of single individuals. To achieve a complete picture, the 'objective' and 'subjective' data must be taken together.

Almost exactly half the respondents were members of a political party before their first candidacy. Virtually all of the party members were activists as well and they include a few who were local party office-bearers. However, these findings conceal substantial variation in both the strength and continuity of party commitment. Two of the party members originally stood for office under a party label, but began their careers as Independents precisely because they had 'fallen out' with, and in one case left, the party concerned (which was Labour). Two others (one Labour,

94

Table 3.4 Party identification of Independent men

Party Identification	%
Conservative	26.7
SNP	13.3
Labour	16.7
Liberal	3.3
More than one party (including Lab + SNP, Con + SNP, Lib + SNP, Con + Lab + SNP)	13.3
No party identification at all	26.7
	100.0

Note: 'Party identifiers' are people who ever been linked or identified with a political paty *at any time*, and therefore include people who now regard themselves as completely non-partisan.

one SNP) would have stood openly for their party, but failed to secure its support, although one of them had actually set up the local party branch with the intention of standing as its candidate. On the other hand, the party allegiance of some of these people – in spite of their activist proclivities – appears tenuous to say the least. A few had already left their party by the time they first stood for office and one left thereafter, finding it too boring to go on with. In at least three cases party identity had been assumed for mainly tactical reasons. What is more, a quarter of the party members had belonged to more than one party – to three parties in one case – and three people were identifiable more in terms of their opposition to another party (two anti-Labour, one anti-Conservative) than by enthusiasm for their own. As against this, three people who were not party members at all turned out to have a very strong party identification indeed and a definite sympathy with one party or another emerged in several other cases. Taking the latter into account as well as the members and activists, just over two-thirds of the respondents expressed some form of party identification, of which the catholicity is shown in Table 3.4.

On this showing the strongest party is the Conservative, but it is followed fairly closely, if we include a history of multiple memberships, by the SNP and Labour. The relationship of party allegiance with occupational group followed fairly predictable lines. Only one busi-nessman and one farmer showed Labour leanings, whereas there were no Conservatives among nationalised industry employees. Among occupational/employment Groups 3 and 4, allegiances were more mixed. There was no clear socio-economic pattern to SNP membership, which may reflect a tendency – frequently postulated by respondents – for people to turn to the SNP in contexts where either Labour or Conserva-

Table 3.5 Proportions (%) of party identifiers and party members among Independent men compared with the adult UK population

Relationship with party	Independent men	UK populations
Party identifiers	73.3%	92.0%[A]
Party members	66.6%	7.4%[B]

Sources: [A] Bo Sarlvik and Ivor Crewe, *Decade of Dealignment: the Conservative victory of 1979 and electoral trends in the 1970s* (Cambridge University Press, 1983), p. 293.
[B] The British Participation Study of 1984–5 (Figure supplied by courtesy of Geraint Parry, Department of Government, University of Manchester).

tive identification, but especially the former, is considered too much of an electoral liability.

Comparing the proportion of party identifiers among these candidates with what is generally found in the population at large, we can see that the Independents are unusual in two rather paradoxical respects. As shown in Table 3.5, they are notably *less* likely than other people to identify with a political party, but *very much more* likely to join one.

The proportion of 26.7 per cent who do not have any party links or identification (however tenuous) contrasts markedly with that of only 8 per cent among the general population. However, we have to set against this the incongruous fact that Independents are no less than 59 per cent more likely than voters to be party members and activists. Although there is clearly a possible foundation here for competitive politics which are substantively non-partisan, there is an even stronger basis for politics which are partisan. Just how strong the latter is emerges when the candidates' subjective assessments of their relationship to parties are reviewed.

Respondents were told that from talking to Independent candidates and councillors I had come to the conclusion that Independents fall into one of three types in respect of their relationship to party politics. They were invited to place themselves in one of these categories or else explain why none was felt to be appropriate. The categories were as follows:-

1 People who have no links with any political party and no particular political alignment. They feel completely independent of party and may even be hostile to the very idea of political parties (Type A).
2 People who have a definite political alignment – they know where their sympathies lie and may even be members of a party – but do not wish to stand for election under a party label because they want to preserve their independence in local affairs. They foresee that they might disagree with their party on public issues and want to be free agents when it comes to council business, to behave as they see fit without reference to a party line (Type B).

3 People who are committed to a political party and stand as Independents purely out of deference to the local tradition; such people will make no bones about their party identity and may be widely known for their party commitment through canvassing at general elections, holding local party office, and so on (Type C).

This typology met with instant recognition from almost all the respondents, and the vast majority were able to place themselves within it without difficulty. The main exceptions were the small group of people who would have liked to stand as official party candidates if only they could. If these people are treated as a sub-category of Type C, then the Independents are found to be not quite equally divided among the three categories, with the largest group classing themselves as Type A – the wholly non-aligned – but nearly two-thirds recognising a strong personal party commitment.

This distribution might seem to accord well with the earlier findings about party membership and identification and for the most part it does. However, close scrutiny and cross-reference with those parts of the interview dealing with party involvement in the initiation and promotion of candidacies revealed some distinct surprises. Of the straightforward Type Cs, one (Labour-aligned) was not even a party member; only two attributed their recruitment in whole or part to party intervention; and only two (one of the latter and another) had ever received any active support from their party in elections. On the other hand, two people who had actually been recruited by a party (the SNP in both cases) and one lifelong member of another party described themselves most emphatically as Type A.

The respondents who saw themselves as Type B, politically aligned but locally independent, varied considerably in the strength of their party commitment, but hardly at all in its direction: three-quarters were Conservatives. This contrasted strongly with Type C, where over half were single-mindedly Labour. In fact an attitude frequently expressed by Labour candidates was one of disbelief in the whole concept of Independence. Seeing it as a smokescreen for Conservative defence of the *status quo*, they tended to emphasise the need for a political line in pursuit of redistributive policies. Conservatives, on the other hand, though motivated in some cases by a strong desire to 'keep the Labour fellows out' were much more sceptical of the ability of any party, including their own, to produce a line which embodied enough flexibility and common sense to be workable at the local level. Both parties seemed to be paying a price for these orientations towards party discipline, the Conservatives in the tendency of their people to drift in and out of party membership and the Labour party in internecine strife. Of the respondents in serious dispute with their local party, three out of four were Labour.[11]

Taking all the indicators of partisanship into account, it is clear that considerable overlap exists between party politics and the local Independent candidacy, enough to throw in question the very concept of non-partisanship in many cases. What is more, some measures of partisanship, like membership of a political party, are found to be considerably more common among recent (post-reorganisation) Independent candidates. On the other hand, there is no corresponding decline in self-perceived membership of the wholly non-aligned Type A. In fact there is a sizeable core of around a quarter of the Independents who lack either any history of party links or any party identification, past or present, and see themselves as wholly independent of party. A further sixth have tenuous and/or fluctuating party ties and stress their individuality in local politics. About the same proportion are definite in their allegiance but equally determined to reserve their freedom of action. However, this leaves a third of the Independents who are quite uncompromising in their partisan loyalties, even if they see them as compatible with a certain amount of individualism in the council chamber. A distinction can be made here between the two Districts included in this study, with non-partisanship considerably more fictional than real in Clydesdale, and the Independent tradition much more substantively non-partisan in Argyll in Bute. In both places non-partisanship is seriously under threat, however, both from the determination of the parties and the pressure of local events.

Routes to recruitment

Notwithstanding the partisan content of non-partisanship, the fact remains that direct party intervention in recruitment is the exception rather than the rule, even among the partisan. We have already seen that the Independents vary greatly not only in the strength of their party commitment but in the strength of their party's commitment to them. The proportion of candidates who said that a party had played any part at all in initiating their original candidacy was very small, amounting to only a fifth of the whole. These ranged, moreover, from the routinely selected party candidate, operating under protective cover as an 'Independent', to the farmer who had been persuaded to stand by the SNP (just as he had formerly been persuaded to come before a Parliamentary selection meeting by the Conservatives) and took great pride in belonging to no party at all, and the ex-Conservative whose sympathies now seemed to be divided equally between Labour and the SNP and who had been 'put up to it' by the former. The latter candidate was somewhat taken aback, however, to find that he was expected to do all his own campaigning without party help.[12] By contrast, three of the candidates with party sympathies (two SNP, one Labour) who did not attribute their original candidacy in any way to party intervention were actually helped by the party in elections. One of these described his candidacy as entirely self-starting but regarded himself as tantamount to an official SNP candidate; another was a former (Independent) burgh councillor whose relations with his local party branch are inharmonious but who usually mounts a full-blown SNP campaign notwithstanding. If we add these two, plus a former Labour candidate who was recruited directly from his trade union by a fellow unionist already serving on a burgh council, to the small proportion of declared party recruits, we have a quarter of the Independents' first candidacies which were in whole or part supported by party intervention in the recruitment process; not an insignificant proportion, but much smaller than might have been expected.

Of course, this takes no account of 'nods, nudges and rumours'. If we allow for any kind of party allegiance or even sympathy as a possible basis for the almost imperceptible kinds of party intervention, then approximately two-thirds of the candidacies might have been affected thereby. It has to be said, however, that a cross-reference between respondents' own accounts of themselves and the incidental remarks made about them by their opponents suggests that such signals, if given, are not very clear. There is in any case a widespread desire to avoid too close an identification with a political party for fear of negative consequences at the polls.

However, political parties are but the consequences of underlying interests and values and in small communities, where people can be known as individuals, their intervention may be superfluous. The respondents were asked to describe the events leading up to their very first candidacy and whether the idea of standing had germinated first in their own minds or in those of other people. Rather less than a quarter saw their candidacies as entirely self-starting, approximately half of the candidates said the idea of their first candidacy had come entirely from others and over a quarter said it was 'a bit of both'. The most frequently cited 'others' – by nearly a third of the respondents – were existing Independent councillors at the time a 'vacancy' arose. In a few cases (under the old system of annual elections for a third of the seats in multi-member constituencies) this had even taken the form of co-option. Of course co-option is not an option nowadays, and the new system of single member seats means that incumbents no longer recruit for their own areas. This may be one reason why direct party recruitment is more common since reorganisation. Next in frequency came 'people in the community'. Pressed to define this category, respondents used expressions such as 'people of standing' and 'people who have an interest in the development of the area', or else explained that 'well, you see, this is a farming community'. Although almost every respondent had been actively involved in the affairs of his community, only a sixth mentioned fellow-members of community councils, ward committees or non-occupational groups as recruiters. In fact Independent incumbents, 'people of standing' and direct party intervention between them were involved in no less than 83 per cent of the cases where external recruitment was reported, which also means two-thirds of all the Independents. It was also interesting to find that in every case where members of the family were cited as influential in recruitment, these people turned out to be either Independent councillors themselves or else party activists.

The central recruitment role of institutions and people of status is therefore incontestable, and the implication is, of course, that political and socio-economic continuity is being ensured by this means. The importance of the recruits' own socio-economic characteristics is implied in this but receives more direct confirmation in other aspects of the data, which also show that it is occupation and property rather than formal education which are the crucial factors in both external and self-selection.

All the landowners made reference to the traditional standing and civic involvement of their kind in the local community. In addition, although no one attributed his personal recruitment to direct intervention by the National Farmers' Union, more than half the farmers were NFU activists who volunteered this information as relevant to the events leading up to their first candidacy. Both the NFU and the Young Farmers were also cited as vehicles for the respondents' original induction into local affairs and an excellent training ground for public life. Several farmers also alluded to their occupational ability to arrange free time as a factor in their self-selection, and some to their ability to capitalise on the 'farming vote'. Prominent professional involvement in the NFU and other agricultural organisations also appeared to have been a major factor in the co-option of a government research scientist to the old County Council just before reorganisation.

While the majority of farmers said that other people played a large part in their recruitment, and a few had even been reluctant at the start, business people were notable for their self-selection. In fact the majority of entirely self-starting candidacies were those of businessmen (mainly from families with a tradition of prominence in local politics) and hardly any of this occupational group were entirely dependent on external recruiting agents; predictably, these agents consisted mainly of Independent councillors, the Conservative party and people of standing in the community. Most of the business candidates were involved in business and property-based organisations, such as Ratepayers' Associations or their equivalents, commercial and trading associations and Rotary-type organisations. Like the farmers, they tended to stress the occupational advantages – control over their time, flexibility and the help of family members also involved in the business – which had played a part in their self-selection and ability to carry on as councillors in the face of the increasing paperwork and other demands of local government. They also stressed the financial costs of diverting time and energy to politics, but in few cases did this seem to have been a serious enough problem to cause more than mild regrets.

Although the nationalised industry employees were not as likely as the businessmen to be party members, most of them were active union members before becoming candidates and in two cases the union had been directly involved in their recruitment. Like the farmers and busi-nessmen, too, they tended to come from families with a history of involvement or at least interest in political affairs, and nearly all said that by the time they emerged as candidates they had already come to see themselves as the kind of person who might, one day, stand for public office. However the most striking and general aspect of this group was the stress they placed upon the supportive attitudes of their employers. Not only were they given time off on pay to attend council meetings, but it was made easy for them to arrange cover for unpaid leave as well, putting them on a level with self-employed farmers and business people in terms of flexibility and control of their time. Even promotion prospects, though damaged by this, were not always destroyed, for as one electricity board employee explained, 'It was to their advantage. They felt that the Board derived quite a lot of benefit by having someone in the position of being able to speak for the Board, forewarn them about things; so it worked quite well.' The same speaker described how this had come about, in terms which illustrate perfectly how rural employees of nationalised industries, though few in number and geographically peripheral, have gained direct access to the political fruits of collective industrial resources. The nationalised industries were the creation of the first post-war Labour government and

> in these days, in the Electricity Board, we had people with a particular interest in politics. Of course you didn't have so many whiz kids then. You had people who had been brought up in the industry and the fair majority of them also had political leanings. It all started of course in the Hydro-Board with Tom Johnston [Attlee's Secretary of State for Scotland] and he instilled into people who came after, that they should let people who were interested in furthering local government *and* the Board have a bit of rein to do as they could.

Whether the sense of active encouragement or supportiveness came primarily from employer or fellow-workers, this group of men has been exceptionally well-placed for political elite recruitment.

Where the employees of other external agencies, such as teachers, civil servants and the employees of private firms (Group 4) are concerned it is immediately apparent that these men (and the residue of cases in Group 5) differ from all the other three groups on several dimensions. In the first place, only one man in Group 4 is a post-reorganisation recruit, which suggests that it has become more difficult for people of this kind to break into local politics. One possible reason for this is a change in the conditions of electioneering, with the disappearance of the public election meetings of the past where a mass audience of apparently anything up to a thousand people (even in a small rural centre) could be swayed by the eloquence of an articulate, educated man who had not lost the 'common touch'. Another problem for this group is that whereas the House of Commons offers the politically ambitious schoolteacher, for example, an alternative career, local government service has to be combined with one's regular job, an increasingly difficult proposition these days. The only practising teacher among the Independents (the above-mentioned sole post-reorganisation entrant in this group) had quite exceptional advantages in this respect; not only had he married into a local political family, but his wife is a former teacher who shares his specialisation and takes his classes for him when he is away on council business. It should be remembered that the distances involved normally make absences from work an even more serious problem in rural than urban areas.

People in both groups 4 and 5 are also distinctive in being late starters in politics, who have been peculiarly dependent on other people to raise their sights to public office. Only one man (from group 4) came from a family where politics was even discussed when he was growing up, only one had thought of himself as the kind of person who might stand for office before he actually came to do so, and more than two-thirds were originally recruited by other people. These 'others' were not party selectors, however. Although, like almost everyone else, groups 4 and 5 had been very active in community affairs before coming forward, they differed from the other groups in their relative lack of party involvement. The identity of their recruiters was extremely varied and the only conclusion supported by the incidental evidence of the interviews is that these two categories, more even than the others, tend to consist of people whose personalities impel them into group activities. They are 'joiners', who by sheer force of activity or visibility come to attention of others who turn their minds to politics.

Thus the overwhelming tendency of the interview data was to confirm that the crucial recruitment dimension was that of occupation. However, there was one rather unexpected aspect of occupational experience which cut right across the main occupation/employment categories but also stood out in the interviews as a major factor in recruitment. From interviews with older respondents, a recurring theme began to emerge of an association between their *return* to the area after a considerable absence and a marked increase in their involvement in local affairs; this arose in no less than half the personal histories of pre re-organisation entrants. In some cases a causal relationship was merely implied, but in several it was made quite explicit that the experience of work or military service elsewhere had opened the respondent's eyes both to other forms of social organisation and to his own potential role in affairs. Two, for example, had served on the Military Control Commission in Germany after the last war, and after helping the defeated enemy construct a new society returned with a consciousness of their experience and skills to find that nothing had changed unless for the worse at home 'That sort of stirred me up.' said one and the other 'naturally assumed I could use the experience to good advantage in my own camp.' Another felt that fourteen years in the RAF had given him his ideas 'about politics and the local government situation' and 'an insight into what to do; how to speak; how to get things done'. Returning to his native island he proceeded to persuade the poverty-stricken distillery workers to join a trade union and the more prosperous islanders to form a Ratepayers' Association. Other returnees had learned new trades which opened up their expectations or had simply developed wider horizons from working in other social milieux. Listening to these accounts, an interesting parallel began to suggest itself; when either war or economic necessity had driven these people away, they returned with something of the same sense of simultaneous 'belonging' and detachment – and the same sense of their own worth – which the landed gentry bring back from their traditional round of public school, 'varsity and a job in the City'. However, where the gentry have an interest to defend and a propensity to get involved with the Conservative party, the more humble returnees are the most likely group of all to stand aloof from party politics and see themselves as genuinely non-aligned Type As. The latter are in fact almost entirely composed of returnees and incomers.

This is not to say, of course, that the effect of war-time or other forms of external experience is not mediated by the socio-economic variables with which this recruitment study started. After all, almost every male between the ages of eighteen and forty was caught up in the Second World War and witnessed the triumph of Labour in 1945, and the rural areas under study here (especially Argyll) have a famous history of military service in both war and peace. The fact remains that out of all those who served and witnessed, it is people from certain very clearly defined occupational groups who end up as Independent political elite recruits.

The changing world of the independent

The world of the Independent is not static. From interviews with older respondents it is clear that the present breed of Independents, Conservatives included, are very different from the authoritarian, ex-army landowners whose determination to maintain the structures of inequality is said by some to have dominated the old County Councils. In the present time, three developments in the broader context are imposing change on the recruitment of Independents. Firstly, the new system of local government, with its fewer seats and growing demands on councillors' time, has had a marked effect on the age at which men first become candidates. This effect is not as drastic as some of the councillors themselves seem to think; the reason existing councils contain so many elderly and retired people is simply the incumbency factor which has kept them in office so long. However, when the candidates (mainly, it should be remembered, councillors) of 1984 are divided into two groups according to whether they first stood before or after reorganisation, the mean age of the former at first candidacy is found to have been 36.4 years, compared with 45.3 years for later entrants. This may benefit late starters, such as the men in Group 5.

The second change relates to the nationalised industry employees. It has been argued here that these men's recruitment advantages have sprung

1 from their share in the collective resources (psychological and material), of occupations which are strategically located in the economy with a large and highly organised work-force; and
2 from the specific way in which the political power of the collectively resourced was used at the end of the Second World War to set up nationalised industries and facilitate their own political recruitment.

The fact that the impact of collective resources on recruitment has been so strong even in rural areas (where there is no large industrial work-force) and without benefit of party organisation attests to both the importance of collective resources and the success of the post-war strategy. However, in the present era of decline for traditional collective resources, accompanied by the abandonment of collectivist values and the actual dismantling and privatisation of nationalised industries, we can expect to see the rapid erosion of these advantages. The reverberations of this are already emerging from the interviews, with respondents reporting increasing difficulties in securing time off, more severe loss of earnings and promotion, and for one British Telecom engineer the prospect of losing his job altogether if he tries to carry on as a councillor. A return to the virtual dominance of non-partisan local government by the individually well-resourced seems to be a distinct possibility.

The third change is a further decline of non-partisanship itself in Strathclyde region. In 1987, Argyll and Bute District Council was set in turmoil by the establishment of a non-party 'Group' by fourteen out of the twenty-six councillors, with the intention of asserting councillor control over officials, advancing the claims of certain areas to a bigger share of the expenditure cake and (it is said) ousting existing chairmen in favour of adherents to 'the Group'. Personal antagonisms, already something of a problem in this council, were soon running high and after the elections of May 1988, in which 'the Group' narrowly failed to secure a majority, confidence in the non-partisan system has been shaken. Some councillors feel that the main effect will be to strengthen the hands of the parties in foisting party labels on the candidates and imposing party discipline in council business. Although the level of non-partisanship merely dropped in 1988 in Argyll, and the Independents have retained their majority in 1992, it appears to be doomed in Clydesdale. In this District, where most of the incumbent Independents were closely tied to the Conservative party, they were able to persuade the latter not to contest their seats. However, this agreement was entered reluctantly by the party and lapses with each councillor's retirement. The great age of many of the Independents means that their era in Clydesdale is virtually over. In 1988, only a handful stood, and they are now a small minority on the council.

The implications for women

As with partisan elections, the implications for women of these patterns of male recruitment are both obvious and discouraging. Female counterparts of the advantaged male groups simply do not exist. It is men who own or tenant land, inherit the local family business, work as engineers and local officers in the nationalised industries, and enjoy the higher personal incomes. As a result it is from men, not women, that the people with a high sense of their civic worth are drawn.

It is also these kinds of men who have the necessary control over their time and movements to convert efficacy into action. The main employers of most women are their husbands, who do not provide such benevolent cover for extra-curricular activities as the nationalised industries. Like crofters and tree-fellers, all that most wives could expect after an afternoon away campaigning or on council business would be to spend the evening catching up with the work they had missed. Indeed, to a greater degree than even the most poorly paid, low-status groups of men, women live at others' beck and call; even in the evenings, when the lowliest of workmen is usually to be found at the pub, they cannot call their time their own. This, of course, is what people mean when they say that women 'do not have the time' for politics. The greater and frequently exclusive earning power of husbands also means that wives are less likely to regard family income and savings as theirs to dispose of in electioneering or support of a public career. On top of this, it seems reasonable to suppose that their nurturing responsibility and attitudes will make them more inhibited about using the money for personal ends. The only promising general development which might benefit women trapped in domestic ties is the recent tendency of men to start their candidate careers later, indeed at about the same age which is characteristic of women. On the other hand, this means that women will be facing men who have had more time to accumulate the personal resources that females are unlikely to have.

We cannot wonder that so few women stand as Independents. Nor can we be surprised to find that those who do are either standing in the unusual circumstances of a dearth of suitable men or on the basis of quite exceptional personal characteristics. In Lowland Clydesdale, where the majority of the small group of Independents who have dominated the Council consists of extremely elderly women (average age well over seventy), a lack of suitable men is the best-fitting hypothesis to explain their presence. The area they serve is predominantly rural, but, although its villages offer little or no career prospects for educated and/or ambitious men, it lies within commuting distance of a major city (Glasgow). The result is that there are resident men of high individual status, but with the exception of farmers they invest their energies and working lives (and have the bulk of their occupational affiliations) outside the area where they live. When a previous generation of Independent councillors (and their Conservative political backers) came to look for their replacements, they turned to women for a solution to this problem. The women they approached were the nearest equivalents they could find to suitable men, people who for women enjoyed unusually high status and visibility within and beyond their communities. Two were farmers' wives with a history of exceptional involvement in the national and regional levels of women's civic organisations. One was the wife of an existing councillor. Another woman who stood as a 'Progressive' (i.e. Conservative) but came to head the 'Independent' group none the less, was a local schoolmistress. Only one member of the group appears to have had a more or less self-starting rather than institutionally generated initial candidacy, which seemingly arose out of intense involvement in a local issue. For the most part their party affiliation is quite clear and they fall into the least non-partisan category of Independents.

Beyond this District, women Independents are few indeed and their candidacies have arisen mainly on the basis of the exceptional civic involvement of exceptional individuals. In so far as such a tiny group of people can be said to supply a pattern, it is that women Independents are more likely than men to be incomers to the area where they stand and to have something of the psychological outlook of the male returnees. Personality factors and special circumstances, such as coming with a teaching background into a community which is preoccupied with a controversial educational issue, or having an unusually strong motivation to create a stable new community (the legacy of wartime experiences) explain the recruitment of the few successful candidates. It is an apt illustration of the kind of compensatory socio-economic attributes women will otherwise require that in Argyll and Bute, where only one woman has served on the District Council since its inauguration in 1974, those women who reached the old County Council were quite exceptionally exceptional – such women as Miss Catriona Maclean of Ardgour, the hereditary chief of her clan and owner of a sizeable chunk of the county, and the landowner, novelist and celebrity, Naomi Mitcheson.

Although these conclusions seem glaringly obvious, it should be said that the priority of socio-economic variables rather than sex itself as the explanation for the gender pattern was not an explanation that came readily to the Independent men themselves when they were asked why they thought there were so few female Independents. So ingrained are our assumptions about the inevitability of male–female differences in status and resources that few even of those respondents who immediately provided a socio-economic framework for their discussion of *male* Independent candidacy and success thought of applying the same criteria to women. This left most of them without any frame of reference for discussing the gender pattern at all, and it was obvious that these men had taken the absence of women (like that of the ordinary working man) pretty well for granted until the question was posed. The answer was usually sought in terms of women's gender role, but respondents found it impossible to explain why gender roles should affect Independent candidacies more than partisan, and the most specific suggestion made, apart from the traditionalism of the local culture, was that rural councillors have to spend more time travelling. However, the bulk of the responses could be summed up in the tautology that 'they do not . . . because they do not.'

It is true that fear of societal punishment for deviant behaviour, especially in the rural areas where Independent candidacies mainly occur, might inhibit women's self-selection. One would expect all the same that if such prejudice exists it would manifest itself in an idiosyncratic rural pattern of electoral behaviour, whereas this is not at all the case. Not only is the success rate of the few women who stand as Independents actually higher than that of the men but a recent American study of voting behaviour in this same set of elections finds no voter bias against women even when controlling for incumbency.[13] Furthermore, the suggestion made by a few respondents in Argyll and Bute that simple sex discrimination is at the root of the matter has been confounded already by the dramatic triumphs there of two Liberal women at the polls, first in a by-election for the Regional Council seat of mid-Argyll in 1986 and then in the General Election of June 1987 when Ray Michie was elected as MP for the constituency, one of only forty-one women members of the then House of Commons.

Since the voters of Argyll and Bute are prepared to send a woman to the most coveted seat of all, at Westminster, the absence of local women councillors can hardly be laid at their door. We must conclude, yet again, that the real source of women's problem is their lack of the resources that underlie the recruitment of men. Although the visibility of Ray Michie may enable her to modify the future gender role inhibitions of some women by acting as a role-model (and it is interesting that the advent of the women Independents in south Lanarkshire, as Clydesdale was formerly known, had been preceded by the election in 1953 of a woman (Judith Hart) as MP for the Lanark constituency) the only sure basis for their progress into non-partisan political elites under present conditions will be their prior advance on the socio-economic front. When there are more women farmers, landowners and business people, (with the job of telephone engineer having become something of a political *cul de sac* nowadays) then we can expect to see more women Independent councillors. The only alternative would be that women should abandon socio-economic criteria of political eligibility, *and* find alternative bases of social support than are provided by the occupation-based networks available to men. Changing the selectors – from parties to non-party institutions or the potential candidates themselves – will make no difference unless the criteria for recruitment are changed as well.

4

MINOR PARTIES AND THE GENDER PATTERN

If the advancement of women is not served by non-partisan elections any more than it is by major parties, the translation to the House of Commons of a woman candidate for a minor Scottish party is an appropriate cue to turn our attention to another kind of variation in the range of selectors which might be supposed to advantage female recruitment. This is the intervention in a competitive electoral system of minor parties which do not appear to be derived from the established hierarchy among men and may even be, to a greater or lesser extent, the institutionalisation of protest against it.

As the following investigation will show, the instances where women have genuinely advanced by means of minor parties are the exception rather than the rule (and great care must be taken to distinguish them from those where an improvement in women's situation is more apparent than real). Few as these cases are, the conditions which give rise to them deserve the most serious consideration. If new and revolutionary social tendencies are at work which favour women, then these presently deviant cases may be the heralds of a general advance for women or even changes in the nature of politics as we know it.

MINOR PARTIES AND THE GENDER PATTERN OF RECRUITMENT

There are three main reasons why the intervention of minor parties might be expected to benefit women. Firstly, their rejection of the *status quo* might make them particularly attractive to potential women candidates who are uneasy with the values of the dominant parties and/or unable to advance within them; the more access women have to education in a society dominated by conventional socio-economic values, the larger such a pool of possible candidates will likely be. Secondly, to the extent that minor parties are opposed to the existing distribution of resources, their interests might seem to coincide with those of women. Thirdly, their limited chances of success should expose party selectors to a shortage of male candidates. Being comparatively unattractive to men as an electoral prospect, these parties may be obliged to recruit more women than the dominant parties whether they want to or not, just in order to field sufficient candidates for 'credibility'; some of these women may succeed against the odds.

Recent events, especially if taken out of context, seem to give credence to these arguments. In Britain, minor parties are credited with a major role in the increase in female candidacies for the House of Commons and one of them (the SDP) was the first to adopt a constitutional commitment to a small measure of positive discrimination in the recruitment process. On the continent, the West German Greens[1] have gone much further, promoting women not just as candidates but into winning positions; the climax came in 1986, with the commitment to ensuring a 50 per cent quota of women in their parliamentary seats.[2] Since the Greens had already proved their ability to win a considerable number of seats at state level and had justifiably high hopes of the outcome of the next round of federal elections, this was no idle gesture. In the event, they won forty-two Bundestag seats in 1987, twenty-four of them going to women. Equally startling was the appearance and immediate success of the all-female Women's List in Iceland, a women's party which won eight out of twenty-one seats in the local council of Reykjavik in 1982 and three seats in the parliamentary elections of 1983. Events like these have helped to create the impression that small parties are generally more sympathetic towards women and have encouraged a sense of optimism about the will and the ability of protest parties to advance their cause.

However, there are compelling counter-arguments and the total facts convey a rather different picture. It does not follow that because a party is not based upon the dominant social groups and values, it is necessarily more attractive, accessible or well disposed to women. After all, most out-groups in a male-dominated society are also dominated by men and (male relationships being what they are) there are plenty of them. It has to be remembered that parties that seek merely to adjust the distribution of political power in favour of, for example, different national or religious groups are not challenging the values on which the socio-economic relations of men are based but acting according to their rules; they are not protesting against the nature of male-dominated societies or the dominance of men in general over women, but the dominance of one set of men in particular. Given that women are only one out-group among many (and in most respects the least-resourced), it seems unrealistic to expect most minor parties to advance them. Indeed, some parties may derive from such exclusively male-dominated social groups (with such intrinsically male-supremacist subcultures), that they can neither invite nor tolerate female candidacies at all.

Even in cases where women are nominated in unusually high proportions, there are likely to be serious constraints on their prospects of success from a minor party base. If the electoral prospects of minor parties are poor (which would seem to be the case by definition), women are obviously not going to win many seats by standing for them. The opportunities they offer will be mainly at the level of unsuccessful candidacy, even where the electoral system favours proportional representation. It is important, too, to be on the lookout for the flexible operation of the second 'iron law', that the dominance of men is correlated with the hierarchy of rewards.

In some parties, a shortage of males who have the 'right' characteristics (whatever these may be) and are willing to face almost certain defeat may greatly increase the opportunities for women to stand. This is what happens in major parties too, and is the most likely explanation for the large number of women nominated by the Conservatives to stand in hopeless seats in Strathclyde. As one Conservative woman put it, 'Men don't want to stand where they have to take a chance. Women are not so afraid of looking foolish as men. If a seat is marginal a man won't push much for it and it'll go to a woman who's willing to do it – but he'll be back next time if it looks more promising'.[3] Similarly, if the electoral prospects of minor parties improve (and their selectors reach a position where they can identify winnable and unwinnable seats) the competition will become more intense. Selectors may begin to differentiate the attributes of winners and losers either along the same dimensions which are the standard in dominant and long-established parties or else on new dimensions which are equally derived from a hierarchical distribution of resources among men. Indeed, unless the party derives from an unusual milieu in which women are not an out-group, or its selectors are subject to revolutionary social pressures which make it in their interests to accommodate female aspirations, this is exactly what we ought to expect.

The complete facts speak strongly in support of these more sceptical lines of reasoning. Minor parties (like proportional representation) have been around for a long time without benefit to women and in spite of the dramatic recent examples cited above the truth is that they are still not generally disposed to favour women's candidacies. Examination of the candidate lists of minor European parties reveals some which have no female candidates at all and many others with a worse record than the major parties. Taking the elections to the European Parliament of 1984 as a recent example (and 10 per cent of the popular vote as the dividing line between the two categories of party) a total of thirty-two major and eighty-two minor parties stood in the ten sets of national elections involved.[4] In only three countries (Britain, Belgium and Eire) was the average proportion of women substantially greater among the candidates of minor parties. In three cases (Italy, Luxembourg and the Netherlands) it was significantly *smaller* and in the remaining four countries (Greece,

West Germany, Denmark and France) it was much the same. British experience is thus untypical, and the West German Greens are exceptional in more senses than one, even in Germany itself.

Within each country, as the German findings suggest, the proportion of women also varied greatly from one minor party to another. It ranged from 15 to 46 per cent in Belgium; from 14 to 25 per cent in Eire; from 10 to 30 per cent in Denmark; from 8 to 45 per cent in France and 50 per cent in Luxembourg; from 1 to 22 per cent in Italy; from nought to 20 per cent in the Netherlands, 25 per cent in Greece and 62 per cent in the UK; and in the extreme case of West Germany (where in addition to the Greens, a Women's Party entered its all-women list) from nought to 100 per cent. Inevitably, very few of these women won their seats and even though the success rate of women in a few minor parties was very high (with a woman being the only candidate to succeed in two cases) these few were vastly outnumbered by women from the major parties. Altogether, seventy-six women won seats in the Parliament, but only seven (9 per cent) were from minor parties. It is a similar effect to that which generally obtains in elections to national legislatures. Even in the Federal elections of 1987 in West Germany, where the Greens made history with the 57 per cent proportion of their Bundestag seats going to to women, the twenty-four women concerned are still outnumbered by the proportionately fewer, but absolutely more numerous contingent of thiry-one female Social Democrats.

A single set of elections cannot throw any light on the longitudinal relationship of a party's electoral prospects with the proportion of women who are given a chance of success by its selectors.[5] However, the volatility of electoral behaviour and party systems in Europe over the last twenty years suggests an inverse relationship between female recruitment and minor party prospects. In Britain, it is well known that minor parties nominate a large proportion of the women who stand for the so-called 'Mother' of Parliaments[6] but the proportion of women within these parties is also observed to fluctuate inversely with their electoral prospects.[7] Throughout the Scandinavian countries, too, Skard et al. have found a strong inverse relationship between party fortunes and women's recruitment, both in candidacy for public office and internal party posts.[8] What is beyond any doubt is the tendency of most minor parties, like their major counterparts, to exhibit a success rate gender gap; men are more likely to be adopted for winnable seats.

It is clear from this evidence that minor parties are not, as a general rule, favourable to women. On the other hand, it is also undeniable that some minor parties depart radically – and consistently – from the norm. Indeed, with careful scrutiny of their electoral histories, minor parties can be divided into three distinct types in respect to gender pattern. The first, and by far the most numerous, consists of parties in which both the candidacy level and success rate of women are either worse than or no better than those of their major party competitors. Since this is doubtless for similar reasons as were demonstrated in the study of major party and non-partisan recruitment, it would be superfluous to dwell upon them. Into the second, and more interesting category fall those minor parties which tend to put up a significantly higher proportion of women than the norm, but target them to lose; either the women are more likely than men to be selected for unwinnable seats (or positions on the party list), or the proportion of men tends to rise when the party's electoral prospects improve, or both. Since a shortage of willing men (in the face of adverse electoral circumstances) is the most likely explanation for this pattern, the main interest where this type of minor party is concerned is to compare their models of recruitment with those at work in parties of the third and final type.

This third and smallest group consists of those very few parties which not only consistently present more women candidates but also target them to win. Within this group, the actual proportions and success rates of women vary greatly of course, from cases where they are impressive only in relation to the other parties in their national system to the instance of the West German Greens, where women stand and win in perfect equity with men. A common feature, however, of nearly all these parties is their commitment to some form and degree of positive discrimination in support of women's candidacies; all-women's parties are of course a special subgroup, where positive discrimination is practised to the ultimate degree by excluding men.

Clearly, a shortage of willing men is not a suffcient explanation for parties which combine high levels of female candidacy *and* success. Instead of lacking value in selectors' eyes (and in their own), women are actually being advanced here on more or less equal terms with men, being apparently exempt from the scissors problem which normally afflicts them. The only possible explanation for this is that women are not, in the context concerned, an out-group any more. Either they have as much in the way of conventional resources as the men, or else the way their party evaluates the socio-economic hierarchy (and possibly the attributes peculiar to the female gender role as well) is fundamentally at odds with the surrounding culture.

It is extremely fortunate that the SDES data, with a wealth of information about winning and losing candidates, allow us to explore these issues in considerable depth. The data include almost all the individuals who stood in Strathclyde for the two main British minor parties in 1984, and since one of these (the Scottish National Party) does not contest seats outside Scotland and over a third of the parliamentary seats held by the other (the Liberal/SDP Alliance) were Scottish too, Scotland is the only setting where the two parties can be strictly compared. Both parties have been credited with a large role in the political advance of women in Britain, such as it is. However, a longitudinal study of their gender and recruitment patterns shows marked differences. Using the SDES data to explore the characteristics of men and women and winners and losers, the contrasting models of recruitment which produce these fundamentally different outcomes can be identified.

SCOTLAND'S MINOR PARTIES: THE SNP AND THE ALLIANCE

The present party system in Scotland dates from the early 1970s, when the Scottish National Party (SNP) and the Liberals (subsequently the Liberal/SDP Alliance)[9] mounted an increasing challenge to the dominant Labour and Conservative parties, with hopes which in certain times and places were not entirely unrealistic. Both are in some sense parties of protest and change.

In the case of the SNP, the challenge is to the constitutional relationship of Scotland to the rest of the UK. The political, economic and cultural domination of Scotland by the English is the grievance which motivates the party, and complete independence is the ultimate (and for many SNP members the only acceptable) goal. Although very divided internally on left–right issues, the strategy of the party in the 1970s was to win seats wherever it could, by simultaneously appealing to all voters as Scots *and* presenting the party as the champion of local interests and needs, in order to displace whichever major party was in possession of the seat concerned.

The challenge mounted by the Alliance was perhaps more diffuse and in consequence less distinct to the electorate. Although at one with the SNP on the need for constitutional change (with federalism rather than independence as the preferred option), the Alliance parties also stressed their rejection of the divisiveness of the left–right dimension in British politics.[10] The Liberals, in particular, were identified with demands for proportional representation, industrial democracy and a more consensual political system; the SDP with hostility to the unions and Labour's left wing, along with a desire for strong government based on rationality rather than partial interests. Both parties, but especially the Liberals, moved towards radical, intellectually based positions on ecological issues. On some major issues such as defence, however, the parties to the Alliance were deeply divided.

On the face of it, there are good reasons for expecting both the SNP and the Alliance to have had a considerable impact on the gender pattern of recruitment in Scotland. Not only is the SNP a party of protest, but two of the most dramatic events of Scottish politics in recent times were the victories of two SNP women in Parliamentary by-elections (Winnie Ewing in Hamilton in 1968 and Margo Macdonald in Glasgow's Labour heartland in 1973) and the rise of the SNP is strongly associated in the public mind with that of these and other prominent women. Although the Liberal party had no particularly female associations, the SDP did. In the first place, one of the Gang of Four who founded it was a woman (Shirley Williams, formerly a Labour Minister) and secondly, the party caused a sensation by committing itself constitutionally to a very small measure of positive discrimination in recruitment, by insisting that women and members of other out-groups appear on candidate short-lists. In addition, both the SNP and the Alliance must be credited with a large role in bringing women into parliamentary contests; approximately a third of all the women who have stood in British General Elections in the 1980s have been candidates of these parties and in Scotland the proportion is well over half.

These parties have also made a large contribution to the role of women in local Scottish politics. In District council elections over the whole of Scotland, the total number of women candidates rose from only 369 in 1974 to 613 a decade later[11] and although all four parties have participated in this development, over half of the additional women are standing for the minor parties, even though the latter contest considerably fewer seats. There are nearly three times as many minor party women candidates now as there were in 1974, whereas the growth for the Conservative and Labour parties has been of the order of 79 per cent and 46.5 per cent respectively . Nevertheless, the factors which account for these developments are complex and the recruitment histories of the minor parties are interestingly different.

In the case of the SNP, a marked increase in the number of local female candidacies certainly took place between 1974 and 1984, the period during which SNP fortunes rose to their all-time zenith (1977) and were abruptly dashed in 1979–80. However, closer examination shows that this was simply the result of an overall increase in SNP electoral activity. The number of male candidacies rose too, at virtually the same rate, and the proportion of SNP candidates who were women stayed almost exactly the same throughout. What is more, although there is no sign overall of an inverse relationship between the party's electoral prospects and the proportion of women among its candidates, there has been a consistent gap between male and female success rates in the SNP, with women 8 to 10 per cent less likely to win than men.

This is not a pattern of female advance at all and its discouraging nature is reinforced by closer analysis of the parliamentary level of SNP activity. The prominence of women there belies their number, which is very small. Over the five General Elections from February 1974 to June 1987, the proportion of female candidates had never been higher than 12.5

per cent and on two occasions (1979 and 1987) had fallen as low as 8.4 per cent. What is more, the proportion of female candidacies was much higher (at 15.3 per cent in 1970) *before* the party's modern renaissance began and the SNP has now been overtaken by all other Scottish parties except Labour (of whose candidates only 4.1 per cent were women). What the rise of the SNP has really done for women is provide a vehicle for a few exceptional individuals, whose parliamentary victories have had in common their unexpectedness and the charismatic personalities of the women concerned. Although the short-term fluctuations in the proportion of women among parliamentary candidates are not consistently related to the party's electoral fortunes, the overall picture is one of decline for women. At the local level, there is no doubt about it that the SNP is a party of the second type, recruiting women predominantly as losers.

The Scottish Liberal party (the older party to the Alliance) is more difficult to classify. Even in the more remote rural areas where a tradition of Liberal voting has survived (or in the case of the Borders, recovered from) the rise of the Labour party, the Scottish Liberal party offered few opportunities of reaching the House of Commons for the individual of either sex who was not prepared to mount something of a personal crusade over a long period. Although the proportion of women among parliamentary candidates was fairly high by the standards of the time (overtaking the SNP in 1979) little significance can thus be attached to the fact that none of them succeeded until 1987. At the local government level, the Liberals have always suffered from the fact that their greatest parliamentary strength is concentrated in the areas of greatest resistance to partisan intervention in local politics, the Highlands and the Borders. Relatively few candidates have traditionally been fielded in local elections, with the proportion of women varying from a sixth to a fifth and their success rate usually trailing that of the men. Although the Liberals certainly did not discourage women in their sometimes desperate search for candidates, it is noticeable that on a local basis the proportion of women was nevertheless inversely related to the party's electoral strength, with Lothian region and Inverclyde (a District of Strathclyde which was under Liberal control for a period in the 1970s) making a particularly poor showing.

There was a marked change, however, with the advent of the SDP and the formation of the Alliance. The number of local women candidates suddenly shot up from a pathetic total of twenty-five Liberals across the whole of Scotland in the District elections of 1980 to 107 Alliance women in 1984 and this was not simply a reflection of the Alliance's greater electoral activity. Unlike the case of the SNP, it involved a sudden, marked increase in the *proportion* of candidates who were women, by nearly 10 per cent. Furthermore, this took place without any fall in the

116

female success rate relative to men. On the contrary, the relative performance of women greatly improved, with the success rate gap narrowing from a 12.1 per cent advantage to men in 1980 to one of only 3.8 per cent in 1984. While the Liberal party on its own had certainly not done much to advance women, the SDP, by contrast, appeared on the scene as a genuine party of the third type, both bringing women into candidacy *and* targeting them to win.

At the level of parliamentary elections, the impact of the Alliance was equally impressive, with the proportion of women among their Scottish candidates rising from 12.5 per cent in 1983 to the quite un-British level of 22.2 per cent in 1987. Interestingly, there were almost as many Liberal as SDP women among them, something which happened at the local level too: the impact of the SDP was on the Alliance as a whole, not simply in itself. The fact that the results of this election were not encouraging (the Alliance won eight out of the seventy-two Scottish seats, but only two were SDP and only two were new seats) should not be taken to mean that this gender pattern was a response to poor prospects either; the party had gone into the election with considerable hopes, fed by favourable mid-term opinion polls and media speculation about a 'hung parliament'.

What was different, then about the SDP? It might seem that the answer must lie partly in its character as a party which, for the first time in Scottish politics, constitutionally obliged selectors to consider women for recruitment. However, this still leaves the unanswered question, why? Why should the SDP, a mixed-sex, male-dominated party with its origins in a breakaway faction of the Labour party, ever have espoused even this mild degree of feminism in the first place and why, above all, was it actually practising what it preached? Why, too, was it the Alliance rather than the SNP with its flamboyant female 'stars', which made a real, positive impression on the proportion and success rate of Scottish women?

For answers to these questions, the best strategy is to turn to the characteristics of the candidates themselves, to identify the differential models of recruitment which are operating in these parties and consider their implications for women. As in previous chapters, the Districts of Strathclyde provide the context for such an investigation, the SDES supplies the data and the first step is to identify the models of recruitment operating among men.

THE GENDER PATTERN IN STRATHCLYDE

The longitudinal gender patterns of SNP and Alliance candidacies in Strathclyde are almost identical to those in Scotland as a whole, with an increase in SNP women forming part of a general increase in the party's electoral participation and a sudden influx of women occurring with the advent of the SDP in 1984.[12] In Strathclyde, as elsewhere, the rise in women's recruitment thus owes a great deal to the minor parties and the SNP and the Alliance between them accounted for 40 per cent of all the women who stood in 1984. In each case, a quarter of the candidates were women, a considerably greater proportion than among Labour and the Independents although still much smaller than that of Conservatives. However, very few indeed of these women were to succeed – so few that even their low success rates of 11 per cent for the Alliance and 4.9 per cent for the SNP give a misleading impression of numbers; there were only five and three successful women respectively. This does not mean that men were any more successful. Both parties were essentially routes to failure, so much so that in 1984 there was no success rate 'gender gap' at all. In 1977, however (the year of SNP triumph, when that party won ninety-one seats overall in Strathclyde) the success rate for men was 39 per cent, but for women only 24 per cent, a more characteristic 'gender gap' of 15 per cent. In the same year, the Liberal 'gap' was 6 per cent.

The close correspondence between the gender pattern in Strathclyde and that of Scotland as a whole makes Strathclyde an excellent base for investigating the character of SNP and Alliance recruitment. As before, the large number of cases involved and the richness of the data allow for detailed analysis. Of the total of 105 women and 324 men who stood for these two parties in Strathclyde in 1984, 84.1 per cent responded to the basic SDES enquiry, giving the same information on their socio-economic background characteristics which the reader has encountered in the studies of major party and non-partisan recruitment. In the following sections, the educational and occupational profiles of male candidates in each party are examined first and then compared with those of women. A marked divergence is found in the socio-economic basis of SNP and Alliance recruitment. Winner/loser comparisons are necessarily tentative in view of the very small numbers of winners involved, but tend to confirm the implication of the first stage findings, that the SNP is in effect competing with the Labour party for the allegiance of its traditional socio-economic constituency, and applying similar selection criteria, whereas the Alliance derives from a very different, and more narrow, socio-economic sector which is more likely to sustain the recruitment of women as candidates. Unfortunately, this sector is equally unpromising as yet – by virtue of its marginal character and numerically weak electoral base – for their access to elected office in significant numbers.

The Socio-economic basis of recruitment: SNP and Alliance men

Like the candidates of the two major parties (and even the less well-educated Independents) SNP and Alliance recruits constitute a socio-economic elite by comparison with the poorly educated and occupatio-

Table 4.1 Proportion (%) of candidates with full-time further education, by sex and party

	Party				
	Conservative %	Labour %	SNP %	Alliance %	Independent %
Men	36.8	26.9	32.7	54.6	15.9
Women	37.8	45.7	48.1	76.9	28.6

Source: SOGS, 1984

nally more diverse Scottish electorate. This apart, however, the two minor parties are extremely unalike, with the patterns of SNP recruitment showing a very close resemblance to those of the Labour party described in Chapter 2, while those of the Alliance are a distinct departure from anything we have seen so far.

The most extreme divergence is in the case of education. Whereas the SNP men fall between Conservatives and Labour in their likelihood of having had full-time further education – and SNP women have an almost identical educational profile to their Labour counterparts – the Alliance candidates were quite remarkably different from any of the rest. As Table 4.1 shows, Alliance men were nearly 20 per cent more likely than their nearest rivals, the Conservatives, to have had full-time further education; nearly 30 per cent more educated than Labour candidates; and 40 per cent more than Independents. The Alliance, compared to all other Scottish political parties, was a party of educated men.

Education, however, does not in itself locate an individual on the dimensions of individual and collective resources. Although having it increases the likelihood of professional employment, there is a world of difference, in terms of socio-economic status, between the lawyer and the schoolteacher, just as there is between the skilled worker and the shop assistant. Yet again, it is the occupational data which we need to interpret these findings correctly. These data make two points very clear. Firstly, the occupational profile of SNP men is almost identical to that of the Labour candidates described in Chapter 2. Table 4.2 shows the almost identical proportions of candidates in what are for both parties key sectors for recruitment; industrial workers, the caring professions and line management/small business.

Industrial workers (28.8 per cent of SNP, 32.2 per cent of Labour) are the largest category in each case, followed by representatives of the caring professions, and although the proportion of the latter is somewhat smaller in the SNP, there are no major discrepancies anywhere in the occupational profile. The slightly greater SNP recruitment (13.8 per cent)

119

Table 4.2 Occupational profiles of male candidates for the Labour party and the SNP

	%	
	Labour	*SNP*
General management/business linked professions	6.6	13.8
Caring professions	26.0	16.9
Science, engineering and technical	11.0	12.5
Line management/small business	7.3	8.1
Service workers	2.6	0.6
Industrial/non-service workers	32.2	28.8
Other	14.3	19.4

Source: SDES, 1984.

from general management and the business-linked professions bears no comparison with the 34 per cent of Conservative candidates who belong to this group. Thus the SNP has the same tendency to modify the standard model of recruitment, in pretty well exactly the same ways, as the Labour party. In keeping with their avowed intention to win the Labour vote in Strathclyde, the Nationalists are self-evidently competing on the same ground as the dominant party, attempting (albeit with very limited electoral success) to draw on similar values and socio-economic sources of support. The fact that in areas of Conservative strength elsewhere in Scotland the SNP are sometimes derisively described as 'tartan Tories' suggests that a similar strategy is being pursued there, with appropriately different recruitment results; where it is the standard model which is locally dominant, they will tend to recruit much more heavily from the managerial and small business categories.

The second unmistakable point to emerge from the occupational data is a marked difference in occupational profile between the Alliance candidates and those of any of the other parties. Some general difference could be predicted from the disparity in educational attainment between the Alliance candidates and the other groups, but what the occupational data show is that even where Alliance candidates superficially overlap with Conservatives and Independents in their generally middle-class identity, in fact they draw on very different socio-economic sectors within that class. Fully 70.5 per cent of the Alliance men are drawn from individually high-status occupations, but although a fifth come from general management and the business-linked professions nearly a quarter are from the caring professions (virtually the same proportion as in the Labour party) and a further 21.3 per cent from science and technology. They are thus particularly distinguished from the Conservatives by the high proportion of caring professionals and the relative absence of small businessmen; from the Labour men by the proportion of high-level managers and professionals; and from all the other groups, Conservative and Labour included, by the proportion drawn from scientific and technical occupations. Whereas the major parties and the SNP are clearly rooted in the traditional economic base of West Central Scotland, the Alliance was a distinctively professional party which also seems to be alone in recruiting from the small, but potentially crucial technocratic element which would presumably be a crucial element in any modernisation of the regional economy.

With so few winners among these men (only twelve SNP and thirteen Alliance) it might be thought that to find predictable patterns of winner/ loser differences would be too much to expect. In the SNP case, nevertheless, although the cell counts in the multiple categories of the occupation variable are indeed too small to be taken seriously, a significant pattern is certainly found where the education variable is concerned. Here, the similar tendencies of SNP and Labour recruitment arrive at exactly the same conclusion, with SNP winners being nearly 20 per cent less likely than losers to have full-time further education.

In the case of the Alliance, there is absolutely no difference between winners and losers in terms of education, over half being highly educated in each case. The tendency of the occupational variable is strong enough, however, to be worth recording. The only successful groups were industrial workers, managers and businessmen, and the caring professions, in that order. Not one of the scientific and technical personnel won his seat.

WOMEN IN THE SNP AND THE ALLIANCE

The patterns of male recruitment in the SNP and the Alliance suggest that these two parties offer very different prospects for women. The SNP, with the resemblance of its modified recruitment model to that of the Labour party, poses them with similar problems. The kind of women who are most likely to self-select are the highly educated, but such women do not have the sort of occupational attributes which are valued by selectors. The predictable consequences are more male than female candidates and a higher success rate among the men. In fact, the resemblance between the educational and occupational profiles of SNP and Labour women is almost exact. Where 45.7 per cent of Labour women had full-time further education, the proportion is 48.1 per cent in the SNP. Although the proportions of both men and women coming from the 'caring' professions are about 10 per cent smaller in the SNP than in the Labour party, the gender gap is the same in both parties; SNP women are 16.4 per cent and Labour women 15.7 per cent more likely to have this occupational background than their respective men. The next largest group of women in the SNP consists of clerical workers and (as with Labour) there is less than a handful of women industrial workers. As we know, SNP women tend to have a lower success rate than the men. Since it is less-educated men who are more likely to succeed, and the women candidates are much more educated than the men, this result is exactly what we would expect. As already noted, the strategy of the SNP is to capture the votes of whatever party is locally dominant, which means Labour in Strathclyde. Extending the analysis beyond the geographical limits of the survey data, we can speculate that the same gender outcome – SNP women less sucessful than men – is achieved in areas of Conservative dominance by the contrasting priorities of the standard model; in those areas, women candidates will have occupations which carry less individual status than those of the men.

In sum, the SNP looks like an excellent example of the kind of party which will do nothing for women as such because it is not challenging the basic socio-economic structure of society or the values on which it rests. In seeking to put the political direction of Scottish society in Scottish rather than English hands, it is in effect seeking a transfer of power from one national group of men to another. Although women may be as attracted as men by the feelings and arguments of nationalism and the general notion of change, there is no guarantee in nationalism of a change in women's out-group status. In fact the catch for women may well be that *plus ça change, plus c'est la même chose.*

The Alliance offers a quite different model and one which is up to a point more promising for women. A context where education is more valued than in other parties (as evidenced by the attributes of male candidates) should be highly attractive to educated women, who will share many of the values and goals of educated men and who may also perceive that their education is an insufficient resource to win them repect elsewhere. The increase in the proportion of women in the population with higher education, especially among the younger age groups, should thus provide a growing pool of potential (i.e. self-selecting) candidates among Alliance members while the selection criteria in use should increase the likelihood of their actual adoption by this party, even for winnable seats.

In fact, the educational qualifications of Alliance female candidates were quite staggering. Over three-quarters of these women had full-time further education – 20 per cent more than even their male Alliance colleagues (who are the next most educated group), about 30 per cent more than SNP and Labour women, and 50 per cent more than Labour men. The SDES data also show an age distribution among Alliance women which differs from that of the other parties in being strongly skewed towards the young. Although the candidates of both minor parties were significantly younger than those of the major parties (with a mean age of 40.3 years in the SNP and 41.0 in the Alliance, compared with 51.0, 46.5 and 56.5 years among Conservative, Labour and Independent women respectively), nearly a quarter of the Alliance women were aged 30 or under, compared with 14.8 per cent of SNP, 8.3 per cent of Labour and only 5.4 per cent of Conservative women. These young Alliance women were exceptionally qualified, with over three-quarters having a university or college degree, compared to 56.7 per cent of their colleagues over thirty.[13]

However, while education was an advantage in becoming an Alliance candidate, it was neutral to success among both sexes, a fact which is readily understood when the occupational characteristics of winners and losers are taken into account. Of the two most successful groups of Alliance men – industrial workers and the managers and business-linked professionals – only the professionals among the latter group are dependent on educational qualifications. If we look at the small band of Alliance winning men as a whole (i.e. including the only other sucessful group, the caring professionals) they divide into two roughly equal little groups: first, workers and businessmen without much education and second, highly educated professionals. While no less than 69.3 per cent of the Alliance women candidates belonged to the second of these occupational groups (59.0 per cent to the caring professions), there was only a single industrial worker among them, and not one general manager. Four out of the five women who won were caring professionals.

With this meagre harvest in mind, it is instructive to compare the absolute results for educated women – and the caring professionals in particular – within the Alliance and the other parties. Although the Alliance contested less than half as many seats as the Labour party and only about two-thirds as many as the Conservatives and SNP, the absolute number of educated women standing as Alliance candidates was greater than for any other party and it was the Labour party, with all its candidates, which put up the least. Even so, an educated woman was more than three times as likely to win her seat – if she could get one – as a Labour candidate than for the Alliance. When this situation is compared with that of the men, however, an interesting fact comes to light. Although far more educated men stood as Alliance candidates than for the Conservatives or SNP, even more stood for the Labour party and more than *six* times as many such men won for Labour as for the Alliance. Although this may look like simple sex discrimination – and maybe has an element of that about it – the main reason for this relative disadvantage of women (which is apparent at the national level of Labour recruitment as well) is really due once more – though at one or two removes – to the importance of collective resources in Labour recruitment.

It has already been observed that the 'right' class origins are an important factor in forming the educated part of Labour elites. A large proportion of educated candidates – and an even higher proportion of those who succeed – have the advantage of non-service worker parentage. However, the bias of recruitment into further education is in favour of working-class boys rather than girls, which means that the proportion of educated women who possess this attribute is necessarily very small. This helps to account for the small number of educated Labour women candidates (small in spite of the fact that they vastly outnumber women manual workers). It also means, however, that educated professional women, as a group, have been even more isolated, politically, than the equivalent group of men. With the advent of the Alliance, the vast majority of educated women have acquired a political outlet (and become an identifiable constituency for a mixed-sex political party), for the first time in British history.

The parental occupations of Labour and Alliance candidates in Strathclyde are a good illustration of this point. Of Labour candidates with full-time further education, 43.8 per cent of the men. and 57.1 per cent of the women were the offspring of non-service workers, compared with 30.8 per cent of Alliance men and only 6.7 per cent of Alliance women. Only 23.9 per cent of educated Labour men and 19.1 per cent of women had fathers in the top five Codot categories, compared with 73.3 per cent of each sex in the Alliance.

Thus it is clear that the Alliance and its successor parties have something new to offer women. As parties of the educated, their values and goals may well be closest to those of most women who want to play a leading role in politics. In recruiting from highly educated members of the caring professions, they are drawing on the only socio-economic sector where women are both likely to self-select *and* be numerous relative to men, a fact which is reflected in their favourable gender pattern. In promoting the success of these people in comparison with some other candidate groups, they are also providing some of these women with a route to local political office. This compensates in part for the lack of collective resources in the family background which closes Labour's door to most educated women, and the lack of very high personal status which makes them largely irrelevant to the Conservatives.

Unfortunately, there are rather more, negative considerations to be taken into account. In the first place, the opportunities for success for these women were still severely limited, both within the Alliance (where some other occupational groups fare better locally) and within the broader context of the party's poor electoral performance against its competitors. As a party which draws heavily on the educated minority for its recruits and includes one sector (the scientific and technical professions) which are scarcely represented in other parties at all, the Alliance certainly offered a partial alternative to the entrenched socio-economic groups, but the price is a narrow electoral base which tends to fluctuate with time and place, gaining short-term votes among those who at the time of an election care for other things more than the traditional socio-economic values, identities and goals. Even then, as we have seen, it may well be those recruits whose attributes are similar to those of the most successful Labour and Conservative candidates (i.e. who are most integrated into the dominant socio-economic alignment) who are most likely to succeed.

In the immediate future, then, the prospects for women *via* the Alliance's successor parties appear to be severely limited. Their advance would seem to depend largely on long-term changes in the socio-economic composition of the electorate which would lead more people to vote for non-traditional parties and in particular to support a party of the highly educated. It is true that there are trends which might favour these developments, such as the higher level of education among the young, the tendency to partisan 'de-alignment'[14] and the rise of issue-voting[15] in Britain. However, the British first-past-the-post electoral system constitutes a major obstacle to the rise of any third party and the results of the 1987 and 1992 general elections also suggest that traditional alignments are very resilient among the electorate.

There is also, of course, the distinct possibility that the future role of women even in a third party advance would be constrained by the limited range of professions they have penetrated. Although unsuccessful in these elections, the scientific and technical professions provided a notable contingent of Alliance men. This is a socio-economic group in the population from which women are largely absent and in this instance provided no female candidates at all. If the economic decline of the traditional industries continues in Scotland and the existing 'frozen cleavage' of management versus labour gives place to new alignments, scientific and technical personnel are likely to be an increasingly important group in the new socio-economic order. They are also crucial agents in the formulation and development of the kind of policy goals (such as those relating to ecological issues) which might attract voters to an intellectually based party which is independent of traditional interests. The role of scientists and other technical experts in issue-oriented parties and movements even now should not be under-estimated. The ecological movement in Germany is well known for its espousal of populist causes and anti-authoritarian values, and yet even this, in the words of a recent analyst, 'has generated its own bureaucracy of experts. The *Environmental Lexicon* (1985) lists thirty-five specialist institutions affiliated to the Ecological Research Institute. It has also led to a veritable flood of books on the subject . . . [and] the development of practical alternatives which are politically extremely important'.[16] In Britain this movement is less politically developed, but anyone who has followed the development of ecological issues here must be aware of the role played by scientifically trained specialists within the framework of organisations like the Conservation Society, the RSPB and the Friends of the Earth (to name but a few) in defining them and supplying the evidence which shapes their political course. Given the scarcity of female scientific and technological experts, it is possible that even the advance of a professionally oriented successor party such as the SLD or the Greens would eventually present new obstacles to women, arising from a new hierarchy of resources among educated men. In those circumstances, it would be difficult for women to maintain even their present level of progress.

CONCLUSION

Cross-national analysis of the gender pattern in minor parties shows that they fall into three categories with respect to the recruitment of women, in only one of which are women genuinely likely to advance, while the advantages of another are more illusory than real. This distinction is perfectly illustrated by the Scottish case, where close study of the SNP and the Alliance have supplied two possible models for a gender and recruitment relationship which seem to depart from the pattern of male dominance. In the first, supplied by the nationalist party, such advantages as there are for women accrue mainly from the party's poor electoral prospects and the success of a few outstanding individuals is therefore deceptive. This is because what the party is striving to capture is exactly that hierarchy of socio-economic values among men in which women are an out-group. Although women are fellow-members of the overarching national group, this is not a passport to status within the group.

In the second instance, a party of the highly educated, we have a more encouraging model. Of all the attributes of socio-economic status it is only in education that women have made up significant ground on men, and in the political environment of a party which values education and recruits from educated people, women have a greater than usual chance of being selected, even to win. Even so, unless education is valued without regard for occupational and/or property status, the crucial socio-economic attributes which continue to elude women, the latter will still be at a disadvantage. The only area where women have so far managed to combine education with relatively high (individual) status occupations in anything like the same proportions as men is that of the caring professions, themselves a relatively low-status group in the broader professional sector. As the case of the Alliance illustrates, a party which draws heavily on professional people for its candidates will be that much more open to women and willing to put them up in winnable seats. However, this very factor can be expected to limit its electoral appeal and make it something of a cul-de-sac for its recruits. Also, the limited range of women's professional employment is likely to keep them at a disadvantage even within a party of this type. As a general rule, we may say that the more highly education is valued *in itself and independently of other measures of socio-economic status* (and is available to women) the more nearly equal the resources of women will be to those of men and the greater their opportunities for political recruitment. Conversely, the more the values of occupation and property interact with that of education in the measurement of status, the fewer these opportunities will be. The corollary is that when significant departures from the usual gender pattern are observed, the most likely explanation is that education is unusually esteemed by men in the surrounding culture.

All three of the empirical studies reported here, of major party, non-partisan and minor party recruitment have thus confirmed the hypotheses proposed in Chapter 1. Given the nature of the competition among men, the universal gender and recruitment pattern is the logical outcome of women's universal out-group status. Lacking the attributes of success, women are by definition losers (even in their own eyes, let alone those of institutional selectors) and in the absence of a spontaneous revolution in either the distribution of resources or the values of selectors, are likely to remain so. The main change in modern women's profile of resources has been their wider access to education and a narrow range of professional occupations and although the study of the minor parties has found one small, slightly open door which has been unlocked by this it has also shown that the parameters of change involved are very narrow. Like any other out-group, women are caught in the vicious circle that if their lack of status denies them access to the political power which could be used to redistribute resources in their favour, it will be self-perpetuating.

Yet can we really leave the matter here? Political scientists are better at explaining the world as it is than at predicting change, yet change is an intrinsic fact of our existence and large changes can have small beginnings. There is that one door which stands ajar. . .and there are the hopes, too, which women in ever-growing numbers are investing in the women's movement. If any general gain at all can be achieved by incremental means (and why else should anyone apart from the individuals involved concern themselves with women's access to political elites?), the role of education in producing the conditions among men which lead to deviation from the gender pattern *and* in mobilising women as feminists may conceivably be the key to radical, unlooked-for changes in the social order. These issues – the conditions for change and how to achieve it – are the theme of Part 2.

Part 2

5

THE RISE OF FEMINISM AND THE PARAMETERS OF CHANGE

The object of Part 1 was to demonstrate the rules governing political recruitment in male-dominated societies and their implications for women. The conclusion was that the grounding of the public sphere in male values, combined with women's invariable socio-economic out-group status in the world of men, inexorably limit women's access to elites: in other words, there is an integral connection between the general condition of women and their representation in politics. Whether the focus was on major party, non-partisan or minor party recruitment the implication was the same: that for women to enter competitive politics on equal terms with men would require either a revolution in the distribution of socio-economic resources which gave women the same profile of attributes as men, or else a revolution in the way that values are ordered in the dominant culture.

Depressing as these findings are, at least from women's point of view, the focus of Part 2 is none the less on change. Nor is this departure felt to be entirely fanciful. It is true that no revolution has occurred either in women's situation or in men; recent studies like that of Fuchs[1] even suggest that the occupational and income gap between the sexes is widening in advanced societies and men most certainly have not abandoned competitive and inegalitarian values. However, human affairs are never static and it is never wise to assume that what is, must be. Even now, there are exceptions to the general recruitment rule, especially in the Nordic countries, which may be harbingers of a new order. There is an active women's movement, too, to challenge traditional assumptions and mobilise women's will for change.

The following chapters concentrate on the exceptions and look to feminism for a change in women's situation. This emphasis on change means a shift of focus away from the demonstration of things as they are (the ways of the world as ordered by men and their effects on women), to the investigation of the reasons for them and speculation on alternatives. *Why* are women always an out-group in a male-ordered world – and on

131

what basis could the world be ordered differently? What criteria should be employed to judge how different policies impinge on women's interests? And what can women do themselves to change their situation? In particular, although we know how closely women's penetration of elites reflects their broader situation in society, can this connection not be put to work the other way? Is it not possible for those women who achieve political influence, however small, to use it in the interests of their sex? One may wonder what other point there is in the struggle for women's access to elites.

The findings of Part 1 should not inhibit this endeavour, for even if the exceptions prove the rule it would be rash to assume that the rule will never change. Socio-economic change is a recurring feature of male-dominated systems, as witnessed by the rise of capitalism and its vicissitudes, and women would not be the first out-group to be its incidental beneficiaries. Nor would they be the first to build on a deterministic basis by taking on the guise of a successful social movement. In fact feminism, as a politically conscious, group-based movement arising out of social change and seeking changes in the social order by means of voluntarist action, seems on the face of it to be a perfect fit for the classic definition of a social movement which was derived by Heberle and others from the model of the European labour movement.[2] If those exceptional conditions which allow more opportunities for women to gain access to elites (and hence perhaps to influence events), are also those which facilitate the rise of feminism as a social movement, should we not expect a relative advance of women politicians to be converted into changes in the social order through their pursuit of policies for women, as would be the case with groups of men? What is more, if women's social base was strengthened in this way, the logical consequence should be a corresponding improvement in their chances of political recruitment. By means of such incremental, mutually reinforcing changes, a social revolution conceivably might be achieved. The contemporary feminist idea of the 'critical mass', according to which the prerequisite for a re-ordering of women's situation is their reaching a certain, irresistible proportion in political elites, is a variation on this theme.

All the same, this optimistic line of reasoning must be set against two awkward facts. Firstly, no such sequence of events has yet occurred, even though organised feminism is well over a century old in most advanced societies and at least on two occasions in the past (to be examined below) has co-existed with unusual levels of female elite recruitment. It is true that the examples of men's social movements warn us not to expect too much, too soon, and to respect the enormous importance of culture in producing different outcomes; capitalism and socialism, for example, have advanced to different degrees, at most unequal speeds and in extremely variable forms in different parts of Europe, let alone the whole developed world. The fact remains, however, that feminist aims have not been realised anywhere and it is the general failure of feminism either to attract a mass following among its natural constituency, women, or to capitalise on women's presence in elites, which give it its distinct historical character.

The second difficulty is that feminists themselves, to say nothing of the mass of women, are not agreed on how they should proceed. This uncertainty is not confined merely to matters of organisational strategy and tactics but extends to the broad aims of the movement and how women's interests should be defined. It is not entirely clear what kind of society women ought, as feminists, to seek, and not at all clear what policies a 'critical mass' of women in elites could use to steer society in the requisite direction. Indeed, the periodic immobilisation of the feminist movement by its pursuit of incompatible values and objectives invites the question: does women's lack of progress have to do with what they are trying to achieve?

Up to a point, the conventional framework of political analysis is useful for attempting to answer these questions. The women's movement can be compared with other groups and movements in male-dominated systems and there is an extensive literature on political socialisation, participation and the rise of social movements on which to draw, some of it relating specifically to the women's movement.[3] This literature has helped to identify conditions favourable to the politicisation and mobilisation of out-groups in general and recent work has added to our understanding of those in which a feminist women's movement in particular can be sustained, both over time and from one level of political action to another. One of the most important issues which emerges from this literature (and is recognised as such within the women's movement) is that of strategy.

In respect of their strategy towards the other elements in a political system, feminists are faced with the same dilemmas as other groups and movements, which are familiar topics in the literature on pressure politics in Britain[4] and social movements on the European continent.[5] In particular, they must decide whether to seek (or accept) the integration of their aims and organisations into the framework of established institutions and values (which may bring incremental gains but undermine their chances of achieving basic aims) or else to stay 'outside' in order to preserve their separate identity and goals, perhaps at the expense of being completely ineffectual. The costs of integration (seeking 'alliances' with men because of feminism's weakness) have been identified by Banks as crucial to the periodic failures of the women's movement in Britain and the USA[6] (although paradoxically unwillingness to integrate is frequently advanced as a reason for the failures of these same movements today). As the history of European feminism shows, its relationship with other social movements arising among men, such as the socialist and labour movements for first-wave feminists and the environmentalists and peace movements today, is a particularly problematical aspect of the integration dilemma. One of the most important lessons we can learn from a study of the past is how far the strategies of feminists contributed to their difficulties and how they compare with those employed today.

Of course, a movement's choice of strategy cannot be independent of its context. Some political systems are characteristically more integrative than others in their response to pressure and there is also considerable variation in the ability of different cultures to assimilate the identity and interests of specific groups. Our particular concern is with those cases where women have gained unusual access to elites and it will be recalled that the conclusion of Part 1 was that short of a revolution in resources and values, the most likely (albeit restricted) basis for improvement in women's political fortunes would be a favourable distribution and evaluation of educational resources. This calls for a special consideration of the role of education in the emergence and development of feminism (a topic which many modern feminists have been reluctant to explore) and of the way that the response of men, whether in defence of the *status quo* or in the context of their own attempts to change it, and has helped to shape the women's movement and its strategy.

The scope of this enquiry obviously transcends the relatively narrow framework of recruitment studies and the kind of empirical research employed in earlier chapters. It must encompass a different sort of material and a wider-ranging analysis of political cultures, social movements and ideas which might lead to or inhibit change. If it is to be successful, however, the difference from Part 1 must be a great deal more profound than this.

One danger of treating feminism as merely comparable to any other social movement is that it leads us to fudge the issue of the nature of its aims. This would not disturb some social movement theorists; it has even been argued that the 'success' of a social movement 'may be due less to achieving what was originally desired than to desiring what it can achieve'.[7] By this yardstick the women's movement has certainly failed, but rather than castigate feminists for their naiveté we ought to ask why it is that feminism obstinately refuses either to be satisfied or die. No movement can be understood in isolation from its aims but least of all that of women, for both the history of feminism and the nature of its social base point to unique obstacles to the achievement of its aims within the framework of existing systems. This is not to say that feminism is unique in being too radical to succeed; men have produced extreme and chronically unsuccessful movements and there is something to be gained from the comparison of feminism with these. However, no examination of feminism gets very far without being confronted by a problem unique to women: that of *gender*. So long as a distinction is made between the male and female genders and their social roles, then it does not matter how active women are in the male-based public sphere, or how subject they become to the rules that govern male affairs; they cannot ever be the *same* as any group of men. Women are, by definition of their gender, *different* from men and this has profound implications for how we should approach the question of their interests and aims and judge the merits of their strategies. These implications can perhaps be best understood if we reconsider the idea of feminism as a social movement in the light of gender roles.

There are really two concepts of the social movement in currency today, those of the 'classic' movement and the 'new', and strangely enough both have been applied at one time or another to feminism. This is because the same conditions which tend to produce a plethora of social movements among men also promote the mobilisation of women;[8] this happened in the nineteenth-century heyday of the 'classic' movement and again today. It is these other movements, however, and not the women's, which inspire the mainstream theories of the nature of the social movement.

Today this means that feminism is often classified as a 'new' movement, which clearly is absurd. In the first place, feminism is *not* new, and explanations for the rise of movements in the 1970s, especially if (like post-materialism or the intervention of the welfare state in previously 'private' areas of life) they are deeply rooted in the context of their time, cannot account for, let us say, the growth of feminist ideas in the eighteenth century. They can only be employed to explain the form the movement takes in particular places and times, as, for example, they are by Banks (implicitly) in her discussion of the sources of the modern movement, or by Hernes in her most convincing exposition of the phases of the Norwegian women's movement.[9]

However, there is another, crucial difference between feminism and the kind of movement typified in recent decades by the Greens. These new movements are defined in terms of common goals and issue-orientations; the constituency of the movement is the people who support its aims and values. The women's movement, with its endemic conflict over basic values and social order goals, is very far from being a movement of this kind. Furthermore, the 'issue' emphasis in the characterisation of the modern movements misses an essential mark where feminism is concerned; were women not a fundamental social group (unlike environmentalists), there would be no such thing as feminism.

The fact that women are a concrete social group, i.e. distinct from men, is why the classic concept of a social movement, derived from social class, seems more appropriate. Here a social movement is conceived as resting on the solidarity of interest and identity which defines the social group of origin. The trouble is, however, that women's social identity has an inherent ambiguity which sits uneasily with such a class-based concept. Women are not a class, and indeed (because of their general condition of dependence on men), they are themselves divided deeply along virtually every dimension of division among men, including that of class. As each feminist generation finds to its cost, the unity of women is thus a fragile one which conflicts with other powerful allegiances and interests. In truth, the common identity of women cannot be discovered inside the male world at all; it lies outside it, in the female gender role.

The central fact of gender is dichotomy; men and women are defined in terms of difference from each other and each sex is located in a different gender role and set of core values. The fact that male-dominated systems are derived from the values of men, not women, is therefore absolutely crucial to the situation of the latter in these systems. Women are not just one out-group among many in the male world order: *they are outsiders too*. As women, it is their female gender which defines their social being and no matter how involved they are in the male-based sphere, whether by virtue of dependence on men or through their own participation, there is no escaping the fact that they are female. Unlike men, they have a dual social basis, inside the system and outside it, a phenomenon which is not contemplated in social movement theory.

In practice, the duality of gender has been an even more profound source of ambiguity and conflict for feminists than the divisions which derive from the relations among men. While some women, consciously or not, have sought assimilation to the gender role of men, and some the adaptation of both gender roles to form a single, adrogynous mode, others – equally committed to the female interest as they perceive it – have tried to reinforce the gender difference and defend traditional roles. In fact these different strands of feminism have reproduced what are essentially the same fundamental conflicts in every generation about the nature of feminism and the kind of social order women ought to seek. Feminists reactions to the gender problem, i.e. their gender strategy, have also had a profound influence on their choices with respect to strategy in the more everyday, organisational sense.

Of course, this does not mean that feminists necessarily have a clear perception of the gender problem and even if they have, it is by no means axiomatic that the policies they pursue, or the strategies they adopt will help them to achieve their goals; feminists like anyone else may exercise poor judgement or get embroiled in the pursuit of incompatible objectives. Indeed it is inevitable that feminists, caught as they are at the intersection of the two genders, will find the whole issue of gender a particularly difficult and psychologically painful problem to confront. We must expect to find that many feminists are unable to do so and that many more could not be said to have a coherent gender strategy at all.

136

It is impossible, therefore, to evaluate the prospects for a change in women's situation without an understanding of the gender problem and a basis for judging how feminist policies and strategies will bear on it. For this a basic change in perspective is required. In Part 1, women were viewed as inhabitants of the male world order along with men and the male-centred perspective of that world was employed for the purpose. However, we cannot understand women's situation in the world *outside* this order unless we move outside that world ourselves: that is, unless we change our perspective from that of the male gender on which the public sphere and its underlying values are based (the first blade of the gender 'scissors') to the perspective of the female gender (the second blade). It is with how *women* experience their situation and want to change it that we are concerned.

Part 2 thus brings together two perspectives, male and female, and two themes – the exceptions to the general recruitment rule and the feminist response. Its four chapters fall into two pairs, in each of which the first lays a theoretical foundation for its more empirically oriented partner. Chapters 6 and 7 focus on the emergence of feminism and the approaches to the gender problem underlying the goals and strategies of 'equal rights' and 'socialist' feminism, strands of feminism which are very much alive today but still most tellingly illustrated by the historical cases of Finland and Russia before and after 1917. Chapter 8 pursues the major problem this identifies with an analysis of women's theories of the formation of gender and their implications for feminist policy-makers. Finally, Chapter 9 investigates contemporary feminism in this light and attempts to assess its potential effect on the parameters of change in three exceptional cases: the West German Greens (where full equality of women in elites has been adopted as a constitutional rule); Norway, where women feel they may have reached the 'critical mass' and have had temporary control of government; and Iceland, where a separatist women's party has achieved what bids to be a pivotal role.

6

EQUAL RIGHTS AND SOCIALIST FEMINISM

The primary concern of this chapter is with the emergence of feminism as a social movement and particularly with the aims and strategy of equal rights and socialist feminism, the two early strands of feminism which continue to dominate much contemporary feminist thought and action and remain problematic even for those who reject them. The role of education in the mobilisation of women and the formation of feminist ideas is a major consideration here and in the following chapter, where two historical cases of deviation from the gender pattern are used to illustrate the questions raised by the discussion of feminist ideas. In both cases, the fact that women reached political elites in unusual numbers did not suffice for them to embark on a radical programme of change, or even, in the long term, to sustain their own advance. Yet feminist ideas were an active political force in the background which brought these women to positions of personal prominence. The question addressed theoretically here, and empirically in the settings of Finland and Russia, is whether it was the nature of their feminism that failed these women.

EDUCATION AND THE ORIGINS OF FEMINISM

For women, as for men, the impact of education is threefold. As well as enhancing the personal aspirations of individuals (including their disposition to participate in politics), education expands their intellectual horizons, developing the capacity to analyse, question and generalise and providing a cultural framework in which to do so.[1] It also helps them to communicate and organise among themselves. When these effects on individual women interact with their experience as members of the female out-group, the result is feminism. General theories are developed to account for women's situation *vis-à-vis* men and give rise to organised efforts to change it. By simultaneously raising individual women's sense of their own worth, confronting them with the lower value put on it by others and developing their capacity for political action, education brings women into the political arena, not only as individuals taking part along with men, but as a politically conscious group, acting on their own behalf.

Of course, not all societies will tolerate a women's movement and we can expect those that hold most strongly by traditional religious values to be the most repressive. However, these are also the societies in which education is least likely to be made available to women. By and large, the conditions in which women can acquire an education (of which secular-isation is perhaps the most important), are precisely those where women can expect to have sufficient freedom of movement and cultural latitude to organise themselves.

This is not to say that feminism is the *invention* of educated women or that education is the only resource which can support it. Although for obvious reasons it is the voices of the highly educated which are most clearly heard (and have most chance of escaping the historical oblivion into which the works of women are generally cast by male-centred cultures), any employment which affords ordinary women economic independence and the opportunity to associate among themselves can be the basis for the development of feminist ideas and action.[2] In fact, wherever women possess the kind of resources which would support political consciousness and mobilisation in the case of men, history shows the same effect for women; the problem is simply that these resources are usually lacking. Thus although not all educated women are feminists, nor all feminists educated, it is inevitable that the development of feminist ideas and the organisation of the women's movement should be associated with educated women and that wherever educated women are to be found, from de Pizan to the present day, so is feminism.

However, the relationship of education and feminism is more complex than this would suggest, for education has divided women as much as it has mobilised them and feminism is even, in many women's eyes, a betrayal of the interests of their sex. As soon as women are able to progress beyond political awareness to the point of identifying their goals, two fundamental, and seemingly irreconcilable contradictions in feminism are invariably revealed. The first concerns the very object that feminists are striving to achieve, and centres on the question posed so frequently by men and so divisive to the women's movement, 'What do women really want?' The second concerns the way that women should organise and prosecute their struggle, 'with men, or against them?'

Conflicting responses to these questions surface at every stage of feminist development. They can be attributed quite simply to the two sets of very different, largely incompatible forces to which all women who step outside their traditional role are exposed, forces which in their different origins and directions recall the 'scissors' metaphor. The first set emanates from the female gender role itself, not only because of the practical constraints it puts on women's lives, but also because of the values which are peculiar to it. The second is derived from the gender role of men, acting through the minds and experience of women who have in part absorbed its values and seek the wider sphere it offers. Feminism is the point at which these forces intersect and it is this crucial, extra ingredient in women's situation – the hierarchical dichotomy of gender roles and the derivation of the public sphere from that of men – which makes the dilemmas which face women, at both the theoretical and practical level, immeasurably more difficult than those of other out-groups to resolve. It is the reason, too, why the political gains of feminism have always been so limited and fragile. The rest of this chapter is devoted to these problems, starting with the essential nature of the gender problem and continuing with an examination of how feminist ideas have coped with this problem at three levels: in terms of the conceptualisation of feminist goals, in relation to the goals of other social movements deriving from the interests of men, and in its effects on feminist choices of strategy.

FEMINISM AND FEMALE GENDER

Women live in two gender worlds, and the 'women's sphere', no matter how little attention it gets or claims, is a potent source of human values and needs which both engender feminism and deny it. The very existence of the female role, and its dichotomy with that of men, has always led the women who enact it to generalise about society in proto-feminist terms. Built as it is on the values of the *male* gender role, the public sphere of social, economic and political life is by definition antithetical to female values. Irrespective of the precise, local content of the male and female genders, the very fact that human attributes and activities are divided in two, with the dominant, public values derived from only one of the resulting roles, ensures that this will be so. Without straying beyond the confines of their role at all, women cannot help but find much that is repulsive, or at least alien, in the way society is run. The standard use of violence in the affairs of men (and its glorification), is just one, obvious example of this dichotomy, and women do not need a formal education or more than ordinary intelligence to be aware of it. Nor can they avoid being aware of the negative view of women which is propagated by men, along with their insistence that women's attributes are incompatible with participation in activities reserved to men. Of course, if each sex is to sustain a different gender role, it follows that unless the differences between them are innate they must be continually stressed, elaborated and reiterated in the surrounding culture, so that individuals do not lose sight of how they ought to think and behave; there is a reciprocal need for women to differentiate men and exclude them from the female sphere. However, if one sex is to dominate and its sphere to expand at the expense of the other, these differences must be seen to be hierarchical: the attributes of one gender role (that of the dominant group) must be judged superior by both sexes and this, too, must be continually communicated and understood. There is ample testimony in the everyday language and lament of women – epitomised by the expression 'it's a man's world' – to the fact that women have needed only the ordinary experience of everyday life, conforming to their role and interacting with men, to become aware of how they are set apart and below.

From this awareness, it is but a small step to wondering what a better world for women would be like, in this life or another. Even in women's historical resignation to their lot (and their tendency to seek solace in religion), there is a kind of political consciousness, albeit one which is imbued with pessimism and withdrawal. Given women's lack of resources in the physical combats which have been so crucial in human history, compounded by their subjection in the past to continual pregnancy and childbirth and their physical dispersal in relations of personal dependence on men, the historically passive political outlook of women can be viewed as both inevitable and realistic.

What education brings is a gleam of optimism and, for many women, a point of no return. Denied the fulfilment of intrinsic needs and aspirations by virtue of their sex, it is inevitable that educated women will wonder why this should be so. It is equally inevitable that they will reject those values in the surrounding culture which are held to justify their out-group status in terms of natural, inherent or necessary differences and inequalities from men (just as these cultures provide similar justifications for the inequalities which always exist among men). After all, the evidence of their own lives will give traditional values the lie, at least as far as they themselves are concerned. Sharing the same knowledge, capacities and interests as educated men and in many cases (because educated women are likely to appear first in the highest social class) the time and energy to pursue them as well, they cannot but question values which not only deny them an outlet for their abilities and the esteem which they deserve, but even deny that they have the abilities in the first place. Like the equivalent members of male out-groups, educated women will come to see their situation as less inevitable than inequitable; unlike uneducated women, they will feel encouraged, or even impelled to do something about it.

In fact, women are likely to reach the point of generalisation about their situation comparatively quickly. Throughout the history of men, many educated (or otherwise capable) individuals of out-group origin have had the possibility of upward social mobility to take the edge off their discontent. Similar rewards for ability are not available to women.[3] Although a very few women may find that circumstances make exceptions of them, so that they are treated as 'honorary men' and can fulfil their aspirations in spite of their sex, it will be extremely difficult, if not impossible, for most women to solve the problem of their out-group origin and status on an individual basis. Like men from racial out-groups, women are trapped by visible difference from the norm, a difference which cannot be shed, like the 'wrong' accent, or glossed over, like the wrong parentage, on a day-to-day basis. They cannot 'pass'[4] and their presence can be accommodated only when they are sufficiently few in number to be treated as anomalies. When the numbers of aspiring women begin to rise they become the outposts of a double rebellion: both *against* the public sphere (by undermining the dichotomy of gender roles on which it is based) and *within* it (against their lowly status in its hierarchy). In spite of the problems of political psychology which this creates for women, for those who are psychologically able to confront and explore their situation as women, these conditions are a forcing ground for feminist thought. If they are going to seek a solution at all it will have to be conceived in general terms, and deal with women as a group, not as atomised individuals who just happen to be female. That is, it will have to admit that very same separate, out-group identity – as women – which so many aspiring women would prefer to put behind them. The trouble is (as the duality of their rebellion suggests) that by paradoxically claiming the identity from which they want to be emancipated, feminists are trapped within the scissors of the gender roles. Although the aspiration which brings feminism to light is to take part in the gender role activities of men, the female identity and values present a powerful challenge to that drive.

The first conflict is that of values. Even if they are educated, women will still have reservations about the competitive inegalitarianism of men, their concern for the general to the exclusion of the particular and the death-dealing methods they so often employ. Their system of rewards may well seem shallow and contemptible by comparison with the values associated with women's role in the family and personal relationships, which emphasise responsibility, individual needs and the affirmation of life.[5] While the male role is incomparably more diverse in the range of activities and stimuli it offers, it may be perceived as much more shallow than the female in its values and this, for many women, will inhibit their ever making a complete commitment to the moral-psychological world of men, or, if they do, from sustaining it throughout their lives. The result is that women in the modern world approach feminism from two entirely different perspectives (sometimes at one and the same time) which seem to lead in different directions, intersecting only at the point of feminism but understanding it in incompatible ways.

From the perspective of the female role, they bring their own values to bear on the scheme of things devised by men and cannot but reject it. The logic of these values seems to lead either to total non-participation in the public sphere (the traditional role) or else to that paradox (in terms of female gender attributes), a women's revolution. In practice, educated women have found a variety of intermediate political forms for the assertion of the female role. Some have turned to comforting fantasies of a separate existence. Others (usually motivated by religious and/or philanthropic values) have sought instead to improve women's lot *within* their traditional role, mainly through social work and legislation. Others still, especially in the earliest generations of politically active women, have attempted to bring men in line with *women*. Thus, for example, a female army of nineteenth-century American evangelical agitators demanded that men abjure such characteristic male behaviour as drunkenness and the 'double standard' in physical sex, which were a universal source of misery to women. Prohibition was their Pyrrhic victory.

From the other perspective, however, it is not the evils of the male world but its attractions which are paramount. Men have succeeded in confining a huge range of human interests to their sphere of activity. Within that monopoly, they have defined, refined and developed areas of endeavour and reward, not least that of simple economic independence, which turn out to be as important to educated women as men. It is not the content of men's world aspiring women want to change, but their exclusion from it. The greater women's drive towards reserved activities, the more likely they are to be infected with men's assumption that there is no real alternative to their world and that change, if it comes, must come within, and not against, that framework.

Faced with this contradiction between their 'female' identity and their 'male' aspirations, and the consequent interplay of roles and values to which they are exposed, it is not surprising that the first generations of educated women did not produce a uniform, feminist response to their situation. What emerged instead were two major schools of feminist thought: 'equal rights' and 'socialist' feminism. Each exhibiting its own peculiar strengths and weaknesses, these ideologies developed in bitter opposition to one other. In retrospect, though, what they have in common is as striking as their differences.

'EQUAL RIGHTS' AND 'SOCIALIST' FEMINISM

For educated women faced with obstacles of law and custom to block their advance into the male system of employment, association and reward, the drive for 'equal rights' was a logical form for feminism to take. Nor, although the contemporary view of 'equal rights' feminism is usually derogatory, should historical hindsight and ideological prejudice be allowed to blind us to its strengths and achievements. Its greatest

143

strength was its truly feminist character. Since the inferior status of women in nineteenth- and early twentieth-century Europe and North America was a general condition which applied to women as a whole irrespective of class, it was impossible for educated women who suffered from their lack of equal rights (especially if they did, in fact, come from the upper strata of society) to avoid facing the central truth of their situation. It was because of their sex – not because they were poor, or working-class, or whatever – that they were disadvantaged. Whatever other handicaps they might possess, *women* were the basic out-group they belonged to. 'Equal rights' feminism was thus a genuinely feminist initiative – a movement *for women, vis-à-vis men* – and it was entirely logical that 'women's rights' groups – the product of educated women's individual experience and interaction among themselves – should have been the earliest manifestation of the movement in most societies. They have also been one of its most successful forms. While it is true that many achievements of 'equal rights' feminism have turned out to be more hollow than their protagonists expected, they have been considerable, all the same. It is no mean feat to have moved from almost total exclusion from civil and political rights to almost total formal *entrée* to the public sphere in less than a hundred years. One of the main reasons for the denigration of the 'equal rights' movement today (apart from the inveterate hostility of the left) is simply that these gains are taken for granted nowadays.

Another reason, however, is the invariable aftermath of disappointment following the victory of 'women's rights'. Typically, the early triumphs have been followed by a setback in succeeding generations. Typically, too, the movement itself has failed in its response to this, either being disbanded before the proportions of the disappointment could be grasped or dissipated in the conflicting aims and issues of welfare feminism, many of them derived from endless permutations and combinations with traditional female values. To understand why this should be so, and in particular why 'equal rights' feminism has not led to that equalisation of male and female activities and resources which it seemed to promise, we have to look more closely at its gender implications.

Paradoxically, the principal long-term weakness of 'equal rights' feminism was (and is) the obverse of one of its short-term strengths, the communicability and logic of the principle of 'equal rights' to men. What feminists were demanding was a new application of an existing principle, not the introduction of a new one. However, along with this ability of the 'equal rights' movement to deal with the male world on the latter's terms went the unfortunate implication that women's interests could be accommodated by that world and that women could accept it at its own valuation without prejudicing their own interests. In some

144

respects this could be quite explicit, as when Mary Wollstonecraft demanded education for women in order to bring them up to the moral, as well as the intellectual level of men[6] (or in the less exalted attempts of many modern feminists to promote their own or other women's professional or business careers), but in fact any argument for equal rights in the public sphere as it stands carries an implicit endorsement of its values.

One consequence is that 'equal rights' feminists are automatically embroiled in inegalitarianism. They may win equal rights of access for women as a group, but these rights are not going to be equal in their effects upon individual women, any more than they are among men; 'equal rights' are not the same as 'equal opportunities', much less equal outcomes. Moreover, by identifying their own goals with the existing system, women will be acquiring a direct, material interest in its continuance; it will become increasingly difficult for them to oppose it. At the same time its values will divide them from the less fortunate members of their sex. As the feminists approach their goal, it may well seem that feminism and self-interest no longer coincide, in which case the initial identification with their own sex will give way to identification with the cross-cutting, hierarchical values of men instead. In extreme cases, self-styled 'feminists' will actively seek to withhold the rights they had previously sought for women as a sex from those categories of women it is in their personal socio-economic interest to keep down,[7] finding common ground with dependent, non-feminist women in the privileged classes. Even without this open treachery, the professional and competitive orientation of 'equal rights' feminism may seem like a betrayal to women who cannot take advantage of it. If they are forced by circumstances to work outside the home in low-paid, soul-destroying jobs and poor conditions, such women may well resent the advance of more fortunate individuals and wonder if what the latter really fought for was the equal right to exploit other women. To the extent that the 'success' of feminism helps to put social and economic pressures on women to work whether they want to or not, these criticisms will have considerable force.

Nevertheless, there is an even more fundamental contradiction in 'equal rights' feminism than this kind of inegalitarianism and in actual fact, concern rather than indifference has been the characteristic response of middle-class feminists to the problems of working-class women, giving rise to a vast philanthropic effort in the late nineteenth century and to much of the later social welfare legislation in Britain and elsewhere.[8] A more fatal flaw is the failure of 'equal rights' feminism to address the underlying problem of the gender role dichotomy.

Although the demand for the 'emancipation' of women from the confines of the female role might seem to confront the gender issue, this

145

impression is misleading. If the height of women's ambition is to occupy the gender role of men, then, by implication, they still accept the dichotomy of gender. If the reason they are trying to escape from 'female' values and activities is because the latter are inferior (and unfit for the public sphere), they are also endorsing the hierarchy of male role over female (a point not lost on housewives who feel devalued by feminism and resent it). Yet their aspirations beg the question, 'Who, in future, will perform the female gender role?' There is no getting round the fact that human life, let alone the public sphere as we know it, cannot survive unless *somebody* performs the 'female' functions which sustain it. *Somebody* will have to rear the children, wash the floor and cook the meals. If there is no place in the male gender role for men to do these things, and now women are not going to do them either, then who will? 'Equal rights' feminism unfortunately has no explicit answer to this question. The implicit assumption is that the answer will continue to be . . . women.

Furthermore, this weakness at the core of 'equal rights' – the expectation that women both will, and will not, continue to behave like women – is where the 'scissors' bite again, in another dimension of the gender role dichotomy. This time, it is the reproductive, sex-role kernel of the gender roles which catches women in its contradictions. The world to which the feminists are seeking access is constructed on the gender role of men, not women. To succeed in that world, at any level, they must behave like men. However, the dichotomy of gender roles means that they cannot behave like men without ceasing to behave like women. Conversely, of course, they cannot behave like women without undermining their 'right' to behave like men. If gender roles were altogether cultural in content, this might be tolerable, but they are not. Their point of origin is not culture itself but the biological difference in the sexes' reproductive roles. In elaborating gender roles, cultures are not only interpreting this difference but creating the framework for reproduction to take place. Because the reproductive role of women, even at its most basic, is incomparably more onerous than that of men, gender roles must take account of this; they must to some extent be different.

If gender roles embodied shared values and an equalising distribution of supportive activities between the sexes, the reproductive difference would be unimportant (and there would be no need for feminism). Men's greater contribution in other forms of domestic service would allow both sexes to play an equal part in the non-nurturant sphere. As it is, men's cultural response to the basic difference of reproductive sex has certainly not been to compensate for it. They have magnified it instead, by evading nearly all the associated parental and service tasks themselves and creating economic dependence and confinement to the service role as the framework – different but not equal – for women's right to reproduce.

They have also, by designing the public sphere around competitive relations among themselves, legitimised the need for such exclusively male forms of service as the military, which help to excuse their dereliction of the rest.[9] Thus, on top of their already unequal reproductive burden, females have had to assume full-time, day-to-day responsibility for the family (in whatever form this takes) as the price of reproduction, an obligation which is in purely practical terms incompatible with full engagement in the public sphere. The problem is compounded, too, by constructing the public sphere upon the male life-cycle. The years of heaviest demand on the participant's time and energies are precisely those when women's reproductive cycle is at its peak. Conversely, the cards are heavily stacked against a career begun in the middle years of life, when the creative energies of women, with their longer life-span, may even be at their height and their freedom of action is at last beginning to expand.

The consequence for women is that 'equal rights' confront them with an appalling choice. In the case of a man, the public sphere imposes penalties (such as non-involvement in his children's lives and the possibility of being forced to engage in warfare) which from a woman's perspective are unnecessary, counter-productive and wrong, but they are at least compatible with his sex, since it is from the male role in reproduction (albeit at its most minimal) that the ground-rules of that sphere derive. A man can be a person and a parent, active in the world and yet enjoying the comforts and companionship of marriage and the family. For a woman, it is otherwise; the price of entry to the wider sphere is to put at risk her role in reproduction and everything that goes with it. Even if traditional values do not impose the choice outright, by refusing women the right to bear children outside marriage and prohibiting married women from the public sphere, (so that working women must remain single and childless, and mothers are virtually under house arrest), the constraints of time, energy and informal social punishment will tend to have the same, indirect effect.

It is this inbuilt necessity of 'choice' (which, it must be stressed, few early feminists intended or foresaw and which even now appears to take each hopeful cohort of young women by surprise) that makes 'equal rights' feminism so divisive and its gains so insubstantial. Those who choose the family and motherhood will be deeply divided by their values and their reproductive role from those who choose the public sphere. If women choose the female role, they lose all the activities and fulfilment which men have monopolised to theirs. If they choose the male, they lose the rewards of their biological function. Neither group will be satisfied with their lot, because each has to deny an essential part of their nature to fit into the chosen role. The political implications of this division are severe. Both groups may claim to represent the interests of their sex but

147

neither can do so effectively because of the existence and legitimacy of the other.

The choice is so unnatural that from the start there have been women who could not make it and (wherever societies have been sufficently flexible to allow this), have fought back by trying to combine both roles. Since each role is designed to be full-time and carries material and psychological penalties for the part-timer, this amounts to trying to live two lives in one. Whether women attempt this uncomfortable feat from economic necessity or are impelled to it by their personal capacities and psychological needs, their reward will most likely be the worst of both worlds. The more that women exercise their 'equal' marital and family rights, too, the larger and more materially circumscribed this category of women is likely to be; the combination of low earning potential and women's continuing childcare responsibility will ensure that divorced, separated or otherwise single parents form a peculiarly disadvantaged female group. If we leave aside the few women who really do not feel the drive to reproduce or live some kind of family life, the only women who can to some extent escape this contradiction will, yet again, be those few who have the means (and the necessary support from their menfolk, if they are married or divorced) to employ other women to perform the whole range of service functions for them.

Thus, as far as women's penetration of the public sphere is concerned, (including, of course, the acquisition of resources which will support their recruitment to political elites), 'equal rights' may look like an indispensable move in the right direction. However, we can expect its gains to be in large part illusory. In purely quantitative terms, the fact that the greater part of the female population will have at least one foot inside their traditional sphere means that women will have a much smaller population base from which to advance than men. Even if the women in this group were to acquire the attributes of success in political recruitment at the same rate as men, there would never be enough of them to achieve parity in political elites with women's presence in the population. In reality, such a rate of advance is most unlikely. Quite apart from the fact that men can be expected to make a vigorous defence of their position behind the smokescreen of equality (and the fact that many dependent women will support them), the survival of the female gender role with its inferior status, 'caring' focus and *de facto* identification with women makes it most unlikely that the content and status of women's training and employment will be the same as men's. Nor will the most ambitious of women find it easy to make the same competitive commitment as men, when the personal costs are so much higher; even 'career' women will combine roles where they can. Thus in men, in society and in themselves, women will encounter forces which militate against advance.

For many women, 'socialist' feminism has been the complete answer to these problems. Indeed, one of the main reasons for its emergence as a belated offshoot of the socialist movement was to refute the errors of this kind of feminism. The result was a set of ideas which not only seemed to re-assert the close links between early socialism and feminism but also seemed to reconcile the aspirations of many educated women with both their gender values and their social conscience, while rendering them acceptable to men as well.

From a socialist perspective, the fundamental failing of 'equal rights' is its attempt to tackle the situation of women independently of the 'broader' society in which they find themselves. The only women who can benefit will be the few who can accommodate their interests to the existing, defective social framework at the expense of the rest. Since society is the source of all oppression, and all non-socialist societies, by definition, oppress most of the people in them, regardless of sex, the place for women to start is not with their own situation as women, but with society. In a socialist society, by definition, no one will be oppressed.

At the level of values, the perfections of socialism ensure that no women need have reservations about working for it, or participating when it arrives, whether they are feminists or not. By struggling for socialism, women will be serving all oppressed humanity, so that even as political activists they will be operating within a legitimate extension of their traditional role. (In fact socialists often voice a sense of moral outrage at the idea of women's pursuing their own interests before all other kinds of oppression have been eliminated; women, in keeping with their gender role, should always abnegate themselves.) Within socialism (a system which is variously held to embody such positive qualities as peace, co-operation, social justice, equality and human happiness and to be distinguished by the absence of such negative characteristics as exploitation, alienation, poverty, conflict and oppression)[10] there can be nothing incompatible with what is good in female values. Women will not only have the right, in a socialist society, to take part in public life along with men; for the first time in their history they will *feel* that it is right to do so.

At the structural level, socialist women have always been particularly alive to the social class dimension of the difference between formal rights and real opportunities. In order to ensure that all women, including those of the working class, can enter paid employment on equal terms, 'socialist' feminists have usually proposed the communalisation of childcare and domestic services. It follows from this that performance of traditional female tasks will become a job like any other, the cost of fair remuneration being borne by the community as a whole. Thus in its structural dimension, as well as values, 'socialist' feminism appears to obviate the need to struggle with the problem of the gender role dichotomy. Its ability to mobilise the support of considerable numbers of educated women, and its evaluation by a modern historian of feminist thought as 'the most whole-heartedly feminist' of the three intellectual traditions which interact within the women's movement (the others being evangelical Christianity and 'equal rights')[11] is not difficult to understand.

Why, then, has 'socialist' feminism not lived up to its promise, 'socialist' feminists being no more successful than their 'bourgeois' rivals in changing women's status? The priority of women and their interests has even tended to recede along with the consolidation of socialist movements and parties and it has proved, if anything, especially difficult for socialist women to defend their status. In the long run, the struggles of 'socialist' feminism have been located as much within their own camp as with the external, 'bourgeois' enemy. The twofold explanation of this problem lies firstly in the way that conceptions of socialism changed along with the development of the socialist movement and, secondly, in the fundamental character of 'socialist' feminism itself.

If the initial feminism of the 'equal rights' movement was to founder on its lack of radicalism, in the case of socialism it was precisely a radical vision of social change which got lost along the way. The result was that from its original, sometimes almost central importance in early socialist theory, an interest in changing the situation of women had been demoted, by the time that 'socialist' feminism emerged, to a position that was marginal, at best, to a doctrine which was increasingly focused on the redrawing of power relations among men. At worst, it was even regarded as anti-socialist. As many socialist women saw it, the advocates of feminism (i.e. 'equal rights') were unacceptable not only because they were bourgeois (in outlook, that is, for both sets of women were mainly middle class in origin) but, strange as it may seem, because they were feminists. Yet, paradoxically, the goal that 'socialist' feminists were pursuing was essentially the same as that of their rivals – the equality of women in a world designed for men. To understand how both these contradictions came about, it is necessary to look more closely at the way that 'socialism' and 'feminism' – the two elements of this polarisation – were understood.

From a feminist perpective, the crucial point in socialist development is the transition in the middle of the nineteenth century from communitarianism to a combination of 'state' and Marxist socialism as the dominant form of socialist theory. The socialism of the Saint-Simonians, of Fourier and the Owenites was essentially communitarian in focus.[12] It looked to the creation of a new society from below, through the development of new social relations of people (in small groups) with each other, not with the state. Selfish individualism was the common enemy, but for the communitarians its roots lay in the whole relationship of individuals to one another and the way to eradicate it was not through class struggle (which both Fourier and Owen specifically rejected)[13] or through the imposition by the state of a sweeping change in ownership (which did not occur to most of them) but by changing the basic elements of that relationship, i.e. its underlying values and the primary social structures which embody them. As an examination of communitarian aims makes clear, what this tended towards was the fundamental rejection of core male gender values. What they proposed to substitute – and, indeed, it was the only alternative – were the values we associate with female gender. In place of competitive values and hierarchical relations, the communitarians advocated co-operation and relative equality; in place of built-in conflict, a structural disposition towards harmony. Instead of the general authority of the state over the members of society, their model was the small self-governing community of equally responsible, participant individuals.[14]

That the structural dimension of communitarianism should have feminist implications was inevitable too. Since the family is the most basic element in social formation and communitarians perceived it variously as the bastion of individualism, the fundamental social obstacle to co-operative human relationships and a major source of psychological repression, every communitarian attempt at a structural revolution inevitably brought women and their status into view. To say that communitarian socialists were invariably feminists would be going too far. There were plenty of instances in which feminism was marginalised, or even repudiated by them, sometimes to placate external critics or under the influence of evangelical Christianity. Also, hardly any serious attempts[15] were made to grapple with the functional dichotomisation of gender, Fourier's theory of 'attractive labour', according to which people in a properly constituted *phalansterie* would work because they wanted to and every type of work would be attractive to somebody, being the most far-reaching.[16] Judging by their practical implementation, what the numerous, but vaguely worded Owenite proposals for the communalisation of housework appear to have intended was the communalisation of these tasks *among women*, whose equal participation in the other work of the community thus acquired the punitive character of a 'double shift'.[17]

In addition, the range of family reforms proposed was often very narrow, or if wider, based in libertarianism, a mainly, (though certainly not exclusively) male perspective from which female emancipation is the instrumental means to greater sexual freedom; indeed, the elimination of sexual repression was the real, half-hidden purpose of Fourier's plans. The potentially negative consequences for women of free sexual choice are usually discounted in libertarianism, a point which was not lost on leading women communitarians; it was the prospect of sexual freedom

151

without responsibility on the part of men which led such prominent Owenite women as Margaret Chappallsmith and Emma Martin to reject complete abolition of marriage and the family, at least in the short term.[18] Yet within the parameters of its time, its limited practical experience and the fact that women were never more than a small minority within the movement, communitarianism had an intrinsic feminist potential, reflected in the unprecedented number of politically active women who were mobilised by the communitarian ideal.[19]

Although communitarian socialism originated mainly with men and commanded considerable respect within the early labour movement, it was inevitably handicapped by its radical, 'female' values, its experimental status and the practical difficulties it encountered. It is not surprising that it was more 'masculine' forms which came to dominate the socialist movement, forms which endorsed traditional male values of conflict, hierarchy and power and had by the same token a more 'realistic' basis for change in the changing distribution of resources among men.[20] The transition was in some cases gradual and incomplete (Marx himself never lost a distinct hankering for what he called the 'poetry' of Fourier, which helps to explain the difficulty of reconciling his form of revolution with the 'utopian' character of his barely sketched vision of a socialist society) but it was marked by a decisive shift in perspective. Where communitarians had stood *outside* the existing society and sought, with different values, to build an alternative, socialist society from the foundations up, later forms of socialism were firmly rooted *inside* it.

The distinctive contribution of Marx to socialist theory was not to question men's history and values and, like the communitarians, to canvass alternatives, but to portray them instead as progressive, inevitable and the prerequisites for socialism. Socialism, for Marx, was the climax and resolution of two continuous, interdependent processes of conflict, of man with his environment and of men with men. The 'oneness' of socialist man with his environment was to result from *conquest*, and indeed the history of man was understood to be the history of his victory over nature. This concept of a struggle against nature, which fits neatly into the classical false dichotomy in European culture of reason versus nature, equated with male versus female, was also predicated on conflict, inequality and hierarchy *among* men. Conflict, for Marx, was the engine of history and socialism, like every previous epoch, would be born out of the existing power relations among men and their forcible resolution. What is more, it would not even be possible without each preceding stage of class division and exploitation, for each of these stages, to Marx, was the indispensable context for progress towards the 'abundance of goods' which was his pre-condition for socialism.[21]

There is no doubt that by elevating a descriptive theory of what had actually occurred in the history of European development to the status of a scientific socialist doctrine which equated all history with economic history and classified all economic history as inevitable, Marx was in danger (as he himself suspected),[22] of taking the past too much for granted. He was also providing an apologia for the survival of that past even into socialism, by simultaneously insisting that every phase of men's development sprang in dialectical opposition from the one before and adopting a materialist view of culture which allowed him to ignore the issue of psychological motivations and grossly underestimate the complex processes of cultural transmission. To anyone unprepared to accept a purely mechanistic explanation of human behaviour according to which a change in property relations will transform cultural values, it seems obvious that the values which have shaped a workers' revolution are likely to survive with the victors (along with a host of other assumptions which the latter share with the general population) to shape the society which ensues. Where the quite different values and behaviour which would sustain Marx's vision of a socialist society were to come from must remain a mystery, not unrelated to that other mystery, of Marx's view of human nature, with which his scholars periodically wrestle.[23]

The appeal of Marxism is only too understandable, however, both to the organised industrial workers whose collective resources it celebrates and to revolutionaries preoccupied with the question of power. His claim that both the revolution and socialism were inevitable was not only immensely comforting to radicals but gained enormous credibility from its reflection of contemporary trends. The most salient of these were the intensification of class conflict in most European countries, the tendency towards ever greater concentrations of capital in large-scale enterprises and the rapidly expanding role of the state. For Marx, class conflict was the avenue to power, capital concentration was laying the foundation for the 'socialisation' of production and the state, in the hands of the workers, would be the principal agent of social transformation. Thus Marx answered the question of power in terms that his contemporaries could understand and encouraged them to believe that socialism was already implicit in the tools that capitalism had laid to hand.

For women, these tendencies in socialism could not but have serious implications. Where the centre of communitarian concern had been the individual (who could be female) and the objective was to build socialism on a foundation of unselfish relationships among relatively small groups of people, now it was the economic relations of classes which were held to determine the character of a society and the only possible basis for socialism was the seizure of the means of production by the working class, a social unit comprising male producers with female dependents. What this amounted to was a reversal of the causal flow between relationships among people and the construction of socialism; socialist relations among people were now something which would come *after* the revolution. Thus the interests of women, like all considerations other than that of proletarian power, must be secondary in the short run to those of the working class. From this, it was but a short step to condemning the pursuit of women's interests as contrary to those of socialism until after the latter had been achieved, a position which was adopted generally by socialist men and accepted by socialist women. By attributing the negative aspects of men's values and behaviour to the existence of a specific set of male oppressors of other men, rather than the other way round, socialist women were able to convince themselves that men's behaviour would be completely different once the formerly oppressed were in charge themselves. It had the unfortunate implication, too, that a socialist society could exist independently of change in gender relations. Instead of being central to socialist theory, the status of women was now a secondary issue, to be resolved by a change in relations among *men*.

This marginalisation of women's interests was compounded by the rejection of the individual in favour of the social interest, with which the former was held to be in irremediable conflict; society, to the socialist would always be greater than the sum of its parts. In the long term, this meant that whoever defined the interests of society 'as a whole' under socialism would *ipso facto* define those of women and determine their status. According to the Marxist sequence of events, this should be working-class *men*, on whose collective resources and seizure of power the achievement of socialism depended. In practice, it would be whoever controlled the socialist state, and there was nothing whatsoever in either Marxist theory or the distribution of resources within the labour movement to suggest that this could conceivably be women.

The emphasis of 'socialist' feminism on the 'communalisation' of childcare and other aspects of the service role actually reinforced the central role of the state in constructing women's future. However, it was not only their consequent dependence on the good will of ruling men which was likely to impose limits on the prospects of women under socialism. Feminism itself, as understood by socialist women, was a limiting factor. Although 'socialist' feminism had the appearance of confronting both the inequities of 'equal rights' and the burden of the female role, this appearance was belied by the fact that for 'socialist', as for 'bourgeois' feminists, the goal of women was the same: the equal right of women to behave like men. Both in the mainstream of male socialist thought (where Engels set the parameters with his premise that the sexual division of labour *in itself* was natural and unexploitative),[24] and among socialist women, feminism was defined in terms of women's access to the economic independence, career fulfilment and sexual freedom enjoyed by men. The result was that 'socialist' feminists were no less inexorably trapped by women's gender role responsibilities than advocates of 'equal rights'. Even if traditional female functions were to be communalised under state control, someone would still have to perform them. Since 'socialist' feminists, like their 'bourgeois' sisters, were not challenging the male gender role but endorsing it, this 'someone' would be women. The difference would lie not in who did what, but in their conditions of employment. Where 'bourgeois' feminists anticipated the direct employment of some women (as nannies, cooks, etc.) by others, so that the latter could enjoy more prestigious and rewarding occupations with an easy mind and society's approval, 'socialist' feminists sought to achieve the same end more equitably by substituting indirect employment (through the medium of the state) in communal services which would be available to everyone. This would have the double advantage of relieving working-class women of the 'double shift' and opening up career opportunities to all those women who had the inclination to compete with men. Their enormous faith in socialism *per se* seems to have lead most 'socialist' feminists, until very recent times, to take it for granted that the standard of public childcare in a socialist society would be very high, that 'women's work' would be appropriately valued and that their conditions of work and home life would be immeasurably improved.[25]

The logic remains, however, that some women, under socialism, would continue to benefit from the services of the rest and that these beneficiaries, as with 'equal rights', would be mainly 'career' women. The bulk of women in employment would be engaged in dreary, unrewarding jobs and it could be argued, too, that for many of these the conditions of life would actually deteriorate as a result of socialist reforms. Although the general entry of women into employment would give them the economic independence many of them badly needed, it would also obviate the need for a 'family wage' for men; thereafter, women would work for pay in order to live. Combine this with communal childcare facilities and women would be under both economic and social pressure to stay in full-time employment, on the same terms as men, throughout their working lives. Whatever the benefits of entry to the public sphere, it is a moot point under these circumstances whether they would outweigh the costs. Instead of bringing up their own children in their own homes, women would be faced with yet another bitter choice: either to forgo their role as nurturing mothers altogether or else to bring up other people's children instead of (or as well as) their own in an institutional setting. Either way, they would have to accept the same, almost total separation from home and family relationships that the male gender role has nowadays imposed on men. (The tendency of socialist women to insist on the availability of childcare twenty-four hours a day implies a very demanding shift system too, both for the caring workers and for the children's mothers.) Caught in this version of the 'scissors' conflict, women might well begin to

155

wonder if there was any point in having children. If, however, this put individual women's interests at variance with those of society – on account, for example, of a general decline in the birth-rate – then the 'public interest', with all the authority and resources of the state behind it, might well demand more babies.

The ability of 'socialist' feminism to add substance to 'equal opportunities' is doubtful too. If both dichotomy and hierarchy of gender roles survived into socialism, it cannot be considered likely that real levels of public spending on communal services would match the traditional obligations of the female role. To male decision-makers, they would always appear marginal in comparison with other priorities, leaving women to meet the shortfall with their unpaid labour. Both this tacitly unequal burden and the survival of gender stereotypes give us every reason to expect that women would be disadvantaged in the labour market too, and that 'women's work' would continue to be badly paid and held in low esteem. Trapped by economic necessity and social values in the gender role of men but obliged to fulfil the female role as well, the probable fate of women under 'socialist' feminism – whether it is viewed from the perspective of 'female' values or the gender role of men – would be the worst of both worlds.

As a basis for women's political advance, 'socialist' feminism thus has serious limitations. Like 'equal rights' it is crippled by its attempt to change the situation of women without changing the gender role of men. The result is, once again, that women are caught in the gender role scissors, expected to be simultaneously *the same* as men, and *different*. The practical consequences of this contradiction can only be exacerbated by the emphasis of socialism on the priority of social goals and the power of the state; in their dual capacity as members of the social work-force and its reproducers, women will be doubly vulnerable. 'Socialist' feminists are likely to find themselves handicapped as a result by the pursuit of inconsistent goals. On the one hand they will wish to enhance the opportunities of women to compete with men (by making their lives more like those of men), but both their social priorities and their social conscience will suggest that the immediate necessity is to protect them within their 'female' role. The issue of protective legislation is a perfect expression of the kind of conflict of egalitarian and welfare principles which is likely to result. The concern of 'socialist' feminists for welfare issues will tend in its turn to reinforce the traditional female role and, with it, their own political marginalisation. Integrated into the structures and programme of the socialist state, the capacity of women to advance into political elites will be limited, of course, by their lack of valued resources; as socialists first, rather than feminists, they will have neither the ideological basis nor the resources to do anything about it. To the extent that women retain any separate identity and voice, it is likely to be confined to the very issues – maternity, childcare and the need of women for protection – which point up and perpetuate their disadvantaged, out-group state.

FEMINIST STRATEGY AND THE PROBLEMS OF POLITICAL INTEGRATION

It is clear that the intrinsic propensity of 'equal rights' feminism to divide women on the dimensions of class, etc. *and* gender identification must undermine its coherence as social movement, while the problem is compounded in the case of 'socialist' feminism by its relationship to socialism. It remains to be seen how far these movements' organisational strategies will reinforce or mitigate their flaws.

From a contemporary perspective, the strategy dilemma for feminists of all kinds is whether to act primarily on their own, or together with men. One path calls for separate, all-women's organisations and presupposes that women have interests so distinct from those of men that they cannot but be lost in integration: the other points to the integration of women into mixed political structures and presupposes the compatibility of their goals with those of men. Superficially, the record suggests that 'equal rights' and 'socialist' feminists are predisposed to respond very differently to this dilemma, but in fact their historical differences have been of necessity rather than principle. Few early feminists saw the dilemma in modern terms; and it was only as a result of their experience that women's contemporary perspective, especially on the risks of political integration, was born.

Although 'equal rights' feminism originated in separate women's groups, its subsequent development in many countries as a militant, separate women's movement, was forced upon it by the intransigence of men. The history of the suffrage movement in Britain and the USA certainly disposed of the myth that women (for reasons of nature or nurture) are incapable of acting militantly on their own behalf, but it gave no reason to suppose that feminism had an inherent predisposition to separatism. On the contrary, political integration was inherent in the logic of 'equal rights'; the integration of women into the world of men was, after all, the ultimate goal. Thereafter, if women sought to preserve their separateness while men were content for them to integrate, was this not tantamount to the negation of their aim? Was it not, too, an admission of inferiority, implying that women were different from men after all and could not sustain 'equality' without special treatment? Even the argument that women needed special treatment, either for the long-term protection of the weaker sisters within their traditional role (in the form of welfare feminism) or temporarily, in order to catch up on men, could militate against separate action. If most women were weak and

157

political power resided in the structures of men, then should leading women not act through the latter, rather than waste their scant resources in fruitless confrontation?

The difference with 'socialist' feminism was simply that the latter never existed as a separate, women's movement in the first place. Although contemporary feminist historians with socialist sympathies have been relieved to discover the extent to which women workers took part in the early labour movement, the origins of 'socialist' feminism as we know it do not lie in the working-class feminists who fought and failed to defend their socio-economic interests against male-dominated trade unionism in the nineteenth century (the kind of women who in 1834 were already asking of their men, 'Surely, while they loudly complain of oppression, they will not turn oppressors themselves?')[26]. They lie instead among the intellectuals who took their cue from Engels, and the whole tenor of 'socialist' feminism, as we have seen, was to argue the *historical necessity* of its integration into the politics of class and socialism first. Structurally, this has nearly always taken the form of absorption in the mixed-sex, but male-dominated labour movement. To be tolerated, women's organisations have had to be auxiliary and subordinate to those of men, and 'working with women' has always had the same paternalistic connotation for socialists as working 'with youth' and other marginal groups. Although the suffrage movement succeeded in drawing considerable numbers of socialist women into separate action on an individual basis (often against their better judgement, since they were sceptical of the value of the vote) this was a short-lived departure from the norm. It was not until the late 1960s that European 'socialist' feminism began the painful process of partial separation which is still going on today.

The practical difficulties facing feminists of either type, doubly isolated in the cleft stick of their sex and their education, inevitably reinforced their ideological predispositions to integrate. As women seeking influence within the world of men, they could be nothing more than the insignificant outposts of an out-group among the educated. As people seeking social transformation in the lives of women, their ideas and behaviour would simultaneously present a threat to men *and* estrange them from the very constituency – womankind – which they must seek to represent. This alienation from the mass of ordinary women (the inevitable consequence, as we have seen, of the 'scissors' problem of the gender roles) and the resulting difficulty in sustaining any kind of popular base, undoubtedly helps to explain why the majority of 'first wave' feminists invariably opted for integration and against the idea of a 'women's party'. How far they could expect to achieve their objectives would seem to depend entirely on how well the latter meshed with those of other, more powerful groups (groups of men, that is) and how easily they could be accommodated within the principles of the prevailing culture. These constraints, plus the fact that educated women were themselves inhabitants of that culture and tended to think within its terms, were bound to weight the scales against the separate path.

These integrative tendencies in feminism were certainly reinforced by the divided responses it evoked in men. It might seem that the radical potential of feminism, with its implicit threat to the essential character of male-dominated societies, would always rule out male willingness to favour integration, but there are several reasons why the response of men to educated women and their feminist demands is never likely to be one of uniform, unmitigated hostility. In the first place, where educated women appear it is only because there are already educated men, whose post-Enlightenment values and logic (those of equal rights, social justice and so on) work against their privileged status as males and whose apostolic belief in the value of education makes it psychologically difficult for them to withhold it entirely from others, even women. The historical record shows that many of the earliest openings for women to become educated in modern times were the result of male initiatives; those of fathers with a strong pedagogical drive, who for want of a son educated their daughters instead, of *savants* who could not resist basking in the role of intellectual mentor to a woman, and of fathers, husbands and lovers who simply wanted someone congenial to talk to.[29] Similarly, when women turn to feminism it is only to be expected that intellectually honest men will find it difficult to refuse the logic of their own enlightened values, especially when these are reinforced by social conscience or personal emotion but stop short of any real threat to the male gender role. Thus for every Rousseau, there will be a John Stuart Mill, and for every Proudhon, an Engels. Few, if any, of these 'feminist' men, however, will expect the emancipation of woman to take a form that has man washing floors in her stead.

There are also conditions in which the education and public role of women will come to have a broader social or political significance to men. If national pride is focused on the educated, civilised character of the nation, then the existence of any uneducated group will detract from this. Men are likely to be particularly vulnerable to the argument that women should have the same 'right' to education as men, for this will be a 'right' which is difficult to distinguish from a civic duty. The argument will gain force, too, from its compatibility with the growing demands that modern conditions make on women, in their traditional maternal role, in the early education of their children.[30] From the right to be educated it is but a small step to the right – or even duty – of professional employment, especially in the role of educator, and especially for women who are unmarried and have no children of their own to educate.

If, alternately, educated men are a beleaguered group, desperately seeking allies in their struggle to bring society in line with their socialist or democratic ideals, then the idea of educating women to play a part in this struggle may be highly attractive and not at all incompatible with the female gender role. If women's role is service, what higher object could they serve than social progress? If this particular service requires education, then let them be educated. In effect, it can be predicted that the more important the personal and social value of modern education in the eyes of men, the more likely it is that some of them will actively seek to extend it to women, even in the face of great hostility from others of their sex.

At the same time, the societies in which significant numbers of educated men exist are also those in which traditional values are being eroded by more flexible political norms. In capitalist systems, the dispersal of resources has created the need for integrative (rather than merely repressive) responses to new socio-economic groups and their demands, in the interests of economic development and political stability. Even socialist systems, with their need to harness a broad range of productive forces under state control, cannot altogether ignore the diversity of social needs. Although the limits of acceptable change will vary greatly from one system to the other, the tendency in each is to seek such a balance between the accommodation and denial of interests as will turn the political edge of dissent and isolate those groups whose demands are deemed too radical. Of course, the exact point where the balance is struck will depend on the resources of the group concerned as well as the nature of the demands. In most advanced societies, equal rights (without equal opportunities) and welfare measures which reinforce the gender role dichotomy have been the points of compromise with women.

Here is the strategic crunch, of course. If the price of integration is accommodation to the gender role dichotomy, then what can women gain? In terms of liberal, humanist values, one might say a great deal. Since men have never needed the protection of divorce, legal status within the family and abortion to secure the 'rights of man', these are objects which feminists of all hues have pursued within the 'equal rights' framework, with considerable success. From this perspective, women's dilemma is just the same, familiar problem of cost–benefit analysis which faces any other aspiring group; whether there is more to be gained by confrontation, at the polls or otherwise, or by seeking to come 'inside' the existing system. They have to weigh up this kind of incremental gain against the enormity of the task involved in making a gender role revolution, and the advantages of legitimation and male sponsorship against the dangers of isolation from other women as well as men. The trouble is that there is always another perspective where women are concerned – that of the gender role dichotomy and women's gender base outside the public sphere. If integration means absorption into systems based on the male role, then the 'scissors' problem goes unsolved and incremental changes will carry this sting in their tail, that they reflect and adapt to the values of men. The idea that integration into male-dominated structures will *empower* women to change them from within seems less convincing than the counter-view of integration, as a strategy of disempowerment[31] which will stop the development of feminism in its tracks. In the following chapter, this proposition and the other arguments presented here are put to the empirical test, in settings where unusual advantages favoured women's access to political elites.

7

FEMINISM IN PRACTICE: NATIONALIST FINLAND AND REVOLUTIONARY RUSSIA

Two of the most striking historical cases of deviation in the gender pattern are those of Finland and Russia in the late nineteenth and early twentieth centuries. In each case, the most plausible explanation for unusually high levels of female recruitment to political elites is the effect on women's status of an unusual emphasis on education, relative to other resources. In one case, a whole nation was carried away by its esteem for education; in the other, it was an intellectual minority which set itself against established values. In both, however, the end of a period of political transition brought the stabilisation of a new socio-economic and political order and with it, an end to the unusual progress which women had made. The establishment of, in the one, a democratic and, in the other, a state socialist system serves as a laboratory in which to demonstrate the reasons for these setbacks and their bearing on the problems facing feminists today. Since the Soviet case involved the conscious attempt to transform society itself, as well as women's situation, it is dealt with here at greater length.

FINLAND

The first case to be examined is that of Finland in the late nineteenth and early twentieth centuries, a nation under alien rule but possessed of a distinct ethnic, linguistic and cultural identity and a strong desire for self-improvement, which turned to education as the repository not only of its national identity but also of its hopes for an emancipated future. For centuries a province of Sweden, with a Swedish minority playing a dominant (and greatly resented) role in its internal affairs, Finland was forcibly incorporated into the Tsarist Empire in 1809. At one stroke the Finns were simultaneously separated from their Scandinavian subordination and, in the Russification policy of their new masters, exposed to yet another alien source of cultural imperialism. The effect was to give birth to a new sense of Finnish identity and political purpose, in which a sense of nationhood was inextricably linked with education and an intense aspiration for a culture that would be both truly Finnish and as civilised as any in Europe.

When Russia in its turn was defeated by Japan and rocked internally by the 1905 revolution, the Tsarist government gave in to the demands of the Finnish independence movement for the establishment of a Finnish Parliament, the Riksdag. One of the most extraordinary aspects of this concession was that the Riksdag was to be elected by truly universal suffrage, with women voting as well as men for the first time in European parliamentary history and women eligible to stand for the parliament too. In the first Riksdag elections in 1907, no less than 10 per cent of the elected members were women, a proportion which was not only exceptional for its time[1] but, as we know, is still unequalled today in Britain and many other parts of the developed world; it presents a particularly startling contrast to the rest of Scandinavia, where in Sweden and Denmark the 10 per cent barrier was not broken by women until 1949 and 1953 respectively, and in Norway not until 1973.[2] In Finland, the proportion rose to 13 per cent in 1908 and fluctuated around an average of 10.25 per cent for the next fifteen years. Throughout this period, too, the success rate of women candidates was consistently slightly higher than that of men. In the 1920s, however, this progress was halted. The proportion of women began to drop and was not to reach double figures again until after the Second World War. The slight electoral advantage for women candidates evaporated, too.

Few attempts have been made to explain this phenomenon, although Haavio-Mannila has recently advanced the argument that because women were given the vote in Finland at the same time as men, politics was never seen there as a male preserve.[3] However, this reasoning ignores the fact that the political organisations which were active in post-independence Finland (to say nothing of politics itself) pre-dated the establishment of the parliamentary system, and it certainly offers no explanation for the development of the gender pattern thereafter. In fact, the original high plateau of female parliamentary representation was associated with the domination of politics by the independence movement, the origins of which went back to the 1860s. It was only after the Civil War of 1917–18, when class-based, inter-party conflict had become the dominant political mode, that stagnation and decline set in for women. As an explanation it therefore begs several questions: why did the Finns want an equal franchise in the first place; why, if politics was not a male preserve, were more women not elected; and why should Finnish politics have gone on to become *more* male-dominated thereafter?

A more convincing explanation can be derived from the most uncharacteristic distribution and evaluation of socio-economic resources, and in particular of education, in pre-independence Finland. As the Finnish sociologist and analyst of Finnish feminism, Riita Jallinoja, explains, the development of the independence movement, the election of the early Riksdags and the rise of women's rights groups (to which several women deputies belonged) all occurred against a quite exceptional socio-historical background, in which Finnish women, relative to their men, had already reached levels of paid employment and access to education which were half a century ahead of other European countries.[4] By 1910, women in Finland already amounted to as much as 39 per cent of the economically active population outside agriculture. This phenomenon was related in its turn to a quite extraordinarily high level of education among Finnish women, who as early as 1930 were to constitute no less than 32 per cent of university students in Finland. As Jallinoja explains, it was the peculiar conditions associated with the drive for independence which had made this possible:

> The high percentage of women studying at universities is due to the country's traditionally great respect for education. The [nineteenth century] national movement understood the high value of enlightenment: Finland's citizens, including women, must be educated, preferably in Finnish. All this created an atmosphere in which the value of education in Finland was if anything almost overestimated.[5]

Since the possession of education was, simply in itself, a source of high individual socio-economic status in such a cultural climate, the drive to educate women could not but alter their socio-economic status, relative to men. This was not all. So long as the simple provision of education was a central political concern, the status of educational issues and even the educators themselves was bound to be high and this, too, could work to the temporary advantage of women. The tendency to look upon the education of children as an extension of the traditional female role was, and is, very strong in Finland, at the level of political elites and national policy-making as well as in employment. As Sinkkonen and Haavio-Mannila have shown, the distinction between 'male' and 'female' topics, with education as one of the most distinctively 'female', has been a particularly marked and consistent feature of Finnish parliamentary behaviour ever since 1907.[6] In recent times, when women have finally gained access to the higher levels of the state bureaucracy, the strength of this association has combined with women's long-standing professional expertise in the education field to produce a proportion of women among senior civil servants in the Ministry of Education which is higher (at 38 per cent) than in any other ministry.[7] In the special circumstances of the early 1900s, when education was such a salient issue, even the negative impact of traditional gender roles (which can normally be expected to work against women by associating them with issues of marginal interest to men) could thus be partially suspended.

Once this context is understood, the high level of female representation in the early Riksdags ceases to be mystifying. On the contrary, it is seen to be the logical effect of the independent status of education in the early 1900s, acting through

1 the drive to educate women as a component of the nation, and
2 the enhanced political salience of a professional area where women could be active without departing from their traditional role *and* have a special, political contribution to make as well.

The only puzzle which remains is why this pattern should have been unique to Finland among the Scandinavian countries. Why, in particular, if the independence struggle was a crucial factor in the case of Finland, was there no similar development in neighbouring Norway, where the dominance of politics by men remained absolutely unshaken in the face of superficially similar political events?[8] As the following comparison will show, the political significance of education and the status of educational resources were an area of such profound divergence between the Finnish and Norwegian independence movements that the differences in gender pattern are exactly what we should predict.

Although Norway, too, was under alien rule (Danish until 1814, Swedish until independence in 1905), and questions of education figured largely in its independence struggle, the provision of education was not a point of conflict between Norwegians and their alien rulers so much as among Norwegians themselves. Indeed the educational issue, in the words of a modern historian, 'opened up a fissure in society which still colour[ed] Norwegian politics in the middle of the 20th century'[9] and produced a strong association between Norwegian nationalism and *anti-*intellectualism.

In pre-independence Norway, feelings of national identity were strongest among the peasants of the western coastal regions, where they centred on an austere and narrow religious sect known as Haugeanism, and on the colloquial peasant tongue, the *landsmaal*, which was descended from Old Norse. When compulsory schooling was introduced to Norway (as early as 1848 in the towns and 1860 in the countryside), the impetus came from above, and met resistance from Haugeans, who were allegedly opposed to the spread of any more education than was necessary to read the Bible and the constitution. Against the paradoxical background of a flowering of middle-class Danish-Norwegian culture into international renown, the subsequent nationalist struggles to have the *landsmaal* adopted as a language of instruction, a subject in the school curriculum and, finally, as a joint official language were thoroughly divisive. Indeed Ibsen, who chose to spend most of his life in Denmark

165

and (like most educated Norwegians) wrote in a language which was almost pure Danish, was to describe the linguistic goals of peasant nationalists as nothing better than 'the primeval right of screech'.[10] As a result, the independence movement was characterised by cultural ambiguity and the fusion of education with Norwegian national identity was not really complete until as late as 1942, when it was accomplished by the Germans' mass arrest of schoolteachers for refusing to teach Nazi propaganda. Meanwhile, it was the Norwegian democratic tradition which was the unifying focus of politics before and after independence and political elites were firmly based in the three principal socio-economic groups: government officals, landholding peasants and the merchant trader/manufacturers, joined in due course by the urban working class.

Women, notwithstanding *The Doll's House* and the existence of a small Norwegian feminist movement, were in no position to compete in such a setting. While Finns were seized with the ideal of the educated nation, the possession of education in Norway, far from being an independent source of status, was in many eyes ungodly, and the education of women aroused especially strong opposition. In contrast to the Finns at the other extreme, Norwegian women were to be notoriously more housebound, uneducated and subject to religious oppression than any of their Nordic sisters throughout the first half of the twentieth century.[11] Yet gender role identities, as we have seen, were also strongly marked in Finland. The difference was that in Norway these tended strongly to reinforce women's exclusion from politics: the first grants of women's suffrage there (and in Denmark) were actually confined to 'female' concerns such as school boards and parochial church meetings, children's welfare and poor relief,[12] and the opportunity to specialise in these matters at the national level could not arise since there were virtually no women legislators to do so until the 1970s.[13] With relatively few women educated and the education of those few a dubious political asset, there was nothing whatsoever in the conditions of Norwegian nationalism to support advance on women's part. By comparison, the role of education in the Finnish independence movement, and its explanatory power where the gender pattern is concerned, are all the more obvious.

Of course, before Finnish women could become legislators, they had to gain political rights, and one aspect of the relationship between education and the gender pattern was, inevitably, the rise of feminism. The first appearance of organised feminism in Finland took the form of small 'rights' groups established in 1884 (the same year in which similar groups appeared in Sweden and Norway) and the first phase of its history, as a separate women's movement, lasted until shortly after the foundation of the Riksdag. Predictably, since the principal movers were educated women, preoccupied with the constitutional issue and their own interests in the labour market, 'equal rights' soon became the central, unifying issue of Finnish feminism.[14] The climate of the independence movement, with its stress on political rights, education and the totality of the nation, was unusually propitious for this kind of feminism, so much so that up till 1907 feminists in Finland were able to enjoy the best of two worlds – integration and separatism – at one and the same time. On the one hand, the common emphasis on political rights (and the spread of education) in both the independence and women's movements meant it was relatively easy to integrate the demands of the women's movement into the constitutional programme. Universal suffrage and the civic rights of women could be seen as a logical expression of Finnish nationalism. At the same time, the emphasis on broad national goals temporarily de-emphasised the cross-cutting identities of class and party and even, to some extent, the internal Finnish/Swedish divide. As a dimension of the nationalist movement fighting the same external enemy as Finnish men, the separate existence of the women's movement was both logical and politically respectable. The result was a network of women's groups which were not only a framework for the political mobilisation of women and the articulation of their demands, but the basis for their further recruitment into political elites. When the Tsarist capitulation finally came, the women's groups could even claim some of the credit and their leaders were sufficiently well known to mobilise a personal vote. Fully a third of the 66 women who were Riksdag deputies between 1907 and 1920 were openly affiliated to separate women's groups.[15] A factor in the higher success rate of women candidates may well have been these groups' ability to mobilise the votes of women: Finland is the only country in Europe where the existence of a 'women's vote', (i.e., women voting for women in preference to men) has definitely been established and it is among educated, employed women that this kind of voting behaviour is most pronounced.[16]

The question that remains to be answered is why women could not sustain this early promise; why, instead of continuing to rise after independence, the proportion of women legislators actually fell slightly and stabilised around this lower level as the system settled down. The evidence suggests that this decline and stagnation was not fortuitous. It coincided with swift and far-reaching changes in the focus and values of Finnish politics, away from the unifying object of independence and towards the goals and values of class-based parties, and was an accurate reflection of the severely circumscribed socio-economic position of women in the new society. In these new conditions, the practical implications and strategic problem of 'equal rights' feminism were thrown into particularly sharp relief.

Independence was no sooner granted than class conflict, exacerbated by the example of the Russian revolution, erupted in Finland in the form of civil war. With the victory of the 'Whites' in 1918, parliamentary forms were resumed, but the polarisation of party politics on class lines was to remain the dominant theme of Finnish politics between the wars. There were two, closely inter-related reasons why the level of women's political recruitment could not continue to grow in these circumstances, and would be difficult even to sustain at the level it had reached. The first was the reality of Finnish women's socio-economic position, as opposed to the appearance of equality achieved in 1906; the second was their lack of a feminist framework in which to try to change it.

As we have seen, the entry of women into the paid work-force in Finland was strongly associated with their access to education and professional employment. However, the battleground of class conflict is defined in terms of property and occupations which are almost exclusively non-professional and traditionally occupied by men. With the relative decline in prestige of educationists, as education and Finnish national independence came to be taken more for granted, and the intervention of class values to emphasise the importance of industrial over professional occupations, it was inevitable that women would be disadvantaged politically by their lack of socio-economic resources. Women had acquired the right to work, but this did not mean their work would be the same as men's or equally rewarded. Even today, when job segregation is less pronounced in Finland than in other Nordic countries, this is because of the higher levels of education and professionalisation among Finnish women (and their recent access to jobs in the state civil service) while the low status of most women's work is reflected in inferior wages and gender differentiation.[17]

In the second place, any further growth in women's occupational or property resources was inhibited not only by the restricting effects of gender on the *range* of women's occupations but also by the fact that traditional gender roles within the family remained entirely unaltered in spite of the high proportion of women who were working. The rule was that women with children did not work, so that women were forced to choose between marriage and employment. Of course, this is the classic choice implied by the philosophy of 'equal rights', and its effects have never been more sharply illustrated than in Finland. In a society too inflexible to allow for working wives and mothers, the result of 'equality' was to divide women into two very different socio-economic groups with largely incompatible needs, and impose an ineluctable ceiling on the proportion of women who could be members of the paid work-force. This ceiling was certainly higher than one might expect. The willingness of Finnish women to opt for a career instead of marriage was quite remarkable, and an indispensable condition for the high levels of female employment which have already been described.[18] 'Even in the latter part of the nineteenth century', we are told, 'it was common among middle- and upper-class women to remain single: about 40 per cent of them were un-married . . . .[and] in the 1920s this phenomenon became common among the population in general.'[19] Although wartime levels of male mortality must have contributed to the large numbers of unmarried women, both the nineteenth century origin of this trend and its strong positive association with higher educational status (and to a lesser extent urban residence) seem to rule out purely demographic explanations for its existence. The tendency was particularly strong among graduates. As late as 1960, when resistance to married women's paid employment was evaporating, 38 per cent of graduates aged 30–44 were single compared to 24 per cent of all women in urban areas. By this time, 82 per cent of married graduates actually were in employment, many of them in state and municipal official posts, and (surely, by no means coincidentally) the proportion of women in the Riksdag had risen sharply. The fact remains, however, that at no time were most women prepared to forego their reproductive role. The exclusion from employment of the majority of women (who did marry), imposed an absolute limit to the proportion of women who could acquire occupational status of any kind.

The situation of women in Finland after independence was thus a classic illustration of the 'scissors' problem of 'equal rights', thrown into especially sharp relief by fact that the rules prohibited trying to combine both gender roles. It was also an object lesson in the contribution feminism can make to shaping this dilemma, and the inability of women who are caught in the logic of 'equal rights' and political integration either to confront or solve it.

As we have seen, the strategy of the first phase of the feminist movement in Finland was admirably suited both to articulate the political demands of Finnish women and take advantage of their relatively favourable socio-economic situation before independence. All this was to change with great, but predictable speed after 1906 – that is, even before independence itself had been achieved. With the foundation of the Riksdag on the basis of universal suffrage and the rights of women, the 'equal rights' movement simultanously gained exactly what it had been seeking (like feminists elsewhere, Finns had exagerated expectations of what could be achieved with political rights) and lost the rationale for its existence. As national unity and the constitutional issue gave way to the priorities of class conflict, the idea of a separate women's movement swiftly acquired an unacceptable, subversive character, even in the eyes of its adherents.[20] Jallinoja expresses surprise at women's willingness to let their movement be destroyed by integration into the mainstream, mixed political parties, but, given the logic of equality, there was really nothing surprising in it. The separate movement had implied a universal female interest, transcending the boundaries of class, and as an adjunct to the struggle of the nation, and before the grant of formal rights, this interest had coincided with, and reinforced the values recognised by men. Afterwards, in the era of class struggle, feminism would cut across the focal conflict. The urgency of this conflict, and the cross-cutting loyalties of class, were acutely felt by women as well as men. In these circumstances, the pressure on women to marginalise their residual feminist aims was so irresistable that its own activists took the lead in undermining the women's movement. As early as 1907, the president of the Finnish Women's Association was advising each woman to 'find her party among the existing political parties' and the residual feminism of the movement's activists was already being concentrated on the formation of women's groups within the parties.[21]

Ironically, the women's movement was subsiding before even formal equality had really been achieved – married women, after all, did not enjoy the right to work and important areas of employment were still closed to women altogether- and at the height of its popular success. This disintegration was not felt so keenly on the left, where women had always eschewed direct participation in the separate women's movement anyway (only one out of the thirty-eight women Social Democrats in the Riksdag from 1907 to 1920 was directly affiliated to the women's movement), but the ultimate result was the same across the board. Within the framework of existing parties, women's issues were of marginal importance at best and were soon being shelved.

Individual women politicians, sharply divided by party loyalties and lacking the motivation to develop a common, women's platform which the pressure of an active, separate movement would have supplied, could do very little about this even if they wanted to. Although the formal equality of women was taken for granted by the political parties and the women's sections survived unchallenged within them, the women politicians seem to have been living on the political capital accumulated by the former women's movement. The parliamentary careers of the first generation of women in the Riksdag were noticeably more distinguished than those of their successors and the right of women's sections to nominate a certain proportion of the parties' candidates at each election (which was secured by the electoral law in operation until 1954) began to take on the ominous appearance of a quota system. The capacity of women politicians to influence policy in women's favour can be gauged by the fact that the situation of women in Finland remained frozen in the same state of partial equality, with all its attendant evils, for nearly half a century after independence. By the time it was evident that the price of integration was the abandonment of further moves towards equality and that women were allowing their party loyalties to be exploited to very little purpose, there was no women's movement left to protest. As in Britain, new generations of educated women emerged who had scarcely heard of their predecessors' struggles and had to start again from scratch (in the mid-1960s) by creating the women's movement anew. Given the legacy of unfinished business, it is not surprising that this new movement was also essentially 'equal rights'-oriented and that the major issues it tackled were married women's right to work and the de-segregation of professional employment.[22]

RUSSIA

If the Finns became enthused with education, so too, ironically, did a small but historically significant minority of their Russian oppressors, a people reduced by the impact of the Enlightenment and their social and economic backwardness to despising their own traditions and valuing instead the very different culture of other, more developed countries. Originally the preserve of the 'enlightened' aristocracy and gentry, education came to be seen by individuals from all classes as the key to social change. It was never available to more than a very small minority, but even so, Russian society was unable to integrate these people with either a satisfying socio-economic role or political toleration. They fell into the awkward category of *raznochintsi* – people without rank – in the highly ordered society of post-Petrine Russia, where everyone else had a specified place and function and the only occupational uses for education were in literature and the arts (which soon became politicised) or in the state bureaucracy, where their task would be to administer a system which was wholly repugnant to their values. As the nineteenth century wore on, the reforms of Alexander II and the advent of capitalism provided slightly more occupational opportunities for the educated (providing, of course, that they were male) but also opened up a divide between the incremental reformers (almost exclusively men who were partially integrated by property or professional employment into the existing social structure)[23] and the relatively rootless advocates of revolutionary change. It was among the latter, whose energies were channelled into illegal political activism (including efforts to educate the peasantry and, eventually, the emerging working class to revolutionary consciousness), that exceptional levels of female recruitment were found. In the levelling conditions of the illegal underground, the prison cell, the renunciation of property and conventional status and the absence of gainful employment, women leaders emerged in status equal to the men even though (since educational opportunities were still infinitely more restricted for women than for men) they tended to come from a numerically smaller social base in the upper reaches of society and could not but be fewer in number.

Although it is impossible to establish just how many people, men or women, were involved in the revolutionary movement, the prominent role of women in its elites is incontrovertible. It is evident from

171

contemporary reports and memoirs that women played a notable part in the formation of the populist movement from the 1860s onwards, often in the role of educationists, preparing educational materials for peasants and workers and organising illegal adult education with a strong political content.[24] As the populists became more organised, many individual women leaders emerged, such as Vera Figner, Marya Oshanina and Marya Kovalevskaya, to name but a few. The movements 'To the People' of the 1870s found women as dedicated as men and give some idea of the quantitative basis of women's involvement; according to police figures, 15 per cent of the 1,611 'propagandists' who were arrested between 1873 and 1877 were women.[25] Of the six leading members of Narodnaya Volya ('The People's Will' revolutionary movement) who were tried and condemned to death for organising the assassination of Alexander II in March 1881, two were female. One, Sophia Perovskaya, was the daughter of a former Governor-General of Petersburg and was the joint leader of the group along with one of the very few people of genuinely peasant origin ever to take a leading revolutionary role, Andrei Zhelyabov; the other, Gesia Gelf'man, was actually pregnant at the time of sentence and although her sentence was finally commuted a few days before the birth of her baby, she died in prison shortly after.[26] Women leaders emerged in more conventional activities too. Vera Zasulich (who abandoned terrorism after publicly shooting General Trepov and receiving an enthusiastic, and patently erroneous, acquittal in one of the first ever trials by jury in Russia) was a leading Populist who went on to become one of Russia's first Marxists and, in 1900, one of the six members of the editorial board of 'Iskra' which included Plekhanov, Lenin and Martov. In 1901, Ekaterina Breshkovskaya (an outstanding populist since the 1870s) was instrumental in founding the Social Revolutionary Party, which soon became Russia's largest mass party with a huge peasant following; by October 1917 another woman, Marya Spriridonova, had become leader of the militant 'left' faction of this party, president of the Peasant Congress and a notable member of the Petrograd Soviet's Military Revolutionary Committee.[27] Even the Bolshevik leaders (who in spite of their fixation on the industrial worker as the paradigm of revolutionary leadership were essentially a group of middle-class intellectuals), included Krupskaya, Armand and Kollontai.

Almost without exception, these women resembled leading revolutionary men in being highly educated.[28] Not a few, like Oshanina, the Figner sisters and Kollontai, had studied abroad, others with outstanding Russian scholars and political thinkers, and some had built on their upbringing in upper- and middle-class homes through self-study.[29] Indeed, their memoirs and political writings are a major part of the source material for the revolutionary movement. From these and other sources, it is clear that education gave women more than the psychological orientations for political action and the framework of ideas in which to work. It was their common ground, as political leaders, with revolutionary men.

It was not merely the possession of education, however, which worked to the advantage of women, but its interaction with a strongly anti-hierarchical current in the revolutionary culture which went much further than simply isolating education from other conventional measures of status. Originating with the so-called 'nihilists', whose object of rejecting existing society and its values *in toto* led them into conflict with the whole concept of hierarchical relations,[30] it amounted to a moral and ideological revulsion from any kind of status which effectively turned the latter on its head, so that people with conventional status were despised and those without it valued. This inversion of conventional values gained political direction and force from populism, with its intellectual identification with the allegedly socialist character of the peasant commune and emotional identification with the peasantry itself. The former answered a deeply felt need among intellectuals for an alternative to the development in Russia of capitalism on the West European model; the latter was derived from the feelings of guilt which motivated young people of privileged background to join the revolutionary movement and was in many ways the other side of the coin from their respect for education. Education, as Lavrov taught them, was the supreme privilege and the only way for the educated few to pay their debt was to put their own, personal development to work 'to diminish evil in the present and in the future',[31] which in practice meant renouncing status to work among 'the people'.

When these perspectives were combined, the result was a belief in the historical and moral superiority of the peasantry, who by the same token had as much to teach as to learn. Tolstoy's portrayal of the peasant Platon in *War and Peace* and the hay-making sequence in *Anna Karenina* are familiar literary expressions of this idea (imbued in his case with respect for the pure religion of the peasantry as well). With the advent of Marxism and Russian capitalism, much the same idealisation was transferred to the industrial worker, celebrated in the works of Gorki and given its ultimate dramatic expression by Trotsky's symbolic representation of Russia at the Brest-Litovsk negotiations of 1918 by an elderly *muzhik*, complete with flowing white beard, and an eager young worker.[32] In practical politics, such values were more difficult to operationalise. Even in literature, Tolstoy had found it difficult to communicate the wisdom of his peasants, and the symbolic negotiators at Brest-Litovsk were soon upstaged by their more educated colleagues. Actual peasant or worker leaders were a rarity within the revolutionary movement; neither peasantry nor workers (until after the industrial action of the 1890s) had the resources to sustain the political mobilisation and organisation which would allow such people to emerge. The most practicable way for revolutionaries to express their solidarity with the lowest orders of the Tsarist hierarchy was not, therefore, to select them as their leaders, but to value people who identified with them. Such people could be distinguished by their uncompromising rejection of worldly status and adoption of the poverty and lowliness of the masses in their own lives. As the Marxist, Akselrod expressed it,' a privileged position, even that of a teacher, would not have helped us to come near to the people, but . . . alienated us . . . and weakened our revolutionary state of mind.'[33] Add to this the spirit of asceticism and self-sacrifice which ran right through the movement from the 'conscience-stricken gentry' to middle-class Lenin, and we have a stereotype which educated, women revolutionaries in Tsarist Russia were unusually well placed and motivated to fit. Even their class origins were no handicap, for they could be renounced. Perhaps the case of Bardina, condemned as 'bourgeois' by a revolutionary fellow-student not for being a landowner's daughter, but because she confessed to a weakness for strawberries and cream, can best convey the flavour of this renunciatory, yet richly cerebral sub-culture.[34]

As in Finland, education, and the way that it was valued, was at the root of this unusual situation. In Finland, however, the status of education interacted positively with the professionalisation of the female work-force and even after class-based politics had become entrenched, Finnish women never entirely lost the political foothold they had gained. In Russia, the context of women's political involvement was more radical, but had the same effect of producing favourable conditions for upper- and middle-class women to become political leaders. It was also, as we shall see, associated with a level of overt commitment on the part of men to 'women's rights' unparalleled in Europe. And yet, in spite of women's pre-revolutionary role, and although nearly all the revolutionaries took it for granted that the revolution would solve women's problems, the outcome was one of the most male-dominated systems in the developed world. The sources and severity of this disaster have never been satisfactorily explained. To understand what went wrong – or how misleading these hopes had been – requires an appreciation of firstly, the false position of feminism in the revolutionary movement and secondly, how the real character and values of the Soviet system developed. Since both the independent status of education and the emergence of anti-hierarchical values among educated, middle-class radicals have been as strongly associated with cases of gender pattern deviance in the 1980s as they were in revolutionary Russia, there are important lessons to be learned from this drastic setback in the past.

In Russia, a commitment to the 'rights of women' was almost as old as the revolutionary movement itself. One reason was probably the openness with which male supremacism was articulated as an integral part of the traditional, autocratic culture the revolutionaries were opposing. In the 1860s, this led the young 'nihilists' to adopt unisex hair styles, dress and manners as a badge of their revolt and, along with the intuitive recognition of the hierarchical character of gender relations which this implied, may help to explain why this generation was to prove so psychologically receptive to feminist ideas. Another reason was the influence of Fourier and other communitarian socialists on the first generation of Russian populists, and in particular on N. G. Chernyshevsky, author of the didactic, feminist novel *What Is To Be Done?*

In the 1860s and 70s, when the influence of *What Is To Be Done?* was at its height, Russian revolutionaries stood at a crossroads between their original, communitarian conceptions of socialism and their growing belief in the need for state power to transform society 'from above'. Chernyshevsky exemplified this paradox.[35] One of the first populists to stress the necessity of state intervention, he also believed that autonomous communes and co-operatives should be the basis of socialism and saw society as 'the sum of individual lives'.[36] His novel is actually about the creation of socialism 'from below', through the spontaneous emergence of 'New People' who establish urban co-operatives. It is also a feminist tract, in which the utilitarian theory of enlightened self-interest is used as an intellectual basis for the emancipation of women and the socio-economic prototype for the new society is an all-women sewing co-operative which is founded by the heroine, Vera Pavlovna, and includes ex-prostitutes among its members. A large part of the book deals with Vera's personal emancipation, women's need for economic independence and the relations of the sexes within marriage.

The effect of this book on Russian revolutionaries was colossal.[37] Intended for the new generation of educated youth who looked to the political intelligentsia for guidance, countless memoirs testify to its extraordinary success. As well as setting up urban co-operatives like Vera's to ease their own financial problems and using the novel as a text to explain socialism to the workers and peasants, succeeding generations found in it a 'blueprint for life' and a crucial stage in their political development. As far as women were concerned, how could any admirer of the book be other than a feminist? Henceforth, it was axiomatic that feminism and socialism were inextricably linked.[38] The truth is, however, that this rapid integration of feminism into the revolutionary pro-gramme gave a very misleading impression of the relative positions of socialism and feminism in the revolutionary scale of values, not least in the case of Chernyshevsky himself, who rebuked a colleaugue's growing preoccupation with feminism as follows: 'The question of women'. said he, 'is all very well *when there are no other problems*'.[39]

The apparently unreserved acceptance of feminism by revolutionaries may have something to do with the failure of a separate, feminist political movement to develop in Russia until nearly the end of the pre-revolutionary period.[40] This belated arrival, which compares unfavourably with the Scandinavian countries as well as Britain and the USA, had unfortunate consequences for both the theoretical and organisational development of Russian feminism. The feminism of *What Is To Be Done?* was a curious mixture of 'equal rights' and Fourierisme and was flawed by its *lacunae*, of which the most important was the total omission of any discussion of parenthood and childcare. This failure to deal with the question of how the 'New People' will nurture and rear their successors is especially startling, not only from a feminist point of view, in view of the emphasis on the socialising effects of a traditional upbringing. The fact that Vera (in her later, emancipated life as co-operative manageress *cum* medical student) and her second husband, Kirsanov, even have a child is only mentioned once and the reader is left completely in the dark as to its upbringing; motherhood seems to have no effect on Vera's life at all.[41] The implication of this omission is that it will be left to women to sort out the problems of reproducing the species on their own. In practice, women of the Russian nihilist and populist movements appear to have accepted this responsibility in their own lives, often choosing single parenthood and (like the mathematician Sofia Kovalevskaya) falling back on female relatives and friends when the problems of combining childcare and career became too much for them.[42] Combining gender roles in this way was a course of action fraught with difficulties, as the historical record of these women's lives attests. A separate women's movement, which could have drawn on this experience to make a critical evaluation of Chernyshevsky's ideas and develop them on a feminist basis, might have had a real and positive influence on the development of Russian socialism. Instead, as Tkachev approvingly observed, when nineteenth-century women looked beyond the formation of co-operatives to the question of the social structure as a whole, they came to share the growing preoccupation of the revolutionary intelligentsia with the question of power and the 'political' solution of transformation 'from above' instead of the 'social' option of revolution 'from below'.[43]

Both the paramountcy of power and the low priority of feminism were strongly reinforced by the advent of Marxism, with its central doctrines of class conflict and the seizure of power, and its Leninist development as a theory of state socialism. In Marxism-Leninism, the interests of women, like all other considerations, were marginalised by treating them as secondary to that of class and defining their oppression as a function of capitalism. It was not relations between men and women which would determine the fate of women, but relations *among men*. Instead of being central to the socialist revolution – the possibility which was always contained in communitarian socialism – the liberation of women had become its by-product. Feminism, in the sense of 'equal rights', might be an acceptable subplot to the socialist drama, but only if the leading role was reserved for the working class and their instrument, the state. The separate organisation of women, like any conflict of their interests with those of the working class, were unacceptable.[44]

The result was that when a separate Russian women's movement made its belated appearance on the scene, it was immediately subjected to virulent attacks for its 'bourgeois' character. As far as possible, Bolshevik and Menshevik women were prevented from participating (a tactic which naturally turned the claim that the movement was non-socialist into a self-fulfilling prophecy) and their 'political work' among women was kept strictly under party control.[45] Ironically, in view of the enormous claims which were later to be made throughout Europe for 'socialist feminism' as the only true doctrine (and Soviet Russia as its principal exponent), the reality was that the concepts of 'socialism' and 'feminism' were deliberately polarised by the socialist movement. Indeed, so great was the male chauvinism of leading Bolsheviks that, but for the determination (or some might argue, self-delusion) of a single woman, it is unlikely that any serious effort would have been made to reconcile them.

The task of integrating feminism into the programme of Russian state socialism was accomplished principally by Alexandra Kollontai and was distinguished, predictably, by the central role in women's liberation assigned to the state. Understanding women's aims in terms of freedom to behave like men, in both work and personal relations, Kollontai's problem was how to translate this objective into social reality.[46] The question of how women could manage to be equal with men *and* remain responsible for the duties of the female gender role had hitherto gone largely unconsidered. Chernyshevsky, as we have seen, dealt with the problem by ignoring it. The Marxist abolition of 'bourgeois marriage' and the traditional family were enthusiastically endorsed by some Russian socialists, Kollontai included, but these were negative policies which would destroy the old order without creating a new one. Nor could Engels' naïve expectation that women's problems would be solved by entry to the paid work-force be convincing to someone who was herself a former wife and mother. The Kollontai solution – and this has been the pattern of 'socialist feminism' ever since – was that the traditional functions of the female gender role – mothering, housekeeping and domestic service – should be assumed by the state.

If one believed, with Kollontai, that there could be no better guarantor of women's needs than a socialist government and that the directorial role of the socialist state would inevitably be softened by the kind of participatory democracy which she herself was to introduce alike to Old

Folks' Homes and the Commissariat of Social Welfare,[47] then this appeared to be the perfect solution. It certainly met the requirements for integration. Far from threatening the male gender role and its values, it endorsed them, as the goal to which women aspired. Instead of depriving men of the personal services to which they were accustomed, these would be performed by the impersonal agency of the state, i.e. by the women it employed. Simultaneously, by making women clients of the state it satisfied the basic expectation of state socialism, that every interest be subsumed in that of society as a whole, as defined and administered by the state. It was precisely these integrative strengths of Soviet feminism, not surprisingly, that were to prove its greatest flaws as a feminist programme in practice.

The new regime got off to a good start, with the appointment of Kollontai as Commissar for Welfare, the immediate introduction of civil marriage and divorce and the enactment of Matrimonial Codes which abolished the penalties of illegitimacy (in 1918) and (in 1926), recognised *de facto* marriages and equalised the property rights of the sexes in marriage.[48] Women were declared fully equal with men and encouraged to participate in the paid work-force and in politics. In the separate framework of improving public health, paid maternity leave was introduced, some measures to regulate working conditions for women were adopted and (in 1920), abortion was legalised.[49]

To appreciate the importance of these reforms, it has to be remembered that the vast majority of Soviet women in 1917, and long thereafter, were peasants. Many suffered the additional disadvantage of belonging to Muslim national minorities. The removal of these women's legal disabilities, and the party's programme for women's family rights had enormous impact in the countryside. Liberal values were the essence of this programme, and its social norms were those of urban, educated Russia. By this token peasant men lost their age-old right to beat their wives, abuse female members of their family sexually and force their daughters into marriage. The wretched cycle of the peasant woman's life ('between the stove and the door' as the proverb had it) was to be broken and there was even a small measure of economic independence in view. The party had a long and arduous struggle (with peasants of both sexes) against the brutal anti-feminism of the traditional peasant way of life, and their achievements in the Russian villages – even if motivated as much by a desire to break the hold of the church and customary authorities on village life as by humanitarian ideals – deserve every credit. Among the national minorities, results took longer to achieve. The institutions of polygamy, bride-price and the punitive segregation of women were savagely defended by the Muslim communities and their religious leaders. Their methods included anti-feminist murders on a horrifying scale; in Uzbekistan, for example, 203 such cases were recorded in 1928 and it was stated that 'the actual number of women murdered on political grounds was considerably larger, for there were also many cases which were not investigated'.[50] Victims, as in neighbouring Azerbaijan, included women party workers and local Soviet deputies, but also women who had simply stopped wearing the veil. Such incidents are not unknown even in comparatively recent times, but the great difference in the present day between the condition of women in Soviet Central Asia and in the neighbouring countries of the Middle East and the Indian sub-continent speaks for itself, and for the continuing relevance of equal rights to women in the Third World today.

The seeds of the Soviet future, however – and the preoccupations of socialist feminism – lay outside the peasant village. The construction of socialism was the real objective and must rest on a developed urban, industrial economy, where the ultimate effects of the revolution on women would be measured and the role of women in a socialist society would take shape. 'Equal rights' might suffice for the backward peasantry but 'socialist' feminism promised far, far more.

The immediate effects of the October revolution on women's role in Russian politics were distinctly adverse, none the less. Because of their precarious, minority position, it swiftly became an object with the new regime to eliminate competition from other political parties altogether. Since the role of women in the Bolshevik leadership was not impressive by comparison with other parties, this closing of all political options other than the Communist party fell unequally on women. The fate of many illustrious women was bound up with that of the Social Revolutionary party, which won the largest share of the popular vote in the Constituent Assembly elections of November 1917. Although these elections were as free and genuine as the conditions of the time permitted,[51] the timing of the Bolshevik revolution had the effect of pre-empting their purpose. Also, by the time the Assembly met in January 1918 the 'Left' faction of the Social Revolutionaries, led by Marya Spiridonova, had broken away to join a coalition government with the Bolsheviks.[52] The Assembly's position, and that of the main Social Revolutionary party within it, was hopeless. When a majority voted against the Left SR/Bolshevik motion and their presidential candidate (Spiridonova), the government had the Assembly dissolved by force and many deputies were later arrested and imprisoned.[53] Ironically, the Left SRs' coalition with the Bolsheviks soon broke up over the Treaty of Brest-Litovsk and, after government measures against the peasants in May, they staged an unsuccessful revolt, which was followed by Dora Kaplan's attempted assassination of Lenin in August. Although Spiridonova survived the subsequent reprisals and was allowed a considerable measure of freedom for a while,[54] the party's prospects were effectively destroyed by these events.

Thus the seizure of power itself was incidentally a defeat for women. This could only be reinforced, too, by its violent aftermath. Faced with civil war and foreign intervention in the immediate post-revolutionary years, it became a priority to exercise political leadership and control of a growing but untrusted army; in this setting, the gender role of women put them at an obvious disadvantage. More fundamental, long-term problems, however, were to arise from the class character of the new regime and its subsequent, state capitalist *cum* socialist development.

The class basis of the revolution and the outright class warfare which ensued had severely negative implications for women. The first derived from the exclusion of people of upper- and middle-class origin from political life. Unlike their Chinese counterparts thirty years later, the Russian communists did not believe in the psychological ability of individuals in general to transcend their family background. People of the 'wrong' class origins were irrevocably suspect and although they might be needed in the short run, as army officers or industrial and scientific personnel, they must always be watched and eventually discarded.[55] The result of this class discrimination (which was written into the Constitutions of 1918 and 1923 in the form of deprivation of political rights) was that political recruitment from the former privileged classes came to an abrupt end. With it, too, came an end to the political recruitment of women on its pre-revolutionary basis. Since educational resources had been its basis, but only upper- and middle-class women were educated, this partly-open door for women's entry into political elites had effectively been closed.

The women left inside the system were the almost entirely uneducated members of the peasantry and proletariat, women who started off at a hopeless disadvantage relative to men in terms of the resources available to people of their class. Within the proletariat, on which Soviet power and values were supposed to hinge, this inequality of resources was exacerbated by the party's stress on the superior value of the skilled industrial worker (almost invariably male) and identification of heavy industry as the basis of socialist development. Combined with the uncompromising statism which was to shape the Soviet system under Lenin's leadership, it created a context in which women could hardly have been more at a disadvantage.

Lenin's post-revolutionary vision of the progression of Russia to socialism – from private capitalism, to state capitalism, to socialism[56] – caused no little consternation at first among his long-time colleagues. What it boiled down to was the rejection of egalitarian, collectivist principles in favour of a system of political economy so unified, centralised and hierarchical (with its emphasis on occupational status as the key to party membership and party membership as the key to promotion and rewards) that the alienation of political activists from the old socio-economic order was to be replaced by their total integration into the hierarchical structures of the new one. The basis of this system was the unequal value accorded to different kinds of work, translated into practical effect by the use of individual material incentives and differential status, secured by the victory of Lenin and state socialism over the residual communitarianism of his colleagues in the period 1918–21.

To Lenin, the decentralised, egalitarian collectivism which had been a fundamental element of Russian populist socialism and found expression in the form of 'workers' control' in the immediate aftermath of the 1917 revolution, was anathema. With democratic centralism, he had already put paid to anti-hierarchical tendencies in the Party itself and although, like most of the 'Old Guard', Lenin followed egalitarian principles in personal life, he utterly rejected them as the basis for economic development and control. Efficiency and discipline were his gods and in industry, state direction and the use of the most up-to-date methods of capitalism, in particular those of material inequality and one-man management, was to him the only sensible way to proceed.[57] The role of the workers was to produce, and that of the unions to see that they did so in a disciplined[58] manner. These Leninist perspectives (which, bar the efficiency, were completely consonant with the Russian authoritarian tradition) found a ready response from the growing administrative element in the party.[59] When the issue of industrial control came to a head at the Tenthth Party Congress in 1921, the 'Workers' Opposition' led by Shlyapnikov and Kollontai was defeated and Lenin also took the opportunity to persuade the party to pass the fateful motion banning factions within the party, which was to be a crucial weapon in Stalin's rise to power. When the latter came to implement the five-year plans, the hierarchical principle of his command economy had been accepted long before (with its attendant bureaucratisation) and the foundations of the competitive inegalitarianism of Stalinist society had already been laid.

The consequences for women were far-reaching. The only way Soviet women's ostensible equality with men could have been translated into anything like equal socio-economic resources in the emerging Soviet system would have been for women to abandon their traditional gender role and throw themselves into gaining heavy industrial skills and administrative experience. There is no doubt that many women tried to do this in the early years, encouraged not only by their own inclinations but also by the party's urgent demand that they enter the industrial work-force. In actuality, however, women's circumstances made it quite impossible for them to compete with men.

Of the two dimensions of the 'socialist' feminist programme – that of Engels, which focused on the destruction of the 'bourgeois' family and the entry of women to the paid work-force, and that of Kollontai, which stressed the positive role of the state in substituting for individual women's female gender tasks – only the former was realised in practice. It was not that the party repudiated Kollontai's glowing vision of women's life under socialism, in which the tasks of housekeeping would 'disappear' into the hands of central laundries, collective kitchens, etc. so that ordinary working women would devote their evenings 'to instructive reading, to healthy recreation'[60] and the mother would not have to worry about her child because:

> Children will grow up in the kindergarten, the children's colony, the creche and the school under the care of experienced nurses. When the mother wants to be with her children, she has only to say the word; and when she has no time, she knows they are in good hands. Maternity is no longer a cross. Only its joyful aspects remain; only the great happiness of being a mother.[61]

Lenin, although never explicitly endorsing Kollontai's goal of the 'withering away' of the family, also spoke vaguely of 'model institutions, dining-rooms and nurseries which will emancipate women from housework', and (more trenchantly) of the effect of housework, and men's refusal to take part in it, on women's physical and mental lives.[62] The trouble was that these institutions did not materialise.

The reason for the failure to communalise housework and childcare was quite simply that the regime had other priorities. The first of these, from which all others flowed, was to stay in power. Of course, by seizing power at all, the Bolsheviks were making themselves responsible for coping with the social and economic problems which resulted from the First World War, the period of revolutionary interregnum and, in the winter of 1917–18, their defeat by the Germans. The civil war brought further death and disorder to millions of ordinary people and in its wake came famine. By 1920, industry and agriculture had collapsed and the major priority became economic reconstruction, followed by rapid industrialisation.

Although these were certainly not optimal conditions for social experiments, plenty of experiments actually did take place in the War Communism period. However, they did not extend to a major diversion of resources to women. Addressing the working women of Moscow in 1919,[63] Lenin told them tersely that if they wanted 'model institutions' they would have to create them themselves. Since he also showed a very clear appreciation (in the same speech) of how completely women's situation deprived them of the material and psychological resources which would enable them to do so, this was tantamount to dropping the communalisation dimension for the foreseeable future. Lest there should be any doubt about the time-scale involved, Lenin ended by making the link between women's domestic servitude and men's priorities absolutely explicit and warning women that their situation could never really change while the gender division of labour survived, for which they would have to wait 'many, many years', i.e. indefinitely.

What then, did Lenin mean by his simultaneous claim that the Soviet Union was 'the only country in the world where women enjoy full equality with men'? As he himself admitted:

> Here we are not, of course, speaking of making women the equal of men as far as the productivity of labour, the quantity of labour, the length of the working day, labour conditions, etc., are concerned; we mean that the woman should not, unlike the man, be downtrodden because of her position in the family. You all know that even when women have full rights, they still remain factually downtrodden because all housework is left to them.

Yet Lenin was simultaneously directing the construction of a society in which all the payments, promotion and rewards on which the individual's material and psychological condition would depend were to be based precisely on the productivity of labour, the amount of it an individual could perform, the length of the working day, etc. In truth, it was the economic *inequality* of the sexes which was being institutionalised.

The conditions in which Soviet women were to pursue their downtrodden lives were extremely harsh. Although Kollontai and also Lenin (by Zetkin's account) talked propagandist nonsense at times, teetering on the edge of a fantasy of Soviet life in which people were flocking to enter communal quarters because they were so convenient and comfortable to live in[63] and 'communal kitchens and public eating-houses, laundries and repairing shops, infant asylums, kindergartens, children's homes' were really being established on an effective scale,[64] both of them knew better. In reality, 'the number of creches, nurseries and maternity homes' was so insufficient, and the inability of financial assistance to keep pace with the cost of living so marked that 'hundreds of thousands of women during this difficult period of transition succumb under the double burden of daily work and motherhood'.[65] As for the 'communal feeding centres', these were simply canteens where the fare was so insufficient and non-nutritious that 'willy-nilly the housewife has to prepare additional food'. As Kollontai also observed, but without drawing the logical conclusion, even the provision of such facilities as there were, was a function of other priorities: 'the Workers' Republic . . . has had to resort to communal feeding as the most economic and suitable form of consumption, requiring a minimum of human labour, fuel and foodstuffs.' But this was a response to economic conditions not feminist goals.

Instrumentalism was to become increasingly characteristic of Soviet treatment of women. While it could be argued, as Kollontai repeatedly did, that the circumstances of war and revolution left the regime no options, eventually this argument had to become a rationalisation. Everyone might agree that firstly economic reconstruction and then industrialisation were necessary, but ultimately what the form and pace of these developments came down to was the choice of rapid industrial growth over women's needs (and other possible socialist goals). From this perspective, women served two social purposes. In terms of production, they constituted a reserve army for the industrial work-force; as agents of reproduction, their social duty was child-bearing. Population planning was an important element in government thinking from the beginning and paid work was not intended as an alternative to motherhood, but, as Lenin indicated, a supplement to it. There was no room here for what women wanted for themselves and in fact the pattern of Soviet spending on creches, kindergartens, etc. would always reflect 'broader' social goals instead.[66]

Unfortunately, 'socialist' feminism could not provide any palliatives for women caught between its dreams and these realities. In the hands of Kollontai, one-time head of the women's organisations and effectively their only spokeswoman, it was hopelessly embroiled in its inherent contradiction between class and hierarchy on the one hand and the interests of women on the other. Although she never ceased to herald the dawn of collective housekeeping and the 'withering away of the family', Kollontai actually explained the situation of women under socialism even more bluntly than Lenin. In *Women's Labour in Economic Development* (1923), where she characteristically presented 'socialist' feminism in the form of a diatribe against women of the former middle class (who used other women to do their housework for them and wanted self-fulfilment as a woman's right), she stated unequivocally that it was women's 'social obligation' to 'provide society with healthy offspring' and that this precluded real equality with men. The latter she derided as an 'equal rights' feminist fantasy, quite contrary to a woman's real interests which demanded protective legislation and a certain amount of job segregation. Child bearing was not enough, however, to justify her bed and board, since Kollontai accepted unquestioningly the hierarchy of 'productive' over reproductive and other forms of labour.

> Motherhood, i.e., women's ability to bear children, is not in itself a sufficient reason for society to support her on an equal footing with the men who bear all the responsibility of maintenance. But if the women share with the men in doing work useful for the society, their additional social responsibilities – child-bearing and child-feeding – undoubtedly entitle them to extra care and special attention from society.

This theme, that domestic labour produced use-values only and hence was unproductive and inferior, is a typical example of how a Marxian

184

explanation of men's historical development (based on the labour theory of value) could be transformed by Marxists into a system of socialist *values* which simply perpetuated those of the previous 'historical epochs'. What Kollontai intended was to integrate women's biological function with a wider fulfilment, but the net result was to perpetuate exactly the same belief in the difference and superiority of the male gender role over that of women which was the central weakness of 'equal rights' feminism too. The only difference was that where 'bourgeois' feminists left it open to women to make their individual, self-denying 'choice' between the gender roles, 'socialist' feminists, in the name of society, denied them any choice at all.

Nor was it only child-rearing which fell to women's lot; under the strains of Soviet reality, the 'socialist' feminist conception of the female role was revealed as embracing the whole gamut of supportive, non-'productive' labour by which women traditionally liberated men to live their superior role. If the state was unable to perform this labour, then it was women's social duty to substitute for the state. A feature of Soviet society in the 1920s and early 1930s was the existence of large numbers of children running wild (the *bezprizorniye*). These children and teenagers were orphans, foundlings and runaways for whom neither their parents nor the state had been able to provide. Their roaming gangs created social problems with which the authorities for a long time were quite unable to cope; in some places, according to von Rauch, they resorted to mowing them down with machine-guns.[68] In a context of civil war, starvation and a housing situation in which housing authorities could allot the living scarcely more space than they would occupy when they were dead,[69] it was preposterous to claim that the emancipation of women was the root cause of this phenomenon.[70] Indeed, when the problem of these children was raised by speakers of both sexes in the Central Executive Committee's discussions of the draft 1926 Family Code, it was linked with the emancipation not of women but of men, who were leaving their families destitute by failing to pay alimony and exploiting the divorce laws to evade parental responsibilities altogether.[71] However, when Kollontai, as mentioned earlier, referred to women's 'succumbing' to the dual pressures of work and motherhood, what she meant was the growing tendency of desperate working mothers to add to this problem by leaving children 'on the doorstep' of the state. Of course, state childcare was exactly what Kollontai had been advocating as the highest form of child-rearing, but now (in spite of her great sympathy for their plight), she criticised these women for reneging on their individual maternal responsibilities. In a context where the state was failing to provide for the children in its care, motherhood, she said, was a *social duty* which obliged ordinary women, starving, over-worked and poverty-stricken as they were, somehow to achieve what men need not, and the state, with all its powers and resources, apparently could not. This was anatomy as destiny with a vengeance and pointed straight back to the same, crucial problem of 'socialist' feminist thinking which produced her thesis of inevitable inequality – its acquiescence in the traditional dichotomy of gender roles.

Women's material inequality hit particularly hard in Soviet conditions but is significant in any economic context. If women have shorter hours for paid employment, are segregated in lower status jobs and are affected by protective legislation which does not apply to men, then they must earn less than men in spite of (really, because of) their extra, individual responsibilities. Ironically, whereas Kollontai had argued that woman's right to work would obviate her traditional need to live by serving men, what these conditions really meant was that woman's surest route to economic security, a higher standard of living and social status must still be marriage. The only society in which this would not be the case would be one in which all the hierarchical distinctions of labour were abandoned and everyone was equally paid for the same amount of work, or else where men spent the same amount of time as women in 'non-productive' labour. It seems unlikely that the one could be achieved without bringing on the other; it is also incontrovertible that the Soviet leaders were determinedly closing the door on any possibility of either.

How, the reader may ask, was it possible that Kollontai did not see this for herself? How could she fail to be aware of the gulf which was opening up between the 'socialism' which she and her colleagues were constructing and the glowing future for women which she kept insisting would come after this 'period of transition'? The answer, oddly, must be that she *was* aware of it. What she could not do was follow her insights to their logical conclusion.

Two separate incidents in 1921 point to the intellectual chasm which was opening up in Kollontai's mind. One was her involvement in the 'Workers' Opposition'. This movement was based in the trade union membership of the party and arose as a grass-roots, workers' challenge to the ideas of the party leadership who were mainly, of course, intellectuals; soon after Kollontai's association with it began she was asked to compose the official, intellectual platform for its views. The resulting document, *The Workers' Opposition*,[72] was presented to the Tenth Party Congress and was the basis for the heated confrontation which took place there, with the results which have already been described. What Kollontai said was extremely revealing. The main objects of her criticism were one-man management, the employment of former bourgeois specialists to induct Soviet socialists into capitalist practices and 'the ridiculously naive belief that it is possible to bring about communism by bureaucratic means'. Attributing the mistakes of the leadership to their difficult situation (faced with economic collapse, foreign intervention and a heterogeneous but predominantly peasant population), she argued that they were carrying adaptation to the point of deviation from Marxism. The workers, who were supposed to be the creative force of the revolution, were actually being excluded from the construction of socialism by 'the gentlemen at the centre'. Her criticisms of Soviet inegalitarianism were especially interesting, for she flatly disavowed the idea that there were no other options, even in wartime. The observant worker, she said, could see that 'so far . . . the betterment of the workers' lot has occupied the last place in our policy', but was always fobbed off with the stock answer that

> 'We could not attend to that; pray, there was the military front'. And yet whenever it was necessary to make repairs in any of the houses occupied by the Soviet institutions, they were able to find both the materials and the labour. What would happen if we tried to shelter our specialists . . in those huts in which the masses of the workers still live and labour? . . . it would become necessary to mobilise the entire housing department in order to correct 'the chaotic conditions' that interfere with [their] productivity.

Nor were these just the workers' grievances; what was breeding and nourishing their dissatisfaction was not simply their sense of injustice but 'the facts of ever-growing inequality between the privileged groups of the population in Soviet Russia and the rank and file workers, "the framework of the dictatorship" '. The essence of the argument was 'who shall build the communist economy and how shall it be built?. . . This question is just as important as the seizure of political power by the proletariat'. Time and again, the initiatives of the ordinary people to build socialism themselves had been stifled by the determination of the centralisers to control and direct everything, by their jealous monopoly of resources and their bureaucratic values. The examples she gave of such initiatives make the communitarian tendencies of her thinking (and its roots in her experience as a woman) very clear.

> Whenever there was an opportunity under the impetus of the masses themselves. . . to equip a dining-room, to store a supply of wood, or to organise a nursery, refusal always followed refusal from the central institutions. . . . there was no equipment for the dining-room, lack of horses for transporting the wood, and absence of an adequate building for the nursery. How much bitterness is generated among working men and women when they see and know that if they had been given the right, and an opportunity to act, they could themselves have seen the project through. How painful it is to receive a refusal of necessary materials when such material had already been found and procured by the workers themselves. Their

initiative is therefore slackening and the desire to act is dying out. 'If that is the case,' people say, 'let officials themselves take care of us.' As a result, there is generated a most harmful division; *we* are the toiling people, *they* are the Soviet officials on whom everything depends. This is the whole trouble.

It is small wonder that Kollontai was to feel profoundly alienated after the Workers' Opposition's defeat. This was not the first time she had challenged the leaders and lost, but what she faced this time was an unbridgeable gulf between their conception of socialism and hers.

The Tenth Congress took place in March 1921. The same year found Kollontai lecturing on women and socialism at Sverdlov University, and here she suddenly revealed another, crucial insight which Lenin had hinted at too in his speech of 1919: that women's problem had deeper roots than property and class.

Many consider that the enslavement of women, her rightlessness, was born with the establishment of private property. Such an attitude is mistaken. Private property only helped enslave women . . . The enslavement of women is connected with the moment of the division of labour according to sex, when productive labour falls to the lot of men and secondary labour to the lot of woman.[73]

The trouble was that this insight was no use to Kollontai, trapped within the ideological framework of Marxism and the practical consequences of state socialism. The only way forward was to link her communitarian platform for the Workers' Opposition with her revolutionary perception of the gender role dichotomy, i.e. by challenging the hierarchy of labour and gender as well as the 'Workers' State', but this was something that she could not do (and indeed her contemporary editor has been able to find only two unambiguous references to the elimination of gender roles in all her works). When the Sverdlov lectures were published two years later (as the earlier-quoted *Women's Labour in Economic Development*) Kollontai was still stuck in the grooves of anti-feminism, the 'period of transition' and the hierarchy of labour, and as unable as ever to accept the fact that what her party was promoting and she herself facilitating, was nothing more (and possibly even something less) than that self-same 'equal rights' feminism she so abhorred.

And yet, why could a woman of such undoubted moral courage and political commitment, 'the woman who defied Lenin' not once but twice, not face the consequences of her own ideas? Why could a woman who had spent her life speaking, lecturing and writing about women not transcend her anti-feminist inhibitions and resolve the contradictions in her thought? And why, if Kollontai could not, were there no other 'socialist' feminists to do it in her stead? Perhaps the answer to both questions is the same: Kollontai was too alone.

All her life, Kollontai was a woman virtually alone among men (and lonely with it).[74] Such contacts as she had with the pre-revolutionary feminist movement were bedevilled by the need to convince her colleagues, and herself, that she had nothing in common with it. Within the party itself, the lack of other women leaders, especially after the death in 1920 of Inessa Armand, left her almost totally isolated. Even the periods of her association with the women's departments were brief and overlaid by other responsibilities. In the first year of the revolution, she and Armand had travelled widely, mobilising thousands of women to participate in local women's commissions. Although Kollontai had always felt obliged to oppose a separate women's movement, in 1908 she had suggested that women might have some organisational identity within social-democratic parties. The women's commissions were intended as rather less than that, being simply a means of recruiting women to support the revolution and work under local party control; as Lenin had put it in 1919, 'political activity for the working woman . . . will consist in . . . using her organisational ability to help the working man'. However, the commissions were no sooner formed than they began to press for a national framework which would allow them to make some input to party policy. In 1919, after considerable opposition from within the party leadership, the commissions were incorporated into the party structure as the 'women's departments'; it was their leading organ, the Central Women's Department, of which Kollontai was head in 1920. This was the most influential period of their existence – the abortion reform of 1920 was partly due to their pressure – and it gave Kollontai the practical experience which bore fruit in *The Workers' Opposition*. The association was short-lived, unfortunately, and so was the heyday of the women's departments. Under the tutelage of the party apparatus, the central departments could not develop any autonomy, and, as Kollontai observed, the initiatives of the local departments in urban areas were constantly frustrated by their lack of control over any resources at all. The effective role of the departments was in rural areas and among the national minorities, working for 'equal rights'.

Thus, if there was no room in the mental world of Marxism-Leninism for a feminist perspective, there was no organisational base for women's action in the Workers' State and party either. If women were to develop their own ideas and act upon their own behalf, they would have to do it from outside, in revolt against the revolution. Oddly enough, Lenin had challenged them to do just that. In the same speech of 1919 which was quoted earlier, and *apropos* of the lack of help women could expect from the government in carrying out the socialist feminist programme, he advised his female audience in the following terms: 'We say that the emancipation of the workers must be effected by the workers themselves, and in exactly the same way the emancipation of working women is a matter for the working women themselves'. The implication, that women's revolution was still to come and it was the rule of men they would have to overthrow, was perhaps not lost on Lenin, but equally, he had no intention of giving women any chance whatsoever, in the form of resources or political autonomy, to act upon it.

For Kollontai herself, like so many of her equally disappointed, but less isolated male colleagues in the Bolshevik Old Guard, the fact that she had joined the wrong revolution was too difficult a truth to live up to. The heart went out of her political commitment. In 1922, she was removed from the revolutionary theatre altogether by her appointment to the Soviet Legation in Norway, the beginning of an almost continuous diplomatic career which lasted until 1945. Her creative energies were devoted at first to the development of her ideas about personal, sexual relations using the medium of the didactic novel; then she lapsed into political silence.[75]

At the same time that Kollontai turned to fiction, so too did the confused and suffering female population, as to an ideological agony column which might supply them with some guidance and might at least reflect their anguish and uncertainties. The 1920s and early 1930s saw the role of women become a major theme in popular didactic literature, where 'proletarian' and, after 1934, Socialist Realist writers achieved a mass readership by focusing on questions of desperate, daily importance to ordinary Soviet women trying to understand and cope with what was expected of them in the new society. However, now that the practical implications of these issues were finally confronted, the discussion was led mainly by men, not women, and the context, yet again, was socialist, not feminist goals. The question was not how best to satisfy the needs of women as members of society, but how to make the best use of them in the cause of 'socialist construction', a cause which was simply equated with that of feminism. What this boiled down to in practice, was an acute conflict between the competing demands of the male and female gender roles in the lives of individual women, a conflict which was tragically exacerbated by the conditions of the time but, as we have seen, was actually implicit in the nature of 'socialist' feminism.

The succeeding phases in the development of the Soviet fictional heroine as a role model for real women (and the debate among Soviet writers, critics and readers on this subject) have been analysed thoroughly by Gasiorowska, and will not be dealt with here.[76] One work, however, stands out for the brutality with which the issues facing women were portrayed; the 'proletarian' novel *Cement* by Gladkov. In this notorious tale, published in 1924, the heroine is Dasha, a working-class woman whose husband, Gleb, is a heroic builder of socialism, constantly at work on the reconstruction of the cement plant which gives the book its title. Then Dasha, whose life has been confined to home-making for Gleb and their little girl, Nyurka, becomes emancipated. She too begins to work heroically for socialism, and although her work is mainly unpaid (in the women's department) she ends up working even longer hours than Gleb. Their home becomes cheerless and dirty (it does not occur to Gleb to use his slightly greater leisure time to clean it up himself) and as there is never anyone at home to care for Nyurka, she is put into a children's home. So appalling are the shortages in these establishments that Gleb is horrified to find the children rooting in the ground for food; in fact, Nyurka dies. Although author and critics alike approved of Dasha's proletarian dedication, the author is honest enough to portray her suffering too: as Gasiorowska points out, 'Dasha lived her Marxist principles as martyrs or revolutionaries live theirs, to a degree unmatched by any other Soviet heroine. But while unflinchingly accepting the hardships of such complete dedication, she suffers', for her daughter and for herself.

All the elements of socialist woman's dilemma were encapsulated here: the illusion of equality, which is only open to the woman who becomes a super*man*; the man who also occupies the gender role of men but, unlike his female companion, neither expects, nor is expected to have, any active, personal responsibility for home or child; the priorities which do not allow the state to support the maternal role it has professed to fill; and the inescapable fact that even if it could – and Nyurka could live – the service of society would irrevocably separate Dasha from her child. Where, in all this, did the 'joys of motherhood' reside? As for those of fatherhood, they did not figure, even as an abstraction, in Soviet thinking.

In the event, it was the Stalin regime which resolved Dasha's dilemma. Building on foundations laid by early practice and ideologically legitimated by Lenin and Kollontai, the financial and social costs of substituting the female gender role with state domestic and child-rearing services were ruled out by a government whose priority was rapid economic development, not women's needs. In the interests of indus-trialisation, Soviet women were given the worst of both worlds; a fiction of equality in the workplace was combined with the return to traditional domestic gender roles (and pressure to have very large families) *without* the provision of a 'family' wage for men. Women had to work, in order to live, and combine this in the 'double shift' with household management and childcare, thus bearing the brunt of coping with the deteriorating material conditions which accompanied the great industrialisation drive. At the same time, women lost what little institutional base they had achieved with the abolition of the Women's Departments in 1929. This blow may have made little real difference to policy inputs at the top, but

191

it removed the only party framework which allowed for women to interact with each other and, conceivably, compensate for their lack of valued resources by mutual support. Women's political role *as women* was reduced to the local soviets, where they could struggle endlessly with the practical consequences of policies decided at a centre from which they had been deliberately excluded.[77] In contrast to Finland, where the identification of women politicians with traditional gender issues was not entirely incompatible with a prominent political role, the ideological hierarchy of labour made women's issues even more of a political cul-de-sac in the Soviet Union than is usually the case.

The power of the socialist state was so great that it could manipulate the behaviour and size of the population by administrative means. As everyone knows, among Stalin's onslaughts on the more liberal Marxist values of his predecessors was his demolition of the structure of women's family emancipation, replacing it with a neo-Victorian system of legislation intended to increase the population while simultaneously using the family as a unit of social control. The only occasion when women were consulted was over the plan to withdraw abortion rights in 1936, and when they showed on balance that they favoured their retention, abortion was withdrawn anyway. Sadly, 'socialist' feminism itself had laid the groundwork for this too.

Along with the emphasis on women's obligation to reproduce went disadvantages in the new, expanding Soviet education system. Although education was to become the pre-condition for personal advancement in the Soviet system, (and a veritable passion with the population, as it remains to the present day) the form of education developed by the Stalin regime was severely functional and its value entirely dependent upon the nature of its occupational deployment. While women of the former intelligentsia (like Evgenia Ginsberg)[78] were being herded in box-cars to the Gulag, a new and functionally educated elite was being formed, of which the archetype was the Soviet-trained (and almost exclusively male) heavy industrial engineer. The focus of educational recruitment was the working class, but as in other countries, working-class students were typically boys, not girls. Although in the late 1920s working-class girls seeking entry to higher education outnumbered boys, this appears to have been an effort on their part to compensate for the fact that they still had 'no chance of forming more than a minority among the skilled workers.'[79] Now the pressure was on men to get an education. A tendency to segregate women in disciplines which reflected their traditional gender role and to give them inferior, or less advantageous training except in marginal areas of education (like arts subjects) was to become an enduring characteristic of the Soviet system; indeed, the reintroduction of segregated schooling in 1943 was specifically intended to foster traditional gender roles. Although divorce and abortion rights were restored to women by Stalin's successors, the post-war growth in female recruitment into higher education did nothing to alter the very real advantages enjoyed therein by males.[80]

The fact that women got the burdens of the male role without its rewards had fundamental consequences for Soviet political life. It meant that Soviet girls could not grow up to be the kind of people of whom party members, let alone leaders were made. In the 1920s and early 1930s they had been disadvantaged by the increasing focus of party recruitment on soldiers and skilled industrial workers, especially those in large-scale heavy industries of strategic importance.[81] In the 1930s, the emphasis shifted to the new 'intellectual stratum of the working class' – engineers, factory managers and general administrators – and the dual pattern of party and elite recruitment described in Chapter 2 (standard and modifying models simultaneously at work) became established. Women, instead of gaining access to these most rewarding jobs (which would have been less physically taxing too) found themselves segregated in low-status, less skilled and/or service sectors of the economy, without careers and lower paid than men. The result was that women's share in party membership stood still after 1934 (at 14.7 per cent) and they vanished entirely from the leadership.[82] Yet the 1930s in the USSR saw a massive expansion of industrial and administrative career opportunities for people with the right qualifications, accompanied by a high turnover in top personnel because of the purges. In these circumstances, the rise to prominence on the part of appropriately trained men was often meteoric.[83]

During the Second World War, criteria of party admission became more flexible in terms of age and occupational status (closely linked in the case of men) and even although the emphasis was on recruiting soldiers, the proportion of women rose as a result to 19 per cent. Afterwards, there was a sharp return to pre-war values. The men of the 1930s maintained their hold on the upper reaches of the hierarchy (a grip which held until their leading members' deaths in the early 1980s) while women's hardships in the lower reaches were if anything exacerbated by the disproportionate loss of young male lives during the war. In a now predominantly female population (particularly in its younger, most active cohorts), the vast majority of new recruits continued to be *men* who had established themselves in the occupational hierarchy; the proportion of women in the CPSU stood still again, for a quarter of a century this time. By 1965, *one in every five Soviet men over 30 was a party member*, but only 3.3 per cent of the equivalent women.

8

GENDER THEORY AND
FEMINIST STRATEGY

The task of modern feminists is not a light one. No matter which way
women move within the framework of existing, male-dominated
societies, the content of the gender roles and their relationship to
reproduction ensure that they are caught within the gender scissors; the
'equal' right to be a man is not the answer for someone who is actually a
woman. Conversely – and this was where the attempt of 'socialist'
feminism to accommodate traditional roles fell down – the kind of society
where men and women could be different but equal is impossible without
a fundamental change in the male role and its values (and hence by
definition, in the female too). The result is that two momentous and
inseparable intellectual challenges face the contemporary women's movement: it has to show how gender can be reconstructed to solve the
problem of the place of motherhood in modern women's lives and it must
conceptualise a workable society based on women's values, as well as or
instead of men's. The closer women get to power, whether this is over
their own, individual lives or the direction of society as a whole, the more
urgent these challenges become.

The modern women's movement might seem well placed to meet them.
For one thing, it has the past to be its guide. Although most contemporary feminists (like those of every previous generation) were raised in
almost total ignorance of their predecessors, the sheer number of educated
women today, along with their spending power, professional skills and
access to libraries, research materials and diverse disciplines has helped
the movement find its roots comparatively fast. It is the size, autonomy
and international character of this new, educated female public which
account for the vitality and scope of the modern movement (a fact
accepted now even by socialist feminists);[1] they are also the foundation of
an unprecedented explosion in the production and communication of
feminist ideas. Truly, feminist perspectives amount to a revolution in our
culture (a fact which even men are now beginning to accept).

Contemporary women have another advantage. Like 'first-wave' feminism, the modern movement arose from separate women's groups, but this

time the crucial role of separate interaction has been recognised. Conscious-ness-raising theory is widely accepted, separatist strategies are accorded some credibility and most feminists (including those whose hopes are pinned on access to elites) would probably agree with social movement theorists and empirical researchers that an autonomous women's move-ment has an indispensable part to play in the political advance of women.[2] Today's feminists are unlikely to fall victim to either the personal isolation of a Kollontai or the deliberate depoliticisation tactics adopted by the Finns, or at least to do so quite so easily. To the extent that they decide to integrate with men, the existence of a separate women's movement will certainly oblige them to defend their choice. In these conditions, the politicisation and mobilisation of women can be expected to continue. There should be every reason, too, to hope they will confront the gender problem and unite the women's movement in resolving it.

Against this optimism, considerable caution is in order all the same. Much feminist energy, perforce, has been expended on what amounts to little more than recapitulation of the past, and where advances have been made the new positions are for excellent reasons insecure. Inhibited as always by their marginality, by renascent female anti-feminism and even by so-called 'post-feminist' complacency, women's commitment to their separate institutions is not dependable. The rise of radical feminism and the ensuing disputes over strategy, although intrinsic to the feminist revival, have proved deeply divisive too, and the lines of conflict are disquietingly reminiscent of the different faces of an earlier feminism. In fact, a general crisis in the women's movement has been perceived by feminists almost everywhere in recent years, accompanied by disillusion-ment at how little they have managed to achieve. Even more frustrating is the sense that feminism has lost its way, that not only its strategy, but its very nature and its goals are in dispute all over again.

Such fragmentation demands the question: is the real reason for this crisis in the women's movement yet another feminist failure to confront and solve the gender problem? If so, it is ironic that it coincides so exactly with the new set of anomalies in the gender pattern of recruitment, in which the levels of female representation in political elites are higher, and expectations of a feminist breakthrough correspondingly greater, than they have ever been before. The object of this chapter is to go beyond the surface of contemporary feminist debate to what should be the basis of a feminist attempt to change the world: women's theories about the formation of gender and their programmatic implications.

FEMINISM AND GENDER THEORY
The problem of biology

Feminist explanations for the origins and character of gender roles and their effect on socio-economic and political relations vary considerably in the weight they give to biological, cultural and psychological factors and have developed at a most uneven pace in different quarters of the women's movement. One reason is that a biological component has been particularly difficult for feminists to accept. This may seem odd, since but for reproductive difference we would not even have the categories of sex at all. However, our culture has invested reproductive roles with such a repressive superstructure of allegedly 'natural' differences between the sexes that women who set a value on equality are reluctant to consider any theory which takes reproductive difference as its starting-point, in case it leads – via 'biological determinism' – to resignation and despair.

Such inhibitions are also very strong for socialists, who have much to lose. Against Engels' comfortable view that the sexual division of labour is inherently unexploitative and that the workers' revolution would restore its 'natural' equality, the idea of a biological component in women's status is intensely pessimistic. Socialist women, who have also had the overt chauvinism of left-wing men to contend with, to say nothing of the repressive, theological tendencies of the socialist movement, have hesitated to explore it. In consequence, what Barrett calls the 'Marxist/Feminist Encounter' of the 1970s[3] found the new-styled socialist-feminists grappling all over again with exactly the same marginalisation of feminism within 'the left', the same male-centred scale of labour values, and the same view of reproduction as a social duty as bedevilled Kollontai. Even to admit that women's problem is independent of capitalism was painful, and the hypothesis (rejected now) that capitalism is a system uniquely well served by women's oppression, either as an industrial reserve army or, within the patriarchal family, as the ideal means of capitalist social reproduction, were last-ditch attempts to avoid this. Having finally, like Kollontai half a century before, accepted that women's status does after all have something to do with their sex, socialist-feminists like Hartmann and Eisenstein maintain that material or cultural relations among men are independent of the gender hierarchy, a thesis known as 'dual systems' theory. Rejecting the logical sequence that sex difference is at the root of gender, and the male gender role, in its turn, explains the nature and development of the systems in which men oppress each other as well as women, they postulate two independent causal models. In one, sex leads to gender and men's exploitation of women. In the other, systems created by men, but independently of gender roles and their exploitation of women, lead men to exploit each other.[4]

Ironically, 'dual systems' theory is a rather good metaphor for the way the contemporary relationship between feminism and socialism has developed. Whereas at the end of the 1970s an atmosphere of optimism prevailed in Britain ('After nearly a decade sexism . . . is now admitted to exist even within the left parties themselves)'[5] and tentative moves were being made to recover communitarian ideas and explore their feminist potential in order to 'pre-figure' a new non sexist society,[6] at the end of the 1980s socialist-feminists are 'increasingly dubious about the hyphen in their politics'.[7] This is not only because of anti-feminist resistance on the left; it also reflects a new humility about the contribution socialism, as presently understood, can make to feminism.

Although Rowbotham insists that among British socialist-feminists 'the question of mothering was a powerful influence in the emergence of the women's movement', this was largely in the negative sense of exposing the myths surrounding it (e.g. that all women want children and automatically love their babies), and women with children were seen mainly as rather boring childcare clients.[8] Socialisation of the traditional female role remained the distinctively socialist-feminist programme, but for Kollontai's full-blooded communalism, under which the family could be expected to 'wither away', socialist-feminists of the 1970s substituted a diluted version (usually in the form of 24-hour creche facilities). This was linked at first with a direct attack on the family, employing a neo-Marxist analysis of its patriarchal character, but latterly, in the awareness that this was undermining the legitimacy of the family without any clear idea of what to put in its place, this onslaught too has petered out in favour of freedom of choice, or 'pluralism'.[9] Even now, when so many socialist-feminists of the 1970s have succumbed to the biological clock and (allegedly) to the 'mystique of motherhood', a special issue of the *Feminist Review* on the past and future of the feminist movement devotes no more than 11 of its 153 pages to the issue of reproduction, in an article significantly entitled 'To Be or Not To Be; The Dilemmas of Mothering'.[10]

Although the ideological inhibitions facing socialist women were never a problem for radical feminists (the premise that sex, rather any other factor, is the fundamental source of women's oppression being the defining characteristic of radical feminism) they too have had their difficulties in facing up to reproduction as a central issue for the future. One reason for this is the relative youth of activists of all persuasions in the women's movement of the early 1970s. This did not prevent the emergence of innovative gender theory: Firestone's *The Dialectic of Sex* appeared as early as 1970. What it certainly tended to do was root this theory early in the female life-cycle, in fears about the trap of reproduction and negligence of its rewards, while simultaneously allowing many feminists, in the optimism of youth, to believe they could side-step the issue: motherhood was not for them. In New York, according to Ehrensaft, the anti-reproductive bias was at one time so strong in the radical movement that motherhood was regarded as 'politically incorrect' (a terminology redolent of these women's previous experience in the 'left') and women who had children kept as quiet about them as they could.[11] Of course, one of the reasons for this political 'line' was the radical feminist belief that all relations with men are exploitative of women, with reproductive, heterosexual sex as the core relation; 'political lesbianism' and the adoption of separatism as a way of life for women were to be the logical extensions of this premise.

The political limitations of such a position are obvious. What anti-motherhood feminists were trying to live was something very close to the gender role of men – freedom from the web of care – and at the identical cost we have seen in 'equal rights': the renunciation of their reproductive role. Like the careers of those few who were in a sufficiently favourable position to exploit their 'equal rights', this set feminists apart from the majority of women, whose behaviour was still incorrigibly 'incorrect' and whose belief in positive aspects of motherhood combined with their increasingly precarious dependence upon men (in the era of separation and divorce) to create that gulf of incomprehension and fear between 'women's lib' and part, at least, of its female constituency which Friedan has observed.[12] It also helped to account for the emergence of a pro-natalist reaction within the women's movement itself.

The anti-motherhood position was not without advantages for gender theory all the same, the nature of which, yet again, underscores its 'equal rights' connection. As young, unmarried, child free agents, radical feminists were peculiarly well placed to explore and defend the interests of women as sexual beings, with the same right to control their bodies, which is taken for granted by males but is so subversive to the patriarchal order when applied to women. Issues such as abortion, freedom of sexual choice, rape, wife-battering and the whole range of men's violence against women could be brought out into the open in a way that would have been more difficult for a movement dominated by more conventionally situated women. Under the stimulus of this new perspective, the sexist frontiers of academic and political thought could be swept away. The appalling catalogue of men's abuse of power over women could be opened up by Mary Daly; Susan Griffin and Andrea Dworkin could expose the violent, woman-hating core of pornography and its deep roots in western culture and Susan Moller Okin could begin that revelation of the misogyny at the heart of male political thought which Carole Pateman is continuing today.[13] What this openness achieved, among other things, was to impart a sense of dreadful urgency to women's search for explanations about gender and its relationship to culture; *why* do men think and do these things, how do they maintain their ill-used power and what, if anything, can women do about it?

There are few feminists now who would not agree that biology has something crucial to do with the answers. Few will deny that the reproductive functions of menses, pregnancy, childbirth and breast-feeding and the physical weaknesses and responsibilities that these entail, make women vulnerable to physical coercion. Most would agree, too, that some form of division of labour between themselves and others, at some points in most women's lives, is a practical necessity. The question for feminists is why women's vulnerability should be met with male aggression and coercion, and why women's occasions of dependence should be translated into a perpetual and oppressive hierarchy of men over women. Are these outcomes 'natural', as men have usually assumed and women been obliged to accept, and if so, natural for whom? Does the apparently universal fact of male power mean that there are two different human natures, male and female, which respond automatically, in programmed ways, to their different reproductive situation? Or are men the norm, with female 'nature' a distortion somehow rooted in biological misfortune? Alternatively, is it women who are 'human' and are the biological casualties really men, because of their peripheral reproductive role? Or are both sexes equally distorted by their failure to cope with reproductive difference, in which case gender is not 'natural' at all? Is it not possible, too, that what was once 'natural', in other circumstances, is now unnecessary or even dysfunctional?

It is the hallmark of feminist gender theory that it has tried to answer these questions, i.e. to make the vexed connection between our natures and the social, economic and political conditions in which we live. Its object, always, is to explore the possibilities of change, for if human relations as we know them are the product of our gender roles, then changing gender is the way to change societies. Thus feminist gender theory is never a purely academic excercise; it actually has in view a social-engineering project on the grandest scale. The fact that very little critical analysis of this body of theory has been attempted so far seems inexplicable except in terms of the same ambivalence among women about their reproductive role that has already been remarked. What follows is an attempt to remedy this lack, by explaining the reasoning behind the main suggestions that have emerged, exposing their intellectual origins and relationships and highlighting the degrees of compatibility and conflict among them, always with a view to throwing light on the implications of the choices women have to make whether in political elites, within the women's movement itself or in their personal lives.

The schools of thought involved are complex, inconsistent and yet overlapping, a problem which is drastically compounded when we review the diverse solutions they propose. In a simple world, there would be a straightforward correlation between one's explanation for the gender problem and the kind of solutions – pro- or anti-natalism, shared parenting or separate parental roles, the biological family or other reproductive settings and so on – that she proposes. One might also expect some systematic relationship between theories of gender and the way it is proposed to disentangle the functions of child-bearing, child-rearing and the other service functions like housework and household management which are associated with them in the traditional female role. To a surprising extent, this is not the case. Nor are the newer options (and very little of note has been added since the 1970s) necessarily the most revolutionary or influential. In purely quantitative terms, we can probably learn as much about the state of mind and social options of educated women today from Mary Wollstonecraft as from Shulamith Firestone or Adrienne Rich; in terms of creative theory, the decisive advances were made mainly by Margaret Mead. Of course, as always, it is invidious to focus on a few outstanding individuals at the expense of other women who have shared or contributed to their ideas. It must be emphasised, therefore, that what follows is not intended for a comprehensive anthology of feminist gender theory and its contributors. Instead, it is a review of the main lines of theoretical development and their practical implications, with the selected thinkers grouped according to a logic which is necessarily, given the overlapping complexities of the subject, somewhat idiosyncratic but is also believed to be the most illuminating possible.

Biology, destiny and emancipation: de Beauvoir, Wollstonecraft and Firestone

The fear of feminists, that the closer they get to a biological explanation of gender the more pessimistic their conclusions will have to be, is most fully justified by those theorists who postulate a single, androgynous human nature, of which women have been dispossessed, more or less directly by biology. Simone de Beauvoir is perhaps the most depressing example of this kind.

According to de Beauvoir, there is only one basic human nature, represented in the modern world by that of men. Women's values and behaviour – the 'feminine' – are a distortion of this nature, resulting from women's subjugation by nature, in the form of pregnancy, childbirth, etc., and by men. The effect of their socialisation to the female gender role, and confinement in it, is that men are capable of being fully human but women – until they are emancipated – are not. In her existentialist explanation of how this comes about,[14] de Beauvoir actually makes biology as much the 'how' as the 'why' of women's status as the second sex. The real first cause is the nature of existence, which leads human beings (irrespective of their sex) to see the world in terms of of 'self' and 'other'. This duality pervades all thought, producing the dichotomies of, for example, culture and nature and male and female gender. The reason these dichotomies are hierarchical is human nature, which unlike that of other animals, responds actively to the conditions of existence; instead of submitting to nature, it struggles for control. The reason why men control women rather than the other way round, and why human culture is male-centred (so that man is the Self and woman the Other) is biology. Women's reproductive role makes losers of them in the struggle for centrality and it is men who cast them in the role of Other; thus, in the often quoted phrase, 'one is not born, but rather becomes, a woman'.

For de Beauvoir, therefore, the *real* world is the world of men ('this male world, which is, quite simply the world itself to a large degree')[15] and woman's problem is exclusion from it. Even after ten years in the women's movement, when she had learned to recognise such shortcomings in that world as men's pomposity, addiction to status and so on from a feminist perspective, de Beauvoir remained convinced that women had nothing to add. 'I believe that liberated women will be just as creative as men. But I do not think women will create new values. If you believe the opposite, then what you are believing in is a feminine nature – which I have always opposed.'[16]

Depressing as this view of women is, there is worse to come. The only solution for women is emancipation from the female role and the rediscovery of their real humanity. As in the basic programme of 'equal rights', they must become educated, economically independent and fully participant in the world of men. The trouble is, of course, that this conflicts with their reproductive role; how is emancipation to be reconciled with motherhood.? De Beauvoir's answer is quite simple: it cannot. Since motherhood is nothing but 'the most skilful way there is of turning women into slaves' (and she does not consider the separation of the reproductive from the other service functions of that role as a practical possibility) it is almost invariably incompatible with self-fulfilment. However, contraception, abortion and divorce give women a wider range of practical alternatives to having children; reproduction has become a matter of choice. Nor is the choice intolerable; motherhood is sufficiently peripheral to women's being that they can reject it without a serious denial of self. De Beauvoir's advice to women is, quite simply, *not to have children* and be men instead.

This might seem to pose a problem for the survival of the human race. However, de Beauvoir does not really expect that many women will follow her advice; the weaker sisters will always give in to motherhood. To the comment that before the women's movement existed, she used to say 'they' when she spoke of women , but now said 'we', de Beauvoir's immediate retort was as follows: ' "We" meaning "we feminists", not "we women".' The assumption apparently is that feminists are 'men-women' and that 'women-women' cannot be feminists – a polarisation in which, it may be observed, there is no place for feminist women. We cannot be surprised to find de Beauvoir extremely hostile to the idea of a women's party, which would restrict her to 'the ghetto of the women's problem'.[17] Apart from paternalist measures to ameliorate their situation, there is really nothing 'feminists' can do for women other than themselves; although de Beauvoir is supremely aware of the part that social experience and men's social interest play in forming men's and women's different family roles, she is resigned to the results.

If de Beauvoir represents the defeatist face of 'equal rights', radical feminism inherits its more positive, woman-oriented side. Mary Wollstonecraft, who is often credited with being the original, archetypal 'equal rights' feminist, exemplifies both the link between the two and the roots of their divergence.

The cultural context of 1790 favoured the language of reason and morality, rather than psychology or existentialism. Nevertheless, (although Wollstonecraft makes the relative roles of human nature and biology in the process less explicit), the central theme of the *Vindication of the Rights of Woman*[18] is the same as that of *The Second Sex*, that women are not born, but made, and male culture is the norm. God created men and women in his image, with the same innate capacities for self-improvement. Since the autonomous exercise of reason was the only path to virtue, and women's lack of education and responsibility for themselves did not permit them this, what women were being denied by their confinement to the female role was the right to a moral existence. What is more, (a point more fully developed in her novel, *The Wrongs of Woman*) women's economic dependence upon men positively fostered duplicity and vice.

The logical solution, that women recover the full range of their natural capacities through emancipation, is the same as de Beauvoir's. However, their views on the future of women's reproductive role could hardly be more different. Where de Beauvoir sees emancipation and motherhood as incompatible, Wollstonecraft takes it for granted that women, emancipated or not, will usually have children. Nor can this be attributed simply to the fact that Wollstonecraft lived before the age of contraceptives, for the option of remaining unmarried and childless was not unknown to her; earlier feminists, like Mary Astell, chose to live this way and so did Wollstonecraft herself in her twenties.[19] Her demands for women's economic independence would also have the result of greatly extending their options. Abortion was readily available, too, as Wollstonecraft revealed, and at a time when death in childbirth was commonplace, was hardly more dangerous than child-bearing itself.[20] Nor can her support of motherhood be attributed to comfortable, middle-class ignorance of its burdens. Wollstonecraft (herself a willing and delighted mother) took motherhood very seriously indeed, as entailing morally imperative, time-consuming obligations, such as breast-feeding one's own young and attending to their education; one of her principal objections to the ignorance and frivolity imposed on middle-class women by their unequal status was that it engendered neglect of these responsibilities.[21] She was very well aware, too, of her own good fortune in having domestic help and the contrasting terms on which most women lived; the common notion of Wollstonecraft as a complacent, middle-class intellectual who saw women through the eyes of a male-centred culture is so ludicrously wide of the mark that it can only be attributed to imperfect acquaintance with her work. No, the real reason why Wollstonecraft's expectations about motherhood are so different from de Beauvoir's is that she sees reproduction (in the sense of bearing and nurturing children) as one of those innate capacities which women will exercise as moral beings; in her own words, 'one of the grand ends of their being'.[22]

As a careful reading of the *Vindication* suggests, and *The Wrongs of Woman* shows beyond any shadow of doubt, Wollstonecraft looked at life in all its rawness through the eyes of ordinary women of her time and what she saw bears a remarkable resemblance to society today, as seen through feminist eyes. Looking around her, she saw women, many of them single-parents, forced to live in poverty or resort to prostitution because they were excluded from decent, well-paid work; women forced to have sex with their employers on pain of losing their servile, low-paid jobs, and then to have abortions at the men's convenience; women driven to social outlawry and even suicide by the double sexual standard; women without rights in their own bodies or (the principal point of difference from today) in their children; and women abused mentally, phsyically and sexually in the unequal state of marriage. She saw women divided, too, by their dependence on men, so that they acted as men's accomplices in the degradation of their sex and hence themselves.[23] The answer for women was not to stop having children, which she did not contemplate, but to escape *with* their children from ignorance, dependence and subordination; and not to identify with men but (like Maria and Jemima in *The Wrongs of Woman*) to overcome the barriers to consciousness among themselves and act in concert against their oppressors.[24]

Of course, Wollstonecraft did not live to explore the contradictions between her radical, feminist consciousne, the male-centredness of the rights she wanted women to enjoy and the maternal and domestic functions of women's gender role, although some of them had already surfaced in her own life. Like many a modern Cinderella, she cherished the idyll of the stable, caring two-parent family as the proper setting for child-rearing, and yet was herself a single parent, with a great distrust of marriage; conversely, although she fought for women's economic independence and was a breadwinner all her life, she automatically assumed the role of housekeeper when she eventually married. Her sternly civic

203

notion of the family (designed to give the private sphere a public content and status) contrasts sharply, too, with the dominance of feelings in her own life.[25]

In fact, the mixture of social realism and feminism in Wollstonecraft's life and works implies a plenitude of options, all of which are available to women today: to have children or not, to live with other women, or with men or alone, to bring up children on their own or with a father, to be independent, dependent, or something in between. What it does not signify, when gender roles are unequal and society ordered around that of men, is real equality between the sexes. In practical, political terms, it points to the familiar bind of simultaneously pursuing emancipation *and* protecting women in traditional roles. The only missing piece of the modern puzzle is welfare feminism; in Wollstonecraft's time, conceptions of the role of the state had not developed to the point where dependence on the state (with all its analogous problems) could be considered an alternative to dependence on men.

What Shulamith Firestone has in common with Wollstonecraft and de Beauvoir is her belief in a common human nature, distorted by biological difference. However, while Wollstonecraft was ambivalent about the gender roles of her time and indeterminate in her conclusions, there is no ambivalence in Firestone. *The Dialectic of Sex* is an uncompromising assertion of biological determinism, according to which the universal characteristic of male–female relations, the 'biological' family and economic class relations among men – their inequality – is the inevitable result of reproductive difference: 'men and women were created different, and not equal'.[26] The only answer is *to give up natural reproduction altogether.*

In spite of the unpopularity of this conclusion, the *Dialectic* and its author (a prime mover of the New York Radical Women, and hence of the modern women's movement itself), have had an enormous impact on modern feminism, and beyond it, on mass perceptions too; to re-read it now is rather like reliving an intellectual revolution which is taken for granted nowadays. This is not because her main conclusion has been widely accepted, for it has not. Nor is the book an even work; though in places trenchant and even brilliant, it is also clumsy and naive. It is woman-centred and iconoclastic as few feminist works dealing with male authorities like Marx and Freud had been before, and yet the argument gets indigestion from swallowing some ideas of these authors whole. It is the sort of book where a whole theory is encapsulated in a footnote,[27] and yet the central thesis, to be examined here, does not stand up. Nevertheless, *The Dialectic of Sex* was a pivotal moment in women's liberation.

Like Wollstonecraft and de Beauvoir, Firestone starts with the premise of a single, androgynous human nature, of which women have been dispossessed by men and biology; it is their different reproductive roles, not their natural propensities, which differentiate the sexes. However, she sees no need for de Beauvoir's concept of 'Hegelian otherness' to account for the duality which runs through everything; the duality of sex is an obvious and sufficient explanation in itself. Transcending Marx, she argues that the real driving force of history is the dialectic of sex, i.e. 'the division of society into two distinct biological classes for procreative reproduction'. The struggle of these sex classes for power over the means of reproduction produces 'modes of marriage, reproduction and childcare' by which men control and exploit women, the 'paradigm of caste' (i.e. discrimination based on biological difference), and the sexual division of labour as the basis of the economic-cultural class system, whereby men control and exploit each other too. Thus men's power over men is derived from their original and underlying power over women, while the fundamental characteristic of men-women relations – that they are relations of power – is the result of biological difference.

Of course, the crux of such a thesis must be how it reasons from *different* to *not equal*, the issue fudged by male political philosophers when they describe women's status as 'natural'.[28] As Firestone is quick to point out, following de Beauvoir, difference of itself cannot necessitate the domination of one group by another. Her answer is that it is not the difference itself, but 'the reproductive functions' of the difference which supply the missing link. These functions lead, inevitably, to some or other form of the biological family, 'an inherently unequal power distribution', of which the formative factors are

1 women's dependence on males (that it should be on males is considered axiomatic) 'for physical survival';
2 the long infancy of human young;
3 a universal, basic 'mother/child interdependency'; and
4 'a sexual division of labour based on natural reproductive difference'.

However (even if we accept the dubious proposition that women must necessarily be dependent on men and follow the author's example in ignoring the fact that men depend on women too), the argument cannot really rest here either. Their biological functions may prevent women from defending themselves against a male 'struggle' for power; what they do not explain is why there should be such a contest in the first place; why should dependence necessarily lead to *inequality*?

If Firestone could accept the idea of innate aggression, at least in men, this particular problem would be solved, but there are two reasons why she cannot. One is the premise of her argument, which is that reproductive functions, not human nature, are the root of inequality. The other is her intended conclusion, for Firestone means to show that by abandoning natural reproduction, humans can escape from inequality altogether and enter a new kind of liberated existence. If she accepts innate aggression as the reason for men's drive for power, then human nature, not sex is the source of inequality. What is worse, if the human race (or the male part of it) is innately aggressive, then inequality can never disappear either; instead of a glorious new life after the sexual revolution, it will be a case of *plus ça change*. In an attempt to bridge the gap between dependence and inequality while simultaneously laying the foundation of her new society, Firestone turns to Freud.

The crux of the matter, she avers, is the biological family and her argument follows somewhat Freudian lines. Because of its need for incest taboos, the biological family requires that infant sexuality be repressed in order to produce the 'normal' individual, i.e. the *ego* must come to dominate the *id*. The effect is different for the sexes. Both start by identifying with the mother (in Freud, desiring her) but then shift towards the powerful father; in so doing, they begin to repress their original identification and sense of themselves (Firestone's version of the *id*). This re-identification process, eventually complete in the case of the 'normal' boy, is a *cul de sac* for the girl; her destiny is to be a woman like her mother. She does not need to repress herself after all, because it is her *ego* which seeks the unattainable (to be like her father) and is weak and permeable as a result. Boys, however, have to repress their original selves almost completely, thus painfully acquiring the famous 'rigidly bounded *ego*' and the negative aspects of 'masculine' behaviour as we know it: the tendency to repress feelings, to be aggressive and domineering – in short, the psychology of power.

From the perspective of Firestone's biological determinism, there are actually two major problems with this approach. The first is that it assumes the 'inherently unequal power distribution' of the biological family as the *precondition* for repression. Freud, of course, took the family of his time as given and located his theory inside it and Firestone needs this framework too, in order to explain why boys are willing to go through with such a painful process of repression; it is the price of entry to the world outside the home, which is controlled by and reserved for 'normal' men. The trouble is, this traps her in a circular argument: each generation of males seeks power because males have power already. Why this power started (what she purports to explain) is still a mystery.

The other problem arises because, as Firestone really knows perfectly well, the biological family is not a constant. Although she insists that no amount of anthropological evidence (not all the tribes of Oceania!) can alter the fact of its ineluctable, universal inequality, she admits that different family and kinship structures actually vary greatly in both their need for sexual repression and the extent of male power.[29] What she does not admit is the logical conclusion, that if the biological family varies, and inequality with it, then it is not so much biology, as a cultural response to it which causes male behaviour and the gender hierarchy.

Firestone, however, is satisfied that Freud has supplied the link between biology and her optimistic vision of the future (for like every good dialectic, that of sex contains the seeds of its own destruction). Both 'masculine' and 'feminine' are distortions of our nature, reflected in two different 'modes' in male-centred culture, the male 'technological', the female 'aesthetic'. Now the male, 'technological' mode has changed the basis of reproduction. It is not just that contraceptives have brought reproduction within the sphere of human will (female as well as male). Reproductive technology has advanced to the point, or nearly there, where the human race can reproduce by artifical means, and although men may not want to give up control of women's child-bearing, which is the basis of their tyranny, a women's revolution can oblige them to. What women must do is seize the means of reproduction (their own bodies, the 'new biology' and child-bearing and rearing institutions) and *stop having babies themselves altogether*. The biological family will wither away as a result and with it not just male privilege, but the whole point of the distinction of sex. Gender will disappear as a result. There will be no further need for psychological repression and the dichotomy of male and female cultural modes; instead, there will be 'an adrogynous culture surpassing the highs of either cultural stream, or the sum of their integration . . . – a matter-antimatter explosion, ending with a poof! culture itself.'[30]

There are obvious parallels with Fourier and Kollontai in this conclusion, as in the libertarian communalist upbringing which Firestone favours for the clones and test-tube babies of the future; she anticipates the same programme of total, communal childcare, the same desegregation of child-rearing roles and the same disappearance of the distinction between family and community as these earlier sexual radicals. Unlike Fourier, however, Firestone thinks that to eliminate repression is to eliminate aggression altogether and, unlike any of her predecessors, she also believes that artificial reproduction is the only way to achieve this. Since these are exactly the points her argument has failed to make, the reader is inevitably left wondering if such doubtful reasoning can really justify such drastic measures. They are measures which are most unlikely to appeal to women who do not share the author's wholly negative views (formed at second-hand) about motherhood or who feel that life is held cheaply enough already without making it any easier to create and Firestone does not explain what basis there would be, in such a society as she envisages, for the values which we presently invest in motherhood and family life. Is there no other, less costly way of reconstructing the psychological development of men? And if men and women became more alike, *what* would they be like?

It is for such reasons, perhaps, that Firestone's reproductive plan has not aroused support. On the contrary, her devaluation of motherhood helped trigger a pro-motherhood reaction, while subsequent feminists (perhaps misguidedly) have paid but scant attention to the new biology. Where Firestone's influence has been much greater, and overlapped with the quite contrary concern of other feminists to support conventional motherhood, is through her emphasis on power, both as a product of male psychological formation and as intrinsic to her theory of the dialectic and women's struggle for control of reproduction.

The political implication of this theory is very clear; power must be met with power. From this perspective, feminism is a revolutionary movement and its aim is the seizure of reproductive power, that very specific, basic power which was originally seized by men. In practice (and in spite of reservations about the very notion of power as an acceptable feminist goal), the recovery of this specific power has become one of the most coherent and identifiable of the women's movement's programmatic goals. Articulated in terms of women's right to control their own bodies, it has engendered worldwide struggles against the the power of the male medical establishment, which alienates women from their reproductive functions and brings them under minute male control, against rape and other forms of violence against women in and out of marriage, against pornography and so on. It has also reinforced the centrality of abortion to feminism and the claim of women to have freedom of sexual choice *and* to have children. The relationship of this particular power to other areas of power, such as the state or economic class, is not so clear, however, and neither is the form that women's 'power' might take. This is what Firestone glosses over with her theory of sexual liberation (and the equally confident assertion that cybernetics will solve the problems of production); for those who do not share her confidence, the dialectic of sex leaves large grey areas where women's strategy and goals are concerned. However, the realisation that there *is* a relationship between all aspects of power, and specifically between men's power over women's bodies and their power over each other, has become a core area of feminist thought.

As to what women should do with reproductive power once they have got it, this remains a separate issue. Firestone had sought the answer in Freud and here, as elsewhere, the *Dialectic* was prophetic; neo-Freudian theories of individual psychology have been a preoccupation of feminist gender theory ever since. It is Margaret Mead, however, rather than Firestone who has been their guide and inspiration, conventional reproduction has been the framework for their arguments and the relativity of culture, so uncompromisingly discounted by Firestone, has been the main source of their optimism.

Culture, sex-roles and psychology: the crucial contribution of Margaret Mead

Although, as Firestone once observed, Freud and feminism are about the same thing seen from different points of view, it was not a psychoanalytical theorist but the anthropologist, Margaret Mead, who set the scene, supplied the material and in *Male and Female* virtually wrote the agenda for the modern feminist debate on gender.[31] This is not to say that Mead was precisely a feminist (she carefully disassociated herself from the feminist movement of her day), but in a sense she did not need to be. A highly successful, professional career woman, her intellectual stature, her long absences abroad and the great interest of the educated public in her books made her to some extent independent of the female role in her own society. Absorbed in the work of comprehending other cultures in their immense variety, she was able to develop an interest in gender which was detached as well as intense; her work is full of what would be described as 'feminist' insights today. Indeed, it was the realisation that her own society had entered a period of great unease about existing sex-roles that motivated her to write *Male and Female* and inspired much of her earlier work. Although the lack of a political dimension to her otherwise immense social science repertoire limited its frame of reference (and her unfortunate readiness to pontificate and extemporise in the mass media has created some confusion about her ideas), her serious work shed a revolutionary light on the significance of sex difference in shaping culture and the gender options that cultures afford.

Mead's contribution is not always freely acknowledged today, all the same, for her academic reputation has been savagely attacked since her death.[32] It is interesting to find, too, how ready some women are to participate in its destruction.[33] In the present context, the issue is her theory of gender and the possibilities it suggests, so that the rights and wrongs of the continuing controversy about her fieldwork are irrelevant. What matters here is that the mature Mead was an outstanding comparative culturalist who had, as she said, spent her professional lifetime thinking about the issues raised in *Male and Female*. In fact, Mead had one of the outstanding intellects of modern times and now looks remarkably like a classic illustration, happening before our very eyes, of how great women's works get written out of history.

In terms of Mead's own theoretical perspective, this would be only too predictable. By achieving anything at all, she had broken the cardinal rule of gender in her society, where maleness was not an absolute quality but something men must earn and re-earn by achievement every day, with achieving more than women an essential element in the definition. By achieving so much, and in the field of intellectual endeavour too, which men in western culture have so unwisely adopted as a major proving-

209

ground of masculinity, she had beaten men in the very competition which they had most reason to fear they could not win and where they had most to lose. The fears and insecurities which plagued American men were not unusual, however, except perhaps in degree. As Mead saw it, the problem of male insecurity is *the* problem of civilisation.

At the core of Mead's analysis are a set of observations which have been the basis of almost all consideration of gender ever since (and will be familiar to the reader as the premise on which the argument in Part 1 was based). The first is that sex-role differentiation is absolutely universal; all cultures, in every known society, have reflected and elaborated on this inescapable fact of everyone's existence, that men and women are biologically different. Gender is never a simple statement of reproductive difference, however: people always build their own elaborate cultural patterns around this difference, so that human beings are never seen simply as individuals, whose store and mix of non-reproductive human attributes vary on an individual basis, but as beings who are sexed, and differ accordingly in a patterned way. Yet a comparison of cultures shows that this patterning is almost entirely arbitrary; attributes assigned to one sex in one culture are assigned to the other elsewhere and the range of activities considered proper to men or to women is variable to the point of absurdity. This makes another observation – that the attributes assigned to men are always held in more esteem – seem all the more surprising.

The explanation lies in the fact that gender roles, in spite of all their variation, are actually always constructed in the same basic way; while the kernel of the female role is the unquestionably female reproductive functions of child-bearing and lactation, the male role, from which these functions must perforce be absent, is always defined in terms of difference from the female. Furthermore – and this is the core of Mead's theory of gender – the male role is invariably constructed in such a way as *to compensate men for the fact that they are not women*. The way this is done is by valuing what men do, not for what it is (it may be dressing dolls or hunting hummingbirds), but simply because it is men who do it. In many cases (but not all), men's security is underwritten by excluding women from whatever activities or feats are identified as male, evidently to ensure that all men can achieve more prestige than can be accorded to any woman.

Thus the existence of the gender roles and their hierarchical relationship are inseparably inter-related and biology is their common root. The specific cause is the universal fact that although everyone, whether male or female, starts life being mothered, only females are mothers; the result is a fundamental difference in the psychological formation of boys and girls.[34] For infants of both sexes, the mother is necessarily the child's first object and motherhood is the first adult role that either recognises, but where the girl's original identification with her mother (and that of the mother with her female baby) is a simple, uncomplicated and enduring base for her reproductive role in adult life, the boy must learn to differentiate himself, or 'never be at all'. As if this inescapable fracturing of his psyche were not enough, it has two further threatening dimensions. Firstly, there is the elusive, negative character of masculinity; if to be a man is simply to be different from a woman, then this is an identity so nebulous that he will have to prove it over and over again throughout his life. On top of this, there is the shock of discovering that he will never be a mother. The discovery of maleness is thus at one and the same time a loss of identity and the loss of potential for that 'solid sense of irreversible achievement, of which his childhood knowledge of the satisfactions of childbearing has given him a glimpse.'[35] The result is that while the little girl learns that she has only to wait for this dramatic and fulfilling role to be hers, the little boy must find alternatives.

Thus it is men, not women, who need gender, and it is not their nature but women's mothering which is at the root of their need. The extra-ordinary cross-cultural inconsistency to be found in ideas of what is possible or appropriate for one sex or the other suggested a prudent scepticism to Mead about innate differences between the sexes. Apart from greater female manual dexterity and male musculatory potential, the possibility of differential skin sensitivity, and differences in body rhythms and endocrine levels of very dubious significance (because cultures can so easily defy them), lack of evidence to the contrary suggested similar capacities of body and mind (although Mead reserved judgment on the possibility that men might be innately more achieve-ment-oriented). The result is that the female sex-role can be more or less punitive for women to inhabit, according to how much and what in life is reserved for males at their expense and how uneven the rewards; cultural patterns can be 'womb-envying' (as in primitive societies where male initiation cults are jealous mimicries of women's reproductive powers), 'lopsided' (as Mead tactfully characterised America) or more 'even-handed'. We may be unable to discover why a culture has developed in one direction rather than another, but once a culture has taken shape, it becomes, as we shall see, a force in the deepest levels of our experience and psychic formation which will make us bring ourselves, much less each other, into line.

Since Mead's is an essentially psychological account of gender, which takes reproductive difference as its starting-point, it is to that extent determinist; men will never be entirely secure.[36] Her stress on the role of early childhood experience in gendered psychological formation is also Freudian up to a point, but selectively so; like almost every woman who has come to grips with Freudian theory, she centres her story of psychological formation on identification more than libidinous sexual drives. This helps to explain why Mead is also *not* a biological

211

determinist, for the formation of identity is necessarily mediated at every stage by actual experience, which is relative. For Freud, the only actor in the drama of maturation was the instinct-driven child himself; for Mead, 'in the whole of human experience this never happens. No boy is asked to interpret his maleness except in relation to other human beings of both sexes; no small girl ever sits attentive only to the rhythm of her own heart'.[37] The great differences to be found in the most basic child-rearing practices (from the Mundugumor women who held their infants at arms' length and the Iatmul who let them scream before they would be fed, to the relaxed communion with their mothers' bodies and permissive feeding experienced by the babies of Samoa) and in the circumstances of childbirth itself had taught her that even earliest infancy is a culturally variable experience. Likewise with sexual behaviour and the gender expectations societies provide as signals to the child; whether, for example, the Oedipus *situation* becomes an Oedipus *problem*, and even when it occurs, depends on family structure, parental input and cultural norms.[38] (In fact, Mead saw it largely as a local, cultural problem of the Occidental nuclear family, where the mother–child relationship is so much more exclusive and intense than in primitive societies.)

Mead's account is balanced, too, by the role of later life experience in psychological formation. This not only gave her insight into gender socialisation in later childhood and adolescence and the problems of rapidly changing societies (where people have to invent their own cultures, like the American 'dream', as they go along),[39] but let her draw on women's adult life experience as well as men's. Like Adrienne Rich and the French feminists, Kristeva and Iragaray, she pointed to our different bodily experiences as a fruitful source of systematic variation in our outlooks.[40] In contrast to the lifelong drama of the female life-cycle, with its abrupt transitions and remarkable physical transformations, there is little men can learn from the development of their bodies; women go on learning all their lives. This particular difference is crucial to Mead's theories of mothering, paternity and the origins of the family.

Mead had no doubt whatsoever that parental roles are based on learning, not instinct, but the way they are learned by women as compared to men, and what is usually meant by 'motherhood' and 'fatherhood', are very different. The fact that women bear and nourish children does not mean they have a compelling drive to do so, or know instinctively how to deal with the events of childbirth and rearing when they occur; Mead found no evidence to support the idea of 'maternal instinct' in either of these senses.[41] However, women can and do learn to *mother* – i.e. to nurture – without being taught; they learn from the profound and prolonged experience of pregnancy and lactation and from the behaviour of the child. Thus although the social setting of motherhood, the child-rearing practices involved and the way that motherhood is valued in a particular society are all cultural matters, mothering itself, in the sense of personal nurturing and responsibility, is deeply rooted in personal experience.

There is nothing comparable in the experience of men. Not only is the male reproductive role limited to a single activity at a single point in time but its long-drawn reproductive consequences are things that happen *to, and inside someone else*. A man may not even know that he has had a child, whereas the same could never be said of a woman. Since fatherhood is something that men cannot learn from their bodies, it must be taught by cultural transmission, and unlike motherhood, paternity is entirely a social institution.[42] Men may experience surges of protective feeling towards a woman and her young (who form the basic nurturing unit) but for these random drives to be turned to good account, the family (in the broadest sense) had to be invented. The role of the family is twofold; to regulate the conditions in which men have sexual relations with women and thus prevent constant competition among males for access to females (an assumption in which Mead follows Freud), and to provide a framework for men to nurture women and their young, which otherwise they would not do. Which men nurture which women and which children is entirely a matter of cultural preference; some kinship systems, for example, are built around nurturing obligations to sisters rather than wives, and the relationship can be as remote as when the modern welfare state acts as intermediary between the men (and better-paid women) and the mothers and children. In the latter case, however, it is becoming dangerously tenuous. The family is the prerequisite for constructive male behaviour, and hence for society itself; it has proved so valuable to men that once discovered it has never been abandoned. It has tottered more than once, however, usually in large, powerful societies like ours, and could conceivably be 'lost'.[43]

Clearly, Mead could not be sanguine about any sex-role change which eliminated the family altogether. The desirability of some kind of stable structure in which both sexes partake followed logically, too, from the need of the child of either sex for a same-sex role-model and for opportunities to adapt to the existence of the other sex. However, Mead's ideas of what might constitute a family were flexible. Almost every criticism that can be levelled at the nuclear family, with its rigidity of roles, segregation of generations, claustrophobic childrearing atmosphere and penalties for women was raised by Mead, and the door left open for looser, more extended structures, in which biological ties would not be so important. None the less, her most revolutionary option, addressed to the traditional division of parental labour between the sexes,[44] clearly fits into the nuclear family framework.

As Mead saw it, if women's exclusive role in mothering is the independent variable behind the problem of male attitudes to women, then the logical way to change these attitudes is by changing mothering. Specifically, if women's mothering monopoly (which includes a 'carry-over' effect from lactation into child care as a whole) could be broken by involving men, the effect would be to present the child with the model of a sexually undifferentiated parenthood with which both sexes could identify throughout their lives. Shared parenting would thus take the pain out of reproductive difference for the boy *and* obviate the need to differentiate himself in order to mature. Growing up in a setting where children's needs were met by men as well as women, boys would feel they had an essential, nurturing part to play in reproduction too. As a result, they would feel less envious and insecure, less defensive against women and more prepared to look at individuals on their merits. Of course, in the process of emulating their fathers in childhood, and caring for their own children in adult life, males as well as females would learn how to nurture, which would have a separate, reinforcing effect on their psychology. Men would become more like women in their values and behaviour, seeking rewards in care for others rather than in personal achievement. Although the latter prospect did not altogether appeal to Mead (who feared to lose the positive side of men's achievement-orientation), she saw every reason to consider shared parenting as a serious alternative to women-only motherhood. Since modern technology enables women to control their fertility and substitute lactation with other forms of infant nourishment, it is becoming ever more reasonable to propose that the roles of father and mother in primary childcare should converge. Mead thought a primitive prototype existed in the Arapesh, a small New Guinean society where men were almost as actively involved in child-rearing as women and (although the gender hierarchy had not altogether disappeared), men's drive for differentiation was correspondingly reduced.

Of course with this proposition, Mead was turning Freud on his head in respect of man and woman, in rather the same way that Marx felt Feurbach had done for Hegel in respect of God and man. To Freud, the experience of the male child was the norm and the results of his painful differentiation both inevitable and admirable. The psyche of the female was unintelligible to him (as he was to become uncomfortably aware in the end) and it was only women's inability to play the cipher part assigned to them by men which he understood, and condemned. To Mead, what she called the 'sureness' of woman's identity was just as striking, in its continuity and wholeness, as the restless search of men for proof of who and what they are, and it was this ability to escape male-centredness (plus, of course, her greater knowledge of the world than Freud's) which made shared parenting, with its implication that women are the norm, not men, conceivable to her.

However, shared parenting was not the only option Mead observed to reduce the gender distance between the sexes; devaluation of motherhood could have the same effect. Where shared parenting de-emphasised the mother–infant bond by embedding it in a wider spectrum of parental nurturance, denigration could reduce it in another way, producing a society where neither sex was nurturant. In such a case, levels of assertiveness and aggression might well be high in both sexes, but envious behaviour on the part of men towards women would be reduced; women would be allowed much the same opportunities as men. Furthermore, if children need parents, it does not necessarily follow that adults need children. Although Mead asserted that the idea of men and women living separate lives was fundamentally flawed and a 'denial of life itself',[45] she did not find any evidence to support the contention that women need to be mothers. The lack of an oestrus cycle in the human female, and her consequently continuous sexual receptivity, certainly mean that women are likely to have children, while the reproductive basis of their mothering means that once started on the child bearing process it will be difficult not to learn to nurture too (though not impossible, as shown when social pressures drive unmarried mothers to infanticide). However, women can learn not to want children much more easily than not to care for the ones they get, and much of the wanting of children (which renders the childless emotionally deprived in societies like ours) she thought was learned as well. In cultures where motherhood is devalued, she observed that women can and do decide not to have children at all, apparently without experiencing deep conflict in their natures.[46] This may occur because society is making life so unpleasant for mothers (the example of Finland comes to mind) or for other reasons; small societies, faced with the extinction of their culture at the hands of ours have been known to give up reproduction, apparently by choice of both sexes, and die out altogether.[47] Furthermore, in pro-motherhood societies less fixated on the biological tie than ours, women who do not have biological children of their own appear to solve the problem quite painlessly by sharing in the general mothering. The reader who has reacted derisively to Firestone may care to think again.

Mead also suggested that a de-emphasis on motherhood could come about as the corollary of a positive stress on the sexual act in itself, so that people are seen primarily as sexual objects rather than as reproducers or achievers. This effect could be reinforced by non-familial social patterns. Specifically, she observed an association between the socially structured relation of the sexes in the period of so-called sexual 'latency' in boys (from about aged five till puberty) and later male behaviour.[48] In societies where the sexes were segregated during latency, adult men appeared to feel less threatened by women, displayed less envious aggression and found it comparatively easy to admit women to their pursuits. She attributed this to the interaction of two factors.[49] Latency is the period when the boy, having discovered his sex, is trying to establish his masculinity among his male peers by competing to achieve something which females allegedly cannot do. If the sexes are not segregated at this point, and worse still if they compete in the same pursuits, the boy is faced with an inexorable, threatening consequence of the different male and female life-cycles; this is the very period when girls mature much faster than boys. Aggression, destructiveness and jeering are his only defence against the appalling discovery that females are actually better at almost everything than he. Even in size and strength, which are pretty well universally taken to be greater in men, he cannot compete. Since latency coincides with the early years of formal education in modern societies, it is not surprising that Mead attributed the aggressive treatment of their women colleagues by professional American men to their humiliating experience of early co-education, exacerbated in her view by the fact that the teachers and ethos in primary education are usually female too. Segregation, the recruitment of male primary teachers or some other compensatory adaptation of the education system, was urgently required to obviate this for women's sake. In fact, this was the most unequivocal advice on women's behalf that Mead ever gave.

Given that men were posited as the gender problem, it was logical enough to concentrate on trying to modify their psychology, but this does not mean that Mead's view of women was unambiguously positive. On the one hand, women are whole and sure and can, if given the chance, behave as assertively as men. On the other hand, women are too ready to settle for the joys of motherhood and regrettably lack the 'divine discontent' which characterises men. Clearly, Mead wished women in general were more like herself and was uncharacteristically unsure why they were not. Perhaps, she rather lamely (if presciently) suggested, education would make all the difference. It is impossible, however, to read Mead's comments on women today without becoming aware of the absence of a crucial factor which might have tempered her account of female psychology. It is the passing references to what men will and will not allow, the occasional startling mention of rape used as a punitive weapon against women and of the origin of the family in male aggression, and the jesting language of wife-beating used by Mead's subjects when she lets them speak for themselves, which supply the clue. The missing dimension is the political, the elusive concept is power and the unexamined area of experience is violence. Mead is taking it for granted that men have *power* over women.[50]

The main reason for Mead's failure to examine this assumption clearly is her phrasing of the male gender identity in terms of achievement rather than aggression or dominance, as in later feminist accounts. This evades the issue of the real asymmetry of power (ironically, almost the only open reference to power Mead makes is to insist that women are not entirely *powerless* within their limited sphere) and thus she never asks what costs there are for women who aspire in a world circumscribed by the power of envious men. Of course, this reflects the limited political vocabulary of her time. The anthropological revolution consisted in showing by means of cross-cultural evidence that what was previously taken to be natural and inevitable was not inevitable at all; the revolutionary conclusion that 'the personal is political' had to wait for Firestone and her feminist generation.

Instead, Mead recognised the facts of power implicitly by basing her argument for change on an appeal to men's self-interest. It is not only women, she points out, who may be penalised by sex-role differentiation. It is a common factor of all sex-roles, male as well as female, that they consist mainly of limitations; they do not tell people what they can do so much as what they must not do. In the process, stereotypes are constructed which are the source of endless frustration and inferiority for the countless men and women who do not fit the norm.[51] Just as societies can organise their work and play in ways which suit the bodily rhythms and life-cycle of one sex better than the other, or of both sexes equally, or of neither, so with the organisation of their personalities. Some societies are easier for women, or men, or neither, or both to live in than others; at the same time, where one sex loses, so does humanity as a whole. If only difference could be celebrated, instead of used against us, everyone would benefit; specifically, men would actually be better off if women could exercise more choice in their lives.

Motherhood vs Parenthood: Nancy Chodorow, Adrienne Rich and Betty Friedan

Mead's motivation for constructing her theory of gender was not so much to make recommendations as to render the unsettled conditions of modern life more intelligible to the people who are caught up in them and to heighten awareness of the diverse and conflicting cultural possibilities – of androgyny or difference, of nurturing or competitive values, of motherhood valued or devalued and of women more or less confined – that they contain. So successful was she that nearly all contemporary feminist works on gender are set within the framework of her theory and elaborate one or another of her projections. However, the most influential of the latter are two striking, mutually incompatible alternatives: that of a society based on shared parenting and one in which motherhood and difference are emphasised and valued. In consequence, it is not only the societies in which feminists live, but feminism itself which is simultaneously facing in quite different directions. With the political dimension which the women's movement has brought to the question of gender, demanding action as well as extending understand-

217

ing, this incompatibility and conflict of ideas has created what may be a set of insoluble and ultimately paralysing dilemmas for feminism.

The leading, although controversial contemporary advocate of 'shared parenting' is Nancy Chodorow. Up to a point (especially in the first and final sections of her celebrated book *The Reproduction of Mothering*),[52] Chodorow is simply restating, with new supporting evidence, the stages of the argument found in Mead:

1 that women's monopoly of mothering produces the characteristic psychological formation of girls (whole, 'sure' and nurturant) and boys (fractured, insecure, and competitive);
2 that this is the reason not only for men's need of gender but also for their hostility to women; and
3 that one way of solving the gender problem on women's behalf is to involve men in mothering too.

The novelty of Chodorow's approach and the source of the argument over her book (described by one reviewer as 'a book on motherhood that few mothers can read')[53] is that where Mead's focus was on men, hers is on women. Her probing and elaboration of the place of women's psyche in the argument (why do women fit in so well with the structure of modern parenting as defined by men?) not only exposes the same ambivalence about women that we find in Mead but also ends up defying the original logic of shared parenting (i.e. that men should become more like women) by suggesting that it is really women who are the problem. The result is that the drift of Chodorow's argument is never altogether clear; is it men who are to change or women? The problem is exacerbated by the nature of her evidence, especially in the coloratura performance on the Oedipus complex which is the central portion of her book.[54] Using clinical psychoanalytical data to illustrate her points, she argues that because women identify more with their daughters than their sons (the same assumption earlier made by Mead) and the 'pre-oedipal' phase lasts very much longer in girls, a woman will always find it difficult to see herself as a person, discontinuous with her mother. The boundaries between her body and ego and those of other people will never be clearly defined and she will always be searching both to escape from and to recover the primary unity she and her mother once experienced. Therefore, she will always find it difficult to realise herself except in relation to others and will reproduce exactly the same problems in her own daughter. Although Chodorow denies that mothering makes women's egos weak[55] (they are rich, empathetic, etc.) this certainly appears to be the gist of what she is saying.

It is small wonder that Chodorow's argument is being taken in two quite different senses by her readers; as a feminist programme for reforming men and as yet another neo-Freudian exercise in 'blaming mother'. Her book is certainly the ultimate essay in guilt for the unfortunate mother with whom her argument strikes a chord. Nor does shared parenting even appear to be the answer to the problem as Chodorow presents it. Although she ostensibly sets out to show that it is the *structuring* of motherhood (i.e. women's exclusive mothering) which leads us to reproduce ourselves in our daughters, what she is really describing much of the time is the effect of same-sex nurturing, i.e. of daughters being mothered by their mothers at all. This is quite a different matter and will survive the introduction of father-mothering, for shared parenting is not the same as role-reversal; women will still mother too. What is more, although the expedient of shared parenting can certainly be expected to relax the rigid boundaries of the boy-child's ego and solve the problem of his 'too much mothering', this must presumably be at the expense of giving him the same problems on account of his fathering as girls get from being mothered by their mothers (and one is reminded that the presumed limitations of the nurturing mentality were precisely the source of Mead's reservations about shared parenting). It is not at all clear what men's mothering can do for girls, unless it obliges them to repress themselves. In short, if men are the problem then 'shared parenting' is the solution that fits, but not if the problem is women.

In the end, Chodorow indirectly acknowledges this by separating the costs of mothering for girls from the role of fathers altogether; in her final chapter the ground shifts to the degree of mothering's intensity, a problem which can be solved by sharing it with 'a network of *other women*'[56] and the biological mother's involvement in 'meaningful productive work'. This merely adds to the confusion, for these are aspects of structure which are independent of heterosexual parenting and would leave the psychological formation of boys unchanged.[57] Indeed, there are many institutions of women's oppression, such as their segregation under Islam for example, which could very well be described as shared parenting systems in this all-female sense yet have the effect of intensifying both the discontinuity of psychological formation among males and their irrational hatred of women. Even in western contexts where women are allowed to work, women's shared parenting is obviously no answer to the problems of male psychology. If nurturing the young is a task for all women to share, then there will be no escape from mothering even for the woman who eschews biological parenthood. By the same token, all men will escape it simply by virtue of not being women.

One way out of Chodorow's difficulty has been proposed by Westkott, who argues that she has overlooked a crucial, contextual factor which distorts the way that women mother; the fact that women have to nurture men as well as children. This leads Chodorow to attribute the faults of women's nurturing disposition (by which Westkott means excessive altruism and dependence on their children) to the psychology of mothering, when they are really caused by their unreciprocated nurturing responsibilities as wives. 'Mothers turn to other women and to their own children to fulfill their emotional needs, not simply because men are not there for them . . .but because men *are* there – too much so – demanding to be cared for.'[58] Of course this argument – which recovers the rationale for shared parenting by identifying the problem as the psychology of men – puts its finger on exactly the same hole in Chodorow's account which is found in Mead's: the absence of any treatment of power and the effect of its asymmetry within the family. Coming as it did eight years after Firestone's *Dialectic*, Westcott is not the only commentator to find this omission most surprising.[59]

This criticism also raises the question of the separation and hierarchy of the public and the private spheres, emphasised by Rosaldo[60] and elaborated in the Parsonian functional dichotomy of the expressive/ nurturant functions privately performed by wives and the instrumental functions of men who mediate between their families and the outside world. These functions are rephrased by Chodorow in terms of their psychological content, to show how modern women, in reproducing mothering, also reproduce their privatisation. Although Chodorow also argues (on rather unconnected grounds) that the separation of spheres is a structural device designed to train men and women for their separate roles in the service of capitalism, her solution is not to abolish the private–public distinction altogether – after all, shared parenting is a form of intra-family structure – but to make the frontier between the spheres more permeable and non-sexist, so that man and woman equally move back and forth between the two. For many feminists, this risks more than it promises to gain, for it increases the exposure of women and their children to the structures and pressures of the outside world without increasing their resources to resist them. Where Westkott stresses how the power of individual men impinges on the home to shape female psychology, Young and others emphasise the power of the public sphere to regulate and shape the lives of both women and men and argue that any attempt, such as shared parenting, to reform outwards from the private sphere is bound to be in vain. It must be preceded or at least accompanied by a separate revolution in the public sphere: a chicken-and-egg problem which is implicit in life as well as 'dual systems' theory.

There is no question that by touching women on their pride and what is surely their rawest nerve, their feelings for their children, Chodorow has helped to bring the whole question of motherhood nearer centre stage. In the process, she has also inadvertently revealed shared parenting as an extremely complex issue with profound and contradictory implications. Faced with the cogency of the argument for the reform of male psychology and its obvious relevance to the feminist goals of a less conflictual, hierarchical and competitive society (to say nothing of the greater individual freedom it promises in the short term), many women with sympathetic partners have felt encouraged to make personal trials of shared parenting. Inevitably, this exercise in the personal as political has brought home the kind of practical problems faced by any radical social engineering project, especially if mounted 'from below', and in the process illustrated many of the points made by Chodorow's critics. As Ehrensaft points out, such projects are typically embraced by out-group individuals, and shared parenting is no exception with its following of feminist women and maverick men, most of whom are intellectuals and relatively powerless, socially alienated and economically unresourced.[61] These sharing parents must maintain their personal revolution in opposition to the current social climate and in spite of the practical difficulty that the public sphere around them is organised on the basis of a very different family principle, with man as full-time breadwinner and woman as full-time mother/housewife (fictional as the latter status so often is). Assuming that if both parents are to nurture equally then neither can work full-time, both will fall through the safety-net of full-time earnings, employment protection, status and promotion prospects into the economic ghetto of the marginal, part-time worker. If both try to work full-time instead, then what they are really doing is de-segregating the superwoman syndrome, so that both parents are equally stressed. One way or the other, shared parenting points to strain and deprivation; to be otherwise, the whole structure of our economic life and social values would indeed have to be transformed in congruence. The loss of status and prospects falls particularly hard on men, whose expectations are the greater, a fact which cannot be lost on male observers; the extension of shared parenting to the general population cannot but bear the implication of a war of sex-interests. It also bears the seeds of a damaging form of male adaptation which could preserve male hierarchy and dominance in a new form. Just as de Beauvoir's advice to women implies a hierarchy of non-mothers over mothers, so shared parenting implies a hierarchy of non-fathers over fathers. Unless the reorganisation of society and culture included severe penalties or internalised sanctions for non-nurturing men as well as greatly increased financial rewards and status for childcare, this outcome would seem to be inevitable.

There is also a danger, pointed out by many critics and supported by historical examples of authoritarian patriarchal involvement in early child-rearing,[62] that the psyche of man as presently constituted may prove too strong for the domestic experiment to succeed. His negative influence may subvert maternal values faster than he can learn them through nurturing and men may even pose a physical threat to their young, on account of the capacity for violence and sexual abuse to which innumerable newpaper accounts of male domestic mayhem attest; dare mothers leave the children they love to the mercies of men?

The problem, however, is not only that social realities impose limits on the capacities of the human will to transform them. More profoundly, shared parenting threatens what many women value most; the uniqueness of their mothering. At the intellectual level, it demands that they devalue their personal role as mothers; at the emotional level it threatens to overwhelm them with guilt about their mothering (at least in Chodorow's version) while depriving them of its joys, not excluding the rewards of the mother and daughter bond which, as Chodorow argues, is often deeper and stronger than the erotic heterosexual bond between a woman and her husband. At the institutional level it intrudes a rival, in the form of man, to the only sphere where women enjoy a measure of authority and power. In fact, there is an astonishing contradiction at the heart of the shared parenting proposition: women are to devalue their own mothering to the point where they are prepared to merge it into parenting along with men, but the reason they are to do this is because they value it so highly.

The crossroads that feminists have reached with the shared parenting proposal, and the ambivalence about women and their values which it has exposed in Chodorow as well as Mead, is thrown into especially sharp relief by Adrienne Rich. *Of Woman Born*, Rich's response to her own experience of motherhood and the radical feminist challenge that women should recover reproductive power, was published in 1976, halfway between Chodorow's original case for shared parenting and the psychoanalytical study of mothering which overtook it in her book. Dismissing Firestone's views of motherhood and her artificial reproduction plan as shallow,[63] Rich's object was to distinguish *motherhood* – a punitive, social institution historically controlled by men and constructed in accordance with their power, perceptions and values – from the *mothering* – a human function and experience of incomparable worth – which it distorts. In the process, Rich presents a celebration of mothering which perhaps comes closer in its conclusions than any other feminist work to identifying what women really want: a world where 'a mother's battle for her child – with sickness, with poverty, with war, with all the forces of exploitation and callousness that cheapen human life – [has] become a common human battle', in which mothers refuse to be victims and where every woman is 'the presiding genius of her own body . . . bringing forth not only children (if and as we choose), but the visions and the thinking, necessary to sustain, console and alter human existence'.

Instead of heaping blame on women, Rich asked why they should feel guilty at all. As a mother, she had discovered that motherhood set her own identity and needs strangely at odds with those of her children; instead of loving them and following her vocation (as a poetess), she had to learn a destructive discipline of self-denial as she ran here and there,

222

always domesticated, always alone, in the service of her children, her husband, the uncaring society around and ultimately of anyone but herself. This unnatural situation did not make her love her children more, but more unevenly and unreliably. On the one hand mothering was the most worthwhile and indispensable of human functions; on the other, motherhood set almost every mother at war with herself.

The explanation, Rich concluded, lay around her, in a patriarchal society which devalued motherhood so much that mothers were powerless, frustrated people and public funds were spent on virtually anything else but their needs, and in patriarchal men who demanded nurturing from women but would not nurture in their turn. Through the institution of patriarchal motherhood, men satisfied their envious, repressed desires by imposing their culture, power and violence on 'the essential human relationship' of mother and child. The only answer was to destroy the patriarchal institution. This would not abolish motherhood itself, but 'release the creation and sustenance of life into the same realm of decision, struggle, surprise, imagination and conscious intelligence, as any other difficult but freely chosen work.'

One of Rich's principal means to this end is the introduction of shared parenting on a massive scale (though not in the conventional family framework), not only because it will change those attitudes of men towards women which result from women's exclusive mothering and thus break the reproductive cycle of misogyny, but also on the grounds that nurturing matures the nurturer, so that shared parenting is the only way for men to grow up.[64] Rich is not sanguine about men's resources for this nurturing task, however, so it will have to be accomplished under women's tuition and control. In fact, although Rich is sceptical about what women's reproductive power really amounts to and unfortunately belongs to the 'far be it from me to provide a blueprint' school of political theorising, power is really crucial to the accomplishment of her ideas.

Rich points in two completely different directions, however, and this is not only because of the difficulty of how women are to make men do what they would rather not. She is envisaging a world where women are really in a position to decide their own lives for themselves, because of their emancipated psychological attitudes, their economic independence and the allocation of public funds to services that mothers need. The possibility this contains, as her own book makes abundantly clear, is that what women may actually choose is to exclude men from the crucial phases of their lives altogether. She shows why women value mothering so much and must liberate it from the culture warp imposed by men, and the trouble is that although controlled male parenting is one way of achieving this, women's single-parenthood is an obvious alternative. Furthermore, one of the most famous and evocative passages in *Of Woman Born* is that in which Rich celebrates the relationship of mother and daughter as the source of sisterhood, starting with Mead's idea that biochemical affinities of mother with baby girl, and differences of mother from baby son, may reach as far back as the womb and ending with her own reconstruction of the religious mystery of Eleusis, which centred on the mother–daughter bond and was destroyed by men.[65] The burden of Rich's song is that women can recover this all-female bond and build on it in adult life, not only through their daughters but also in sexual relationships with other women. Rich is certainly not suggesting that women's relationships should be exclusively non-heterosexual (and she herself is one of a celebrated group of leading radical feminists whose lesbianism was preceded by a heterosexual phase and motherhood in marriage), but there is surely something piquant, to say the least, about the suggestion of shared, heterosexual parenting coming from a lesbian. Not surprisingly, a school of thought which vehemently advocates single-mother or lesbian-couple parenthood, and sees motherhood as empowering in itself, has arisen in her wake.

For many feminists, separation from men is exactly what women's liberation means. Yet, paradoxically, if women pursue the fullness of their lives independently of men, the feminist gender theory which Rich herself endorsed suggests that this is the very path which is most likely to reproduce the misogynist cycle of gender, for what independent single-motherhood paradoxically implies is the most extreme necessity for boy-child differentiation, and the most complete loss of reproductive role for males, of any childrearing option which is contemplated. It also denies men the possibility of acquiring the nurturing experience which might lead them of their own accord to modify their values into less competitive forms. It is thus the course which can logically be expected to produce the greatest hostility on the part of men towards women and the most intense, competitive rivalry among men towards each other.

Paradoxically, the best way to temper these adverse effects would be if women's single-parenthood were accompanied by a *devaluing* of motherhood, as something to be avoided (on account perhaps of socio-economic penalties), for these are the only circumstances (following Mead) in which the primacy of the basic mother–child relationship is compatible with greater freedom for women to participate with men in non-reproductive pursuits. Since this would not provide a basis for women either to enjoy their mothering, or to temper the public sphere with female gender values, and would be accompanied (as indeed we see it is) by growing insistence of the role of women as sex objects in the misogynist fantasies of men, the prognostication for a society compatible with feminist values is, however, correspondingly poor. A society where motherhood is devalued and women disempowered by difference is the opposite of what separatists seek. It would seem to follow, too, that attempts to ameliorate the material and social disadvantages of single-parenthood for women would logically be matched by male attempts to re-restrict their lives.

Not surprisingly, the combination of feminist separatism, the growing instability of modern marriage and the rise of single-parenthood among the general population has not only provoked an anti-feminist reaction among women but also a pro-family, 'revisionist' response among feminists themselves, conspicuously led by Betty Friedan and *The Second Stage*. Friedan's is not a closely reasoned, theoretical work, and she has aroused considerable anger among feminists for her complacency and the ambiguity of her support for feminist causes. Arguing from an impressionistic database and in defiance of widely available evidence to the contrary, she presents an exaggerated picture of feminist achievements, especially in the field of equal opportunities, overstates the nurturing revolution in American fatherhood and seems to advise women to abandon the separate women's movement on the spurious grounds that its main objectives have already been secured. In so far as she is taken seriously by feminists, it is out of recognition that her book reflects the gut reaction of most women to the extremes of 'political lesbianism' and articulates the aspirations many people of both sexes invest in the idea of 'the family', a concept which Friedan extends to include non-biological and non-heterosexual groups and partnerships, but which for most of the women for whom she speaks presumably signifies the traditional, heterosexual nuclear family.[66]

There is slightly more to feminist 'revisionism' than this, however. A modest degree of shared parenting within the family framework is the cornerstone of the future Friedan envisages, but what she is proposing is not the elimination of gender but a new sexual division of labour, in which the roles and values of the sexes are modified by what they share, but stop short of convergence. Women want to live in families, and this is not only out of need for enduring relationships with other adults but because they value the intimacy of the 'private sphere' more than they will ever value equal rights and want to preserve the uniqueness of their role within; the fact that the family still comes first for most women is not just a cultural hangover but a reflection of the values women want to see preserved. The family is also the only framework in which they can construct a future which allows for the existence and needs of men (for whom Friedan thinks that women must assume responsibility). Sexism and the post-war cult of domesticity had made the family unbearably restrictive, but feminism will have accomplished its historic task if it has supplied those needs in women's lives which make it tolerable again. These are basically the right to work and a supportive husband but, like another recent feminist critic of the women's movement in the USA, Sylvia Ann Hewlett,[67] Friedan also directs attention to the costs of feminism and the question of the infrastructure for the family it has revised; too much focus on the personal as political has left individual women carrying the burden of a social revolution without essential social and state support, which both women principally understand in terms of optional childcare facilities, employment protection and social welfare on Scandinavian and British lines (which from the American perspective of most contemporary feminist theory look a lot more substantial than in European women's eyes). In this they echo almost every feminist who has ever addressed the practical question of government intervention, but are outstanding for their castigation of the women's movement's failure to achieve it.

Feminism at the crossroads

There is no question that women's gender theory has enormously enriched our understanding of the relationships of reproduction, gender and politics, but it is equally clear that it has failed to provide any single, clear sense of direction. It is difficult to avoid the conclusion that the reproductive issues of motherhood, the family and parental roles, which should be at the core of the feminist programme, are actually its weakest points. Indeed, if there is any single explanation for the fact that the women's movement has shown signs of faltering and disintegration at the very moment when its efforts are beginning to bear some political fruit, this is surely it.

As the deadlock reached by 'equal rights' and 'socialist' feminism has shown, as long as women go on having children then the situation of all women, whether they are mothers or not, is mediated by the female gender role and its relationship with the male. The de Beauvoir solution is therefore no solution at all and unless women are prepared to follow Firestone into the elimination of natural reproduction (which they do not appear to be) the central task of feminism must be to deal in some new way with the problem of natural, biological motherhood and its relationship to gender. Unfortunately, this is precisely where gender theory has diverged in two incompatible, mutually exclusive directions: first, those of shared parenting, with its emphasis on androgyny, and second, that of independent motherhood, which institutionalises differences between the sexes.

It is important to understand that this is not really a question of nature versus nurture, as the disputes within feminism are so often represented. Although there undoubtedly are women who assume the existence of insuperable, innate differences between the sexes, all the major theorists examined here either assert a single, androgynous human nature (de Beauvoir, Wollstonecraft and Firestone) or like Mead, Chodorow and Rich are more concerned with differences which are learned or constructed than those which may or may not be innate. It is not innate

226

difference, but the fact that 'difference' is inextricably linked in the psyche of men with 'inequality' (a point on which virtually all feminists agree, even if their explanations vary) that they must reckon with. In fact, the inescapable conclusion of the psychological explanation for gender, whether in the phrasing of power used by Firestone and Rich or that of achievement employed by Mead, is that gender difference equals gender hierarchy as far as men are concerned, whether they are innately more aggressive than women or not. Women are therefore confronted with the absolutely fundamental dilemma, that the celebration of difference – of motherhood and its values, and of the unique learning and insights that women's bodily and nurturing experience yields – is the most politically dangerous path that women can take. The only way to minimise the aggressiveness of men, either towards each other or against women, is to renounce the difference that they value. Whether women can or cannot converge with men, it is politically expedient for them to make the attempt. The trouble is that the more women value themselves, as Rich has shown, the less willing they will be to do this; the more determined they will be to achieve a world where they can simply be themselves, where there is no intrinsic, institutionalised contradiction between their motherhood and their nature. The metaphor of gender as a scissors, in which women are inextricably caught, remains only too grievously apt where basic differences of sex are concerned.

The resulting pitfalls for women, whether as individuals faced with the political implications of their personal dilemmas or as policy-makers with a general remit, are clearly legion. Both Firestone and Rich suggest that women's political power supplies the way out of the scissors, but even in a utopian setting, where women's power to influence events was sufficient to outweigh that of men, the advantages of bringing up boys and girls to parent equally and indistinguishably would have to be weighed against the loss of mothering this must entail; conversely, support for the joys and cultural rewards of motherhood would have to be set against the envious aggression they must be expected to arouse (and have historically aroused) in men. In the real world, where men, their values and their institutions are more powerful than women, where people cling to customs even when they recognise the harm they do themselves thereby and where the social fabric is constantly being rewoven by the personal decisions of millions of ordinary people, their task is immeasurably more difficult. In particular, they are faced with the problem that the polarisation of feminist thought around the alternatives of independent motherhood versus shared parenting is reflected in a growing polarisation of actual social trends in the western world. As Friedan observed, there are more and more marriages (with the remarriages of divorced people being the most significant factor in this trend) and, in addition, the drive for separate home-ownership on the part of nuclear families remains the biggest single reason for the housing booms and shortages of industrialised countries. Within this trend, shared parenting is being attempted at least to some degree by an increasing number of couples, not only for ideological reasons and because of the self-assertion of educated wives but because of economic trends: the realities of male unemployment and female part-time working are forcing some people to compromise with their gender expectations. Fragile as this tendency may be, the fact that so many people are choosing the nuclear family as the framework for their adult lives demands that feminist policy-makers accept their choice and pursue the possibilities for gender change that it affords.

Yet at the same time the rate of divorce (mainly initiated by women, too) is constantly increasing and the most revolutionary change in reproductive practice within the industrialised west is the growth of women's single-parenthood, especially among the young.[68] Although men's lack of interest in fatherhood and the opportunities to evade personal responsibility afforded them by easier divorce must be part of the explanation for this, it is incontrovertibly also the case that large numbers of young women are deliberately choosing to have children out of wedlock and/or bring them up alone. A decade ago Chodorow expressed surprise that girls were still growing up with a heterosexual erotic identification in spite of the increasing physical absence of fathers from the family scene and their consequently minimal performance in the Oedipal role assigned to them by Freud. Perhaps she had not allowed sufficient time for the lesson of the nuclear family, that family life is altogether women's business while fathers are dispensable, to take effect; the single-parent family may be its social, rather than erotic fruit.

With such divergence among public trends and feminist signals alike, the quandary of women policy-makers is obvious. Are they to support the single-parent mother, attempting to create a population of ungendered equals in the public sphere in defiance of the fact that half of these people will spend a large part of their lives locked in an intensely private nurturing relationship with children while the other half will not? Or should they try to structure the economy, taxation and family support towards shared parenting in defiance of the facts that increasing numbers of women are obviating this possibility altogether through single-parenthood and that welfare feminism is a two-edged sword which, like the nuclear family itself, is as likely to perpetuate the gender hierarchy as undermine it? The only areas of consensus remain those which feminists inherit from equal rights and socialist feminism – the need for equal opportunities in the public sphere and for publicly funded alternatives to women's traditional service functions – but here too they are faced with new forms of the same old dilemmas. Is the object of an equal opportunities policy to help women compete with men or to eliminate competition altogether? Is everyone to nurture, or no one? And although all are agreed about the need for public childcare facilities, are these to be constructed as an alternative to the family, or in support of it? And are improved pay and conditions for caring and service workers to be construed as an equalising reward to women for their uniquely 'non-productive' work or as a device to lure men into nurturing and service roles by non-familial means? If the former, then a male invasion of this women's sphere in search of its increased rewards is the last thing they should be seeking to achieve; if the latter, then it is precisely the uniqueness of this sphere and its control by women that they should be trying to undermine. At its most fundamental, affecting every dimension of the male and female roles and functions, public and familial, their dilemma seems to be whether to help women to enhance their motherhood or share it, to foster difference or androgyny. Both feminist theory and the divergent trends of social change seem to constrain them to try to do both things at once.

These were academic questions as long as women were powerless to influence events but in recent times they have become central to the lives of increasing numbers of women as matters of personal, political choice. Now, in a few isolated cases, there are also feminist women in political elites who may have reached the 'critical mass' in numbers (as in Norway and the German Greens) or else achieved a sufficiently pivotal role in terms of political leverage (as in Iceland) to confront the problem at the policy-making level. It is to these women's efforts to identify and pursue feminist goals, and the implication of their choices in the light of gender theory, that the next and final chapter is addressed.

9

WEST GERMAN GREENS, NORWEGIAN FEMINISTS AND THE ICELANDIC KWENNALISTINN

The focus of this chapter is on contemporary feminism in action, and the settings are three outstanding modern deviations from the gender rule; the Green party in West Germany, the Norwegian political system and the Icelandic Kwennalistinn. These are exceptions which in many respects recall, but in others certainly surpass those witnessed in the past. For one thing, women's recruitment has reached much higher levels than before; some Norwegian feminists have even wondered if they have achieved the 'critical mass' they need to integrate pro-woman pro-grammes. The settings and strategies involved are also slightly more diverse. In Scandinavia, women have advanced within the framework of traditional mixed parties and an integrationist strategy, but in co-operation with a separate, women's movement. In West Germany, women's exceptional progress came about through the medium of a mixed-sex party but one which is derived from radical 'new' social movements and is ostensibly 'anti-system' in spite of its conventional success. Iceland, however, is something altogether new, with the meteoric rise of a separate, unequivocally feminist women's list to what may be a pivotal role in the Icelandic parliament.

These circumstances have inevitably led to speculation that underlying forces are at work which favour women, so long as they are sufficiently aware and flexible to seize political opportunities when they arise. Furthermore, the declared feminism of nearly all the women politicians advancing in these special cases has roused high hopes that their intervention will achieve a fundamental shift in public values and, ultimately, a reformation of the social order which may influence events in other countries too.

There are some grounds for optimism. If gender is the rock on which past feminists have foundered, women should be better placed to solve this problem now. For one thing, they have the experiences of the past to instruct them. They also have a separate women's movement of unprecedented size and international character to mobilise support, sustain a feminist political consciousness and communicate ideas among a far more generally educated female population. Since these ideas include radical feminists' insistence on the importance of women *as such*, with their own distinct experience and values (and not as men *manquées*), it should be more difficult than formerly for any feminist to reject what women value in their traditional role and ignore the central place of motherhood in shaping women's lives. Above all, they have the insights of gender theory to guide them in the policies they should adopt to foster change. The opportunities that women have to influence events may be severely limited, but nowadays they should be more equipped to make the most of those that do arise.

Against these hopes, however, women have to set the inherent limitations to change imposed by the nature of male-dominated systems and bear in mind that the exceptions are mainly in small countries clustered on the northern periphery of the industrialised world. They also have to recognise that the development of the contemporary women's movement has, yet again, revealed sharply conflicting feminist conceptions of its goals and profoundly different strategies on the part of different groups of women. The danger is, as in the past, that when the favourable opportunities prove to be short-lived and the male order settles down in its new, adjusted form, the efforts of women will have been in vain. Divided among themselves and pursuing inconsistent and ill-founded aims, they will have foundered on the gender problem yet again and their policies, instead of extricating women from the scissors of the male and female gender roles, will have lead them right back to where they started from: the situation of a female out-group in a man's world.

This chapter therefore has two objects. One is to identify the specific cultural, or sub-cultural conditions which gave rise to these exceptions and the parameters of change that such conditions, of themselves, are likely to support. The other is to evaluate the feminist response to them and assess the prospects for more radical and long-term change.

These objectives clearly cannot be achieved without engaging the themes of both parts of this work – recruitment and feminism – and all the strands in its research. Particular consideration must be given to the role of education: as a resource which may acquire a heightened, independent significance in some recruitment contexts, as an influence on the attitudes of privileged men towards the rights of others and as a vital force in the political mobilisation of women and the development of feminist ideas. The tendency of feminism to thrive in the same conditions that produce radical social movements among men, and the role the latter have been seen to play in both promoting and setting limits to the advance of women, must be considered, too. In each case, the strategy that women adopt with respect to the existing political system and its institutions *and* the relationship of feminism with other social movements will be crucial to their prospects of success.

In the last analysis, however, what women get depends on what they want. The theory and practice of equal rights and socialist feminism provide a set of fundamental questions to be answered in evaluating feminist goals and strategies. What is the attitude of feminists to women's traditional role and values and on what basis do they appeal to women for support – as women, or as would-be men? How do they define the interests of women and how do these reflect upon the gender basis of society? Do their aims, implicitly or explicitly, reinforce or challenge the dichotomy of gender roles? If the former, they face the insuperable problem that this dichotomy of roles is intrinsically hierarchical as well. If the latter, the trouble is that even if they are agreed on the reformation of gender as the precondition for a better world, they also must agree on the direction this reform will take and bring the mass of ordinary women with them.

The theories reviewed in Chapter 8 indicate that changes in parental roles are the key to a well-founded gender strategy. Unfortunately, they also reveal profoundly divergent feminist conceptions of what changes are desirable and/or possible and the means to be employed. These discrepancies are reflected in the different choices ordinary women make and at the level of public policies may all too easily result in inconsistency and the neglect of long-term goals. Whether contemporary feminist politicians address the problem directly and consciously through an articulated gender strategy, or indirectly and unwittingly through the effects of second-order policies, the effect of their intervention on the gender basis of society will be the acid test of their success.

In what follows, the intention is not to give exhaustive accounts of feminism and women's situation in the three selected vanguard cases, but rather to isolate those elements in both which bear upon these themes. This is not always easy, given the idiosyncratic settings and the nature of the sources; politicians, even feminist ones, do not always express themselves in theoretical terms or relate specific policies to fundamental, long-term goals. Also, continuing events are obviously more difficult to categorise than finished episodes. The prospects of the Greens, as either a conventional party or a radical movement, are far from clear. The success of Norwegian women in achieving entry to elites has been phenomenal, but their recent electoral setback makes it impossible to say if their 'feminist experiment' has already peaked or just begun. In Iceland, women have made an isolated gain rather than a broad advance and it is too early to judge how far they can consolidate their position. The conclusions reached here must be tentative.

WOMEN AND FEMINISM IN THE WEST GERMAN GREENS

Like every aspect of German life this century, the role and aspirations of German women have been in a state of periodic turmoil ever since the First World War. In the Weimar period, the traditional values of the German population were severely shaken and an attempt was made to construct a new political system based on parliamentary and social-democratic norms. This drew on the support and values of the educated and professional classes rather than traditional military, administrative or business elites and consequently, as we should expect, it proved a relatively favourable context for women's political recruitment; as in Finland eleven years before, the first elections under the new constitution in 1919 produced a women's parliamentary representation of 10 per cent. The Weimar period of transition was also short-lived, however, and led not to a stable, democratic system as in Finland, but to Nazi Germany, a prospect which was in fact foreshadowed in the German women's movement as early as 1914 by the victory of the proto-fascist ideas of Gertrud Baumer over its original 'equal rights' feminism.[1] The latter cause was inherited in Weimar by the social democrats and 'socialist' feminists, who thus tended to occupy the same position in the feminist spectrum as 'bourgeois' feminists elsewhere.

In the cultural regression which marked the Third Reich, the gender role foundations of society were exposed with unusual clarity and crudity. It may be (as is sometimes suggested), that those women (relatively very few, of course, compared with men) who voted for the Nazis were those who felt most threatened by Weimar's undermining of the traditional female role; with high and growing unemployment, the feminism of 'equal rights' must have appeared particularly hollow. However, the Nazi view of women as the home-based bearers of the 'master race', while it may have provided a spurious sense of security for some and helped to solve the male unemployment problem, was also associated with a reassertion of the traditional male role in pathologically exaggerated form. The Nazis' glorification of the violence and domi-nance components of male gender and the deep-seated fear and hatred of women which their pornography exposed, was to provide the psy-chological basis for the SS, the death camps and the ill-judged aggression which ultimately led to the destruction of the German state itself.[2]

The more conventional society which emerged in the Federal Republic after the further upheavals of defeat was constructed on the basis of reversion to a more moderate version of the male gender role, but women's role remained comparatively unreformed and their resources consequently few. Political elites were dominated firstly by the CDU, a party focusing on economic growth and drawing on the support of established business interests and diverse local elites, and latterly also by the SPD with its traditional base in the male-dominated workers' organisations. Although both came to draw increasingly on the service professionals and mushrooming bureaucracies for activists and candidates, this had no effect on the role and recruitment of women, whose mobilisation and prospects were inevitably circumscribed by lack of education and professional employment, even in the service sector. In spite of proportional representation and the fact that the war left the German population demographically askew (even now, as much as 54 per cent of the electorate are women), the proportion of women in the Bundestag did not pass 10 per cent until 1987.

The Federal Republic was thus an excellent illustration of how proportional representation does not, of itself, bring women into public life. However, subsequent events there were also to show how useful PR can be once women have been mobilised. In Germany, the factors which achieved this mobilisation were the spread of education to the female population, the growth of extra-parliamentary political movements based in the very same sector of the population – young, university-educated, and weakly integrated into social roles – to which the newly educated women belonged and finally the appearance of the Greens, a mixed-sex, minority party which used these movements as the basis for electoral advance. The sudden influx of women into regional and national representative bodies which has taken place in the 1980s can thus be attributed indirectly to the workings of a PR system, but has been entirely incidental to the electoral success of the Greens, a party by whose lights its women members are unusually well-resourced.

Although the intellectual roots of the West German Greens can be traced to such remote and diverse sources as Nietzsche, William Morris and the Expressionist movement of the 1920s, their recent origins lie in the emergence of the overlapping ecology, anti-authoritarian and peace movements in the 1970s.[3] The ecological movement arose in mass response to the broad environmental issues of nuclear energy and the ecological impact of policies for infinite economic growth and developed through the medium of protests against their specific local consequences. The anti-authoritarian movement derived in part from the protest and hippie movements of the 1960s but was also a response to the growth and bureaucratisation of central and regional government in the 1970s, which was continuing unabated under SDP control. It ranged from the student movement's Sponti groups, which aimed to create alternative communities in which individual differences, subjective consciousness and emotional feelings could be liberated from the rule of order, reason and the state, to the less alienated Citizens' Initiatives (*Burgerinitiativen*), through which people tried to get more say in local affairs; it was from the latter that the original Green lists emerged to contest Lander elections. Disillusionment with both the conventional, Marxist left and the *embourgeoisement* of the SDP played a significant part in the emergence of these movements, as well as in the rise of left-wing terrorism and the cult of violence. The latter was soon offset, however, by the appearance of the mass peace movement, triggered by Nato's adoption of the dual-track weapon system (involving Pershing and Cruise missiles) in 1979. All these strands combined to produce the Greens.

Clearly, feminism was not a primary motivation for the formation of the Green movement, even if women may be held to have a special gender interest in some of their concerns, such as peace and the environment. With the one exception of those communalist groups which sought alternatives to the traditional family and whose attempts to reconcile the needs of the individual and the community within a non-hierarchical framework contained the same, largely unrealised potential for gender change as those of earlier communitarians, feminism was a peripheral issue. It would not be true to say that the women's movement had no impact on Green thinking at all (as male accounts imply by omission),[4] for when the Green Party was formally constituted in 1980 the founders included feminists from the women's movement who pressed successfully for abortion reform to be an unqualified party commitment. Furthermore, the Green party programme was later to give more prominence to the 'women's issue' (and other movement themes such as industrial relations) than to environmental issues. However, the 'women's issue' did not finally emerge as a central topic for the Greens until the mid-1980s, by which time women were already in leadership positions.

This early prominence of women among the Greens requires to be explained but, given the party's values and its socio-economic and demographic profile, this is not too difficult.[5] If ever there was a party of the highly educated, it is the Greens; in fact the party's strongest centres are the medium-sized university towns, along with areas where a high percentage of the electorate are engaged in service occupations. In effect, the Greens are a party of the Alliance type and although men are still more likely than women to vote Green, the movement of highly educated women into the party is very marked.[6] The result is that when it comes to candidate recruitment there is an available pool of women who are mobilised and possess the most highly valued conventional attribute among the Greens: a high degree of education.

However, there is one major difference between the Greens and the Alliance, which gives women an additional edge in the former and recalls conditions in the Russian revolutionary movement. This is the very noticeable lack of *occupational* status among Green voters and activists and the low esteem in which socio-economic integration, and indeed the very concept of a socio-economic hierarchy, are held by them. In spite of the similarities of educational profile and economic sectoral location between the Greens in West Germany and the Alliance in Britain, the former has been emphatically a party of the young and where both voters and activists are concerned there is this signal difference, that where the typical educated Alliance activist was a teacher or other professional employee, the Green counterpart is a student.[7] Indeed, with about a third of their supporters in the process of higher education or training and a higher proportion unemployed than vote for any other party, the Greens have been characterised as a party of the socially un-integrated.[8] In this context, the characteristically female combination of higher education and lack of commensurate occupational status is not a handicap, but may even be an asset. This is not to say that the 'alienation' of the Greens is unambiguous: their ecological and social proposals and the regulatory role of government which these imply are strongly biased towards respect for expertise, further economic growth (to meet the demands of a conservationist market) and an increase in state bureaucracy. Also, in spite of the adoption of measures such as rotation of posts to prevent the entrenchment of leadership, it appears that an inner party elite is consolidating itself by the simple device of its members' rotating posts among themselves. Obviously, too, today's young Greens cannot be expected to be immune from the integrative effects of growing older and unless the party continues to recruit students in sufficient numbers to maintain its present demographic profile, its values can be expected to change. In the meantime, however, the anti-hierarchicalism of the movement is not only reflected in the character of its membership, but at times of expanding candidate lists, in gender patterns of recruitment too.

The socio-economic characteristics of the Greens not only explain why they are *finding* women who fit their model of a successful Green candidate but also help to explain why they are deliberately *looking for* them too. Like most people who are highly educated in the European cultural tradition, the radical West German intelligentsia is highly susceptible to the principle of equal rights. The Greens appear to have taken the equality of women for granted from the start and, in a society where equality was enshrined in the constitution but rarely exercised in practice, they have been quick to radicalise this into a demand for equal opportunities. However, the fact that this has not remained an empty rhetoric is due to the concerted action of Green feminists in putting forward women's lists of candidates for local and inner-party elections, including the successful bid of the six-woman 'Das Feminat' for the parliamentary party leadership in 1984. Like the Social Democrats in Britain, the Greens have found the arithmetical approach of using quotas an acceptable method of achieving equity but, again in response to the separate action of Green women, they have gone even further, demanding positive discrimination in every area of life. Where political candidacies are concerned, their simple and effective method is the 'zip', in which women and men are placed alternately on the party lists, always starting with a woman, and in 1986 they adopted a quota of 50 per cent for all their lists. The 'zip' works fairly well in practice, with some exceptions. In non-city areas where Green initiatives have attempted to build bridges with local communities, including the recruitment of disgruntled members of local socio-economic elites, the proportion of women candidates has tended to be low, presumably because of shortages of female farmers etc. as well as a corresponding shortage of highly educated women. Also, in order to find sufficient women Bundestag candidates in 1987, the Greens were obliged to draw on movement activists with relatively little standing or experience in the party. Now a male reaction has surfaced, with the demand that future candidates should have time-served status in the party itself, a provision which would favour men. The fact remains, however, that the Greens have tried to meet their quotas and were almost entirely responsible for the increase of women in the Bundestag (up from 9.8 to 15.3 per cent) in 1987.

In the wider context of German party politics, where demographic and economic pressures were already directing the attention of the other parties to the 'women's issue' on purely instrumental grounds, the effect of this was catalytic. Concern about the falling birth-rate had already led the CDU to formulate an essentially conservative, pro-mother family policy in the 1970s. In March 1985, alarmed by the exodus of women's votes to the SPD and subject to pressure from industrialists seeking to attract female employees, the CDU unprecedentedly invited a non-party assembly of politically active women, including well-known anti-CDU feminists, to discuss the future role of women in German society. The result was legislation introducing parental leave for men and making child rearing a pensionable occupation. This was followed by the first of the recruitment quotas, in which the CDU, now seriously alarmed by women's attraction to the Greens, voluntarily undertook to field a proportion of women candidates equal to the proportion of women in their membership. Shortly after came the Greens' 50 per cent rule and a more complicated and over-ambitious quota system in the SDP. As a result, the 1987 elections produced the interesting spectacle of the two major parties' competing to pre-empt a (largely non-existent) feminist vote but failing to deliver their recruitment commitments. The CDU fell considerably short of the due proportion of women candidates and neither party could produce women who fit their model of a winner; most were put in losing situations and the number of CDU and SDP women in the Bundestag remained almost unchanged.

In terms of overall political recruitment, then, the effect of the Greens has been to raise the stakes for women albeit without (because of the party's minority position in the Bundestag), spectacularly affecting the level of female representation. They have also stimulated general interest and movement on some feminist issues by invoking the typically integrative response which the major German parties bring to any movement for change or protest which may affect their vote. The Greens may well continue to act as this kind of catalyst, but with what long-term effect on gender roles in Germany or the nature of its politics is not so clear. It is not even clear what direct effects the Greens would have – or seek to have – if they could come to power, for the more involved they have become with the 'women's issue', the more divisive they have found it to be.

The relationship of Green feminists with German feminism is not a happy one. One reason for this is that it is the Greens, rather than the women's movement which has provided contemporary German feminists with their main political base. Although the women's movement was stirring in the 1970s, it overlapped in membership with the main radical movements in German politics and was effectively pre-empted by the Greens. As a result, it was one of the smallest and weakest of its kind in Europe and by 1980, when the Green party was formed, it was disintegrating into the fragmented activities of local women's groups.[9] Its greatest impact was in the pro-abortion campaign and, as observed above, the commitment to abortion was also its most notable contribution to Green policy. Relations deteriorated thereafter. Whereas the vast majority of German women who sympathise with feminism apparently support the Greens, the leading women's movement feminists, such as Alice Schwarzer,[10] reject them as essentially no different from other mixed-sex parties. Yet it is within the Greens that the central dramas of West German feminism have been enacted, with Green women being divided vehemently on all three of the basic feminist dilemmas: separatism versus involvement in mixed structures, participation in the existing system versus the creation of 'alternatives' and finally and most divisively of all, gender difference versus gender androgyny.

On the issue of whether to organise separately from, or together with men the spectrum is wide. At one extreme are those women on the fringes of the party who condemn participation in mixed structures altogether, the Greens included; at the other are those Green women who wholeheartedly subordinate women's aims to party interests. For the latter, feminism is a secondary goal which depends on Green success and too much emphasis on women's interests will only undermine their essential unity with like-minded men. Most leading Green women, however, appear to fall into an intermediate category. While identifying their hopes for women with Green objectives and accepting that this necessitates working with men, they are cynical about what can be achieved if women do not take their interests upon themselves. As a result, they are positive, but pragmatic, in their approach to separate organisation. While their primary aim is to work effectively (and this

238

means lead) in mixed-sex settings, they will use separatism to achieve this when it suits them. This is how the women's lists and quotas were accomplished and it is inner-party women's organisations, official and unoffical, which have been the basis of their policy-making inputs too; the anti-discrimination proposal of 1986, which is one of the party's major policy initiatives of recent years, is entirely the product of co-operation between separate women's groups and agencies within the parliamentary group and the party's organisational structure.

It is striking, all the same, that Green women's recruitment efforts and the anti-discrimination policy are specifically designed to enhance female participation in the conventional (i.e. mixed-sex, hierarchical and competitive) political and socio-economic systems to which both feminist and other Greens are in principle opposed. The issue of whether to participate in order to change the system from within or create an altogether new society from the grassroots up is a source of endemic conflict in the Greens but judging by the relatively low proportion of women supporters who are involved in party as opposed to 'alternative' political work, the Green women are even more chary than the men of working in conventional structures.[11] These issues of separatism, alternativism and the real commitment of the Greens to social transformation recently came to a head together over the question of finance. Under the generous terms of the FRG's electoral law, the Green Party's success had secured it considerable public funds to spend as it saw fit. Naturally, every group within the Greens had its own idea of how the money should be used, including some who felt it should be refused as binding the movement ever more tightly to the existing system. The most militant Green feminists have made a test case of this funding, demanding that if the party is sincere, then all or most of it should go to separate women's projects. The rejection of their demands as unreasonable has intensified intra-feminist contention in the party.

At the heart of the dissension, however, is a deeper conflict over what is meant by feminism. There is no question that the main burden of Green party feminism has been a highly developed form of 'equal rights', essentially aimed at securing women's access to what their gender has reserved for men. The result has been a counter-reaction from women who see this as a programme for the childless woman, which evades the central reproductive issue and denies the value women really set on motherhood.

In November 1986, a 'Mothers' Manifesto' was published by a group of women in the party, calling for a new women's movement to represent 'the wishes and hopes of mothers with children as consistently and emphatically as the interests of women without children';[12] to the dismay of party leaders, this initiative met with an immediate grass roots response within the party. They should not have been surprised; it was a similar reaction which alienated many American women from the feminist movement of the 1970s and led to such diverse results as the radical feminist celebration of motherhood and Betty Friedan's 'feminist revisionism' of the 1980s. The Mothers' Manifesto, however, has been described as no less than a 'declaration of war on non-mothers'[13] and the fact that the mothers not only aim to dilute Green anti-discrimination policy but support restrictions on abortion has been particularly alarming to many in the light of German history. To its opponents, the mothers' initiative is not just a conservative restatement of traditional roles but a reversion to the pre-war proto-fascism of the *Mutterschutz*. Such fears were exacerbated by the electoral campaign of 1986–7, in which Green women leaders sought to re-unite the party with its feminist grass roots, attract a new female following and outflank the separate women's movement by concentrating on the abortion issue. Instead, it was the anti-abortion mothers' faction which gained ground in the parliamentary party and since their success has obliged reluctant party organisers to finance them, the problem of the mothers is most unlikely to go away.

In truth, the objectives of the mothers' faction and the conflict it has aroused are as ambiguous as anything in the annals of the women's movement. Their criticisms of the equal rights tendency in Green feminism are almost exactly those advanced in Chapter 6, while their insistence on the centrality of motherhood and its caring attributes in the construction of a new society resembles radical feminism at least as much as a retreat into traditional roles. Nor does the solution they propose recall the Nazis, for it is to reward, liberate and empower mothers: financially by paying them for their caring and domestic work, socially by changing the hours and conditions of employment and public life to suit their needs and politically by means of women's quotas, of which from a half to three-quarters would be reserved for mothers.

Of course there is a central ambiguity in this feminist programme for it ignores the question; what of men? In fact the mothers' faction have combined insistence on the unique value of women's motherhood with some recognition of how this has affected men. Like Adrienne Rich, they want men to participate in parenting under the direction of women but, again like Rich, they treat this as a secondary consideration. Social respect and monetary reward for caring are expected to act as inducements to male participation and the mothers' centres run courses in housework for men, but the whole idea of men's parenting sits uneasily with the mothers' emphasis upon their own, definitive maternal role. It is difficult to see how the empowerment of mothers in the public sphere could be achieved without a transformation of the male psyche, but the question of how the latter could take place without the mothers' renunciation of their mothering role is being evaded.

The 'mainstream' Greens have been quick to seize upon this flaw and regard themselves as incomparably more consistent on the question of parental roles. This is because although the fortified version of 'equal rights' which is their dominant trend would seem to leave gender roles *au fond* unchanged, they also advocate shared parenting (with the inducement of parental leave for men) as the foundation for a gender reformation. In practice, however, the social trend in Germany since the early 1970s is to single parenthood, as it is throughout the industrialised world.[14] Like socialist-feminists, the Greens have endorsed this trend with attacks on marriage and the family as patriarchal institutions serving capitalism. They also advocate the same kind of extensive state-based childcare and welfare programme as the social-democrats. In practice, such help is desperately needed by most single mothers as a substitute for the traditional dependence of married women on individual men. In the Greens' consciousness of this need, the fact that single-parenthood is the antithesis of shared parenting and can only support a highly gender-differentiated society (because it offers no parental role to men at all), is simply not being faced. No matter how we interpret the conflict among Green women – in terms of German history, traditional feminist alignments or the fragmentation of the Western women's movement – the verdict has to be the same: neither side has a coherent, long-term gender strategy. Each has other priorities which preclude it, and on the basic gender question each, like Western feminism as a whole, is unfortunately heading in two different directions at the same time.

THE 'NORWEGIAN EXPERIMENT'

Of all exceptions to the gender pattern, past and present, the case of Norway is outstanding. Three factors have been pivotal in the transformation of this country in little more than a decade (1972 to 1986) from the most traditional and male-dominated of all the Scandinavian nations, to its present status of world-leader in female representation and even government: the immense respect in which education has been held in post-war Norway; the 'passion for equality' with its far-reaching effects on women's access to resources and to formal rights; and the intervention of the new Norwegian women's movement.

At the end of the Second World War, a profound change was seen to have taken place in Norwegian politics. The old political elites had been displaced, and the dominant theme of the new politics was a profound commitment to reducing the inequalities in Norwegian society. Extensive social security programmes were immediately adopted, the structures of the welfare state were swiftly created and a new concern for social consensus led to the rapid development of the now typical Scandinavian corporate structures which enable government, unions and industry to reach a negotiated settlement of key economic policies. Along with this went a quite exceptional respect for education which was reflected in new patterns of government spending and the rapid integration of the educators themselves into political elites. By the late 1960s Norway ranked sixth among the twenty-three member states of the OECD in percentage GNP allocated to education[15] and teachers had become the third largest occupational group among the members of the Storting.[16] The result was a dramatic improvement in the general level of education of the general population and their leaders which had two predictable effects; firstly on the mainstream culture through the attitudes and political recruitment of educated men and secondly on the socio-economic status and political behaviour of Norwegian women.

In a culture already imbued with the desire for social justice, it was only to be expected that educated men would be particularly susceptible to the principle of equity in public life. It was also logical in a society as proud as Norway of its democratic tradition that this should lead to questions about how disadvantaged groups are represented in a democratic system.[17] In 1966, these concerns prompted the Norwegian Labour party to establish a committee to report on the composition of the Storting and suggest ways of rendering the parliamentary Labour party more strictly representative of its electorate. As expected, the report found that workers, women and the young were grossly under-represented; the essence of its recommendations, accepted to some extent by nearly all the parties, was that selectors should mount a conscious drive for greater equity.

This initiative was to have important long-term effects and is worth examining more closely, for the considerable light it sheds on Norwegian attitudes and what it took for women to achieve their present position. The spontaneous discomfort of Norwegian political leaders about the existence of oligarchical tendencies in their representative system is one of its most striking aspects. Whether, as Valen thinks,[18] they were simply unaware that these are typical of western democracies or whether it was a consciously different, Norwegian conception of democracy which inspired the investigation, the fact is that the politicians understood the ideal of democracy in Norway to be a system in which all groups were represented *directly*, not by others, and in proportion to their numbers in the population.

It was equally important that the committee helped to prepare Norwegians for the idea of women as a legitimate socio-political group, no different from any other group which might be considered eligible for equitable representation. In the first three post-war decades, women had been almost entirely absent from Norwegian public life, a fact which reflected three fundamental, inter-related aspects of Norwegian women's immediate post-war situation: their traditional gender role and religiosity (which was also reflected in a typically conservative pattern of

242

female voting); their extreme lack of education relative to men (especially where further education was concerned); and their lack of paid employment (in which Norway was well behind the rest of Scandinavia). In a recruitment context where 'social group' was understood in terms of *occupational* criteria and the typical recruit of all main parties was a 'middle-aged male of middle-class background',[19] women's exclusion from public life was all too easily rationalised in terms of gender difference. Although a public debate on gender roles took place in Norway in the late 1950s and early 1960s (part of a wider Scandinavian debate and largely led by social democrats) this failed to reach any clear conclusions. Now, in terms of the new debate about recruitment, women's legitimacy as a political group was seen to depend precisely on their not being 'different' after all, a proposition which the small Norwegian feminist movement, with its typically Scandinavian, equal rights orientation had been promoting vainly all along, but which now reflected the ideas of educated men as well.

In some quarters, this went very much against the grain. Skjeie reports that when the former Labour leader Gerhardsen was invited to lead the first campaign for an increase in women candidates, his immediate reaction was to refuse, in the belief that the entrée of more women was undesirable. He expected them to undermine the party system by voting across party lines, a tacit admission that the interests of women were different, at least in his view, from those of men and that the existing party cleavages did not represent them.[20] Although his fears turned out to be unfounded (Norwegian women politicians being determined to work with the existing party framework), they probably were widely shared among the old establishment. Certainly no enthusiasm was shown for implementing the committee's recommendations, for the proportion of women candidates and winners remained virtually unchanged in the elections of 1969. So did the under-representation of young people and the working class; party leaders found it difficult to exercise much influence on local selectors (whose hand was actually strengthened as a result of the report's recommendations) and the committee proved to be a toothless watchdog over the recruitment process, finally fading away in 1980.[21] Indeed, no improvement in the representation of workers has occurred to this day and women are, ironically, the only group whose access to political elites has changed significantly since the report. Norwegian analysts are agreed that a great deal of the credit for the latter must go to the appearance on the scene of the women's liberation movement.[22]

The modern women's movement emerged in Norway around 1970, under the dual impact of education and the rapid communication of feminist ideas from America throughout the Scandinavian countries. The movement was vastly more radical than anything in Norwegian feminist history but paradoxically its most immediate and profound effect was to turn the public conception of gender right around again, from the 'enlightened' notion that women were really no different from men back to that of gender difference. This process took only from five to eight years, between 1972 and 1980,[23] and one of its immediate effects was to strengthen the hand of women politicians in pursuit of *equity*. Like the Green women in West Germany, the Norwegians found that the existence of a separatist movement made an immense difference to their own effectiveness within the system. Women whose primary political involvement was in the separate movement were often profoundly alienated from conventional public life and consequently were not interested in getting into parliament themselves, but as Skjeie puts it, 'the distance between top and bottom is short in the Norwegian society . . . and the meeting-points are numerous.'[24] Although movement women regarded the 'thematisation' of gender issues as their primary objective (and still do), they soon found themselves drawn into consultation on legislation and readily campaigned for party women in elections alongside the traditional women's organisations. Where the latter were concerned, the readiness of the party women to build their feminism on gender difference was also to have far-reaching consequences. It meant that ordinary women could identify with feminism as reflecting their own highly gendered lives and interests and that 'party' feminists in an increasingly educated and secular society could work constructively with traditional organisations because (in sharp contrast to, for example, British feminists) they saw their 'philanthropic' caring work as a legitimate expression of women's political identity.[25] The result was a degree of unity among women, and a level of mass support which no feminists, anywhere, ever had enjoyed before.

The possibility that a frustrated women's vote might undermine the existing party system, the galvanising effect of the movement on women inside the political parties and the sense that here was evidence of a major failure of the system to do justice to all social groups made a tremendous impact on male party leaders. As in West Germany, they moved swiftly to turn the edge of women's radical potential and enhance their own competitive electoral edge by rapid integration (though not, perhaps, quite so much from expedience in the Norwegian case as in the German); as in Germany and the other Nordic countries too, the Norwegian system of proportional representation was a facilitator of this process, but not a primary cause.

The first result was a sudden rise in the proportion of women candidates in 1973, from 20 to 32 per cent. The absolute increase was even greater than this suggests, since the number of men candidates rose dramatically too (as in the UK around the same time, and apparently also reflecting the general spread of education and fluidity of party alignments); more than two and a half times as many women stood as before, but also one and a third times as many men. However, most of these women were targeted to lose; in spite of a sharp fall in the success rate of men (from 9.3 to 6.4 per cent between 1969 and 1973) that of women also declined and the proportion of women in the Storting consequently rose only to 16 per cent. The real crunch came later, when the pressure of the women's movement was beginning to bite and the broader processes of socio-economic change were simultaneously producing a pool of women who fit the part of elite recruits.

The first women's quotas were adopted by the Labour and Liberal parties in the mid-1970s. At the same time, the effect of what has been described as the 'massive' move of women into higher education and paid employment[26] (the latter especially between 1975 and 1979 and in the case of professional women particularly in the public service sector), was having its effect. Now, for the first time in Norwegian history, there was a pool of women who resembled winning men. In the elections of 1977 the gender and recruitment pattern suddenly began to change; the female success rate began to rise and the proportion of women in the new Storting jumped dramatically to 24 per cent.

By the early 1980s, under severe pressure from the separate women's organisations within the parties, the idea of formal rights was giving way among party selectors to a belief in the urgent necessity of accommodating women's 'difference' inside the system. In 1983, the Labour quota was increased to 40 per cent and though the Conservatives resolutely refused to adopt any quota at all[27] they made a strong commitment in principle and practice to greater female representation.[28] In the crucial election of 1985 which produced the Brundtland government, the proportion of women rose to 34 per cent. At the election of September 1989, it climbed to 36 per cent.

A similar progression from formal equality to positive discrimination simultaneously took place within the very highly educated party organisational elites[29] (where the proportion of women was negligible before 1970 but rose to 40 per cent with the use of quotas in the early 1980s) and in the state and corporate sector. As early as 1973, a Royal Decree enhanced the powers of ministerial appointment and directed that two people, one of each sex, should be nominated for every post. This ineffective gesture was followed by a general drive for equity in law, in which the object was to gender-neutralise legislation by removing discriminatory wording or indeed any distinction of sex at all in most instances. (Thus the laws of inheritance were amended to provide for gender-neutral primogeniture, women gained the right to keep their own names after marriage and pass them to their children if the latter chose, and so on.) The climax was the Equal Status Act of 1979, passed in a climate of high expectations and considerable pressure from feminists within the system. A programme for equity on the grand scale, it was embellished by a form of government-sponsored positive discrimination which began under the Conservatives and proved effective even in appointments to the corporate structures. By 1981, the proportion of women on public boards, councils and committees had reached 27 per cent in Norway, compared with 16 per cent in its nearest rival, Sweden; by 1985 it was 30 per cent.[30] What is more, real efforts were made, albeit with very variable success, to achieve a standard level of representation across the board, even in subject-areas such as industry where the pool of women conceivably in line for appointment was inevitably very small.

The climax came on 9 May 1986, when the Labour Party gave Norway its first government headed by a woman. Mrs Gro Harlem Bruntland adhered strictly to her party's 40 per cent quota in the appointment of her government. In the cabinet, this meant that half the ministers, herself included, were women; Mrs Bruntland had achieved the goal she had been working for ever since becoming involved in politics.[31] Norwegian feminists could no longer see themselves as simply struggling to get in; they had arrived.

1986–9: the feminist 'political experiment'

To some outside observers it may have seemed that 1986 marked the triumph of Norwegian feminism, but the Norwegian women themselves had no such illusions. In the first place, equity itself still had very far to go. When half the population, but only about a third of Storting representatives and still less of state and corporate appointees were women, Norway was obviously still a male-dominated society. In the economic, academic and scientific elites there were hardly any women at all and in terms of women's access to education, employment and property, Norway still lagged markedly behind Finland, Sweden and Denmark, with the shortage of children's day-care facilities relative to working mothers' needs being particularly acute.[32] An element of fantasy, too, clung about some of the equity legislation; as late as 1988, a professor of public law was still speculating on how the gender-neutral primo-geniture law of 1974 might be received in rural areas, as if it had just reached the statute book.[33]

Women's advance into elites also vividly illustrated the social inequalities of equal rights and the high price individuals have to pay for their success. As advocates of incremental change had accepted all along, the only way for women to advance by means of integration would be if 'more women should be nominated from those who have already gained access to the male system'.[34] This, of course, was exactly what happened, not only in the corporate structures (which bring together representatives of business interests and the occupational sectors as well as civil servants), but in the Storting and the party organisational elites as well; the attributes of successful women were the same as those of winning men.[35] The similarity could not extend to their 'personal' circumstances, for the demands of public life are compatible with the male gender role, but not the female. Exactly as we should expect, the private lives of Norwegian women who achieve access to elites and/or material rewards for work commensurate with men's are not only different from those of other women, but from men's as well; they are far more likely to be childless and/or living on their own than their male counterparts.[36]

To 'anti-system', non-participating feminists, this was enough to show that 1986 was an entirely empty triumph. Where the 'party' women differed from the 'movement' women was in their hopes for incremental change, and their faith in existing institutions as their instruments.[37] The point of equity was not numerical justice in itself, but the 'feminisation of power' it brought in train. With power came the risks of integration, but the party feminists were confident that all of these could be outweighed by the nature of their links with other women and the women's movement. The real question facing them in 1986 was how to use their power; the really disconcerting thing was that they had no complete and ready answer.

Up till 1986, the focus of feminist efforts within the conventional system was so overwhelmingly on 'justice' that the question of what women would do with power, when they got it, was not effectively addressed. As recently as 1984, Helga Maria Hernes (now a leading theorist of the new Norwegian feminism), could find no clear evidence as to what women's entry to public life would bring in terms of political change[38] and a year later, another academic study concluded that it was 'difficult to perceive the sort of society [the national equality policies of all the Nordic countries] are striving towards.'[39] In 1986, this had to change. Conscious of a unique responsibility to Norwegian women and impelled to think on their feet by the extra edge of urgency – the opportunity, once lost, may not return – Norwegian feminists set out with immense intellectual energy to map the outlines of a new, 'woman-friendly' social order which could be engineered by means of public policies. This order, by definition, would be one in which women would enjoy 'a natural relationship to their children, their work and public life' and not have harder choices forced on them than society expects of men. What has emerged from the theory and practice of the last few years, however, is not one programme but two. The first is for the development of 'state feminism' as a system which incorporates gender difference into the public sphere and reconciles it with the principle of equity. The second is a more tentative project for transcending gender difference by using public policy to make the gender roles converge. How compatible these programmes are, or, more properly, how feasible it would be to

247

make the transition from the one to the other, is obviously open to question. The contradiction is perhaps more apparent than real, since the second programme is a response to the limitations of the first. The following account will therefore approach them in their logical sequence.

It is not surprising that the Norwegian women who participate in conventional politics should become 'state feminists' in spite of the militant anti-statism of some women's movement radicals; after all, post-war Norwegian politics have been dominated by the social-democratic ethos and its most characteristic institution, the welfare state. The object of state intervention has been to 'equalise' society, by means of material transfers which reduce the distance between the more and less advantaged social groups. As one of the latter, Norwegian women have a strong material interest in welfare programmes and party feminists of all persuasions are united in their support. 'State feminism' therefore involves a special commitment to the maintaining and improving the level of services in health, education and the other social services. However, the 'state feminist' programme is not simply an amalgam of welfare feminist and socialist ideas; it does reflect the strong impact the state has had on women's lives and project a central role for it in engineering social change, but in new, more radical ways.

One of the principal objectives of 'state feminists' is to employ the state to liberate women from dependence upon men. State intervention in the areas of education, childcare, maternity leave and employment protection has always had the side-effect of weakening the family power and status of men, by increasing the economic independence and life-choices available to women. The intention of 'state feminists' is to develop these forms of support for women to the point where the dependence of women on individual men, within the family, can be entirely substituted by dependence on the state. This does not involve questioning the special gender responsibility of women for maternal care as well as child bearing, and the assumption is that motherhood cannot be other than a condition of dependence. The reasoning is that once women's dependence, as mothers, is on the state and not on men, it can be seen in the same light as other sources of dependence, such as age, ill-health and retirement, which affect men as much as women. The optimal arrangement will be one in which women can move freely between economic independence, state dependence and family dependence according to their maternal responsibilities, their position in the life-cycle and their personal inclination.[40] The implication is that women's dependent relation to the state will be no different from that of men's.

There is obvious common ground in this proposal with both traditional socialist feminism and modern equity ideas, but Norwegian feminists have realised they cannot stop at this. Considering that gender difference is the basis not only of the lives of women but of the welfare state itself, they have had to recognise that the *outcome* of dependence can never be the same for women as it is for men until either the state, or society is constituted differently. Since the object of 'state feminism' is to incorporate gender difference, rather than to challenge it, it is the reform of the state rather than society on which the second pillar of their liberation programme rests.

Feminist analysis of the welfare state[41] starts with the sexual division of labour associated with the industrial revolution, a dichotomy between male 'productive' and female 'non-productive', i.e. reproductive work. The effect of this division was to exclude women from the 'public sphere' and thus from politics, but it has lately been the means, ironically enough, of drawing them inside it. The reason for this is the post-war expansion of the public service sector. Although the first phase of the Nordic welfare state was firmly based on the 'productive' public sphere, being designed to insure the male industrial worker (in his role as sole breadwinner and head of household) against the failure of the market to provide him with employment, the second phase of health and other welfare policies invaded what had been the 'private' women's sphere. Although the 'private' sphere was really always more regulated than its terminology suggests, the post-war welfare state is such a massive change in the degree of intervention that it amounts to the 'deprivatisation' of reproductive labour. Unfortunately, this has been at the instance of the state, which is controlled by men, and touches women within their traditional role, for it is women in their roles of mother, wife and widow who are the objects of the transfers involved. Welfare programmes not only keep women and their children from the extremes of poverty and deprivation but in effect they regulate their reproductive work within the framework of traditional roles. From being the dependents of individual men, women have become the clients of the state, but this is still dependence on men, albeit in a new, impersonal form.

The paradox is that the state cannot perform its new, paternal role without recourse to women's traditional skills; women are needed in the new role of employees to regulate women in their other, traditional guise. Thus the 'mature' welfare state has had a twofold impact on the lives and consciousness of women. On the one hand, it has drawn them into paid employment, still performing their traditional gender functions of caring and service, but now as paid employees and increasingly as educated professionals. At the same time, it has generated public policies which are extremely salient for women and has consequently mobilised them into politics.

Women's difficulty is that they have not been strong enough to control public reproduction policy themselves or regulate their own employment. This is because they lack the institutions – and their labour lacks

249

the strategic value in the eyes of male-dominated culture – which made this possible for men. Women's traditional work-based organisations, engaged in voluntary self-help and public service, were always defined as 'non-political' and consistently devalued as 'charities' so that they have faced the state without the kind of power-base the labour movement has been for working men. When they turned to the unions for the promotion of their interests, women found themselves excluded by the oligarchical hold of men on union hierarchies. Finally, and more effectively this time, they have turned again to separate organisations of their own. Norwegians therefore see the contemporary women's movement as being partly the result of welfare policies, as a reactive movement by women to empower them *vis-à-vis* the state.[42] As the pursuit of equity brings more women to decision-making roles a corresponding sea-change will take place in how the state performs its role; instead of merely reflecting male values, it will respond to those of women too. Where reproductive labour is concerned, women will be able to direct their own affairs, autonomous from men.

While this seems to provide for women *within* the context of their gender, feminists still have to deal with policies which are 'gender-neutral', in the sense that they apply to men as much as women. The problem is that these have not provided women, in or out of the family, with the same degree of independence and reward for labour as the organisation of society accords to men. One reason is that the level of services provided is simply insufficient to meet the demand. The more fundamental reason is that the fragmented reality of women's lives, compared with those of men, defeats their 'equal' purpose. The 'state feminist' solution is to infuse these 'gender-neutral' policies with the reality of gender difference in order to achieve equality of outcome. This is not as easy as it sounds, however, as the case of pensions serves to illustrate.

Norwegian state pensions incorporate the features of both state and private pension plans in Britain; a basic, subsistence pension is augmented according to an individual's accumulated work-points (i.e. lifetime history of earnings). At present, women, unlike men, rely on three sources of income and support: the family (i.e. men), the state and their own paid-work earnings. Because of time spent in child bearing and the extended reproductive role, paid work cannot in most cases suffice for their support. As well as having to move in and out of their condition of dependence on the family and/or state at various points in their lives, they also find it easier to work part-time in paid employment, where the norm for 'full-time' work is that which is convenient and feasible for men, not women. The result is that women's ability to earn is restricted by their working hours and the discontinuity of their employment, both of which also disqualify them from promotion. Job segregation in the labour market is a factor too.

It is this that makes nonsense in practice of the ostensible equality guaranteed by gender-neutral social legislation. At the core of social security construction in Norway as elsewhere are the values of the labour market, where it is only paid work which counts as work of public value. In spite of the relative egalitarianism of the welfare state, the idea that earnings are the proper yardstick of the individual's right to receipts from the public purse remains central to it. The result is that the higher pensions go to men (ceasing on their death); women as widows or as earners in their own right almost always get the lower. In Sweden and Norway, three-quarters of the lowest pensions paid are those of women,[43] and of the roughly 30,000 Norwegians who received the highest pension level in 1988, fewer than 100 were women.[44] Of course, this is not because women are congenitally incapable of working as long and hard as men, or because they are lazy. In reality, they work much harder, and the only reason they cannot work as much for pay is because they are working such long hours without it. The net result is that 'in all the Scandinavian countries, as in most industrialised societies, gender is the best predictor of a person's social status.'[45]

The problem is clear, but what is not so obvious is how to solve it. If the state is to incorporate the difference by giving women equal pensions, then, it is men who will have to pay for it. Indeed, as society is presently constituted, any expansion of the welfare state (including better pay for its employees) has the same, disturbing implication. A conflict of material sex-interests, between just rewards for women and higher taxes for men, is inherent in the 'state feminist' programme. The only alternative is to change the material basis of these interests and in Norway, the facts about women's unpaid, caring labour have provided the premise for a set of three inter-related policy proposals which would transform the public value given to different kinds of work. Women are proposing a general six-hour day, such recognition and reward for unpaid care-work as would create a genuine 'care-culture' and, ideally, a universal, citizen's wage.

The proposal for a universal six-hour day in paid employment is one in which women typically find themselves ranged against the interests and perceptions of the employed, industrial male worker but in alliance with a variety of other social groups, such as the young, the elderly and the unemployed, who share their relative lack of integration into the labour market and its values. For the latter, the main object of a shorter day is to spread the available employment more widely (although in fact Norway and Sweden have largely escaped the unemployment crises of the past two decades) and the reluctance of the presently employed to agree to this is quite comprehensible; in the market, time is money and shorter hours means less pay. They also signify more leisure time, but this has never been an object for men to compare with higher pay.

To women, the point of shorter hours is not more leisure time but greater flexibility, to help them synchronise their unpaid work with paid employment. As every woman knows who combines a family and job, the synchronisation of these different kinds of work is very difficult. The reason is, as European feminists are increasingly aware, that they are governed by two quite different kinds of time: cyclical (or natural) time which regulates most natural processes, like life itself, and is the dimension of most care work and (even in this age of mechanisation) much agricultural activity; and linear time, the open-ended, purposive and man-made kind of time which came into its own with the industrial revolution, regulates the labour market and the public sphere and can be stopped and started (e.g. by office hours or clocking in and out) independently of natural processes.[46] Of course, linear time is possible only for those individuals or groups who can evade responsibility for the sphere of cyclical events and the production/reproduction division of labour achieved this very neatly for men, by making cyclical, natural time a female ghetto. Now that women have entered paid employment they are constantly crossing and re-crossing the bounds of cyclical and linear time-frames, and are actually being penalised for the conflicts which occur (e.g. if a carer arrives late for paid work because an elderly dependent has fallen out of bed this is regarded as *her fault*). The six-hour day is a device designed by women, for women and is intended not to eliminate the conflict, which is not possible, but ease it.

Of course, this is a problem which scarcely touches men at all, whereas the proposed solution would change their lives considerably by reducing their incomes and extending their leisure. It may be questioned whether they would know what to do with the extra time, especially on a reduced budget; it is also doubtful if their use of it would have a social value. Women, on the other hand, would go on using their time to contribute to the welfare of society through care-work, in the family and wider community, just as they do now. To understand the full significance of this proposal, however, it must be seen in relation to a second feminist demand, for recognition of the value of this caring work.

In Norway recently, the expression 'the care-culture' has become a catch-phrase for the kind of society Norwegians admire and even claim to have created, but women dispute the latter claim most strenuously. Although the state is committed to caring as a social obligation, the result has been to create a set of citizen expectations without the money to pay for it. In reality, it is calculated that 67 per cent of all the health care done in Norway is privately performed as women's unpaid labour, the greater part of the rest being carried out by part-time female workers.[47] Ironically, while the perennial problem of the labour market is too little work to support sufficient jobs for those who seek them, the problem of the caring sphere is too few jobs for all the work there is to do. What feminists want is to turn the fiction of the caring society into a reality by recognising and rewarding women for their care-work, either by turning it into a 'job' which they are paid for, or giving the carers social vouchers against their own future care and welfare needs, or even by the indirect means of a *tax on time*. In this, they have been moving rapidly towards the concept of 'welfare citizenship', according to which the citizen is defined as someone who gives care and receives it.[48]

The irony of this proposal is that 'state feminism' has been constructed on the differences between the genders, of which the principal is that women care while men do not. If women continue to be the carers then men will end up less well-off than women because they do not care-work, in which case it will be men, not women who are caught in the gender scissors. The only solution for men in this unprecedented scenario will be to abandon their uncaring gender role and behave as women do, just as women, by entering the public sphere, have voluntarily converged with men. Then the ultimate feminist alternative to the division of labour, the universal civic wage, will become a practicable proposition. In truth, although Norwegian feminists are insistently promoting the idea of gender difference as the proper complement to equity, their vision of the long-term future is really one where 'equal participation in the culture of care and the culture of more traditional work by men and women . . . will be the clearest expression of a new gender solidarity'.[49] That is, it is a vision of androgyny.

The question is, how can such a radical vision be realised? The 'state feminist' answer is to try to do so 'from above'. The six-hour day and material rewards for care are conceived as mechanisms for manipulating men's behaviour, by giving them a strong self-interest in modifying their gender role in order to partake of women's rewards. Of course, this strategy implies a rational choice model of behaviour and presupposes that *either* women will control the environment in which men make their choices *or* that the changes will be introduced with the consent of men. There are two obvious dificulties in this. One is the socio-economic and political reality, that men are still the dominant group. When it comes to paying for care, men and women will have the same conflicting interests as they do in the case of pensions and the other welfare programmes; no matter how it is done, women will gain but men will lose. Once men already have converged with women, they may not count the cost, but until that has happened, is it realistic to expect them to consent? The other problem is that the idea of reforming gender 'from above' is not consistent with women's gender theory. It is the *psyche* of men (formed in the earliest experiences of the individual and his childhood perceptions of the adult role his culture will afford him) which is identified in this theory as the driving force of gender difference, which means the only certain way to build a new society is by reforming gender 'from below', through the formative effect of changes in parental roles. Not only are Norwegian feminists putting little emphasis on this approach; many of their policies run counter to the direction a well-grounded gender strategy should take.

What grounds are there, then, for optimism? In truth, Norwegian feminists are not particularly hopeful (and never were, even in 1986–9). Curiously enough, however, such guarded optimism as they have expressed reflects a keen appreciation of the importance of male gender values in determining their prospects of success. The basis of their hopes is the belief that the gender role of Scandinavian men *already has* converged with that of women to such an exceptional extent that it will not stand in women's way. In particular, Norwegian men are perceived as having been more inclined towards co-operation and non-violence than men of other countries ever since the end of the Second World War, which explains the concern for social justice and consensus they brought to post-war politics. This is also regarded as the reason for the readiness of men to acquiesce in women's recent rapid access to elites. In the most hopeful scenario, as outlined by Skjeie, these attitudes will enable women to 'feminise' the parties and their policies from within.

Nowegian 'party women' have been determined to work through the existing party system for more than one reason, but the most important from a feminist perspective are the desire to avoid antagonising or alarming men and the belief that this is possible. The integrationist strategy is based on the premise that the internal workings of the parties are imbued with the same modified male values as the system as a whole. The expectation is that as the proportion of women in the party groups and organs grows to the point of 'critical mass', yet these women are seen to be loyal to traditional ideologies, accommodating to the interests of others and willing to abide by party discipline, the male response will be consensual and democratic too. Men will feel impelled by their values to accept specifically female gender interests as constraints on public policy and even welcome women's inputs to decision-making. The feminisation of a party and its policies will be mutually reinforcing, so that although, in the end, the parties will have changed dramatically – incorporating not only women as individuals but their gender difference too – but they will have done so in a very undramatic way, simply by the operation of their inner-party norms. Even the fact that women will still be divided by the boundaries between the parties is sometimes seen as an advantage. Norwegian feminists are less prone than most to expect more unanimity from women than they do from men and some see the party system as a useful way of legitimising conflicts which must arise within the female sex, e.g. between women with different life-experiences or located at different points within the life-cycle.

The modified male gender role has also given hope to those with the most radical objectives in view. Once started, the process of gender convergence is seen as having gained momentum from the growing emphasis on social policy as the focus of civic solidarity. The state's assumption of responsibility for the bodily needs of the individual has begun to erode the traditional boundaries between family, market, state and public sphere and even the 'mind-body' (reason versus nature) distinction which has been fundamental to European culture since Plato. The normative values are still those of males (and in particular, those of capitalism and the labour market) and men are still dominant, but by their actions they have created conditions in which it will be difficult for them to maintain their separate status. The basis for a genuine care culture may have emerged.

Unfortunately, recent events belie this optimism; Norwegian men, it seems, have not converged that far. Instead, the development of 'state feminist' ideas has taken place in an atmosphere of growing crisis about the future of the welfare state. It is true that Norwegian men are not actually demanding that women return to the home, even though, according to some, the movement of women into the labour market has made a major contribution to the welfare problem by exacerbating the social burden of a disproportionately ageing population. They are jibbing, however, at the size of the welfare state and the level of taxation required to pay for the high costs of care *as they are now*. Although apparently committed to the welfare state and even to 'state feminism' in principle, the established parties are now seeking what are euphemistically described as 'organisational' alternatives like privatisation, ostensibly to foster free enterprise. Irrespective of their motivation, this has aroused acute anxiety among women of all parties about the possibility of a forcible return of caring to the 'family', i.e. to women. In these circumstances women of virtually all political persuasions are the defenders of the state and instead of gender solidarity, it is the lines of that objective conflict of sex interests which is implicit in 'state feminism' which are coming to the fore. At the same time, a new generation of young men is beginning to make its mark with very different values. What women did not seem to reckon on is the fact that gender changes, party systems and electoral cleavages are not irrevocably fixed. If a new cleavage should develop along sex and gender lines, then the party system may be realigned.

It is a pity that no one has provided a satisfactory explanation of why the post-war modification of the male gender role ever took place, for this has allowed Norwegians to assume the trend was independent of parental roles and also fixed. They have been able to overlook the fact that post-war welfare policies, along with women's drive to liberate their motherhood from its traditional bonds, are more likely to reverse, than reinforce the trend. By producing a greater need in males to differentiate themselves from women in order to find a non-maternal, masculine identity, such developments can logically be expected to reassert the competitive, aggressive and misogynist components of the male gender role. Furthermore, since the highly developed welfare state gives men the possibility of having no direct paternal role at all, we can predict from Mead (fatherhood being a social institution) that without the traditional obligations imposed on fathers by society, it will be difficult for the new generation of young men to understand and accept paternal responsibilities at all; the relationship of men to their children will be determined on an individual rather than a social basis.

In fact, this seems to be happening throughout the western world, wherever employment, welfare and housing patterns allow young men to drift away from a family relation with their girl friends and babies, back to the irresponsibility of the juvenile male culture. Although feminists offer entry to childcare and the caring, reproductive role as a 'good' to men – sometimes as a kind of *quid pro quo* for giving women access to paid work, promotion and political elites – the men are not obliged to take the offer up. The only incentive is individual attraction to the caring role but in Sweden, where men have been able for some time to take the same parental leave as women, they do not do so to a significant degree. No more do Norwegian men take up that of part-time work to spend more time in the family and it seems obvious that the more feminists stress the female gendering of care-work, the less inclined to do so they will be. In the long run, men may feel that their exclusion from the family of the mother and child has gone too far for them to bear. In the meantime, feminism, the welfare state and current social trends, in Norway as elsewhere, are all going in the opposite directions of shared parenting *and* women's exclusive motherhood at the same time, with the cards stacked heavily in favour of the latter.

The marked polarisation of young people's votes which has been observed since 1983 in Norway, with young women voting social democrat or further left and young men for the right, especially the 'new right' Progress party,[50] looks very like the electoral manifestation of this trend. The Progress party almost exclusively consists of men, condemns the welfare state and pays lip-service to the image of the 'caring mother' without showing that interest in the traditional family (i.e. in some kind of fatherhood) which is characteristic of the traditional right. In other words, it presents the very worst combination of ideas for women, that of women's caring unsupported by either men's direct responsibility or state support, *and* without any modification of the values of the market which would allow them the opportunity to support themselves on equal terms with men. Given the time the 'mature' Norwegian welfare state and feminist movement have had to form the experience and expectations of the present younger generation, this male reaction is only too predictable.

The Progress party is not part of the established system but an external challenge to it and even if it is not strong enough to be a party of government, it represents enough of a threat to influence the composition of the government (in 1989 the electoral shift to the right resulted in the temporary replacement of the social democratic government by a centre-right coalition) and the policies of other parties. It is significant that rightward parties have been unwilling to commit themselves constitutionally on such feminist issues as the use of gender quotas, leaving themselves just the room for manoeuvre they need to respond to pressure from the further right. Norway's 'state feminist' experiment is certainly not over (and once again, over half the present government are women), but these events undoubtedly have jeopardised its gains.

ICELAND: THE REFORMATION OF POLITICS

The most isolated and undiluted of the early Scandinavian, or indeed European cultural communities, Iceland has preserved much of its language and lore from medieval times and in spite of many kinship features to the other Nordic countries (which include its small size, democratic tradition, relative fluidity of class boundaries and contemporary prosperity), Icelandic society is sharply distinguished by its secular tradition and basis in pre-Christian social norms. It was this cultural distinctiveness which led Lipset to see Iceland as the ideal setting in which to show how over-simplified and parochial the usual western assumptions about the relationships among social variables often are; what he had particularly in mind was the idiosyncratic gender basis of Icelandic society.[51]

One of the most striking features of the Icelandic social heritage is the relative weakness of the family and marriage as social institutions and the extreme differentiation of parental roles associated with this. Icelandic society traditionally includes a large proportion of families headed by women single parents (estimated at 25 per cent of families in 1983)[52] while the incidence of natural fathers performing no paternal role at all is also very high. However, this does not mean that women have enjoyed a higher status than elsewhere. On the contrary, to Lipset's great surprise, the freedom of Icelandic women to engage in extra-marital sex and have 'illegitimate' children (which he assumed to be the essential stuff of sex equality), has been combined with the almost total domination of economy and polity by men. From the perspective of present-day Europe and North America, *traditional* Icelandic society looks remarkably like what other western societies are rapidly heading towards. The result is that although the development of women's relationship to politics has not been the same in Iceland as elsewhere (which is as we should expect), it has lessons for the women's movement everywhere today.

The first lesson is that the combination of independent motherhood with socio-economic deprivation and political exclusion has made it easier for Icelandic women to be conscious of their separate, political identity as women and perceive the conflict of male and female interests and values in their society as public and political in character (rather than as the private problem of individuals within the family structure). The idea of a separatist strategy not only emerged as soon as Iceland's modern democracy began to take shape but has survived to become the distinguishing characteristic (along with the unparalleled degree of mass support it has received) of Icelandic feminism today.

The first attempts of Icelandic women to bring separate structures directly into conventional politics actually go back as far as 1908, when women's lists were nominated in local elections and met with some success. Then women got a limited parliamentary suffrage along with men in 1915, and in the parliamentary elections of 1922 a women's list was put forward and one of its members elected to the Althing. In spite of this unique success, the political consciousness and mobilisation of Icelandic women was insufficient to sustain it; their sole representative eventually joined an existing male-dominated party and the list was abandoned after 1926. This was followed by a long hiatus, in which the political movement more or less subsided until the great reawakening of Western feminism in the 1970s. As elsewhere, it was to be the spread of education and the rapid communication of ideas among highly educated women which precipitated the re-emergence of the Icelandic women's movement.[53] Since many of these ideas were of North American and continental European origin and bore the hallmarks of their different cultures, the initial effect was to divert the course of the Icelandic movement into unfamiliar channels.

It was returned students from abroad, especially from European centres of feminist activity such as Denmark and the Netherlands, who were responsible for the formation of the Icelandic Redstockings in 1970 and the influence of radical feminism was immediately apparent in the deliberately non-hierarchical basis on which the new movement was organised internally. In other respects, however, these Redstockings were a striking departure from the model of their ultra-radical, New York namesakes and from the Icelandic feminist tradition as well. The influence of the European left, with its insistence on the illegitimacy of separate action, had been imported too, so that the Redstockings' surprising emphasis was on lobbying the system rather than rejecting it, and on integrating women into mainstream socialist politics rather than proclaiming their separate values.[54] Putting pressure on the political parties for a commitment on abortion, equality and childcare allocations and on the unions for action on the issue of women's low pay, the new feminists had some success. Where the allocation of public resources was concerned promises were honoured more in the breach than the observance, but equality legislation was passed and although this had little or no immediate effect on women's very low socio-economic status it helped to open doors for younger women. Attempts to reform the abortion law foundered on divisions of opinion among women and among the Redstockings' left-wing parliamentary allies but even so, a tacit change in medical practice gave women most of what they wanted without formal amendment of the law.[55]

These achievements, however, brought crisis in their train, in the form of a startling popular manifestation of the potential of ordinary Icelandic women for direct, separate action and the capacity of women's organisations, traditional and new, to act in unity; this was the one-day women's strike which brought Iceland to a virtual standstill on 24 October 1975. In resorting to separate action, Icelandic women were reverting to their former practice but one which was unacceptable on principle to many Redstocking socialists. Not for the first time or the last, Icelandic feminism found itself at a strategic crossroads, and in this instance the integrationists prevailed. Without any Icelandic equivalent to those developments in mainstream political culture which made Norwegian men so susceptible to the demand for equity, this strategy led the movement straight into the *cul de sac* of left-wing class politics in which it would stagnate for the next five years or so. In spite of proportional representation, the unchanging composition of the Icelandic political elite in these years of Scandinavian advance was very marked. Throughout the period 1970–83, only three women were elected to the Althing and the improvement in local politics was very slight.

It was not until 1981 that Icelandic feminism recovered and resumed its march of success, in and out of conventional politics, with the formation of the separate, women's party known as Kwenna Frambothid (KF). The protagonists were a small group of radical intellectuals incensed by the lack of progress being made by 'equal rights' and left-wing feminism. Although these women were deeply alienated from the conventional political system and advocated a new kind of non-hierachical, participatory democracy in its stead, one of the spurs to their action was the success of Vigdis Finnbogadottir's Presidential bid in 1980 (an event which stressed women's right and fitness for elite positions even though her platform was not overtly feminist), and one of their immediate decisions was to fight the forthcoming local government elections in Reykjavik and Akureyri. Their overnight success in these elections, achieving 11.7 per cent and 18 per cent of the votes respectively, not only put KF representatives into both councils but revealed a potential separatist power base in women voters the size of which took Icelanders by surprise. The following year, a parliamentary women's list, the Kwennalistinn, was formed amid heated controversy inside Kwenna Frambothid and proceeded to cap all previous electoral achievements by winning three Althing seats in its very first appearance at the polls.

The background to these startling events was the striking change in Icelandic women's socio-economic situation which had been occurring since the 1970s. The education of women had greatly improved, with the proportion of women among *gymnasium* graduates up from 24.8 per cent in 1960 to 59 per cent by 1983. There was also a vast increase in the proportion of married women in paid employment, up from 28 per cent in 1964 to 65 per cent in 1980. This actually represented a movement of women *back* into employment, for although women in Iceland had experienced the same post-war isolation in the home as British and American housewives this was a striking departure from the old Icelandic pattern. Now, the difference was that many women entering the labour market were educated, with specialised skills and qualifications.[56] However, the Kwenna Frambothid feminists did not confine their social appeal to the material interests of this new and mainly younger stratum. Putting comparatively little emphasis on equity, they took their stand on gender difference instead, stressing the traditional female values of caring, responsibility and desire for peace and demanding recognition for them in the public sphere. The result was an extremely effective electoral alliance between a few highly educated and untypical radicals and a significant proportion of the ordinary female population. Although the alliance proved short-lived, this was not due to any loss of popular support (in spite of the fact that the traditional women's organisations held aloof from Kwenna Frambothid). It was the activists who withdrew from it, because they felt unable to cope with the two sets of contradictions to which they had exposed themselves: between participating in the system and rejecting it, and between women's liberation and the traditional values of their gender role.[57]

In making their bid for access to the system on the grounds of gender difference, the new feminists were returning to the idea underlying the older tradition of the women's lists – that women have something different to say from men – but with a crucial difference. Unprepared to settle for women's simply having the opportunity to speak in their own voice, they wanted to ensure that women's voice was *heard and acted on*.[58] The fact that men, in their entrenched positions of power, could afford to ignore the voice of women led the feminists to conclude that the only way to end the power of men was to seek power for themselves. Rejecting power and hierarchy on principle, they intended to use them to carry out a revolution from within the public sphere, firstly by gaining access to the council chamber and then by refusing to follow its procedural rules and accept their own superior status. The feminist councillors would share this status and decision-making role with the women's movement as a whole, by taking council business to the mass meeting and implementing its decisions as its delegates, not representatives. If possible, they would also share their council seats with other women on an informal basis. Thus the voice of women would be heard directly in the centres of political power but at the same time women would be destroying the basis of that power.

In the event, this project failed disastrously. In the first place, their power was insufficient; a programme of procedural reform which might have been feasible for a majority party was quite beyond the powers of a minority group whose ideas were received with hostile incredulity by the dominant male majority. Instead it was the KF councillors who had to adjust to an unwelcome set of norms. In the second place, the development of their relationship with the movement was severely disappointing. The problem was not a loss of popular support, for both activists and sympathisers continued to endorse their councillors' actions on the whole, but the passive nature of this support. Increasingly, as they became more skilled in following and transacting council business, the councillors found that their responsibility and expertise were isolating them from their grass-roots base. While factionalism and acrimony emerged among the most committed activists over fundamental aims, other women found the volume of council business discussed at KF meetings both intimidating and boring. Instead of becoming more involved through the movement's participatory model of democracy, they began to plead ignorance, to pass the buck tacitly to the councillors and eventually to stay away from meetings altogether, even pleading their traditional, domestic duties as an excuse. In so doing, they were of course behaving according to the conventional political expectations of the Icelandic citizen of either sex, according to which the role of voters is to vote while that of councillors is to take decisions in their name. As one of the women councillors expressed it, 'My feeling is that this damned representative system is one of the most effective means of neutralising people and making them powerless. In itself it is absolutely anti-feminist and our experience has taught me that we were actually helpless within it.'[59] Instead of bringing power to all women, it encouraged grass-roots apathy.

At the same time, the very stress on gender difference which was the root of their electoral success seemed to have led the feminists into a gender *cul de sac*. Instead of developing a radical feminist analysis of the family and sexuality, they felt obliged to side-step these issues for fear of losing mass support.[60] This tacit endorsement of traditional values came to be seen as tantamount to reinforcing patriarchy and an important factor in their inability to maintain a dynamic relationship between the activists and their grass-roots support. The result was that although Kwenna Frambothid continued to delight and encourage women with its creative flair (as in the 'Supermarket Demonstration' of 1984, in which women shoppers announced at check-outs that since women's average wage was only 66 per cent of that of men they would not pay more than 66 per cent of the marked prices for their goods), the heart went out of it. For many disillusioned activists, the only answer was to withdraw from conventional politics.

This conclusion, worlds away from that of Norwegian feminist politicians in pursuit of the 'critical mass', was not unanimous, however. In 1986, Kwenna Frambothid decided not to fight local elections in spite of the sizeable vote it could expect and in the face of accusations of defeatism and an abdication of responsibility, but the result was simply that Kwennalistinn emerged as the foremost feminist group, rallying the less disillusioned KF activists as well as new, less militant support. In spite of very limited success in the few local seats they could contest in 1986, Kwennalistinn went on to fight the parliamentary elections of 1987 with astonishing results. Six KL feminists were elected to the new (63-seat) Althing with 10 per cent of the popular vote and because of the distribution of seats among the other parties these women found themselves catapulted into a pivotal parliamentary role.

The post-election crisis, which led to their being courted as potential partners in a coalition government not just by the Social Democrats but even by the right-wing Independence party, confronted Kwennalistinn right away (and in the glare of maximum publicity), with the same basic contradiction between their desire to participate in the existing system and their objective of transforming it on which the Kwenna Frambothid had foundered. The problem had two dimensions. One concerned the frontier between separatism and integration: Kwennalistinn must decide whether it was more important to achieve the status of a government partner or to retain a separate stance; if the former, the terms on which participation in a government would be acceptable must be agreed. The other dimension was that of democratic theory and practice, for against the conventional Icelandic conception of democracy as the representation of the masses by their leaders, the KL feminists, like their KF predecessors, were proposing a feminist alternative in which there were no leaders and no decisions either until the popular movement as a whole could be agreed.

Both dimensions, and the strengths and weaknesses of the feminist position, were vividly exposed by the coalition negotiations. Since the KL parliamentary group refused to make any commitments without referral back to the movement, where decisions were reached by talking the matter out exhaustively in a non-hierachical, unregulated meeting until consensus of opinion was achieved, the inter-party talks were protracted.

From the perspective of the other parties, this conception of democracy was incomprehensible; the women were accused of being indecisive and wasting time.[61] However, the result was a solid basis for the decision when it came and neither the decision itself (to withdraw from the negotiations) nor the manner in which it was achieved appeared to have done the Kwennalistinn any harm, in the eyes of the electorate at least. Although the other parties accused the feminists of showing an inability to compromise and unwillingness to take responsibility, successive opinion polls showed that mass support for KL was mounting quite dramatically throughout the spring of 1988; by May this reached the point where 29.7 per cent of those polled said that if an election were held immediately, KL would get their vote.[62] This would have made them the biggest parliamentary group.

Nevertheless, their popularity cannot disguise the fact that Kwennalistinn's fundamental conflict of pragmatic participation versus outright rejection of the system is unresolved. As repeated statements by participants make clear, the talks did not fail because the KL rejected the idea of government in principle, but because the other parties would not agree to the feminists' demand for a mininum wage to help that 90 per cent of Icelandic women workers who are low-paid.[63] (The discussions never reached the thorny subjects of disarmament and peace.) What this means, of course, is that it was not power nor the system which the feminists rejected, but their *lack* of power to strike the bargain they wanted with the other parties in the system. Their justification was not that they were helpless in a representative system (as the KF councillor quoted above had said), but that they could be *more* effective (and responsible) inside it as a 'sincere opposition force'.[64] This claim seemed to be borne out by their subsequent success in presenting bills on maternity leave and minimum wages over and over again until (at least in the former case) public clamour persuaded the government to bring in a bill itself. It has to be said, however, that the role of opposition lends itself particularly well to evading the issue of participation versus transformation. The test of radicalism is when it comes to exercising power directly and if the opinion polls are to be trusted, that day may not be very far away.

In fact, Kwennalistinn activists are well aware that they have entered on a dangerous path of compromise. Their best insurance against being captured by the system, as they see it, is to try, like the KF councillors before them, to import their version of democracy into the system along with themselves. The determination to stand firm on the democratic, consensus mode of decision-making, the formal commitment of elected Althing members to relinquish their seats halfway through the life of the parliament to the women placed below them on the list (a device adopted also by the West German Greens) and the rule that no women should serve more than two parliamentary terms, are all regarded as evidence of their ability to infiltrate the new democracy into the male-dominated system. As well as spreading parliamentary experience more widely and preventing the emergence of individual leaders, rotation is also seen as introducing into public life a principle of 'come and go' more in harmony with the realities of women's lives than the male conception of politics as a continuous, full-time 'career'.[65] As for the principle of continuous grass-roots participation, only time will tell whether the KL can strike a better balance between the principle and the demands it makes on their supporters than their KF precursors were able to achieve.

Of course, no amount of democratic purity inside Kwennalistinn will be sufficient in the long run unless these new principles effectively undermine and substitute existing values, i.e. unless they are adopted by the other actors in the system. Otherwise, the feminists might find themselves obliged by their electoral success inside a competitive system to act as a conventional party of government, while the other parties persisted in their appetite for representative norms and exercised the same right to oppose which Kwennalistinn is exploiting at the moment. It seems that what the KL feminists most need is not to win an election too decisively, too soon, but to gain time instead to change the system as they go, by a combination of their own example and a steadily mounting electoral threat which will induce the other parties to take it seriously. So far, their main impact on partisan politics has been in the recruitment field, where virtually all the other parties have produced a token woman in the Althing, bringing the female total to thirteen seats. Although this is only 20.6 per cent, it raises the long-term possibility of a cross-party 'critical mass' of women who might also lend support to value change. As yet, women in the other parties are prepared to collaborate on what they see as 'women's issues' only so long as there is no clash with the dominant male ideological cleavages and party discipline. Success for the feminists seems to depend on a very tricky feat of synchronisation, in which their impact on the values of the system, their electoral performance and the political consciousness of women in the other parties all reach the threshold which will support a feminist consensus government at the same time. So far, only the local council in Akureyri (where an untypical consensus-building approach to decision-making existed already and the separatist feminists are able to collaborate with a very much larger group of women councillors) has come anywhere near meeting these conditions.

The question that has to be asked, however, is what 'success' in these terms would really signify. The overwhelming emphasis of Icelandic separatism in both its contemporary phases has been on the transformation of the *political system*, i.e. on a reformation of male gender values 'from above' and by means of a mixture of feminist example and coercion, but this has tended to distract attention from the very fundamental problem that the root of gender is not in public life but in men's and women's different reproductive roles. No authentic revolution in male values can occur independently of a fundamental change in gender roles, just as no authentic revolution in the distribution of political power can occur independently of changes in the distribution of socio-economic resources *which is also gender-based*. Any advantage that the Kwennalistinn feminists can obtain will be merely temporary unless it can be used to set in motion very basic changes which will reshape gender roles and values 'from below'. Otherwise they will simply meet the same brick wall as the women's list in 1926 and Kwenna Frambothid in the early 1980s; that the values and behaviour of men and women – and their access to resources – can only be as similar as their gender will allow.

The parliamentary focus and more pragmatic, policy-oriented style of Kwennalistinn may help to explain why they have experienced the relationship of feminism and the traditional female gender role as, so far, less problematic than the KF did. The problems are not far to seek, however. It is not that Icelandic women underestimate the importance of motherhood in defining women's role. On the contrary, they recognise that the existing gender role of women is an extension of their child-bearing and nourishing functions into those of social care in general[66] and see the resulting difference in gender perspective as so profound that women need a different policy from men on virtually everything. In fact they go much further than most women would to identify women with their mothering role; where most feminists would agree that a male-dominated society like Iceland which is fundamentally hostile to women's interests must *ipso facto* be hostile to children too, it seems unlikely that many would be comfortable with Kristmundsdottir's statement that 'the situation of women is closely tied to the situation of children, so we don't distinguish between the two.'[67] Given the real weakness of paternal values in the male Icelandic gender role, this attitude is understandable, but it also, even more starkly, raises the same problems as in Norway of potential incompatibilty between the emphasis on gender difference, which recognises that a separate women's voice exists and must be heard, and the need to modify both gender roles to the point where men will willingly support a woman-friendly order. Parental roles will be the crucial factor here.

Icelandic feminism has always stressed the need to relieve women of some part of their unshared parental burden through public childcare agencies but latterly a strong Scandinavian influence has given this concern a wider focus. The principal childcare goal pursued by Kwennalistinn is the rapid proliferation of day-care centres, to be available 'regardless of location, job status, financial status and marital status of the parents', but along with this goes the demand that the salaries of nursery school teachers be raised to a level which will attract people into the profession and be commensurate with the importance 'to the nation' of their work.[68] Standards of private day-care should be improved as well and in the consensus-oriented town of Akureyri, Kwennalistinn has won special assistance for single-parents in the form of cash payments to recompense those who cannot use existing public day-care centres. Like the Norwegians, Icelandic feminists also allude to the part the state has played in drawing women into public-sector employment with low wages and no decision-making role and they, too, demand that 'women's jobs, in all their forms, must be given more value and prestige', so that the whole extended range of care-work, while remaining in the women's sphere, will bring rewards commensurate with those of men.[69] Like their Scandinavian mentors, Icelandic feminists are also looking to a vision of the future in which women will share their mothering with men (to the 'liberating' advantage of the latter) and consequently propose that *parents* (i.e. of both sexes) should have the option of shorter working days and flexible working hours so as to give families more time together. They have not so far found any means of ensuring that this will actually happen on a significant scale. The competitive, inegalitarian values of the labour market, as always, are against them; men will be reluctant to take advantage of a leave which will endanger their future earning capacities and careers. In so far as any answer to this problem has emerged, it is the Norwegian feminists' sophisticated concept of the genuine 'care-culture' and their proposals for the six-hour day and material inducements for men to modify their role. Hopes are already receding in Norway, however, and although Kwennalistinn shows every sign of following this lead, the Icelandic cultural climate is obviously even less congenial. It is difficult, too, to see these new concerns as other than peripheral compared with the central Icelandic feminist project of transforming the political system. The fundamental gender problem of parental roles is all too clearly unresolved.

10

CONCLUSION

The problem facing feminists is indeed daunting, and may even be insoluble. It is impossible to analyse the development of the women's movement without arriving at the same conclusion reached by gender theorists, that women cannot change their situation without a fundamental change in men's. Although, from the perspective of existing systems, women's situation resembles that of other out-groups and the dilemmas of feminism can be compared with those experienced by other social movements, this is only half the picture. Women are not just one of many out-groups in these systems but stand outside them too, and society, economy and polity are not just dominated by men but are the product of the male gender role and values. Any feminism which fails to recognise these facts and tries to integrate women and their interests into the structures and ideologies devised by men will be trapped in the scissors of conflicting gender aspirations and identities. Women in general, the supposed beneficiaries, will end up where they started from.

The logical way forward is for feminists to face the facts of gender difference and take their stand on the female identity, organising separately and articulating their interests in a distinctive, female voice. In practice, this is almost as difficult a step for women who participate in politics today as for Finns and Russians a hundred years ago. The fears and assumptions of equal rights and socialist feminism are still very much alive and, as the West German Greens vividly illustrate, even those who admit the force of separatism as a strategy are prone to falter at the hurdle of the female gender role. Yet when women take the kind of unequivocal stand on gender difference that Norwegian and Icelandic feminists have done, enormous dividends accrue, both in terms of unity and mass support from ordinary women and in the ability of feminists to articulate female interests and clarify the gender issues they involve. Where loopholes in male-dominated systems afford unusual access to political elites, this is the feminism which has most to gain.

The trouble is that gender difference in itself cannot provide the long-

267

term answer. It is not only that when women bring their voice and interests into the public sphere these are at odds with those of men. The crucial insight of women's gender theory is that gender difference is intrinsically linked with the drive of men for dominance and the profoundly gendered basis of the public sphere. The inherent paradox of feminism based on gender difference is that it serves to reinforce the basis of the gender hierarchy.

Even when feminists are aware of this problem and committed in principle to the long-term aim of an androgynous society, the transition to a strategy of gender convergence is very difficult to make. The methods employed are often strangely inappropriate as well. A well-founded gender strategy would use the opportunity to make incremental changes 'from above' to initiate a long-term process of gender convergence 'from below', by means of changes in parental roles throughout society; these would enable adult men to learn from 'mothering' as women do, but have their most profound, sustainable effect through the psyche of the caring fathers' offspring. Yet this is not what the most advanced contemporary feminists are trying very hard to do; their efforts for shared parenting stop with enabling legislation, which extends the options open to individual men who are uneasy in their gender role but leaves the system to exact a heavy price for such behaviour and reward the majority who do not seek a 'mothering' role. The active emphasis is on changes 'from above' which will act on the behaviour of male adults through the *superstructure* of their gender rather than by striking at its roots, and thus on rational choice rather than reshaping the male psyche; men will *consent* to changes in their role (not understood primarily in terms of parenting) because women politicians will be sufficiently powerful to manipulate the environment in which their choice is made.

Although these short-cuts to a gender revolution are unlikely to meet with much success, women need not despair on that account; if the 1980s have proved anything it is the creative capacity of modern feminists to share ideas and experience and learn from past mistakes. The more intractable problem is still the question of what women really want and how compatible their aspirations are.

So far, the personal choices made by ordinary women in the western world, like feminism, point different ways. Most women choose marriage as the framework for motherhood, at least initially, but wish to make it a less unequal relationship with men. However, although their ideas may encompass some degree of shared parenting this is something few couples can seriously attempt and still fewer achieve within existing socio-economic systems and male-centred cultures; marriage for most women is tantamount to settling for traditional roles. At the same time, the rapid growth in single parenthood suggests that women's liberation is not understood, especially among the young, in terms of fundamental changes in both gender roles so much as in the sense of separating motherhood from relationships with men.

If this reflects a real incompatibility between women's deepest aspirations (or natural inclinations) and sharing their mothering role with men, the feminist problem is not merely daunting but insoluble. However, it evidently has not occurred to many women, including feminists, that both single-parenthood and dependence on the state are dramatic re-affirmations of women's traditional role; nor are the consequnces of liberating *men* from a paternal role receiving the consideration they deserve. In any case, the full implications of the gender role dichotomy – for the gender hierarchy *and* for the nature of relations among men – are still not widely understood by either sex. Until they are, women cannot really make a choice.

NOTES

1 GENDER AND RECRUITMENT: THE NATURE OF THE PROBLEM

1 Samuel Lipset, *Political Man* (New York, Doubleday, 1960) chap. 3.
2 In the United States this happened even before the enfranchisement of women, which took place in 1920; Jeannette Rankin, the first woman elected to the US House of Representatives, won her seat in 1916.
3 Sidney Verba, Norman Nie and Jao-on Kim describe the gap in the United States as 'strikingly narrow' in their *Participation and Political Equality: a Seven-Nation Comparison*, (Cambridge, Cambridge University Press, 1978:267); the data for this study were collected between 1966 and 1971. See also Susan Welch, 'Women as Political Animals? A Test of Some Explanations for Male–Female Political Participation Differences' (*American Journal of Political Science*, XX1, 4, 1977, 711–730) and the same author's 'Sex Differences in Political Activity in Britain' (*Women and Politics*, 1, 2, 1980, 29–46). Most recently, Carol Christy's meticulous study of the available cross-national evidence also supports the conclusion that '. . . sex differences in political participation have usually decreased' during the last thirty years or so (but not the widespread assumption that they will necessarily continue to do so in the future). Carol Christy, *Sex Differences in Political Participation: Processes of Change in Fourteen Nations* (New York, Praeger, 1987).
4 Norway in 1981 and Iceland in 1983. See Elina Haavio-Mannila *et al.* (eds), *Unfinished Democracy; Women in Nordic Politics*, (Oxford, Pergamon, 1985:173).
5 Over the period 1982–4, a bare 10 per cent of candidates for the US Senate, but only 7.9 per cent of those for the House of Representatives, were women. See *The Congressional Quarterly's Guide to U.S. Elections*, 2nd edn, (Washington, 1985), pp. 609–36 and 1057–61.
6 Haavio-Mannila (1985) 60–4.
7 Calculated from Alan Wood (ed.), *The Times Guide to the House of Commons June 1987* (London, Times Books, 1987).
8 The former Soviet Union, controlled as it was by the CPSU, provided one of the best models of recruitment in a one-party state. This book concentrates on the available data on the Soviet Union as an historical case-study. Any mention of the USSR refers deliberately to this one-party era, and unless stated otherwise to the years before any of the Gorbachev reforms.
9 Vicky Randall, *Women and Politics*, 2nd edn (London, Macmillan, 1987) pp. 97–101.

270

10 For the Soviet Union, see David Lane, *State and Politics in the USSR* (Oxford, Basil Blackwell, 1985) p. 185; for Scandinavia, see Haavio-Mannila (ed.) (1985) pp. 184-5; Scottish figures calculated from John Bochel and David Denver, *The Scottish District Elections 1988: Results and Statistics*, (University of Dundee, Dundee, 1988). For the USA, see Susan Carroll and Wendy Strimling, *Women's Routes to Elective Office*; a Comparison with Men's, (Rutgers, Center for the American Woman and Politics, 1983) p. 5.

11 Among the material rewards of local office which contestants are seeking to control, a recent work lists 'appointive and elective positions in government, contracts or other preferments supplied by government, economic opportunities that result from working in and around government, and exemptions from strict law enforcement on such matters as vice and taxes.' David R. Mayhew, *Placing Parties in American Politics; Organization, Electoral Settings, and Government Activity in the Twentieth Century* (Princeton, Princeton University Press, 1986) pp. 20-1. The rewards go with the office, so that their use and enjoyment is as open to individual and group-based candidates as those backed by political parties; as Mayhew points out, party organisations use these assets to reward their supporters but even they may lose control of them to individual office-holders once elected.

12 Naomi Lynn, 'Women and Politics; the Real Majority' in Jo Freeman, (ed.), *Women; a Feminist Perspective*, 3rd edn, (Palo Alto, Mayfield, 1984) p. 414.

13 Susan Welch and Albert K. Karnig, 'Correlates of Female Office Holding in City Politics', *Journal of Politics*, 41, 1979, 478-91.

14 Deportation (into exile in the West) was the fate of Tatyana Mamanova and other leading feminists associated with the periodical *Zhenshchina i Rossiya* (Woman and Russia) in 1979. See Tatyana Mamanova, *Women in Russia* (Oxford, Blackwell, 1984), p. IX.

15 Wilma Rule, 'Why Women Don't Run: The Critical Contextual Factors in Women's Legislative Recruitment', *The Western Political Quarterly*, 9, 1974, 171-84.

16 Torild Skard and Elina Haavio-Mannila 'Women in Parliament' in Haavio-Mannila (1985) p. 54 and Table 4.3. Denmark and Norway have had proportional representation systems since 1920 and 1921 respectively, but women were never more than 3 per cent of the Danish Folketing or 2 per cent of the Storting until after the Second World War.

17 Gabriel Almond and Sidney Verba, *The Civic Culture* (Princeton, Princeton University Press, 1983) p. 379.

18 Maurice Duverger, *The Political Role of Women* (New York, Unesco, 1955); Angus Campbell, Philip Converse, Warren Miller and Donald Stokes, *The American Voter* (New York, Wiley, 1966) pp. 484-9; Verba, Nie and Kim (1978).

19 Verba, Nie and Kim's *Participation and Political Equality* is devoted to the demonstration of this thesis.

20 Ibid. p. 250.

21 Ibid. p. 265.

22 A pioneering discusssion of the variation in male–female roles in primitive and modern societies is to be found in Margaret Mead, *Male and Female*, (Harmondsworth, Pelican, 1971). A remarkable recent treatment of this subject is Sheila Lewenhak's *Women and Work*, (London, Macmillan, 1980). See also Ann Oakley, *Sex, Gender and Society*, (London, 1972), the review of this topic in Randall, op. cit, pp. 15-49 and Henrietta Moore, *Feminism and Anthropology* (London, Polity Press, 1988) Chapter 12 and passim. Most

271

recently, the scholarly review of anthropological literature in Cynthia Fuchs Epstein *Deceptive Distinctions: Sex, Gender and the Social Order* (New Haven, Yale University Press, 1988) comes (p. 71) to exactly Mead's original conclusion.

23 Lewenhak, op. cit pp. 42–3

24 Mead, op. cit, pp. 161–76; Sherry Ortner, 'Is female to male as nature is to culture?' in M. Rosaldo and L. Lamphere (eds) *Women, Culture and Society* (Stanford, Stanford University Press, 1974). This may not always have been the case. Although the origin and timing of male dominance are questions which presumably can never be resolved, the anthropological evidence can be used to support the view that Stone Age societies varied from the patriarchal to the genuinely matriarchal with examples of different but equal roles for the sexes as well. For an impressive treatment of this evidence, using a feminist perspective in contrast to the usual male-centred assumptions, see Lewenhak, op. cit, 19–71. For an excellent short account of the origins and development of two opposing interpretations of the relative effect on women of the rise of capitalism, see the Introduction by Miranda Chaytor and Jane Lewis to Alice Clark, *Working Life of Women in the Seventeenth Century*, (London, Routledge and Kegan Paul, 1982) pp. IX–XLIII.

25 Elizabeth Vallance, *Women in the House*, (London, Athlone, 1979) pp. 12–15.

26 Ibid., pp. 6–12.

27 Jill Hills, 'Lifestyle Constraints on Formal Political Participation; Why So Few Women Local Government Councillors in Britain?' *Electoral Studies*, 2, 1983, 39–52.

28 See, for example, David Easton and Jack Dennis, 'The Child's Acquisition of Regime Norms: Political Efficacy', *American Political Science Review*, LXI, 1971, 36–8; Lynne Iglitsyn, 'The Making of the Apolitical Woman: Feminity and Sex-Stereotyping in Girls' in Jane Jacquette, (ed.), *Women in Politics*, New York, Wiley, 1974, 25–36; Robert Dowse and John Hughes, 'Girls, Boys and Politics' (*British Journal of Sociology*, XXII, 1971, 53–67) and 'Pre-Adult Origins of Adult Political Activity' in Colin Crouch, (ed.), *British Political Sociology Yearbook, Volume 3, Participation in Politics* London, Croom Helm, 1977, 202–21; Welch, 'Women as Political Animals' and 'Sex Differences in Political Activity in Britain'. See also the review of the literature in Randall, op. cit, 83–5.

29 Joni Lovenduski, *Women and European Politics: Contemporary Feminism and Public Policy*, (Brighton, Wheatsheaf, 1986) pp. 226, 231; Haavio-Mannila *et al.*, (eds), op. cit, 52–3; Randall, op. cit, 72–3.

30 Helge Maria Hernes *et al.*, 'Women in the Corporate System' and Drude Dahlerup and Elina Haavio-Mannila, 'Summary', both in Haavio-Mannila *et al.*, (eds), op. cit, 106–32, 163–4. At the level of grass-roots participation, the finding of Lafferty's Norwegian research (William Lafferty, 'Social Development and Political Participation: Class, Organisation and Sex' Scandinavian Political Studies, 1, 4, 1978.) that '. . . sex is the most important "structural" determinant of participation in Norway' appears to corroborate the pessimistic views of these authors.

31 T. T. Mackie and F. W. S. Craig, *Europe Votes 2: European Parliamentary Election Results* 1979–1984, (Chichester, Parliamentary Research Services, 1985).

32 Robert Dahl, *Who Governs?*, (New Haven, Yale University Press, 1961), pp. 11–86.

33 Kenneth Prewitt, *The Recruitment of Political Leaders; a Study of Citizen-Politicans*, (Indianapolis, Bobbs-Merrill, 1970) 27–50.

34 Sidney Verba and Norman Nie, *Participation in America; Political Democracy and Social Equality* (New York, Harper and Row, 1972) 125–37.

35 Lester G. Seligman, Michael R. Kim, Chong Lim Kim and Roland E. Smith, *Patterns of Recruitment: a State Chooses its Lawmakers* (Chicago, Rand McNally, 1974) pp. 15–28.

36 Michael Rush, 'The Members of Parliament', in S. A. Walkland and Michael Ryle, (eds), *The Commons Today*, London, Fontana, 1981, p. 48.

37 Rush, ibid., 46–53. For an immensely stimulating and scholarly examination of the evolution of the British labour movement in respect of its location in the working class and the development of attitudes within it to the prevailing social structure and its hierarchy of values, see also Zygmunt Bauman, *Between Class and Elite: The evolution of the Labour Movement. A sociological study* (Manchester, Manchester University Press, 1972, translated by Sheila Patterson).

38 The 1930s were the crucial period in the formation of the Soviet bureacratic elite (which Milovan Djilas went so far as to call a 'new class' of controllers, rather than owners of property) and the enduring pattern of CPSU composition. See T. H. Rigby, *Communist Party Membership in the USSR, 1917–67* (Princeton University Press, 1968).

39 Vallance, op. cit, p. 6.

40 Susan Welch, 'Recruitment of Women to Public Office: a Discriminant Analysis', *Western Political Quarterly*, 31, 1978, 372–80.

41 Raisa Deber, 'The Fault, Dear Brutus: Women as Congressional Candidates in Pennsylvania', *Journal of Politics*, 44, 1982, 463–79.

42 Sharyne Merritt, 'Winners and Losers: Sex Differences in Municipal Elections', *American Journal of Political Science*, XXI, 1977, 731–43.

43 Helga Maria Hernes and Eva Hanninen-Salmelin, 'Women in the corporate system' in Elina Haavio-Mannila (ed.), *Unfinished Democracy: Women in Nordic Politics*, (Oxford, Pergamon Press, 1985), pp. 106–33.

44 Jorgen Rasmussen, 'Female Political Career Patterns and Leadership Disabilities in Britain: The Crucial Role of Gatekeepers in Regulating Entry to the Political Elite', *Polity*, XIII, 4, 1981, 600–20.

45 John Bochel and David Denver, 'Candidate Selection in the Labour Party: What the Selectors Seek', *British Journal of Political Science*, 13, 1983, 45–67.

46 The points raised here will be examined in more detail in a subsequent work, using data from the same Scottish study which is reported later in this book.

47 The low-point in post-war Parliamentary candidacy was 1951, when 1,376 people stood, compared to a high of 2,578 in 1983. Only in 1987 has the rise of 77 per cent in the number of men (from 1,299 in 1951 to 2,302 in 1983) been offset by the continuing rise in female candidacies and a fall-back in the total number of candidates in that year. Of course, these changes have meant a severe drop in the success rate of male candidates, while their almost exclusive control of the seats has remained unbroken. For raw data, see F. W. S Craig, *British Electoral Facts, 1885–1975* (London, Macmillan, 1976); *British Parliamentary Election Results, 1974–1983* (Chichester, Parliamentary Research Services, 1984); and *The Times Guide to the House of Commons 1987, op. cit.*

48 See K. Lawson and P. Merkl (eds) *When Parties Fail: Emerging Alternative Organizations* (Princeton, Princeton University Press, 1988).

49 Jean Martin and Ceridwen Roberts, *Women and Employment: A Lifetime Perspective* (London, HMSO, 1984).

50 As Dennis and Easton found in their study, cited earlier, of political efficacy among American adolescents.

51 For a detailed historical analysis of women's industrial organisation and difficulties in Britain, which also distinguishes the attitudes and behaviour of different sections of the trade union movement towards women, see Sarah Boston, *Women Workers and the Trade Union Movement*, (London, Davis-Poynter, 1980). See also the excellent comparative analysis of women's work and organisation in the early period of industrialisation in Jane Rendell, *The Origins of Modern Feminism: Women in Britain, France and the United States, 1780–1860* (London, Macmillan, 1985), pp. 150–88, where the political implications of women's domestic and employment situation and the policies pursued by working men are more fully explored.

52 Yet again, it should be stressed that the physical representation of a group is not being equated with the exclusive representation of its interests; not only political movements but even quite narrow socio-economic groups may exhibit, for example, concern for the underdog; a broad class identification which extends to the less fortunate; or a sense of reciprocal responsibilities with less advantaged groups. It has to said, however, that this normally goes no further than is compatible with preserving of their own relative advantage.

53 For example, it has frequently been observed in Britain that a higher proportion of women elected to the House of Commons is from marginal seats than is the case for men. This is not because more women win marginal seats than men – the absolute number is actually very much smaller – but because there are so few women elected from safe seats. Taking the election of 1987 as an example, fourteen women were elected with majorities of less than 10 per cent, which is 34 per cent of the whole female representation in the house. The number of men with such small majorities was much greater – 137 – but this is only 22 per cent of male MPs. The size of the statistical advantage possessed by winner-type women over the rest is thus more dependent on the relative number of these loopholes in a particular political context than is the case for men.

54 Randall, op. cit, p. 87.

55 Carol Gilligan, *In a Different Voice*, Cambridge, MA, Harvard University Press, 1982.

56 M. Kent Jennings, 'Another Look at the Life Cycle and Political Participation', *American Journal of Political Science*, 23, 1979, 755–71.

2 MAJOR PARTIES AND RECRUITMENT: THE USA, SCOTLAND AND THE SOVIET UNION

1 Interview with Labour councillor, 28 April, 1986.

2 A few Scottish Conservative councillors encountered in the course of this research had no history of party involvement at all before being approached by party selectors; others were so marginally involved that the approach came as a considerable surprise. Some of these people said they were initially reluctant to stand.

3 Martin Holland, 'British Political Recruitment: Labour in the Euro-Elections of 1979', *British Journal of Political Science*, 17, 1, 1987, 53–70.

4 It is this which makes it a study of recruitment rather than elite composition and not, as Holland seems to suggest, the fact that it encompasses more than

one stage of the selection process. In any case, the majority of Holland's aspirants were people who had already stood for public office, and included MPs as well as local councillors, so that a complete study of their recruitment would have to look much further back than the selection process in 1979.

5 Ronald J. Hill, *Soviet Political Elites* (London, Martin Robertson, 1977).
6 Verba and Nie, *Participation in America*.
7 Verba, Nie and Kim, *Participation and Political Equality*.
8 Dahl, *Who Governs?*.
9 Suzanne Keller, *Beyond the Ruling Class* (New York, Random, 1963).
10 Donald Matthews, *The Social Background of Decision-Makers* (New York, Doubleday, 1954; Keller, op. cit; Kenneth Prewitt, *The Recruitment of Political Leaders*; Carroll and Strimling, *Women's Routes to Elective Office*.
11 Prewitt, op. cit, p. 50.
12 Prewitt, ibid., p. 35.
13 Prewitt, ibid., pp. 40–1.
14 Richard J. Tobin and Edward Keynes, 'Institutional Differences in the Recruitment Process: a Four-State Study', *American Journal of Political Science*, 19, 1975, 667–92. The confusion in these authors' minds has given rise in turn to a good deal of confusion in the reporting of their work and accounts for some erroneous references to 'candidate' studies which are sometimes encountered in the American literature. See for example, Malcolm Jewell and David Olson, *American State Political Parties and Elections* (Homewood, Ill., Dorsey Press, 1982) pp. 100–1.
15 The attitude studies are John Kingdon, *Candidates for Office* (New York, Random, 1968) and Chong Lim Kim 'Political Attitudes of Defeated Candidates in an American Election', *American Political Science Review* 64 (1970) pp. 879–86. I take no account here of candidate studies, mainly focused on incumbency, which use no data beyond what is contained in election returns and public records of campaign expenditures. Susan Carroll's *Women as Candidates in American Politics* (Bloomington, Indiana University Press, 1985) is, of course, a candidate study, but of women only.
16 Warren Miller and Donald Stokes, *American Representation Study, 1958: the Candidate File* (ICPSR no 7726); Deber, 'The Fault, Dear Brutus'.
17 The weighted n=1364. By adopting weights of 4 and 7 for the parties' candidates rather than 1 and 1.75, the authors of this dataset create an illusion of numbers which might trap the unwary researcher into attaching unwarranted significance to the inflated numbers they will find in their cells. It has to be handled with extreme caution.
18 R. Davidson and W. Oloszek, *Congress and its Members*, 2nd edn, (Washington, Congressional Quarterly Inc., 1985) p. 110.
19 Deber, op. cit.
20 Seligman, Kim, Kim and Smith, *Patterns of Recruitment*.
21 Author's italics.
22 Frank Sorauf, *Party and Representation; Legislative Politics in Pennsylvania* (New York, Atherton Press, 1963) pp. 75–81.
23 Merritt, 'Winners and Losers'.
24 Prewitt, op. cit, p. 26.
25 Oliver Williams, Harold Herman, Charles Liebman and Thomas Dye, *Suburban Differences and Metropolitan Policies: The Philadelphia Story* (Philadelphia, University of Pennsylvania Press, 1965); Bryan Downes, 'Municipal Social Rank and the Characteristics of Local Political Leaders' *Midwest Journal of Political Science*, 12, 4, 1968.

26 Prewitt, op. cit, p. 38, n. 18.

27 The results of each set of District elections from 1974 onwards are available in a series of volumes by John M. Bochel and David T. Denver: *The Scottish Local Government Elections 1974: Results and Statistics* (Edinburgh, Scottish Academic Press, 1975); *The Scottish District Elections 1977: Results and Statistics* (University of Dundee, 1977); *The Scottish District Elections 1980: Results and Statistics* (University of Dundee and University of Lancaster, 1980); The Scottish District Elections 1984: Results and Statistics (University of Dundee and University of Lancaster, 1984); The Scottish District Elections 1988: Results and Statistics (Election Studies, 1989). These are the sources for election data used in this and the following chapters, with one minor amendment. An SNP candidate who stood in the elections to Glasgow District Council in 1984 and was also a respondent in my own research is wrongly identified as a man by Bochel and Denver due to her ambiguous first name. The corrected figure of 260 is used throughout my analysis for the number of women who stood in Strathclyde in 1984.

28 Information was not requested on income because this is considered to be a very delicate subject in the local culture and it was feared that its inclusion would have a seriously adverse effect on the survey response rate. The lack was not considered particularly important for two reasons. Firstly, income is less informative in the context of this study than either education or occupation and is heavily dependent on the latter anyway. Secondly, in Britain election expenditures are strictly limited by law and in partisan elections are normally met by the party, not the candidate.

29 Data from the 1981 Census is available in *The Scottish Summary of the Census: Strathclyde Region* (Her Majesty's Stationery Office, Edinburgh), in the reports of the 10 per cent sample of the census population; and in the *Small District Statistics*.

30 A simple barchart has been used to illustrate this point rather than the more sophisticated technique of multivariate regression analysis for two reasons. In the first place, in a regression equation the occupation variable can be used only in a dichotomised form, where much of its explanatory power is lost by contrasting a single occupational category with all the others lumped together in disregard of their varying relationships with the dependent variable. In the second place, although regression analysis is useful for distinguishing the variable which has the most explanatory power, which in these circumstances has to be education, and it confirms that both education and occupation have an independent effect on success, it makes the interaction effect of the two related variables very difficult to illustrate. Several versions of a regression equation with winning as the dependent variable and measuring the effect of education and occupation, controlling variously for age and incumbency or both, were carried out nevertheless. Although incumbency dwarfs any other variable as a predictor of success, we could hardly expect anything else in an election which saw virtually no change in the party votes and where most of the incumbents stood again; controlling for incumbency in these circumstances comes close to the tautology of asking who wins when we control for who won. However, in every case, including the subsamples of young candidates (up to 30 years old) and non-incumbents, the socio-economic variables were good independent 'predictors' of success.

31 Being 'male, militant and middle-class' in Whiteley's famous phrase. See Michael Rush 'The Members of Parliament', pp. 49–53 and Paul Whiteley, *The Labour Party in Crisis*, (London, Methuen, 1983).

32 Rush, op. cit, p. 51.
33 Ibid, p. 52.
34 Even now, the working-class beneficiaries of the education system are almost always male and it is only recently that working-class women have begun to penetrate higher education as 'mature students' who lost out earlier in life because of their sex. No wonder, then, that the upwardly mobile Labour MPs are nearly always male and that scornful reference to their women activists as 'middle-class intellectuals' is so often heard within the Labour party.
35 With the quadruple handicap of further education, a professional occupation, the wrong family background and the wrong sex, the average educated woman has little to hope for (and may have ill-disguised resentment to endure) in the Labour party as things stand. These points were perfectly illustrated by the remarks of a female Labour councillor interviewed in the course of this research. A 'caring professional', this woman lived in a solidly middle-class area and her children attended a prestigious school; by any objective criteria she was middle-class herself. In her own eyes, however, her present circumstances were outweighed by her (non-service) working-class origins, which she stressed as a key factor in her route to a successful Labour candidacy. One of those successful women who blame others for not succeeding so well as themselves, she showed little insight into either the predicament of most working-class women or the role of education in her own development. Her parting question (with accents of positive revulsion on the last two words) was, 'But *why* are the women who come forward always *middle-class*?'
36 See Stephen White, *Gorbachev in Power* (Cambridge, Cambridge University Press, 1990) pp. 23–53 and Richard Sakwa, *Gorbachev and his Reforms: 1985–1990* (Hemel Hempstead, Philip Allan, 1990) pp. 126–99.
37 The outstanding analysis of the pre-Gorbachev Soviet political system is Jerry Hough and Merle Fainsod, *How the Soviet Union is Governed* (Cambridge, MA, Harvard University Press, 1979). See also Bogdan Harasymiv, 'Nomenklatura: The Soviet Communist Party's Leadership Recruitment System', *Canadian Journal of Political Science*, 2, 3, 1969.
38 Ronald J. Hill, *The Soviet Political Elite.*
39 Hill, ibid., p. 74.
40 Hough and Fainsod, op. cit, p. 343.
41 White, *Gorbachev in Power*, p. 48.
42 Izvestia, 4th February, 1990.
43 Isobel Lindsay, 'Constitutional Change and the Gender Deficit' in (ed.) Jackie Roddick, *Women and Scottish Politics* (Polygon, forthcoming).
44 Katherine Kleeman, *Women's PACs*, (Rutgers, Centre for the American Woman and Politics, 1983); Kathy Stanwick, *Getting Women Appointed; New Jersey's Bipartisan Coalition*, (Rutgers, Centre for the American Woman and Politics, 1984).
45 The main conclusion of Victor Fuchs, *Women's Quest for Economic Equality*, (Cambridge, MA, Harvard University Press, 1988).

3 CHANGING THE SELECTORS: NON PARTISAN RECRUITMENT

1 Bochel and Denver, *Scottish District Elections*, op. cit.
2 For these interviews, I used a slightly expanded form of the basic schedule which was designed for the systematic, stratified random sample of the main survey population. In the questions pertinent to the present enquiry, respon-

dents were asked to describe the extent of political discussion or involvement, if any, in their family background; to itemise their party, civic, trade union and other group affiliations and experience before their first candidacy; to explain in detail the events leading up to their original decision to stand; and to describe their subequent candidate history. After a detailed exploration of the range and financing of their electioneering activities, non-partisan candidates were asked if they ever drew on the help of other people or organisations outside the immediate family in mounting a campaign. Later in the interview, they were invited to place themselves in one of three categories of 'Independent', according to their relationship with political parties and perspective on their role in local politics. Finally, they were asked whether they thought it was more difficult to stand as a non-partisan candidate; whether there are any particular obstacles to deter people from standing as Independents; and for their opinion as to why so few of those who do are women.

3 As well as those who use the label 'Independent', there are non-partisan candidates who present themselves variously as 'non-political'; under a variety of idiosyncratic descriptions which amount to the same thing; or with no label at all. For the sake of convenience all these categories of non-partisan candidate are described here as Independents. Excluded from this category are the various conventional pseudonyms used by Conservatives (such as 'Progressive' or 'Moderate') and people who describe themselves as Independent/Conservative/Nationalist/Labour, etc. In this I am coinciding with the classification used by Bochel and Denver, (op. cit) whose 'Independents' include the people who did not stand under precisely that description.

4 Donley Studlar and Susan Welch, 'Understanding the Iron law of Andrarchy: Effects of Candidate Gender on Voting in Scotland', *Comparative Political Studies* 1987, 20, 2.

5 It is not that urban-dwellers are necessarily more attached to party politics; many party candidates, councillors included, who were interviewed in this research expressed nostalgia for the 'good old days' of the Independents, and a few younger councillors who had had strong partisan motivations for seeking office said that their council experience had made them wonder if party politics is good for local government. The problem is that urban 'communities' appear to have have no alternative.

6 Interview with Independent councillor, 26th February, 1988.

7 Of the twenty-six councillors on this council, only one was unemployed. A further two had taken early retirement, in one case perforce, the other from choice. Three farmers and two businessmen who referred to the role of family members in running the business and providing cover for time spent on council business appeared to be semi-retired.

8 Yet this is exactly what one pair of analysts understandably conclude, working purely from election returns. See Studlar and Welch, op. cit The in-depth interviews with Independent councillors do not support this interpretation at all. With the exception of a single very remote community, the level of Councillor satisfaction was found to be extremely high in the 'Independent' areas, (although declining due to the policies of the Thatcher government) with particular stress being placed by respondents on the scope for a sense of personal achievement.

9 In this respect the 1984 entrants may be somewhat uncharacteristic. Seven men stood in this election for the first time, of whom four were elected; of the other

three, one has already fought a regional by-election and another has left the area but hopes to return and fight again.

10 This total is confined to defeats up to, and including 1984; defeats while standing as a non-partisan candidate; and defeats for levels up to and including the District Council level. It therefore excludes (a) a few District councillors who have failed in attempts (as party candidates) to reach the higher level Regional Council and (b) the single case of a man who was defeated in a District Council election while standing as an 'Independent Labour' candidate against his party's official nominee. (This man thereafter abandoned the Labour label to stand as a wholly non-partisan candidate, thus qualifying for inclusion in the present study.) As it turned out, there was no one who had lost an election, in any guise, before re-organisation.

11 Although the disputes appeared to involve personal ambitions as much as ideas or policies.

12 This contrasts curiously with the experience of some other people – mainly not party identifiers – who have been embarrassed by the eagerness of political parties (in some cases more than one party at the same time) to leap to their aid at elections and thereby compromise their Independence in the eyes of the electorate. Such offers are sometimes refused, as are those of friends with political leanings, and with good cause. One of the women candidates who thought she had been compromised by the *religious* beliefs of one of her canvassers was actually being accused by each of her opponents of belonging to a different political party, simply because of friends who had accompanied her round the doors.

13 Studlar and Welch, ibid.

4 MINOR PARTIES AND THE GENDER PATTERN

1 The analysis of Green politics in this book refers entirely to the period before German unification. It remains to be seen whether the Greens can maintain their success in a unified Germany.

2 By adopting the 'zip' method of placing women and men alternately on the party list, starting with a woman in first place.

3 Interview with Conservative candidate, 19 April, 1985. Athough this woman did not win her seat, she gained 40 per cent of the vote and had won the nomination in competition with two men; her remarks cannot be attributed to sour grapes.

4 Data from T. T. Mackie and F. W. S. Craig, *Europe Votes 2* (Chichester, Parliamentary Research Services, 1985) In the case of the UK, these authors treat the Liberals and SDP as separate parties and as such both qualify as minor parties under the rule adopted here. However, even if the Alliance parties were taken together, the 10 per cent rule would have to be waived in the peculiar conditions of the UK with its 'first-past-the-post' electoral system. Although between them these parties achieved not far short of 20 per cent of the popular vote (and this share of such a large electorate as the British would have ensured a party several seats in any other country of the EC) the Alliance did not win a single seat and must be regarded as a minor party in the idiosyncratic UK system.

5 Nor, of course, does the single set of elections reviewed here necessarily represent the typical gender pattern in all the parties concerned. Plaid Cymru, for example, with women constituting 17 per cent of its candidates in the General Election of 1983, had no women candidates at all in 1984; other

parties presented considerably more than on other occasions. However, with such a large number of parties these variations tend to cancel each other out.

6 In 1983, for example, the proportion of the women candidates nominated by parties other than Conservative and Labour was 57.2 per cent.

7 Vallance, *Women in the House*, p. 33. How secure this generalisation is depends, understandably, on the time-frame adopted.

8 Torild Skard and Elina Haavio-Mannila, 'Mobilization of women at elections', in Haavio-Mannila, (ed.), op. cit, pp. 42–3.

9 The Social Democrat Party (SDP) was created in 1981 by a breakaway faction of the Labour party which included two former Cabinet Ministers (Roy Jenkins and David Owen). Later the same year, the Alliance with the Liberals was formed and this lasted until 1988, when it was superseded by the Social and Liberal Democrats (SLD), a new party formed by a merger of the Liberals and the majority of the SDP. The Owenite faction of the SDP, who resisted the merger, continue as a separate party. All these changes create something of a nomenclature problem. In this text the terms 'Liberal', 'SDP' and 'Alliance' refer to the parties as they existed before the merger of 1988. In the analysis of the 1984 election and SDES data, the Alliance is referred to in the singular and treated as a single party. Where reference is made to the post-merger parties (the SLD and the rump SDP) this is clarified by using the adjective 'successor'.

10 Although both parties are understood to be 'centrist' by the electorate, this view is not shared by many of their activists. Liberals tend to see themselves as a radical alternative, while SDP activists believe they are distinctly left-of-centre and are rejecting the *polarisation* of right and left rather than the dimension itself. See the Note by J. M. Bochel and D. T. Denver, 'The SDP and the Left–Right Dimension', *British Journal of Political Science*, vol. 14, no. 3, 1984.

11 The pattern was exactly the same in Strathclyde, with figures of 170 and 259 respectively.

12 The only minor divergence is that the proportion of women among SNP candidates rose in Strathclyde when the party's fortunes collapsed in 1980, in keeping with the hypothesis that this proportion will be inversely related to the prospects for success but at odds with the pattern across the country. This was not the result of greater female recruitment, however, but came about because the candidacies of men fell away in these adverse circumstances.

13 The women candidates of both minor parties were on average younger than the rest. The mean ages of SNP and Alliance women were 40.3 and 41.0 years respectively (compared with 46.5 for Labour, 51.0 for the Conservatives and 56.5 for the Independents), but the standard deviation was much greater in the case of the Alliance than the SNP, reflecting the more skewed distribution of age in the former. The series of interviews conducted later with women candidates showed that Conservative women were more likely than those of other parties to have postponed seeking candidacy until their children had grown up. However, we should not necessarily conclude from this that Conservatives are more inhibited than others by traditional family roles, but should note instead that the Conservative party seemingly offers older women more opportunities for first-time candidacy. In the case of the Independents, prolonged incumbency was also a factor in their greater mean age.

14 See Bo Sarlvik and Ivor Crewe, *Decade of de-alignment: the Conservative victory of 1979 and electoral trends in the 1970s* (Cambridge University Press, 1983).

15 Mark Franklin, *The Decline of Class Voting in Britain: Changes in the Basis*

of Electoral Choice 1964–1983 (Oxford, Clarendon Press, 1985), especially Chapter 6.
16 Werner Huhlsberg, *The German Greens: a Social and Political Profile*, trans. Gus Fagan (Verso, London, 1988), p. 67.

5 THE RISE OF FEMINISM AND THE PARAMETERS OF CHANGE

1 Fuchs, *Women's Quest for Economic Equality.*
2 Rudolf Heberle, *Social Movements* (New York, Appleton Century Crofts, 1951).
3 See, for example, Olive Banks, *Faces of Feminism: a Study of Feminism as a Social Movement* (Oxford, Blackwell, 1986); Jo Freeman (ed.) *Social Movements of the Sixties and Seventies* (London, Longman, 1983); Drude Dahlerup, *The New Women's Movement: Feminism and Political Power in Europe and the USA* (London, Sage, 1986); Jenny Chapman, 'Adult Socialization and Out-group Politicization; an Empirical Study of Consciousness-raising', *British Journal of Political Science*, vol. 7, no. 3, 1987.
4 See, for example, Samuel Finer, *Anonymous Empire: A Study of the Lobby in Great Britain* (London, Pall Mall, 1958); Grant Jordan and Jeremy Richardson (eds), *Government and Pressure Groups in Britain* (Oxford, Clarendon, 1987); Wyn Grant, *Pressure Groups, Politics and Democracy in Britain* (London, Philip Allan, 1989).
5 For recent reviews of the issues raised in European social movement theory, see the section on 'Social Movements: a Theoretical Framework' in Wolfgang Rudig, *Anti-Nuclear Movements: a World Survey of Opposition to Nuclear Energy* (London, Longman, 1988); Dieter Rucht (ed.), *Research on Social Movements: the State of the Art* (Frankfurt/Boulder, CO: Westview, 1990); and see also Elim Papadakis, *The Green Movement in West Germany*, (London, Croom Helm, 1984), pp. 18–63.
6 Banks, op. cit, pp. 248–9.
7 Ruth Levitas, 'Some problems of aim-centred models of social movements', *Sociology*, 1977, vol. 2, pp. 47–63.
8 Freeman, op. cit, p. 196.
9 Helga Maria Hernes, *Welfare State and Woman Power* (Oslo, Norwegian University Press, 1988).

6 EQUAL RIGHTS AND SOCIALIST FEMINISM

1 It is education in the European tradition of the Enlightenment, or what we loosely call a 'modern' or 'Western' education, which is intended here; the effect on political behaviour of other, non-Western systems of education may be quite different. To contemporaries of the Enlightenment, it was the ability to generalise which seemed to be the essence of that great intellectual movement from which so much of our modern political and educational values derive and Mary Wollstonecraft identified this as the crucial resource which was reserved to men by making education a male preserve. Mary Wollstonecraft, *Vindication of the Rights of Woman* (London, Penguin, 1982) pp. 104–6, p. 317 and *passim.*
2 For the links between employment and the emergence of feminist ideas, see especially Barbara Taylor, *Eve and the New Jerusalem*, (London, Virago,

NOTES

1983) Chapters 1, IV and V, pp. 1–18 and 83–182, and Jane Rendell, *The Origins of Modern Feminism*. Chapman, 'Adult Socialization and Out-Group Politicization' deals with the specific point of free association among women as the prerequisite for politicisation, in a modern setting.

3 Marriage, of course, is supposed to be the equivalent for women.

4 Or at least they cannot do so without a human cost beyond the capacity of ordinary individuals to pay There have been a few well-documented cases of women who successfully 'passed' as men in order to pursue the avocation of their choice, but the price was, inevitably, a total renunciation of physical intimacy, unguarded relationships with other people and reproduction.

5 The 'family' takes innumerable shapes and forms, across and even within cultures. However, the universal child-rearing core of women's gender role gives a seemingly constant psychological character to her relationships within the family, even if she is also occupying the breadwinning role which some cultures would reserve to men. In this light it is easier to understand why Carol Gilligan's study of the values and psychological development paths associated with the male and female genders strikes such a universal chord, so resonant of other cultures, past and present, in spite of its narrow (and some have argued, questionable) empirical basis in one particular time and place. See Carol Gilligan, *In a Different Voice*.

6 Mary Wollstonecraft, *Vindication of the Rights of Woman*, pp. 120–2, 139 and *passim*. Of course Wollstonecraft was also a radical republican, sharply critical of the society she lived in; her enthusiasm was for the relative rationality of men, because of their education, and the potential of reason to bring about a radical improvement in human affairs.

7 It is well known that this occurred in the case of some of the well-to-do suffragists in Britain and America at the turn of the century, and white supremacism also intruded in the latter case. Banks, *Faces of Feminism*, pp. 124 and 140–1.

8 Ibid., pp. 153–79.

9 The idea that the whole range of public rights is inextricably linked with military service goes back at least as far as ancient Greece and was recently used as an argument in the successful campaign against the Equal Rights Amendment to the American Constitution. Logically, of course, one might as well argue the more morally defensible case that they should be dependent on bearing life rather than taking it.

10 R. N. Berki, *Socialism* (London, Dent, 1975) pp. 9–10.

11 Banks, *Faces of Feminism*, p. 58.

12 For a guide to communitarian ideas and selections from the original texts, see Jonathan Beecher and Richard Bienvenu, (eds), *The Utopian Vision of Charles Fourier: Selected Texts on Work, Love and Passionate Attraction* (London, Jonathan Cape, 1972); A. L. Morton., *The Life and Ideas of Robert Owen* (London, Lawrence and Wishart, 1962); J. F. C. Harrison, *Robert Owen and the Owenites in Britain and America* (London, Routledge and Kegan Paul, 1969); and Barbara Taylor, *Eve and the New Jerusalem*. The ideas of Saint-Simon and the Saint-Simonians are summarised in Frank Manuel, *The Prophets of Paris* (New York, Harper and Row, 1962) pp. 103–48 and 149–93 respectively.

13 Fourier believed that there was room for a measure of private enterprise within the phalange system and Owen that the intensification of class struggle would make socialism difficult if not impossible to achieve.

14 Within these general tendencies communitarian plans exhibited considerable

282

variation (and no little eccentricity). There was also some overlap with the early forms of 'state' socialism derived from the thought of Saint-Simon and Babeuf. However, Buonarotti was quite mistaken in implying (in his *History of Babeuf's Conspiracy for Equality*, quoted by Morton, *Life and Ideas of Robert Owen*, p. 181) that there was no difference in principle between Babeuf's design for 'one single and grand community' and that of Owen, who 'would multiply in a country small communities' or between the former's plan to 'seize on the supreme authority . . . to effectuate the reform they had projected' and the latter's reliance on persuasion and example.

15 If we except the naive, if charming expectation of the Pantisocrats that two hours individual labour a day would see off the entire gamut of female role tasks. See Taylor, *Eve and the New Jerusalem*, pp. 8–9.

16 For this theory, see Beecher and Bienvenu, 'Introduction', *The Utopian Vision of Charles Fourier*, pp. 43–53, and the translated texts in Parts IV and VI of this collection. Fourier made a point of stressing the desegregation of childcare ('Nurse-men' as well as 'Nursemaids') and its partial communalisation but left the role of mothers and the ultimate responsibility for small children unclear. His view of the family was explicitly male-centred and mothers (unlike fathers whom he wished to detach from their children as much as possible) are a practically invisible element in his thought.

17 In practice, the women who entered communes and might, from a modern feminist perspective, have been expected to find the new society most congenial, were more often than not the wives of communitarians, brought in to communal life by economic dependence on their artisan husbands rather than committed to the enterprise themselves. Their lives inside the New Moral World were often harder than they had been outside and instead of seeking to develop the communities on a more feminist framework, they were often the first to want to leave when economic difficulties arose. See Taylor, *Eve and the New Jerusalem*, pp. 238–60.

18 As twentieth-century hippies were to demonstrate, an egalitarian community of men serviced by female helots *cum* concubines may not seem inconsistent or morally unacceptable to the former. Even Fanny Wright's Nashoba commune in the 1840s seems to have displayed the exploitative tendencies often associated with a stress upon sexual freedom, judging from Frances Trollope's eye-witness account in her *Domestic Manners of the Americans* (London, 1832) cited in Alice Rossi (ed.), *The Feminist Papers; From Adams to de Beauvoir* (New York, Bantam, 1974), p. 95. See also Taylor, *Eve and the New Jerusalem*, pp. 67–8. Owen backtracked on the marriage question, although his main motive was probably a wish to contain the damaging publicity resulting from his *Lectures on the Marriage of the Priesthood in the Old Immoral World* (1835). In the experimental Owenite communes in Britain, participants appear either to have ignored his views on marriage, entering as married couples and tacitly refusing to depart from the conventional married state thereafter (a fact to which Owen actually attributed the failure of these experiments), or else to have embarked on a male-centred libertarian life which certainly contributed to the break-up of the communes. In Fourier's amazing schemes for the sexual liberation of both sexes, which one feels would prove to have more drawbacks and less universal appeal than he imagined, there is more than a hint of compulsory libertarianism.

19 They included Anna Wheeler, mentor of Saint-Simonism in Britain and associate of William Thompson, Owenite author of the *Appeal of One-Half the Human Race, Women, against the Pretensions of the Other Half, Men, to*

retain them in political, and thence in civil and domestic slavery
(London,1825); Emma Martin, Margaret Chappallsmith and Frances
Morrison, who worked as lecturers and publicists for the Owenite movement
in Britain; Frances Wright, Scottish founder of the Nashoba commune in
Tennessee in 1825; and the circle of French feminists associated with the
Tribune des Femmes. In the heyday of Owenite public meetings in Britain,
observers were struck by the number and enthusiasm of its women adherents,
for which see Taylor, *Eve and the New Jerusalem,* p. 57 and *passim.*

20 Although Taylor makes a point of the 'solid', skilled artisan background of
the bulk of British communalists (the same background which produced all
the radical working-class movements of the nineteenth century) it is also clear
from her account that there was a tendency for commune memberships (which
were in any case very small), to be recruited from occupations such as textile
working and skilled tailoring which were in serious economic decline at the
time. While this meant that the participants had less than other people to lose,
it was also a reflection of economic trends which it was quite beyond the
capacities of the communes to solve within the broader framework of the
private economy outside, and, more significantly still, it pointed to the
absence of men whose interests these trends were serving. The tendency to
draw on failure rather than success was particularly pointed in America,
where (as the Owens found to their cost), the New Harmony community was a
magnet for the kind of unskilled drifters and incorrigibles who were the least
suitable material for such a difficult social experiment. See Robert Dale Owen
Threading My Way (New York, 1974).

21 The idea that socialism depended on a level of production which could not be
achieved without industrialisation was not, of course, specific to Marx. He
shared this view with his precursors, Saint-Simon (who was also, unlike
Marx, an explicit advocate of hierarchy inside the new society), Owen and
even Fourier (whose phalansteries, however, would attend to the question of
higher yields from agriculture and the creation of 'industrial armies' only
after the establishment of correct relations among the people and for whom
the necessary minimum had been achieved by the ancient Greeks). See *The
Utopian Vision of Charles Fourier,* pp. 238-9 and 326-8). Where Marx
differed was in his 'scientific' integration of industrialisation, economic
determinism and class conflict.

22 'Letter of Karl Marx to the Editorial Board of the *Otechestvenniye Zapiski,*
November, 1877', in Karl Marx and Friedrich Engels, *Selected Correspon-
dence,* (Moscow, Foreign Languages Publishing House, and London,
Lawrence and Wishart, undated), pp. 376-9.

23 This is not to say that communitarians were necessarily more sophisticated in
their conceptions of the roots of human behaviour. Fourier certainly was, but
Owen's faith in the immediate impact of environmental change and the
perfectability of human nature was both naive and, according to his son, the
root of the American disaster at New Harmony.

24 Friedrich Engels, *The Origin of the Family, Private Property and the State*
(New York, Pathfinder, 1972).

25 A notable exception was Suzanne Lafollette, who commented that 'If experience teaches anything, it is that what the community undertakes to do is
usually done badly'. and advocated a system of child allowances sufficient to
allow parents a choice of parental or public care. Rossi, *The Feminist Papers,*
p. 561. Another American socialist, Charlotte Perkins Gilman, seems to have
assumed that mothers would continue to take the bulk of parental

responsibility and occupy both gender roles at once; her ideas about the optimal living arrangements to support this contributed to an active American school of innovative women's architecture and design in the early years of this century which feminist eyes are only now rescuing from historical oblivion. See Betty Friedan, *The Second Stage* (London, Michael Joseph, 1982) pp. 293–303.

26 Letter from 'A Woman' which appeared in the *Pioneer* in 1834, *apropos* of the London tailors' strike, quoted in Taylor, *Eve and the New Jerusalem*, p. 108.

27 Banks, *Faces of Feminism*, pp. 247–8.

28 Translated into the jargon of contemporary political science, they will seek to 'mobilise the bias' of the society they live in (to use Schattschneider's overworked expression) by 'piggy-backing' on more powerful interests.

29 See, for example, Phina Abir-Am and Dorinda Outram, (eds), *Uneasy Careers and Intimate Lives: Women in Science, 1789–1979* (London, Rutgers University Press, 1987), pp. 9–16 and *passim*. Of course, as the latter point out, these were the exceptions in the pattern of male resistance to women's desire for education which persists in most parts of the world even now, and often went hand-in-hand with determined opposition to any attempt on the woman's part to develop her intellectual interests independently or break from the traditional pattern of marriage and economic dependence. These authors also note the association of successful women's careers with a destabilised middle-class family background, in which financial necessity and the family's 'decreased capacity for social conformity' create new options for young women. This factor can be observed in the case of feminist political thinkers too, for example, Christine de Pizan and Mary Wollstonecraft.

30 It follows, too, that the more fervently men believe in the social value of education, the more preposterous it will seem to leave the care of their sons, even in infancy, in the hands of wholly uneducated mothers. The conditions of modern life have made this particularly problematical. The separation of home and workplace gets in the way of paternal supervision and the increasing sophistication of educational precepts makes it impossible for uneducated mothers (or nannies) to implement them. In the Middle Ages, similar problems (fathers away fighting and education conducted in Latin) were solved by sending children into monasteries for their education, but the secularisation of education, the desire to educate vast numbers of the general population and the emphasis of psychologists on the very earliest years as crucial to the formation of the personality rule this out as a modern option. Even the preparatory schools favoured by the English upper classes do not admit boys until they are seven years old.

31 Else Barth, Keynote Address to the International Congress of Women, Gottingen, 1986.

7 FEMINISM IN PRACTICE: NATIONALIST FINLAND AND REVOLUTIONARY RUSSIA

1 Only in the German Reichstag was a similar proportion reached. The case of Germany will be reviewed in Chapter 9.

2 Haavio-Mannila (ed.), *Unfinished Democracy*, pp. 62–3.

3 Ibid, p. 162.

4 Riitta Jallinoja, 'Independence or integration: the women's movement and political parties in Finland' in Dahlerup (ed.), *The New Women's Movement*, pp. 158–78. This early advance is still reflected in socio-economic differences

between Finland and other Nordic countries, as shown in data collected by the Nordic Council and Nordic Statistical Secretariat.

5 Jallinoja, op. cit, p. 166.

6 Reported in Haavio-Manila (ed.), *Unfinished Democracy*, pp. 73–4.

7 In 1981, 38 per cent of higher level Education officials were women. Helga Maria Hernes and Eva Hanninen-Salmelin 'Women in the Corporate System', in Haavio-Manila (ed.), *Unfinished Democracy*, pp. 106–32. See Table 6.3.

8 Although it is true that 'In Finland and Norway it was the national struggle that politicised women, and these were the only countries to grant women the vote before the First World War' (Randall, *Women and Politics*, p. 211) the implication that the two women's movements were similar and the causal inference which the reader is led to make between this and the granting of the suffrage are somewhat misleading.

9 T. K. Derry. *A Short History of Norway* (London, Allen and Unwin, 2nd edn, 1968), p. 172.

10 In Act IV of *Peer Gynt*, cited in Derry, *History of Norway*, p. 171. The leading figures in the linguistic revival were the philologist Aasen and the poet Vinje. To a Scot, the Norwegian parallels with Scotland's fractured linguistic and cultural identity are striking. Like the *landsmaal*, both the Gaelic and our so-called Lallans are the surviving forms of great literary languages of the past which have failed to win a general acceptance in modern times, against an all-pervading and ostensibly more 'cultured' language of external origin. The parallel even extends to the 'rediscovery' of Scottish culture by the Anglo-Scottish romantic school of Walter Scott. In Norway, one of the earliest attempts to revive and romanticise the past was the establishment of the 'Norwegian Society'. Its members, ironically, were mainly officials serving the Danish government and many were not even of Norwegian extraction; their historical vision of the 'Norway of the Heroes' was as tendentious as Scott's.

11 Haavio-Mannila (ed.), *Unfinished Democracy*, pp. 1–4 and *passim*.

12 Torild Skard and Elina Haavio-Mannila, 'Mobilization of women at elections', in Haavio-Mannila, op. cit, pp. 37–50.

13 A curious contrast arises too with respect to the political repercussions of variation in economic gender roles. In Finland's eastern provinces, the lengthy absences of men in fishing, trading, forestry, etc. often devolved responsibility for farming operations for long periods on women and Skard and Haavio-Mannila have suggested that this has a causal relationship with the fact that these districts are the most strongly associated with women's recruitment to elites, especially by non-socialist parties. Yet in Norway's coastal provinces, where exactly the same delegation of responsibility prevailed, women were not recruited; instead, men's control of land was the basis of their access to the Storting. The fact that Finland's eastern provinces were also characterised by 'generally liberal and radical attitudes', whereas the coastal provinces of Norway were the centre of Haugeanism, suggests strongly that the spread and evaluation of education are, yet again, the independent variables behind these very different outcomes.

14 Jallinoja, op. cit, p. 166.

15 Ibid., p. 162, Table 1.

16 Skard and Haavio-Mannila report a Gallup Poll of Finnish voters in 1979, which found that 40 per cent of the women, but only 7 per cent of the men, had voted for a woman candidate. Haavio-Mannila (ed.), op. cit, p. 58. The proportion of women candidates in 1979 was 26 per cent, so the consider-

able 'women's vote' was actually outclassed by the discrimination of male voters in favour of men.

17 Ibid., pp. 4 and 32.

18 This background also explains why there is very little history of part-time work among Finnish women, in contrast to the other Nordic countries.

19 Jallinoja, op. cit.

20 As in similar situations elsewhere, hardly any feminists wanted to set up a Women's Party and the attempt was abandoned after its first failure at the polls.

21 Jallinoja, op. cit, p. 162. The three main organisations of the separate movement were not actually disbanded, but were increasingly disregarded.

22 The main object (in which they succeeded) was to gain access for women to posts in the state bureaucracy.

23 The ultimate expression of this trend was the Constitutional Democrats (Kadets), who have been described as 'a proud and influential party, numbering among their members the cream of the intellectual and business spheres of Russian society'. See O. H. Radkey, *The Election to the Russian Constituent Assembly of 1917* (Cambridge, Mass., Harvard University Press, 1950) p. 10. Practising lawyers (of whom Kerensky was one of the most famous and more radical) were often politically active, usually as reformists or revolutionary 'moderates'.

24 Franco Venturi *Roots of Revolution: A History of the Populist and Socialist Movements in Nineteenth Century Russia*, (London, Weidenfeld and Nicolson, 1952) pp. 525–32 and *passim*. This immense and scholarly work is unsurpassed in its field and although some of the material cited below is also available from other sources, it has seemed most appropriate and helpful to the reader to draw mainly on this source for the majority of references in this section.

25 Ibid., p. 595.

26 Ibid., p. 720.

27 For a journalist's interesting pen-portraits of these and other women involved in the events of 1917, see Louise Bryant, *Six Red Months in Russia : An Observer's Account of Russia Before and During the Proletarian Dictatorship* (London, Journeyman Press, undated).

28 Gesia Gelf'man may be the exception. According to Soviet biographical sources, Gelf'man (whose name is sometimes transliterated into English as Helfman) was the daughter of a rigidly orthodox Jewish family who disowned her when she ran away from home to live among the goyim. She worked in a garment factory for a time but was drawn into the political 'underground' by her acquaintance with two young women populists who had been imprisoned in the movement 'to the people'. Gelf'man quickly gained a wide experience of the whole range of revolutionary activity and had already served a prison sentence before her part in the affair of the 'First of March'. I am indebted to Nyole White for some of this information.

29 The paths open to nineteenth-century Russian women seeking education and the difficulties they encountered are discussed in Ann Hibner Koblitz, 'Career and Home Life in the 1880s: The Choices of Mathematician Sofia Kovalevskaya' in Abir-Am and Outram, *Uneasy Careers and Intimate Lives: Women in Science* 1789–1979. (London, Rutgers University Press, 1987), pp. 172–90.

30 The label of 'nihilist' could not have been more inappropriate, for the 'nihilists' believed in a great many things; even the arch-'nihilist', Pisarev,

was a passionate believer in the uses of reason, and especially in the capacity of scientific understanding to transform the condition of the human race.

31 P. L. Lavrov, *Filosofia i sotsiologiia* (Moscow, 1965) vol. 2, p. 81, available in English translation in J. Edie *et al.*, *Russian Philosophy* (Chicago, 1965), vol. 2, p. 138, quoted in Walicki, *A History of Russian Thought*, p. 237.

32 Thereafter, the conventions of socialist realist art were to substitute the familiar duo of young male worker and female peasant, which is less obviously masculinist, but an evocative symbol of Russian sexism all the same, given the hierarchy of worker and peasant in the Marxist-Leninist canon.

33 The remark was made *apropos* of Zhelyabov, who had staggered Akselrod and his circle by declaring that it did not matter what occupation a revolutionary pursued; he could even be a professor (Venturi, *Roots of Revolution*, p. 823, n. 30).

34 Ibid., p. 526. The story was told by Vera Figner, in her account of the female student colony at Zurich in the 1870s. These young women wanted to renounce marriage as well as strawberries, but were persuaded against it by the revolutionary men; the argument was quite irrelevant, however, since few opportunities for an ordinary family life were to come the way of either men or women in the group. There is a considerable irony in the story of the strawberries, too, for Bardina's colleague would have had to search far and wide to find a peasant or worker who shared her austere morality.

35 Venturi gives a very interesting, scholarly account of the influences which shaped the thought of Chernyshevsky, the development of his ideas and their impact on the revolutionary movement in Russia (*Roots of Revolution*, Chapter 5 and *passim*). A somewhat different perspective is to be found in Andrzej Walicki, *A History of Russian Thought From the Enlightenment to Marxism* (Oxford, Clarendon Press, 1980) Chapter 11. Typically, neither of these male authors discusses the feminist content of the novel, in which the influence of John Stuart Mill sits uneasily with that of Fourier.

36 N. G. Chernyshevsky, *Izbrannye filosofskie sochineniia*, quoted in Walicki, *History of Russian Thought*, pp. 196–7.

37 For references to the documentary evidence, see for example Venturi, *Roots of Revolution*, pp. 178–9 and *passim*; Walicki, *History of Russian Thought*, p. 190.

38 The term feminist is being used here as a convenient anachronism, since it did not come into general use until a later date.

39 My italics. Quoted from the correspondence of N. V. Shelgunov (the colleague in question) in Venturi, op. cit, pp. 244–5. In *What Is To Be Done?*, Chernyshevsky was in many respects turning nostalgically to the Fourierist ideas of his youth rather than his later, statist economic theories and the idea of using the emancipation of women as the framework for his novel may also have been suggested by the fact that, as editor of the journal *Sovremmennik*, he had recently (and somewhat reluctantly) published a series of articles on the subject written by the poet Mikhailov. The latter had been strongly influenced by Fourier and Saint-Simon and was responding to the fanatical anti-feminism of the French anti-Fourierist socialist, Proudhon, who wanted Frenchmen to have the same rights as Roman husbands (which included those of capital punishment) over their wives (Henri de Lubac, *The Un-Marxian Socialist: a Study of Proudhon*, (1948) p. 51).

40 The neglected story of this much-vilified 'bourgeois feminist' movement can

now be found in Linda Harriet Edmondson, *Feminism in Russia*, 1900–17 (London, Heinemann, 1984).

41 The child's existence is so casually treated that E. H. Carr actually overlooked it altogether in his Introduction to Nikolai Chernyshevsky, *What Is To Be Done?* (London, Virago, 1982), p. xviii. Indeed, Carr's comments on the sexual relations between Vera and her two husbands are strangely at odds with the text, even in the edited version (London, Vintage, 1961) for which they were originally prepared. The reference to the child, Mitya, is on p. 300 of both editions and is followed by a passage which dwells pointedly on Vera's wholly unchanged lifestyle and makes several references to the household servants – a peculiar contrast with both the simple collectivism of Vera's sewing co-operative and the communitarian dream of the future (for which see pp. 308–28 of the Virago edn). Although there was ample allowance for personal service in Fourier's *phalansterie*, its framework was completely different from the nuclear family, middle-class household depicted here.

42 See note 28, above.

43 Quoted in Venturi, op. cit, p. 410.

44 See Alexandra Kollontai, *The Social Basis of the Woman Question* (1909). In fact the basic argument of this book, which set the tone of Bolshevik orthodoxy, was that there was no such thing as a 'general' woman question and in her later work *Towards a History of the Working Women's Movement in Russia* (1921) Kollontai was to ascribe the anti-feminism of male socialists to their 'easily understandable fear that the working women might leave their class movement and become entangled in the snare of feminism'. Translated extracts from these works are to be found in Alix Holt (ed.), *Selected Writings of Alexandra Kollontai* (London, Allison and Busby, 1977). For the above quotations, see pp. 61 and 53 respectively of this work. Contradictions within the thought of both Kollontai and Lenin, on this and other issues, will be explored below.

45 When the first All Russian Women's Congress was held in 1908, it was only with great difficulty that Alexandra Kollontai persuaded the social democrats firstly to take part at all and then to send women who would do more than stage an immediate 'walk-out'. Some leading Bolsheviks were hostile to any kind of work among women at all and unpleasantly sexist attitudes were openly displayed in the party. See the discussion by Alix Holt, 'Social Democracy and the Woman Question' in Holt (ed.), op. cit, pp. 32–8.

46 The main documentary sources for Kollontai's policy ideas and programme for women are her *Working Woman and Mother* (1914), *Society and Maternity* (1916), *Communism and the Family* (1919) and *The Labour of Women in the Evolution of the Economy* (1923) extracts from all of which are available in Holt, op. cit, pp. 127–49. Somewhat different selections from the two latter texts are also available in Rudolf Schlesinger, *The Family in the USSR* (London, Routledge and Kegan Paul, 1949).

47 Vividly described by Bryant, op. cit, pp. 93–7.

48 Many of the original texts of these and other reforms relating to the emancipation of women are translated in whole or part in Schlesinger, *The Family in the USSR*.

49 It is not strictly true, as stated by Rauch, that abortion was available thereafter 'without restriction' (Georg von Rauch, *A History of Soviet Russia* (London, Pall Mall, 1967) p. 139); at various times and places it was restricted to certain categories of women (e.g., those who had three or more children already) or

allocated by a medical commission which judged the claims of individual women against competing demands for hospital resources.

50 S. Yakopov, *The Struggle against Offences Rooted in the Traditional Way of Life* and I. Babintsev and V. Turetsky, *On the Emancipation of Women in Azerbaijan*, trans. Schlesinger, *The Family in the USSR*, pp. 188–203 and 204–23 respectively. The lack of investigation, and frequently of effective punishment too, was said to be due to the feet-dragging of locally recruited officials.

51 The conclusion reached by Radkey, op. cit.

52 In which they proved just as willing as their Bolshevik allies to suppress the other parties and their publications.

53 Breshkovskaya, who by 1917 was an ageing popular idol, often described as the 'grandmother of the revolution' and generally feted by all parties, refused to endorse the Bolshevik seizure of power. She went into voluntary exile abroad, where her anti-Bolshevik stance earned her Trotsky's furious soubriquet of 'godmother of the counter-revolution' (Leon Trotsky, *History of the Russian Revolution* (London, Gollancz, 1934) p. 246).

54 Leonard Schapiro, *The Origin of the Communist Autocracy: Political Opposition in the Soviet State, The First Phase, 1917–22*. (London, Macmillan, 1977) p. 125. The revolt in Moscow was led by Spiridonova in person.

55 As even those intellectuals whose pre-revolutionary political credentials seemed to immunise them from the effects of class discrimination were to learn, no one was to be exempt in the long-run; the surviving intelligentsia of Bolshevik sympathies were to be a principal target of the purges in the early 1930s.

56 *'Left-wing' Childishness and the Petty-bourgeois Mentality* (1918), available in translation in V. I. Lenin, *Collected Works*, (Moscow, Progress, 1965 and London, Lawrence and Wishart, undated), Vol. 27, pp. 323–54. This pamphlet (not to be confused with his later *Left-Wing Communism: an Infantile Disorder* which dealt with international communist affairs and is the better-known abroad) was in direct contradiction to much of *State and Revolution*, which many of his colleagues had hitherto taken to be the definitive statement of Lenin's views on socialist development. In particular, 'workers' control' was now condemned as 'petty-bourgeois', and Lenin's earlier advocacy of it cast in the light of a tactical device. Lenin now stated that 'Socialism is inconceivable without large-scale capitalist engineering based on the latest discoveries of modern science' and, in a depressing vision of the future socialist society, 'inconceivable without planned state organisation, which keeps tens of millions of people to the strictest observation of a unified standard in production and distribution.'

57 The system of economic management and payment by results which was introduced closely resembled the American methods of 'scientific management' known as Taylorism, which were greatly in vogue on both sides of the Atlantic at the time and much admired by Lenin. See Maurice Dobb, *Soviet Economic Development since 1917* (London, Routledge and Kegan Paul, 1948) pp. 91–2.

58 The word 'discipline' and its derivatives appear with obsessive regularity in Lenin's writings and speeches of 1918, especially those addressed to party or industrial workers.

59 Whether, as Narkiewicz suggests (Olga Narkiewicz, *The Making of the Soviet State Apparatus* (Manchester University Press, 1970) pp. 49–57) Lenin was too fundamentally opposed to industrial democracy from the start to care that the case against it had not been proven, or whether Roberts is nearer the mark in

claiming that he set off with the same ideas as his colleagues and became disillusioned in stages with his Marxist heritage (Paul Craig Roberts, *Alienation and the Soviet Economy* (Albuquerque, University of New Mexico Press, 1971) pp. 20–47), the outcome for the Soviet Union was the same, but the weight of the evidence favours Narkiewicz. The principle of 'one-man management' was actually adopted by the party Central Committee as early as April, 1918, although not put into general practice until after the Ninth Party Congress in 1920.

60 Alexandra Kollontai, *Communism and the Family*, in Schlesinger, *The Family in the USSR*, p. 63.

61 Alexandra Kollontai, *Working Woman and Mother* (1914) in Holt, *Selected Writings*, p. 134.

62 'The Tasks of the Working Women's Movement in the Soviet Republic: Speech at the Fourth Moscow City Conference of Non-Party Working Women, September 23, 1919', in Lenin, *Collected Works*, Vol. 30, pp. 40–6.

63 Ibid.

64 Alexandra Kollontai, *Women's Labour in Economic Development*, (1923) in Schlesinger, *The Family in the USSR*, p. 50. The extract given by Schlesinger is used here in preference to the selections from various works provided in Holt, op. cit, which make the same points more diffusely.

65 Zetkin, *Reminiscences of Lenin*, (1929) in Schlesinger, op. cit, p. 79.

66 Thus the number of factory creches etc were sharply increased in the period of the First Five Year Plan, after the abolition of abortion rights in 1935, during the war when women were needed to run the economy and thereafter to encourage unmarried mothers to help reproduce the population. The sudden increase in spending on childcare facilities in the 1970s was part of this pattern too. The authorities were alarmed by the low birthrate among its European citizenry and hoped that an improvement in the quality of public childcare (which they admitted was very low) would encourage women (who now had been given legal abortion rights again) to have more children.

67 Holt, *Selected Writings*, p. 212. In 1917, Kollontai called on the trade unions (without success) to adopt the principle of 'equal pay for equal value', but this must be assessed in the light of her scale of labour values.

68 Rauch, *History of Soviet Russia*, p. 140. The lowering of the age for the death penalty to 12 years old in 1936 was the final act in this violent drama.

69 Statement by the Chairman of Erivan (*sic*) Town Executive Committee, quoted by Dr. G. J. Areshev, Director of the Women's Clinic in Erivan, in the paper he presented to the First Ukrainian Conference of Gynaecologists, Kiev, 1927, on Experience with Abortion for Social Indications. (See Schlesinger, The Family in the USSR, p. 180.) In the cemetery, the space per corpse was 1.8 square yards while the normal housing allowance for the living was 2.5 square yards.

70 Schlesinger, *The Family in the USSR*, p. 95 and *passim*.

71 One of the recurring themes in the discussion of the 1926 Family Code was the fear expressed by men that the new law would make it easier for women to get their hands on men's higher earnings.

72 Holt, *Selected Writings*, pp. 159–200.

73 Quoted by Holt, ibid. p. 211.

74 Ibid., p. 18.

75 Much has been said by others on the subject of her novels and as they are not particularly germane to the present discussion, I shall say no more. At the risk of being cynical, I cannot help observing that although many western

economic and political analysts of Soviet development adopt Kollontai's analysis of the Leninist system, as expressed in *The Workers' Opposition*, as their own, the origin of these views is seldom acknowledged. (Leonard Schapiro's *The Origins of the Communist Autocracy* is a notable exception). Her 'socialist' feminist ideas are never examined. The emphasis (usually derogatory) is nearly always on her role as the literary proponent of 'free love'.

76 Xenia Gasiorowska, *Women in Soviet Fiction*, 1917–1964 (Madison, University of Wisconsin Press, 1968).

77 The adverse effect of the loss of the women's departments would have on the pace of emancipation in the national minorities was remarked on at the time. Yakopov, op. cit, in Schlesinger op. cit, p. 203

78 Evgenia Ginsberg, *Into the Whirlwind* (London, Penguin, 1968).

79 Schlesinger, *The Family in the USSR*, p. 21.

80 As a student in the USSR in the Brezhnev period, it was impossible not to be struck by the intense and widespread bitterness of young Soviet women, especially in the fields of science and engineering, about the blatant discrimination in favour of males. Irrespective of their school-leaving qualifications, it was boys rather than girls who were accepted by the more prestigious institutes of higher education and the more rewarding branches of their subjects. As one friend put it to me, 'When the lecturer comes down from the university to give us his lectures, he thinks of it as "slumming" because we are all girls. He is only doing it for the money and he hardly bothers to teach us anything. There is no future for us.'

81 From the Civil War onwards, Communists were dispersed throughout the Red Army to exert political control and thereafter party representation and recruitment remained more intensive in the army than in any other occupational sector. For a detailed analysis of this and the shifting patterns of party enrolment under NEP and the first five-year plan, see Rigby, *Communist Party Membership*.

82 *Pace* the brief role of Nina Furtseva as culture overseer under Khrushchev. Gorbachev appointed Alexandra Biryukova, a party leader in the trade union organisation, as a Central Committee Secretary and Politburo member.

83 In 1939, only twelve years after joining the CPSU and four years after graduation as an engineer, Kosygin was already a government minister (People's Commissar for Light Industry) and although other cases were less spectacular, the first generation of the new Soviet intelligentsia was to dominate Soviet public life until the 1980s.

8 GENDER THEORY AND FEMINIST STRATEGY

1 Frigga Haug, 'Lessons from the Women's Movement in Europe', *Feminist Review*, no 13, 1989, pp. 107–16.

2 Drude Dahlerup. *The New Women's Movement*, p. xx. Chapman, 'Adult Socialization and Out-Group Politicization' is a study of the political orientations of local women candidates (using interview data from the same study which provided the Scottish material used in Chapters 3–5), which provides startling confirmation of the consciousness-raising hypothesis and its continuing relevance for women in political elites.

3 Michele Barrett, *Women's Oppression Today: The Marxist/Feminist Encounter*, Revised edn (London, Verso, 1988).

4 Zillah Eisenstein, *The Radical Future of Liberal Feminism* (New York, Longman, 1981) p. 20. See also Iris Young, 'Beyond the Unhappy Marriage: A

NOTES

Critique of the Dual Systems Theory', in Lynne Sargent (ed.), *Women and Revolution: A Discussion of the Unhappy Marriage of Marxism and Feminism*, (Boston, South End Press, 1981). Ann Ferguson goes even further, arguing that only a 'multi-systems' approach will do justice to the autonomy of the different spheres of human relations; see her 'On Conceiving Motherhood and Sexuality: A Feminist Materialist Approach' in Joyce Trebilcot (ed.), *Mothering: Essays in Feminist Theory* (Totowa, N. J., Rowman and Allanheld, 1984), pp. 153–82.

5 Sheila Rowbotham,'The Women's Movement and Organising for Socialism' in Sheila Rowbotham, Lynne Segal and Hilary Wainwright, *Beyond the Fragments: Feminism and the Making of Socialism* (London, Merlin, 1980), p. 145.

6 Ibid., pp. 132–49 and *passim*.

7 Barrett, *Women's Oppression Today*, p. xxiii, and Lynne Segal, 'Slow Change or No Change? Feminism, Socialism and the Problem of Men', *The Feminist Review Special Issue*, 31, 1989, pp. 5–21. See also Lynne Segal, *Is The Future Female? Troubled Thoughts on Contemporary Feminism* (London, Virago, 1987) and, in rather different vein, Anne Phillips' sensitive treatment of the historical relationship between feminism and the labour movement in *Divided Loyalties: Dilemmas of Sex and Class* (London, Virago 1987).

8 Sheila Rowbotham, 'To Be or Not To Be: The Dilemmas of Mothering', *The Feminist Review*, 31, 1988, p. 83.

9 Barrett, *Women's Oppression Today*, p. xx.

10 *The Past before Us: Twenty Years of Feminism*, Special Issue of *The Feminist Review*, 31, 1989. This simple arithmetic is not misleading either, as the issue rarely surfaces at all throughout the other 142 pages.

11 Diane Ehrensaft, 'When Women and Men Mother', in Trebilcot (ed.) *Mothering*, pp. 41–61.

12 Betty Friedan, *The Second Stage*, p. 38 and *passim*.

13 Mary Daly, *Gyn/ecology: The Metaethics of Radical Feminism* (Boston, Beacon Press, 1978); Susan Griffin, *Pornography and Silence* (London, The Women's Press, 1981); Andrea Dworkin, *Pornography; Men Possessing Women* (New York, Perigree, 1981); Susan Moller Okin, *Women in Western Political Thought* (Princeton, Princeton University Press, 1978); Carole Pateman, *The Sexual Contract* (Stanford, Stanford University Press, 1988).

14 Simone de Beauvoir, *The Second Sex* (Harmondsworth, Penguin,1972), translated and edited by H. M. Parshley. *Le Deuxième Sexe* was first published in 1949.

15 Interview of 1984 in Alice Schwarzer, *Simone de Beauvoir Today*, (London, Chatto and Windus, 1984) p. 116.

16 Interview of 1972, Schwarzer, p. 46.

17 Interview of 1980, Schwarzer, p. 98.

18 Mary Wollstonecraft, *Vindication of the Rights of Woman* (London, Penguin, 1982).

19 Mary Astell, who argued strongly for the right to remain single, settled alone in Chelsea in the 1690s, although she later moved into the household of her friend and patron, Lady Catherine Jones. Mary Wollstonecraft, with her sisters and close friend, Fanny Blood, set up a school in London in the 1780s; when it failed, she turned to her pen for a living. She was extremely critical of marriage as it was in her day – an institution based in property and dominated by greed, usually at the expense of women.

293

20 For an indication of how easy it was to procure a drug-induced abortion, see Mary Wollstonecraft, *Mary, a Fiction and The Wrongs of Woman* Gary Kelly (ed.) (London, Oxford University Press, 1976), p. 109. Wollstonecraft died of the puerperal fever introduced to childbirth by male general medical practitioners.

21 For the development of Wollstonecraft's feelings as a mother, see Mary Wollstonecraft; *Love Letters of Mary Wollstonecraft to Gilbert Imlay*, with a prefatory memoir by Roger Ingpen, (London, Hutchinson, 1908), especially p. 42. The duties of motherhood are a recurring topic in the *Vindication*.

22 Wollstonecraft, *Vindication*, p. 249.

23 Thus, in the *Vindication*, middle-class girls compete in folly with each other, to win a husband; in *The Wrongs of Woman*, the sexually exploited servant, Jemima, is cast out by her employer's wife but ends up working as a wardress in a madhouse, where she is the jailer of Maria, a wronged wife, on behalf of the latter's husband.

24 Initially set apart by the barriers of class, education and their respective roles as prisoner and wardress, Maria and Jemima reach a mutual consciousness as women by sharing their life-histories and discussing them together. Finding that their common womanhood is stronger than the wedges life has driven between them, they conspire together to effect Maria's escape and defeat her husband's plans. It is a perfect illustration of contemporary consciousness-raising theory.

25 The relationship between the domestic and civil orders in Wollstonecraft's thought is analysed by Miriam Brody in 'Mary Wollstonecraft: Sexuality and Women's Rights' in Spender (ed.), *Feminist Theories*, pp. 40–59. Wollstonecraft's attempted suicide of 1795 (which of course meant abandoning her much loved child) was an apt illustration of her case against the passions.

26 Shulamith Firestone, *The Dialectic of Sex* (London, The Women's Press, 1980), p. 16.

27 The theory of consciousness-raising, in a note on p. 57.

28 This is a central theme of Carole Pateman's *The Sexual Contract*; see especially pp. 77–115.

29 Firestone, *The Dialectic of Sex*, pp. 51–2.

30 Ibid., p. 182.

31 Margaret Mead, *Male and Female: A Study of the Sexes in a Changing World* (London, Pelican, 1962) This book (first published in 1950) drew extensively on material already used in earlier works, the most important of which were her *Coming of Age in Samoa* (1928), *Growing up in New Guinea* (1930) and *Sex and Temperament in Three Primitive Societies* (1935).

32 Derek Freeman, *Margaret Mead and Samoa: the Making and Unmaking of an Anthropological Myth* (Cambridge, MA, Harvard University Press, 1983). Freeman is an Australian anthropologist who is convinced that Mead's interpretation of Samoan culture was naive and ill-informed. The anthropological controversy over his evidence and motivations seems unlikely ever to be resolved but there is no doubt that Mead's reputation as an anthropologist has been seriously shaken.

33 See, for example, Phyllis Grosskurth, *Margaret Mead* (London, Penguin, 1988) a biography which is remarkable for its author's overt animosity towards her subject and startling disregard for the content of her work.

34 Mead, *Male and Female.*, pp. 147–8 and *passim*.

35 Ibid., p. 158.

36 In which connection the statement made by Grosskurth, attributing to Mead a 'categorical espousal of the primacy of social environment, totally excluding biological variables' is positively breathtaking in its inaccuracy. Grosskurth, op. cit, p. 84.

37 Mead, *Male and Female* p. 146. In the frightful jargon of present-day psychoanalytical theory, hers is an 'object-relational' account of psychological formation.

38 Ibid., pp. 112–31.

39 Ibid., p. 234–45. Mead's account of the 'American dream' is a *tour-de-force* of cultural analysis.

40 Ibid., pp. 161–76 and *passim*.

41 Ibid., p. 179 and pp. 218–9. Mead also observed how cultural interpretations of women's reproductive experience tend to be based on the fantasies of men and how in modern times women have had the 'simple power of bearing their own children . . . practically taken away from them' by the medical establishment.

42 Although at one point Mead qualified this assertion by speculating that men's original infant identification with their mothers may be a source of men's wanting children too.

43 Mead, op. cit, pp. 177–91.

44 Ibid., pp. 148–9 and *passim*.

45 Ibid., p. 331.

46 Ibid., p. 218.

47 Ibid., pp. 222–3. A recent instance of this phenomenon among South American Indians was described in the BBC Radio programme, 'Head On', 12th May, 1989.

48 Ibid., p. 260.

49 Ibid., pp. 286–94. The effect on girls, of course, is to stunt their creative powers and confidence, as in the heartbreaking case, described by Mead, of the teenage Bali girl whose natural creative gifts were systematically denigrated and destroyed by her male 'peers' (Mead, op. cit p. 336). Modern playgrounds and classrooms abound with similar behaviour.

50 The subject of rape is a notable blind spot of Mead's, and her assertions about male violence in the western world do not stand up at all in the light of recent information.

51 In small, genetically homogeneous, primitive societies, Mead thought this was not much of a problem, but saw it looming as an enormous shadow on the lives of people in heterogeneous modern societies like the United States.

52 Nancy Chodorow, *The Reproduction of Mothering: Psychoanalysis and the Sociology of Gender* (Berkeley, University of California Press, 1978).

53 Pauline Bart, 'Review of Chodorow's The Reproduction of Mothering' in Trebilcot (ed.) Mothering, pp. 147–52.

54 Chodorow, op. cit, pp. 57–170. The first and last parts of the book largely restate the argument of two earlier articles in which the debt to Mead was made explicit: 'Being and Doing: A Cross-Cultural Examination of the Socialization of Males and Females' in Vivian Gornick and B. K. Moran (eds), *Woman in Sexist Society: Studies in Power and Powerlessness* (New York, 1971) and 'Family Structure and Feminine Personality' in Michelle Rosaldo and Louise Lamphere (eds), *Woman, Culture and Society* (Stanford, Stanford University Press, 1974). The central part of Chodorow's book is an *ex post facto* neo-Freudian embellishment of ther theme, which seems to have taken

on a life of its own as the author (a sociologist to trade) became more deeply involved in psychoanalytical material.

55 Ibid., p. 167.
56 Ibid., p. 213 (my italics) although she also states that women would develop more individuated sense of self simply by virtue of having men as primary parents (p. 218) this appears to be mainly because any diffusion of mothering, irrespective of the sex of motherers, will reduce the impact of the biological mother.
57 There is more than a hint here too of the notion of the mother as role-model, an idea Chodorow has earlier rejected (ibid., p. 31) on the highly questionable grounds that socialisation by role-models is a cognitive, non-psychological process based on 'intention'. It begins to seem that shared parenting will allow mothers more time for their own pursuits and present them as more differentiated, bounded individuals for their daughters to emulate (pp. 212–3).
58 Marcia Westkott, *The Feminist Legacy of Karen Horney*, (New Haven, Yale University Press, 1986) pp. 125–34.
59 Iris Marion Young, 'Is Male Gender the Cause of Male Domination?' in Trebilcot, (ed.) *Mothering*, pp. 129–46.
60 Michelle Rosaldo, 'Woman, culture and society: a theoretical overview', in Rosaldo and Lamphere (eds.), *Woman, Culture and Society*, pp. 17–42.
61 Ehrensaft, op. cit, p. 42. Lenin's animadversions on male reluctance to partake in housework presumably help to legitimise and facilitate women's demands for shared parenting in the left.
62 Ferguson, 'On Conceiving Motherhood and Sexuality', pp. 166–7.
63 Adrienne Rich, *Of Woman Born: Motherhood as Experience and Institution* (London, Virago, 1977) p. 174.
64 Ibid., p. 215. This is also a theme of Carol Gilligan's study of sex differences in the paths of moral-psychological maturation, *In a Different Voice*.
65 Rich, op. cit, pp. 225–40.
66 Friedan, *The Second Stage*, p. 108.
67 Sylvia Ann Hewlett, *A Lesser Life: The Myth of Women's Liberation* (London, Sphere Books, 1987).
68 In the UK, divorce rates continue to rise, while marriage is now on the decline in favour of cohabitation with about 25 per cent of births occurring outside wedlock. See John Haskey and Kathleen Kiernan, 'Cohabitation in Great Britain – characteristics and estimated numbers of cohabitating partners', *Population Trends*, 58 (Winter 1989), published by HMSO.

9 WEST GERMAN GREENS, NORWEGIAN FEMINISTS AND THE ICELANDIC KWENNALISTINN

1 For a detailed treatment of the development and decline of German feminism in the face of German nationalism, Social Darwinism and the glorification of motherhood and gender difference, see Richard Evans, *The Feminist Movement in Germany 1894–1933*. German 'socialist' feminism withstood these trends, but its doyenne was Klara Zetkin, whose scorn for the more radical ideas of Kollontai has been referred to above.
2 Numerous feminists have examined the relationship between gender, pornography and anti-Semitism in Nazi attitudes and the part played by repression and psychological insecurity in the Nazi psyche; exceptionally interesting, for its breadth of cultural perspective, is Susan Griffin's *Pornography and Silence*.

3 Elim Papadakis, *The Green Movement in West Germany* (London, Croom Helm, 1984).

4 Werner Huhlsberg, for example, devotes precisely *one paragraph* of the 220 pages of his book *The German Greens* (which ironically bears the sub-title of *A Social and Political Profile*) to the question of feminism and although mentioning in passing that the entire party leadership was composed of women at one time, makes no attempt to consider the policy implications of this. Papadakis is not much better. Fortunately a serious treatment of women and the Greens is now to hand in Eva Kolinsky's, 'The West German Greens: A Women's Party', *Parliamentary Affairs*, vol. 41, no. 1, 1988, pp. 129–48.

5 Detailed discussions of the socio-economic and demographic characteristics of Green support, which agree in most essential points, are to be found in Papadakis, *The Green Movement*, pp. 71-2 and *passim*, Hulsberg, *The German Greens*, pp. 113-18, Kolinsky, 'The West German Greens', pp. 129-48, and William Miller and Charles Taylor, 'Structured Protest: A Comparison of Third Force Challenges in Britain, Germany and the USA during the Eighties', a paper presented to the 13th World Congress of the International Political Science Association, Paris, July 1985.

6 Kolinsky, 'The West German Greens', pp. 135-7.

7 Miller and Taylor, 'Structured Protest' p. 14.

8 W. P. Burklin, 'The German Greens: The Post-Industrial Non-Established and the Party System', *International Political Science Review*, 1985/4. Kolinsky is almost certainly right in regarding estimates of one in five Green voters as unemployed as being exaggerated but German data (see Hulsberg, *The German Greens*, p. 114), confirm that the true proportion is still considerably higher than for any other party.

9 Lovenduski, *Women in European Politics*, pp. 100-3.

10 Editor of the radical feminist journal, *Emma*.

11 On the other hand, when women's 'alternative' projects are successful, especially if these incorporate some improvement on a social service function, they still fall victim to the characteristic German integrationist response. Approved by the authorities for accommodation, funding or whatever else they need to ease their precarious existence, such projects lose their political, transformational edge and the initiators wake up to find themselves working for a pittance to provide an improved and cut-price service for the state; such women may well feel that they have simply created a new vehicle for their own exploitation.

12 Quoted in Kolinsky, 'The West German Greens', p. 143.

13 Prue Chamberlayne, 'The Mothers' Manifesto and Disputes over 'Mutterlichkeit', *Feminist Review*, no. 35, 1990, pp. 9-23.

14 Huhlsberg, op. cit, p. 73.

15 OECD statistics, quoted in T. K. Derry, *History of Scandinavia*, p. 373. The fact that the level of education in the Storting was at this time still slightly lower than in many other industrialised countries (as observed by G. Sartori, 'Members of Parliament', in *Decisions and Decision-Makers in the Modern State*, Paris, Unesco 1967) has to be seen in the light of the low levels of pre-war education affecting middle and older age-groups at that time.

16 K. Eliassen, 'Rekrutteringen til Stortinget og Regjeringen 1945–85' in T. Nordby (ed.), Storting og Regjering (Oslo, Kunnskapsforlaget, 1985), pp. 109-30. See especially Table 3a, p. 114.

17 It has also been suggested cynically that the corporate structures left the parliamentarians in need of something to restore their high public profile;

hence the latter's unusually developed concern with representation and social justice policies. See Maud Edwards, Beatrice Halsaa and Hege Skjeie, 'Equality: How equal?', in Haavio-Mannila *et al.*, (eds), *Unfinished Democracy*, pp. 136–7.

18 Henry Valen, 'Norway: decentralization and group representation', in Michael Gallagher and Michael Marsh, *Candidate Selection in Comparative Perspective* (London, Sage, 1988) pp. 210–35.

19 Henry Valen, 'The Recruitment of Parliamentary Nominees in Norway' *Scandinavian Political Studies*, pp. 121–66. Valen listed the main occupational groups 'to which attention is given at nominations' as 'manual workers (trade unions), white collar workers, farmers, fishermen and private business people in industry and commerce'.

20 Hege Skjeie, *The Feminization of Power: Norway's Political Experiment (1986–)*, (Oslo, Institute for Social Research, 1988), p. 65.

21 Valen, 'Norway: decentralization and group representation', p. 230.

22 Skjeie, op. cit, p. 24; Helga Maria Hernes, *Welfare State and Woman Power: Essays in State Feminism*, (London, Norwegian University Press, 1987) p. 26 and *passim*.

23 Hernes, ibid., p. 22.

24 Skjeie, ibid. p. 24.

25 See especially Hernes, ibid., pp. 56–61.

26 Ola Listhaug, Arthur Miller and Henry Valen, 'The Gender Gap in Norwegian Voting Behaviour', *Scandinavian Political Studies*, vol. 8, no. 3, 1985, pp. 187–206.

27 Conservative women typically have been prepared to accept the party's preference for an informal commitment. However, when the proposal was made and rejected yet again as recently as 1988, some rebelled.

28 The Labour party is typically the pace-maker at the national level, and in 1985 the proportion of Labour representatives in the Storting was 42 per cent, compared to 30 per cent for the Conservatives. However, the Conservatives have always had the highest proportion of women in local government, so the national gap may reflect differences in the geographical distribution of party support as well as ideological and socio-economic resource factors. Obviously a Conservative woman with family responsibilities living in a rural area will find it easier to become a local rather than national representative, whereas the kind of highly educated urban professional who typifies the female Labour activist will find national politics more feasible, especially if she lives in the capital.

29 Knut Heidar, 'Party Organizational Elites in Norwegian Politics: Representativeness and Party Democracy', *Scandinavian Political Studies*, vol. 9, no. 3, 1986, pp. 279–91. No less than 42 per cent of organisational office-holders in the early 1980s were college graduates.

30 Hernes, op. cit, p. 78.

31 She had entered politics as late as the 1970s. Interview with Gro Harlem Brundtland in the *Wall Street Journal*, 5 July, 1987, p. 1.

32 Hernes, ibid, pp. 87–95.

33 Tove Stang Dahl (Professor of Public Law, University of Oslo) in Tove Stang Dahl and Helga Maria Hernes, *After Equality (Scandinavian Political Review*, Summer 1988) p. 1.

34 Hernes, *Welfare State and Woman Power*, p. 98.

35 The author is greatly indebted to the Norwegian Social Science Data Services for their efforts to provide the Storting data on which this statement is loosely

NOTES

based. It had been hoped to carry out a detailed study of post-war male and female Storting recruitment patterns, but the appropriate data was not available. For party organisations see Knut Heidar, 'Party Organizational Elites'. There is not a perfect match of course, since there are still virtually no women in several of the categories (e.g. farmers) which provide success-ful male recruits; as we would expect, women are even more likely than men to be employed in the public sector and especially at its lower professional levels.

36 Hernes, op. cit, p. 88. For comparison with the USA, see Carroll and Strimling, *Women's Routes to Elective Office*, pp. 24–30.
37 In particular, it is worth noting that the Norwegian incrementalists do not accept the common view of the Storting as a 'shrinking' institution, preferring to accept the evidence of academic studies which show an 'ebb and flow' of power between the legislature and the corporate sector. The equity pro-gramme itself appears to illustrate their point, for the changes of the early 1980s were pushed through in the teeth of vehement opposition from the corporate sector, not least (to the chagrin of the social democrats), from the trade union movement. See Skjeie, *The Feminization of Power*, p. 19 and references.
38 Hernes, op. cit, p. 48.
39 Maud Edwards *et al.*, 'Equality; What Next?', p. 141.
40 Skjeie, *The Feminization of Power*, p. 56 and *passim*.
41 See especially Hernes, op. cit, pp. 31–71.
42 Similar arguments about the impact of state intervention have been advanced by social movement theorists to account for the rise of new social movements in general, as Hernes, a principal Norwegian women's movement theorist, clearly is aware.
43 Hernes, ibid., p. 125.
44 Dahl and Hernes, *After Equality*, p. 3.
45 Hernes *Welfare State and Woman Power*, p. 28.
46 See L. Balbo and H. Nowotny, (eds), *Time to Care in Tomorrow's Welfare Systems* (Vienna, Eurosocial, 1986) and Hernes, 'Chronopolitics: A Time to Live and a Time to Work', in *Welfare State and Women Power*, pp. 101–18.
47 Hernes, ibid., p. 127.
48 The concept of citizenship proposed by Hernes and other Norwegian femi-nists has been further developed by the Danish academic Birte Siim in her 'Welfare State, Gender Politics and Equality Principles: Women's citizenship, participation and interests in the Scandinavian welfare states', Paper presented at the ECPR Joint Sessions, Paris, April 1989.
49 Hernes ibid., p. 134.
50 See Listhaug, Miller and Valen, 'The Gender Gap in Norwegian Voting Behaviour'. This polarisation is not unique to Norway of course; it has been marked in Britain, too.
51 Seymour Lipset, 'Foreword', in Richard Thomasson, *Iceland: The First New Society* (Reykjavik, Icelandic Review in association with University of Minnesota Press, 1980).
52 Lena Dominelli and Gudrun Jonsdottir, 'Feminist Political Organization in Iceland: Some Reflections on the Experience of Kwenna Frambothid', *Feminist Review*, no. 30, 1988, p. 41.
53 For readily accessible accounts of Icelandic feminist history and some socio-economic data, see Audur Stryrkarsdottir, 'From social movement to political party: the new women's movement in Iceland' in Dahlerup (ed.), *The New*

299

Women's Movement, pp. 140–57 Dominelli and Jonsdottir, 'Feminist Political Organization in Iceland'; and Haavio-Mannila *et al.* (eds), *Unfinished Democracy*, pp. 27–8 and *passim*.

54 Sigridur Kristmundsdottir, 'Outside and Different: Icelandic women's movements and their notions of authority and cultural separateness of women', Paper presented to the Conference on the Anthropology of Iceland, University of Iowa, May 1987, p. 13.

55 Stryrkarsdottir, 'From social movement to political party', p. 145.

56 Kristmundsdottir, op. cit, p. 11.

57 See especially Dominelli and Jonsdottir, 'Electoral Politics in Iceland'.

58 Kristmundsdottir, op. cit, p. 20 and *passim*.

59 Quoted by Dominelli and Jonsdottir, op. cit, p. 53.

60 Dominelli and Jonsdottir, ibid., pp. 40–1.

61 'Women's politics are here to stay', *News from Iceland*, May 1988, pp. 16–17.

62 Ibid.

63 Madge Kaplan, 'Iceland's Feminist Parliamentarians', *Sojourner: The Women's Forum*, April 1989, pp. 17–19.

64 Kristin Halldorsdottir, quoted in 'Women's politics are here to stay', p. 17.

65 Gudrun Agnarsdottir, quoted in Bernard Scudder, 'Althing being Equal', *Iceland Review*, 1988.

66 *Kwennalistinn: The Women's Alliance Policy Statement 1987*, p. 1.

67 Quoted in Kaplan, 'Iceland's Feminist Parliamentarians', p. 17.

68 The idea of child-rearing as a function of the public interest surfaces in Norway, too, where anxieties have been expressed (and deliberately fostered by feminists) about the increasing reluctance of Norwegian women to have children. The fact that these anxieties are often linked with the demand for a population policy is a reminder – if one is needed in the light of Soviet experience – of just how dangerous it can be to women's interests to recognise a public interest in their reproduction of the social stock.

69 *Kwennalistinn: Policy Statement*, p. 4.

BIBLIOGRAPHY

Abir-Am, P. and Outram, D. (eds.) *Uneasy Careers and Intimate Lives: Women in Science, 1789–1979* (London, Rutgers University Press, 1987).

Almond, G. and Verba, S. *The Civic Culture* (Princeton, Princeton University Press, 1983).

Balbo, L. and Nowotny, H. (eds.) *Time to Care in Tomorrow's Welfare Systems* (Vienna, Eurosocial, 1986).

Banks, O. *Faces of Feminism: a Study of Feminism as a Social Movement* (Oxford, Blackwell, 1986).

Barrett, M. *Women's Oppression Today: The Marxist/Feminist Encounter*, revised edn (London, Verso, 1988).

Bart, P. 'Review of Chodorow's *The Reproduction of Mothering*' in J. Trebilcot (ed.) *Mothering: Essays in Feminist Theory* (Totowa, N.J., Rowman and Allanheld, 1984), pp. 147–152.

Barth, E. Keynote Address to the International Congress of Women, Gottingen, 1986.

Bauman, Z. *Between Class and Elite: The evolution of the Labour Movement. A sociological study* (Manchester, Manchester University Press, 1972, translated by Sheila Patterson).

de Beauvoir, *The Second Sex* (Harmondsworth, Penguin,1972), translated and edited by H.M. Parshley.

Beecher, J. and Bienvenu, R. (eds) *The Utopian Vision of Charles Fourier: Selected Texts on Work, Love and Passionate Attraction* (London, Jonathan Cape, 1972).

Berki, R.N. *Socialism* (London, Dent, 1975).

Bochel, J. M. and Denver, D. T. 'Candidate Selection in the Labour Party: What the Selectors Seek', *British Journal of Political Science*, 13, 1983, 45–67.

—— *The Scottish Local Government Elections 1974: Results and Statistics* (Edinburgh, Scottish Academic Press, 1975); *The Scottish District Elections 1977: Results and Statistics* (University of Dundee, 1977); *The Scottish District Elections 1980: Results and Statistics* (University of Dundee and University of Lancaster, 1980); *The Scottish District Elections 1984: Results and Statistics* (University of Dundee and University of Lancaster, 1984); *The Scottish District Elections 1988: Results and Statistics* (Election Studies, 1989).

—— 'The SDP and the Left–Right Dimension', *British Journal of Political Science*, vol. 14, no, 3, 1984.

Boston, S. *Women Workers and the Trade Union Movement*, (London, Davis-Poynter, 1980).

Brody, M. 'Mary Wollstonecraft: Sexuality and Women's Rights' in D. Spender (ed.) *Feminist Theories*, (London, The Women's Press, 1983), pp. 40–59.

Bryant, L. *Six Red Months in Russia : An Observer's Account of Russia Before and During the Proletarian Dictatorship* (London, Journeyman Press, undated).

Burklin, W.P. 'The German Greens: The Post-Industrial Non-Established and the Party System', *International Political Science Review*, 1985/4.

Campbell, A., Converse, P., Miller, W. and Stokes, D. *The American Voter* (New York, Wiley, 1966).

Carroll, S. *Women as Candidates in American Politics* (Bloomington, Indiana University Press, 1985).

Carroll, S. and Strimling, W. *Women's Routes to Elective Office; a Comparison with Men's*, (Rutgers, Center for the American Woman and Politics, 1983).

Chamberlayne, P. 'The Mothers' Manifesto and Disputes over "Mutterlichkeit"', *Feminist Review*, no. 35, 1990, pp. 9–23.

Chapman, J. 'Adult Socialization and Out-group Politicization; an Empirical Study of Consciousness-raising', *British Journal of Political Science*, vol. 7, no. 3, 1987.

Chaytor, M. and Lewis, J. 'Introduction' in Alice Clark, *Working Life of Women in the Seventeenth Century*, (London, Routledge and Kegan Paul, 1982) pp. IX–XLIII.

Chernyshevsky, N. *What Is To Be Done?* (London, Virago, 1982).

Chodorow, N. *The Reproduction of Mothering: Psychoanalysis and the Sociology of Gender* (Berkeley, University of California Press, 1978).

Craig, F.W.S. *British Electoral Facts, 1885–1975* (London, Macmillan, 1976).

—— *British Parliamentary Election Results, 1974–1983* (Chichester, Parliamentary Research Services, 1984).

Christy, C. *Sex Differences in Political Participation: Processes of Change in Fourteen Nations* (New York, Praeger, 1987).

Dahl, R. *Who Governs?*, (New Haven, Yale University Press, 1961).

Dahl, T. S. and Hernes, H.M. 'After Equality', *Scandinavian Political Review*, Summer 1988.

Dahlerup, D. *The New Women's Movement: Feminism and Political Power in Europe and the USA* (London, Sage, 1986).

Dahlerup, D. and Haavio-Mannila, E. 'Summary', in E. Haavio-Mannila (ed.) *Unfinished Democracy: Women in Nordic Politics*, (Oxford, Pergamon Press, 1985), pp. 163–4.

Daly, M. *Gyn/ecology: The Metaethics of Radical Feminism* (Boston, Beacon Press, 1978).

Darcy, R. and Sarah Slavin Schramm, 'When Women Run Against Men', *Public Opinion Quarterly*, 41, 1, 1977, pp. 1–12.

Davidson, R. and Oloszek, W. *Congress and its Members*, 2nd edn, (Washington, Congressional Quarterly Inc., 1985).

Deber, R. 'The Fault, Dear Brutus: Women as Congressional Candidates in Pennsylvania', *Journal of Politics*, 44, 1982, pp. 463–479.

Derry, T.K. *A Short History of Norway* (London, Allen and Unwin, 2nd edn, 1968).

—— Derry, T.K. *History of Scandinavia: Norway, Sweden, Denmark, Finland and Iceland* (London, Allen and Unwin, 1979).

Dobb, M. *Soviet Economic Development since 1917* (London, Routledge and Kegan Paul, 1948).

Dominelli, L. and Jonsdottir, G., 'Feminist Political Organization in Iceland: Some Reflections on the Experience of Kwenna Frambothid', *Feminist Review*, no. 30, 1988, pp. 36-60.

Downes, B., 'Municipal Social Rank and the Characteristics of Local Political Leaders' *Midwest Journal of Political Science*, 12, 4, 1968.

Dowse, R. and Hughes, J. 'Girls, Boys and Politics', *British Journal of Sociology*, XXII, 1971, 53-67.

—— 'Pre-Adult Origins of Adult Political Activity' in C. Crouch (ed.) *British Political Sociology Yearbook, Volume 3, Participation in Politics* (London, Croom Helm, 1977), 202-21.

Duverger, M. *The Political Role of Women* (New York, Unesco, 1955).

Dworkin, A. *Pornography; Men Possessing Women* (New York, Perigree, 1981).

Easton, D. and Dennis, J. 'The Child's Acquisition of Regime Norms: Political Efficacy', *American Political Science Review*, LXI, 1971, 36-8.

Edmondson, H. *Feminism in Russia, 1900-17* (London, Heinemann, 1984).

Edwards, M., Halsaa, B. and Skjeie, H. 'Equality: How equal?' in E. Haavio-Mannila (ed.) *Unfinished Democracy: Women in Nordic Politics* (Oxford, Pergamon Press, 1985), pp. 136-7.

Ehrensaft, D. 'When Women and Men Mother', in J. Trebilcot (ed.) *Mothering: Essays in Feminist Theory* (Totowa, NJ, Rowman and Allanheld, 1984), pp. 41-61.

Eisenstein, Z. *The Radical Future of Liberal Feminism* (New York, Longman, 1981).

Eliassen, K. 'Rekrutteringen til Stortinget og Regjeringen 1945-85' in T. Nordby (ed.) *Storting og Regjering* (Oslo, Kunnskapsforlaget, 1985), pp. 109-30.

Engels, F. *The Origin of the Family, Private Property and the State* (New York, Pathfinder, 1972).

Epstein, C. F. *Deceptive Distinctions: Sex, Gender and the Social Order* (New Haven, Yale University Press, 1988).

Evans, R. *The Feminist Movement in Germany 1894-1933* (London, Sage, 1976).

Ferguson, A., 'On Conceiving Motherhood and Sexuality: A Feminist Materialist Approach' in J. Trebilcot (ed.) *Mothering: Essays in Feminist Theory* (Totowa, NJ, Rowman and Allanheld, 1984), pp. 153-82.

Finer, S. *Anonymous Empire: A Study of the Lobby in Great Britain* (London, Pall Mall, 1958).

Firestone, S. *The Dialectic of Sex* (London, The Woman's Press, 1980).

Franklin, M. *The Decline of Class Voting in Britain: Changes in the Basis of Electoral Choice 1964-1983* (Oxford, Clarendon Press, 1985).

Freeman, D. *Margaret Mead and Samoa: the Making and Unmaking of an Anthropological Myth* (Cambridge, MA, Harvard University Press, 1983).

Freeman, J. (ed.) *Social Movements of the Sixties and Seventies* (London, Longman, 1983).

Friedan, B. *The Second Stage* (London, Michael Joseph, 1982).

Fuchs, V. *Women's Quest for Economic Equality*, (Boston, Harvard University Press, 1988).

Gasiorowska, X. *Women in Soviet Fiction, 1917-1964* (Madison, University of Wisconsin Press, 1968).

Gilligan, C. *In a Different Voice*, (Cambridge, MA, Harvard University Press, 1982).

Ginsberg, E. *Into the Whirlwind* (London, Penguin, 1968).

Grant, W. *Pressure Groups, Politics and Democracy in Britain* (London, Philip Allan, 1989).

Griffin, S. *Pornography and Silence* (London, The Women's Press, 1981).

Grosskurth, P. *Margaret Mead* (London, Penguin, 1988).

Haavio-Mannila, E. (ed.) *Unfinished Democracy; Women in Nordic Politics*, (Oxford, Pergamon,1985).

Harasymiv, B. 'Nomenklatura: The Soviet Communist Party's Leadership Recruitment System', *Canadian Journal of Political Science*, 2, 3, 1969.

Harrison, J.F.C. *Robert Owen and the Owenites in Britain and America* (London, Routledge and Kegan Paul, 1969).

Haskey. J. and Kiernan, K. 'Cohabitation in Great Britain – characteristics and estimated numbers of cohabitating partners', *Population Trends*, 58 (Winter 1989).

Haug, F. 'Lessons from the Women's Movement in Europe', *Feminist Review*, no. 13, 1989, pp. 107–16.

Heberle, R. *Social Movements* (New York, Appleton Century Crofts, 1951).

Heidar, K. 'Party Organizational Elites in Norwegian Politics: Representativeness and Party Democracy', *Scandinavian Political Studies*, vol. 9, no.3, 1986, pp. 279–91.

Hernes, H. M. *Welfare State and Woman Power: Essays in State Feminism*, (Norwegian University Press, 1987).

Hernes, H. M. and Hanninen-Salmelin, E. 'Women in the corporate system' in E. Haavio-Mannila, (ed.) *Unfinished Democracy: Women in Nordic Politics*, (Oxford, Pergamon Press, 1985), pp. 106–133.

Hewlett, S. A. *A Lesser Life: The Myth of Women's Liberation* (London, Sphere Books, 1987).

Hill, R. *Soviet Political Elites* (London, Martin Robertson, 1977).

Hills, J. 'Lifestyle Constraints on Formal Politicial Participation; Why So Few Women Local Government Councillors in Britain?' *Electoral Studies*, 2, 1983, 39–52.

HMSO (Edinburgh) *The Scottish Summary of the Census: Strathclyde Region*.

Holland, M. 'British Political Recruitment: Labour in the Euro-Elections of 1979', *British Journal of Political Science*, 17, 1, 1987, 53–70.

Holt, A. *Selected Writings of Alexandra Kollontai* (London, Allison and Busby, 1977).

Hough, J. and Fainsod, M. *How the Soviet Union is Governed* (Cambridge, MA., Harvard University Press, 1979).

Huhlsberg, W. *The German Greens: a Social and Political Profile*, trans. Gus Fagan (London, Verso, 1988).

Iglitsyn, L. 'The Making of the Apolitical Woman: Femininity and Sex-Stereotyping in Girls' in Jane Jacquette (ed.) *Women in Politics* (New York, Wiley, 1974), 25–36.

Izvestia, 4 February, 1990.

Jallinoja, R. 'Independence or integration: the women's movement and political parties in Finland' in D. Dahlerup (ed.) *The New Women's Movement*, pp. 158–78.

Jennings, M. K. 'Another Look at the Life Cycle and Political Participation', *American Journal of Political Science*, 23, 1979, pp. 755–71.

Jewell, M. and Olson, D. *American State Political Parties and Elections* (Homewood, Ill., Dorsey Press, 1982) pp. 100–1.

Jordan, G. and Richardson, J.J. (eds), *Government and Pressure Groups in Britain* (Oxford, Clarendon, 1987).

Kaplan, M. 'Iceland's Feminist Parliamentarians' in *Sojourner: The Women's Forum*, April 1989, pp. 17–19.

BIBLIOGRAPHY

Keller, S. *Beyond the Ruling Class* (New York, Random, 1963).

Kim, C. L. 'Political Attitudes of Defeated Candidates in an American Election', *American Political Science Review* 64 (1970) pp. 879-86.

Kingdon, J. *Candidates for Office* (New York, Random, 1968).

Kleeman, K. *Women's PACs*, (Rutgers, Center for the American Woman and Politics, 1983).

Koblitz, A. H. 'Career and Home Life in the 1880s: The Choices of Mathematician Sofia Kovalevskaya' in P. Abir-Am and D. Outram (eds), *Uneasy Careers and Intimate Lives*, pp. 172-90.

Kolinsky, E. 'The West German Greens: A Women's Party', *Parliamentary Affairs*, vol. 41, no. 1, 1988, pp. 129-48.

Kristmundsdottir, S. 'Outside and Different: Icelandic women's movements and their notions of authority and cultural separateness of women', Paper presented to the Conference on the Anthropology of Iceland, University of Iowa, May 1987.

Kwennalistinn: The Women's Alliance Policy Statement 1987.

Lafferty, W. 'Social Development and Political Participation: Class, Organisation and Sex' *Scandinavian Political Studies*, 1, 4, 1978.

Lane, D. *State and Politics in the USSR* (Oxford, Basil Blackwell,1985).

Lawson, K. and Merkl, P. (eds) *When Parties Fail: Emerging Alternative Organizations* (Princeton, Princeton University Press, 1988).

Lenin, V.I. *Collected Works*, (Moscow, Progress, 1965 and London, Lawrence and Wishart, undated).

Levitas, R. 'Some problems of aim-centred models of social movements', *Sociology*, 1977, vol. 2, pp. 47-63.

Lewenhak, S. *Women and Work*, (London, Macmillan, 1980).

Lindsay, I. 'Constitutional Change and the Gender Deficit' in Jackie Roddick (ed.), *Women and Scottish Politics* (Polygon, forthcoming).

Lipset, Samuel *Political Man* (New York, Doubleday, 1960).

Lipset, Seymour, 'Foreword', in Richard Thomasson, *Iceland: The First New Society* (Reykjavik, Icelandic Review in association with University of Minnesota Press, 1980).

Listhaug, O., Miller, A. and Valen, H. 'The Gender Gap in Norwegian Voting Behaviour', *Scandinavian Political Studies*, vol. 8, no. 3, 1985, pp. 187-206.

Lovenduski, J. *Women and European Politics: Contemporary Feminism and Public Policy*, (Brighton, Wheatsheaf, 1986).

Lynn, N. 'Women and Politics; the Real Majority' in Jo Freeman (ed.), *Women; a Feminist Perspective*, 3rd edn, (Palo Alto, Mayfield, 1984).

Mackie, T.T. and Craig, F.W.S. *Europe Votes 2: European Parliamentary Election Results 1979-1984*, (Chichester, Parliamentary Research Services, 1985).

Mamanova, T. *Women in Russia* (Oxford, Blackwell, 1984).

Manuel, F. *The Prophets of Paris* (New York, Harper & Row, 1962).

Martin, J. and Roberts, C. *Women and Employment: A Lifetime Perspective* (London, HMSO, 1984).

Marx, K. and Engels, F. *Selected Correspondence*, (Moscow, Foreign Languages Publishing House, and London, Lawrence and Wishart, undated).

Matthews, D. *The Social Background of Decision-Makers* (New York, Doubleday, 1954).

Mayhew, D. R. *Placing Parties in American Politics; Organization, Electoral Settings, and Government Activity in the Twentieth Century* (Princeton, Princeton University Press,1986).

Mead, M. *Male and Female: A Study of the Sexes in a Changing World*, (Harmondsworth, Pelican, 1962).

Merritt, S. 'Winners and Losers: Sex Differences in Municipal Elections', *American Journal of Political Science*, XXI, 1977, 731–43.

Miller, W. and Stokes, D. *American Representation Study, 1958: the Candidate File* (ICPSR no. 7726).

Miller, W. and Taylor, C. 'Structured Protest: A Comparison of Third Force Challenges in Britain, Germany and the USA during the Eighties', a paper presented to the 13th World Congress of the International Political Science Association, Paris, July 1985.

Moore, H. *Feminism and Anthropology* (London, Polity Press, 1988).

Morton., A.L. *The Life and Ideas of Robert Owen* (London, Lawrence and Wishart, 1962).

Narkiewicz, O. *The Making of the Soviet State Apparatus* (Manchester University Press, 1970).

News from Iceland, May 1988.

Oakley, A. *Sex, Gender and Society*, (London, 1972).

Okin, S. M. *Women in Western Political Thought* (Princeton, Princeton University Press, 1978).

Ortner, S 'Is female to male as nature is to culture?' in M. Rosaldo and L. Lamphere (eds) *Women, Culture and Society* (Stanford, Stanford University Press, 1974).

Owen, R.D. *Threading My Way* (New York, 1974).

Papadakis, E. *The Green Movement in West Germany* (London, Croom Helm, 1984).

Pateman, C. *The Sexual Contract* (Stanford, Stanford University Press, 1988).

Phillips, A. *Divided Loyalties: Dilemmas of Sex and Class* (London, Virago 1987).

Prewitt, K. *The Recruitment of Political Leaders; a Study of Citizen-Politicans*, (Indianapolis, Bobbs-Merrill, 1970).

Radkey, O.H. *The Election to the Russian Constituent Assembly of 1917* (Cambridge, Mass., Harvard University Press, 1950).

Randall, V. *Women and Politics*, 2nd edn (London, Macmillan, 1987).

Rasmussen, Jorgen 1) 'Female Political Career Patterns and Leadership Disabilities in Britain: The Crucial Role of Gatekeepers in Regulating Entry to the Political Elite', *Polity*, XIII, 4, 1981, 600–20.

—— 'Women Candidates in British By-Elections: A Rational Choice Interpretation of Electoral Behaviour' *Political Studies*, 19, 2, 1981, pp. 265–274.

von Rauch, G. *A History of Soviet Russia* (London, Pall Mall, 1967).

Rendell, J. *The Origins of Modern Feminism: Women in Britain, France and the United States, 1780–1860* (London, Macmillan, 1985).

Rich, A. *Of Woman Born: Motherhood as Experience and Institution*, (London Virago, 1977).

Rigby, T.H. *Communist Party Membership in the USSR, 1917–67* (Princeton University Press, 1968).

Roberts, P.C. *Alienation and the Soviet Economy* (Albuquerque, University of New Mexico Press, 1971).

Rosaldo, M. 'Woman, culture and society: a theoretical overview', in M. Rosaldo and Lamphere, L. (eds), *Women, Culture and Society* (Stanford, Stanford University Press, 1974), pp. 17–42.

Rossi, A., (ed.), *The Feminist Papers; From Adams to de Beauvoir* (New York, Bantam, 1974).

Rowbotham, S.) 'The Women's Movement and Organising for Socialism' in S.

Rowbotham, L. Segal, and H. Wainwright, *Beyond the Fragments: Feminism and the Making of Socialism* (London, Merlin, 1980).

—— 'To Be or Not To Be: The Dilemmas of Mothering', *The Feminist Review*, 31, 1988, p. 83.

Rucht, D. (ed.), *Research on Social Movements: the State of the Art* (Frankfurt/ Boulder CO: Westview, 1990).

Rule, W. 'Why Women Don't Run: The Critical Contextual Factors in Women's Legislative Recruitment', *The Western Political Quarterly*, 9, 1974, 171–84.

Rush, M. 'The Members of Parliament', in S.A. Walkland and Michael Ryle, (eds), *The Commons Today*, London, Fontana, 1981.

Sakwa, R. *Gorbachev and his Reforms: 1985–1990* (Hemel Hempstead, Philip Allan, 1990).

Sarlvik, B. and Ivor Crewe, I. *Decade of de-alignment: the Conservative victory of 1979 and electoral trends in the 1970s* (Cambridge University Press, 1983).

Sartori, G. 'Members of Parliament', in *Decisions and Decision-Makers in the Modern State* (Paris, Unesco 1967).

Schapiro, L. *The Origin of the Communist Autocracy: Political Opposition in the Soviet State, The First Phase, 1917–22.* (London, Macmillan, 1977).

Schlesinger, R. *The Family in the USSR* (London, Routledge and Kegan Paul, 1949).

Schwarzer, A. *Simone de Beauvoir Today*, (London, Chatto and Windus, 1984).

Scudder, B. 'Althing being Equal', *Iceland Review*, 1988.

Segal, L. *Is The Future Female? Troubled Thoughts on Contemporary Feminism* (London, Virago, 1987).

—— 'Slow Change or No Change? Feminism, Socialism amd the Problem of Men', *The Feminist Review* Special Issue, 31, 1989, pp. 5–21.

Seligman, L. G., Kim, M. R., Chong Lim Kim and Smith, R. E. *Patterns of Recruitment: a State Chooses its Lawmakers* (Chicago, Rand McNally,1974).

Siim, B. 'Welfare State, Gender Politics and Equality Principles: Women's citizenship, participation and interests in the Scandinavian welfare states', Paper presented at the ECPR Joint Sessions, Paris, April 1989.

Skard, T. and Haavio-Mannila, E. 'Women in Parliament' in E. Haavio-Mannila (ed.), *Unfinished Democracy; Women in Nordic Politics*, (Oxford, Pergamon) 1985.

—— 'Mobilization of women at elections', in E. Haavio-Mannila, (eds.), *Unfinished Democracy; Women in Nordic Politics*, (Oxford, Pergamon) pp. 42–3.

Skjeie, H. *The Feminization of Power: Norway's Political Experiment (1986–)*, (Oslo, Institute for Social Research, 1988).

Sorauf, S. *Party and Representation; Legislative Politics in Pennsylvania* (New York, Atherton Press, 1963) pp. 75–81.

Stanwick, K *Getting Women Appointed; New Jersey's Bipartisan Coalition*, (Rutgers, Center for the American Woman and Politics, 1984).

Studlar, D. and Welch, S. 'Understanding the Iron law of Andrarchy: Effects of Candidate Gender on Voting in Scotland' *Comparative Political Studies* 1987, 20, 2.

Stryrkarsdottir, A. 'From social movement to political party: the new women's movment in Iceland' in D. Dahlerup (ed.) *The New Women's Movement*, pp. 140–157.

Taylor, B. *Eve and the New Jerusalem*, (London, Virago, 1983).

Tobin, R.J. and Keynes, E. 'Institutional Differences in the Recruitment Process: a Four-State Study', *American Journal of Political Science*, 19, 1975, 667–92.

307

BIBLIOGRAPHY

The Congressional Quarterly's Guide to US Elections, 2nd edn, (Washington, 1985).

The Past before Us: Twenty Years of Feminism, Special Issue of *The Feminist Review*, 31, 1989.

Trotsky, L. *History of the Russian Revolution* (London, Gollancz, 1934).

Valen, H. 'Norway: decentralization and group representation', in M. Gallagher and M. Marsh, *Candidate Selection in Comparative Perspective* (London, Sage, 1988).

Vallance, E. *Women in the House*, (London, Athlone, 1979).

Venturi, V. *Roots of Revolution: A History of the Populist and Socialist Movements in Nineteenth Century Russia*, (London, Weidenfeld and Nicolson, 1952).

Verba, S. and Nie, N. *Participation in America; Political Democracy and Social Equality* (New York, Harper and Row, 1972).

Verba, S., Nie, N. and Kim, J. *Participation and Political Equality: a Seven-Nation Comparison*, (Cambridge, Cambridge University Press, 1978).

Walicki, A. *A History of Russian Thought From the Enlightenment to Marxism* (Oxford, Clarendon Press, 1980).

Welch, S. 'Women as Political Animals? A Test of Some Explanations for Male-Female Political Participation Differences', *American Journal of Political Science*, XX1, 4, 1977, 711-730

—— 'Sex Differences in Political Activity in Britain', *Women and Politics*, 1, 2, 1980, 29-46.

—— 'Recruitment of Women to Public Office: a Discriminant Analysis', *Western Political Quarterly*, 31, 1978, 372-80.

Welch, S. and Karnig, A.K. 'Correlates of Female Office Holding in City Politics', *Journal of Politics*, 41, 1979, 478-91.

Westkott, M. *The Feminist Legacy of Karen Horney*, (New Haven, Yale University Press, 1986) pp. 125-34.

White, S. *Gorbachev in Power* (Cambridge, Cambridge University Press, 1990).

Whiteley, P. *The Labour Party in Crisis*, (London, Methuen, 1983).

Williams, O., Herman, H., Liebman, C. and Dye, T. *Suburban Differences and Metropolitan Policies: The Philadelphia Story* (Philadelphia, University of Pennsylvania Press, 1965).

Wollstonecraft, M. *Vindication of the Rights of Woman* (London, Penguin, 1982).

—— *Mary, a Fiction and The Wrongs of Woman*, Gary Kelly (ed.) (Oxford, Oxford University Press, 1976).

—— *Love Letters of Mary Wollstonecraft to Gilbert Imlay*, with a prefatory memoir by Roger Ingpen, (London, Hutchinson, 1908).

Wood, A., (ed.), *The Times Guide to the House of Commons June 1987* (London, Times Books, 1987).

Young, I.M. 'Beyond the Unhappy Marriage: A Critique of the Dual Systems Theory', in Lynne Sargent (ed.), *Women and Revolution: A Discussion of the Unhappy Marriage of Marxism and Feminism*, (Boston, South End Press, 1981).

—— 'Is Male Gender the Cause of Male Domination?' in (ed.) J. Trebilcot, *Mothering: Essays in Feminist Theory* (Totowa, N.J., Rowman and Allanheld, 1984), pp. 129-46.

INDEX

Abir-Am, P. 285
abortion 192, 198, 202, 289-90, 291, 294; and feminism 208; and Greens 240; Iceland 259; reform 235
age of candidates 280
Akselrod 174, 288
Alliance Party (Britain) 84, 113, 114-17, 279, 280; socio-economic factors 118-26; women nominated 44
Almond, G. 7
androgyny 217, 226, 268
Argyll and Bute 84, 86, 88, 103, 105, 107, 108; independents 98; *see also* Scotland
Armand, Inessa 172, 189
Astell, Mary 202, 293

Babeuf, F.N. 283
Banks, O. 133, 135
Barrett, M. 196
Bauman, Z. 273
Baumer, Gertrud 233
Belgium 111, 112
biological determinism 196, 204, 206
biology and gender roles 195-208
Biryukova, Alexandra 292
Blood, Fanny 293
Bochel, J.M. 278
Bolsheviks 289, 290
Boston, S. 274
Breshkovskaya, Ekaterina 172, 290
Brezhnev, L. 63, 64
Britain 11, 22; cabinet ministers 4; electoral system 125, 276, 279; European elections 111, 112; House of Commons candidates 17, 28, 273, 274

Bundestag, women in 110, 112, 234, 237

capitalism 16, 22, 23-4, 132; effect of 14, 272
caring professions 120, 126; Russia 66, 69; and success 58, 61
caring role 255, 256; *see also* childcare; responsibilities; women
Carr, E.H. 289
change and rise of feminism 131-7
Chappallsmith, Margaret 152
Chernyshevsky, N.G. 6, 175, 176, 177, 288, 289
childcare 157, 184, 200, 282, 283; allowances for 284; communalisation of 149, 154, 155, 182, 207; constraints of 10, 11; Iceland 265-6; Mead on 214-15; Norway 300; state 185, 191, 226, 229
Chodorow, N. 217-22, 226, 228, 295-6
Christy, C. 270
civic activism 15, 81-2, 101, 102-3
class conflict 167-8, 169-70, 176, 180
Clydesdale 86, 88, 105, 106, 108; independents 98; *see also* Scotland
communes 283
communitarians 150-2, 284
competition on male terms 12
conflict, institutionalised 13-14
Congressional elections (US) 38, 39-40
consciousness-raising 195, 292
conservation issues 125-6
Conservative party (Britain) 32, 44, 48-51; and independents 95, 97, 98, 100; occupation of candidates 46-7,

Firestone, S. 197, 200, 204-8, 215, 217, 220, 222, 226
first-past-the-post system 125, 279
Fourier, Charles 150-1, 207, 282, 283, 284; influence of 152, 175, 176
France 112
Freeman, D. 294
Freud, Sigmund xiii, 204, 206-7, 208, 209, 211-12, 213, 214, 228
Friedan, Betty 217, 225-6, 227, 240, 285
Fuchs, V. 131
Furtseva, Nina 292

Gasiorowska, X. 190, 191
Gelf'man, Gesia 172, 287
gender pattern of recruitment 6-12; explanations 8-12; and hierarchy of office 5; and minor parties 109-27; research 6-8; Strathclyde 117-21
gender roles 194, 267; and biology 195-208; characteristics 9-10; constraints 139-40, 145-7, 149-50, 200; cultural constitution of 9; diffusion of female 296; economic 286; female 140-3, 283; and feminism 135, 136-7; Finland 168, 169; future of 207-8; historically 272; male 27; Mead on 209-17; Russia 180, 184-5, 186, 192; Scandinavia 254-5; socialisation 11; and socialism 156-7; as unequal 148
gender scissors 25-8, 137, 143, 146, 194, 227, 267; and feminism 158, 160-1; hypotheses 18-20, 45, 53-62; and recruitment 3-28; and standard model 20-2
gender theory and feminism 195-229
Germany 112; ecological movement 125; Federal elections 112; historically 233; see also West German Greens
Gilligan, C. 282
Gilman, Charlotte Perkins 284
Ginsberg, E. 192
Gladkov 190
Gorbachev, Mikhail 63, 69, 70, 71
Gorki, M. 173
Greece 11, 111, 112
Griffin, S. 198
Grosskurth, P. 294, 295

Haavio-Mannila, E. 163, 164, 286
Hanninen-Salmelin, E. 19
Harlem-Bruntland, Gro 4, 246, 298
Hart, Judith 108
Heberle, R. 132
Hegel, G.W.F. 214
Heidar, K. 299
Hernes, H.M. 19
Hewlett, S.A. 225
Hill, R. J. 34, 64-7, 69
Holland, M. 33, 274-5
House of Commons 17, 28, 273, 274

Ibsen, H. 165-6
Iceland: xxi, 74, 137, 229, 232; feminism 258-66; Kwennalistinn 230; reformation of politics 257-66; Women's List 110; women's strike 259
Illinois study 41, 79
income 78, 276; inequalities 76
independent candidates 32, 74, 278; changes 103-5; financial requirements 85; male 87-94; and NFU 100; number of women 82-3, 84; party identification 94-7; socio-economic factors 87-90, 118, 119, 120, 123; women as 82-3, 84, 105-8
institutions: selection criteria 15-16; see also political parties
Islam and women 178-9, 219
Italy 11, 111, 112

Jallinoja, R. 164, 169, 285-6
Jennings, M.K. 76
Johnston, T. 101

Kaplan, Dora 179
Keller, S. 37
Keynes, E. 38-9
Kim, J. 7, 76, 270
Kollontai, A. 172, 177, 178, 181-91, 195, 196, 197, 207; on anti-feminism 289
Kovalevskaya, Marya 172
Kovalevskaya, Sofia 176
Kristmundsdottir, S. 265, 300
Kwenna Frambothid (KF) 259-65
Kwennalistinn 262-6

Labour party (Britain) 17, 18, 19, 20, 31-2; characteristics of candidates